The Blossom Avenue For better human living

Marco Facchinetti   Marco Dellavalle

The Blossom Avenue

For better human living

SKIRA

Art Director
Marcello Francone

Design
Luigi Fiore

Editorial Coordination
Emma Cavazzini

Editing
Silvia Gaiani

Layout
Antonio Carminati

Translations
Paul Metcalfe on behalf of *Scriptum*, Rome

The drawings on pages 13–16 are the work of the Milan Polytechnic department of architecture and planning

The photograph on page 290 is by Antonio Marogna

First published in Italy in 2013 by
Skira Editore S.p.A.
Palazzo Casati Stampa
via Torino 61
20123 Milano
Italy
www.skira.net

© 2013 Marco Facchinetti and Marco Dellavalle
© 2013 Skira editore

All rights reserved under international copyright conventions.
No part of this book may be reproduced or utilized in any form or by any means, electronic or mechanical, including photocopying, recording, or any information storage and retrieval system, without permission in writing from the publisher.

Printed and bound in Italy. First edition

ISBN: 978-88-572-2102-1

Distributed in USA, Canada, Central & South America by Rizzoli International Publications, Inc., 300 Park Avenue South, New York, NY 10010, USA.
Distributed elsewhere in the world by Thames and Hudson Ltd., 181A High Holborn, London WC1V 7QX, United Kingdom.

The work accomplished, the projects carried out and the experiences recounted in this book would have been impossible without the help and commitment of the many people who have worked with Marco Facchinetti and Marco Dellavalle but above all without the expertise and patience of those working with us today, namely Nicola, Lorenzo, Luca, Francesca and Francesca, Tommaso, Raffaele, Alessio and Guglielmo. It is to them that the work is dedicated.

Contents

6	Introduction
12	Dialogue on the City
28	Imagination and Design in Urban Planning
38	Architectural Design and Construction
	ATLAS OF PROJECTS
46	**1. URBAN PLANNING**
156	**2. ARCHITECTURE**
268	**3. INTERIOR DESIGN**
291	Biography
293	**4. LIST OF PROJECTS**
327	List of Associates

Introduction

The projects illustrated in this book tell the story of ten years in the careers of the author and Marco Dellavalle, a decade in which many things have changed, as always happens simply through the passing of time and the flow of history. A small revolution has taken place in the order of things, however, if we consider both the framework of Italian legislation before the reforms that made urban planning simultaneously a focal point of regional laws and almost forgotten at the national level, and what remains today, after nearly five years of international crisis, of the plans, projects, and expectations around which that institutional reform was largely conceived.

The shift of urban planning, the sphere of all our activities, to the regional scale has meant a great deal and led at least in certain regions to a change in attitude towards the dynamics of transformation of the cities. Many regions have experimented with programmes and tools of implementation differing greatly from the old town planning scheme that all municipalities were required to draw up by law 1150 of 1942; many have experimented with new, rapid and intense forms of planning; and many others have reiterated old dynamics and slow, rigid ways of planning. All the regions have unquestionably concentrated on giving their territories the best normative structure, focusing on the municipal planning instrument as the only one really capable of an effective response to their needs. The intermediate levels between the towns and the region and the tools of implementation – in other words, everything that should exist above the municipal plan and that must exist inside it and ensure that it is put into effect – have not received the same attention as the municipal instrument. Between territorial management plans, urban plans similar to the old town planning scheme and structural plans, regional legislation has focused on the municipality and its territory with a view to obtaining the best possible planning. In ten years of activity, we have realized that the municipal framework, even though reformed and transformed as it has been in Lombardy with the transition from the old town planning scheme to the territorial management plan, has proved incapable of extricating itself from certain not necessarily positive approaches and dynamics of Italian history. The emphasis on the programme and the associated anxiety that the municipal plan involves in any case – the knowledge that after the municipal budget, this is the most important public action for the local authorities – have made it possible through all these years not to feel deprived of a level of intermediate planning, which has in reality even lost further power in certain contexts (like Lombardy), and not to feel deprived of certainties for not having reformed all the tools of implementation, the prerequisite for meeting targets, with the same attention. The resulting urban planning is peculiar in character. The municipalities have continued to feel at the centre and in full possession of their powers to modify the territory; the provinces and intermediate agencies have maintained radar alert against all municipal action, both negative and positive; the regions have withdrawn since the passing of the law into a strange role of supervision and coordination; and the state has literally disappeared from the urban-planning scene. And yet, this is the reform and this the urban planning that *reformers* have helped for years to bring to life, characterized by decentralization and flexibility, the structure rather than the whole, the process rather than the plan. In the meantime, the territory crumbled and has gone on crumbling to no small degree over these ten years from one municipality to another, with no intermediate plans, no design, no attention. The processes, the ones that really do alter the everyday panorama outside our windows, have found it easy to develop within this odd framework.

The agenda has also changed over these ten years. Emphasis on the environment and attention to sustainability have informed much of building regulations and planning to the point of structuring the overall practice of planning. The results are, however, not what we would have expected to see, at least in general terms and at least not everywhere. The focus on sustainability has certainly not made it possible to reduce the consumption of building land and aim at a different model of development, nor has it imposed building regulations now in force for years in other countries of the European Community. Concentration on strengthening infrastructures has absorbed Italy's tardy discovery of the need for railways and rail services, which informed the debate and work of many cities in the 1990s and the early 2000s, and in some way made it accepted that is better to work around stations than build without infrastructures. At the same time, the municipal contexts are still too occupied with solving more basic questions – like the presence of traffic in their historical centres, the lack of policies connecting the use of parking space to the services and commerce present in the same towns, and the low efficiency of road-based public transport services – to absorb more evolved canons deeply enough to reform the conception of planning in general.

Settlement policies have seen some new developments over the decade, such as the need for agreements with private builders or a ceiling on prices. In many contexts, however, they have not proved so effective in addressing the problem of revitalizing historical centres with a view to protecting the territory or, at a deeper level, the need to revise the supply in relation to type of context and thus avoid the ugly, monotonous repetition of small villas and condominiums, not least because of the lack of communication between building regulations and tools of planning for built-up areas. To be blunt, though generated by the reform, many tools of municipal planning have not proved very effective over the last ten years in altering the Italian panorama and producing a landscape different from that of the previous decade.

As regards the difficulty of understanding all these themes, together with others precisely listed on the reform agenda, and within the general framework of freedom from regulation imposed by decentralization, as stated above, at a certain point in the last decade we are observing together, something broke down to the point of causing a crisis that has had a great deal to do with settlement contexts and towns. Above and beyond the origin and genesis of the crisis, it was clear that many projects and programmes would be interrupted and then definitively dropped. Mediocre projects that small firms were no longer able to keep going and major operations blocked by far deeper financial crises began to appear on the always positive and progressive panoramas of municipal plans, causing a crisis in the mechanism upon which the plans themselves have always rested, and still more so since the creation of tools by regional laws: planning provisions, implementation and gain for the municipality in terms of responsibilities and standards. This mechanism was struck by the collapse of the certainty that once a provision was included in a plan, there would be a firm ready to put it into effect, and indeed that there would be a firm ready to ask the municipality to be remembered in the planning phase with its own initiatives ready for implementation. This was no longer the case. The firm no longer came knocking at the door of the town hall or suspended its plans while awaiting resources and clients. At a deeper level, the interruption of this natural process upon which Italian urban planning had rested for years has led to a collapse of collaboration on the part of the private sector in the construction of the city. Due also to the world-wide crisis of resources, agreements and partnerships have been halted, shelved and interrupted or still proceed but at a slower rate. Given in addition the continuing lack of involvement at the national level, it is easy to see on the evidence of the last ten years that we are now a long way away from the period of the complex programs, the stimulus for redevelopment that the state provided in certain phases, and the action of the private sector, ready to step in and build entire urban sections, albeit driven by speculative aims. Two key words appear to emerge from this panorama, namely *design* and *feasibility*, and it is on them that we have endeavoured to concentrate in our work, intent as we have been on observing the evolution of the decade.

Design is the most powerful tool our discipline and practice can have. It is through design that we speak, describe the structure of a context, highlight its problems and strengths, the easy angles and points of tension. With design we imagine what must happen both through an ideal vision of our own and above all by taking into account the data of the problem, putting things in place, working for the best and seeking a functional balance through constant adjustment of the forces in play. We have gone back to design in these years of work. Precisely because we felt overwhelmed by a problematic normative and administrative framework and deterred from setting our sights high by the economic and social context, we have recalled the power of our work through design. It is design that makes it possible to imagine a different form for a context. Just as form was once the expression of the wishes of a single power structure capable of constructing a city, today the form developed by design can express the balancing of the many forces that have acquired the right to participate in running the city, a set of forces of variable geometry, changing and discontinuous but always present and always capable of offering so many data on the problem, which design alone can organize. Design is strongly present in the works carried out. Every assignment undertaken in these ten years has started from design as a tool of vision and organization. In recounting the vision, we found ourselves working as technicians to help overwhelmed contexts of little quality to acquire more and more, to stand out as centres of urban quality in a discontinuous, irregularly concentrated and badly connected territory. Design has been used as a tool to oragnize and ensure implementation. No vision made sense and had the honour of being included in an instrument of planning over these years if its implementation could not be guaranteed. The two spirits and the two key words have thus been built up and consolidated through the master plan and the development of plans by means of master plans. The master plan defines the structure of a context without over-determining it and lays down basic principles with a view to its possible transformation. As a tool, it ascertains the applicability of the rules it puts forward and builds up consensus by involving the parties concerned in the physical aspect. Above all, it provides a visual picture of the result in advance and generates a convergence thereon of the forces in play, with their varying degrees of capacity to put the design into effect and strength to modify it or accept it as it stands.

The aim of the design is the construction of connected urban corners for areas generally

INTRODUCTION

Renovation of the Linificio factory, Cassano d'Adda (Milan). Overall planimetric and volumetric plan. Definitive hypothesis, renovation of historical buildings and additional volumes

termed suburban, as in the past. The activity of planning for municipalities of varying size around more consolidated metropolitan areas, such as Milan, Novara, Monza and Florence, has brought realization that the albeit "parochial" characterization of every single part of territory is still strong, marked and recognizable. Amid the defence of environmental values, protection of historical elements and creation of quality of life, many areas reveal a search for a different form of urbanity with respect to the city, less crammed with things and events, more organized on the human scale, small and compact, made up of usable spaces, relations and greenery. On the one hand, this strange kind of urbanity is paradoxically sought within a focus on naturalness, the absence of pressure and distance from "strong" and congested contexts. On the other, precisely because of its need for spaces, meeting places, piazzas, connections and services, it must be designed because it cannot be generated spontaneously by the current processes of these contexts, and must indeed be produced precisely as a defence against the ordinary ugliness that these areas continue to bring forth.

At the same time, the tool has invested in implementation, focusing attention no longer onto the plan and the process but onto the evolution of the plan within the process. A design has life if its implementation is guaranteed. Far away from the possibility of using designs solely in order to imagine, invent and stimulate, forced by action to make effective every design and every provision it expresses, we have believed in the ability of a design – the master plan, for example – to adapt within the process that drives it to transform its provisions into reality. No longer therefore the rigidity of a design to be pursued, not only attention to the formation of a process, but above all the correctness of a design, with its rules, norms and points of equilibrium, capable of modification within the complexity of the process. With no sharp edges or hardness, flexibly able to redraw its horizon in response to changes in the forces and intensities in play.

Through implementation, design has generated the architecture that we have conceived, planned and built over these years.

INTRODUCTION

Our architecture is born out of the care with which we have conceived and addressed the planning processes in which we have been involved. The volumes, spaces and relations designed in our master plans have taken concrete shape thanks to the correctness of the pathways of implementation plotted in relation to the requirements of design. Here too we have drawn upon history and tradition. If our use of the plan as a tool and the design as the necessary ambition of every space is rooted in the urban planning of post-war Italy, when the form of settlements created by the great masters endowed the provisions with their essence and was accompanied by a host of references, our daring to undertake architectural design expresses our essence through a rational, balanced arrangement of spaces, working on the organization of pathways, exchanges, flows and relations as dynamic forces capable of giving shape to space as well as rational, canonically correct development in which openings and closings, materials and compositional elements respond to a tranquil undercurrent already tried and tested and already appreciated (by the Italian Rationalist movement, to which we are still so close) but susceptible of being disturbed by what these forces can bring about. The resulting architecture is thus: it speaks of the design that we had in mind and through which we developed it, of how the planning process modified that design and made it feasible, of how objects were arranged and space was organized so as to function and give noble expression to the uses for which it was conceived. Finally, with its skin, volume and forms, it speaks of how the forces and variables in play today are capable of giving shape to the Italian tradition of composition, returning to the sharpness, order, rigour and correctness of now historic compositions and recounting the modern world. It is unquestionably true that no architectural work conceived and designed by us over these years stands alone on a *tabula rasa*. Precisely because it is born out of an urban-planning process, each work of architecture erects a volume that is born out of the ground level of urban planning, designing the spaces at the foot of the buildings, piercing the ground and laying bare what lies beneath, opening up the base to design spaces so as to increase the number of relations and exchanges and give meaning to the concept of small-scale

Development of the main building in the renovation of the Core area of Verano Brianza (Monza and Brianza). Volumetric concentration and gateway to the municipal settlement system

urbanity sought after by many of these contexts. The elements designed and built have the merit of contributing to the creation of urban places within the open and discontinuous space of the suburb, of which they constitute an important part. Our architectural projects have therefore carried within them the very elements of that urbanity – like compactness, the proximity of things, the relation between open space and relational space, and the equal dignity between constructed elements and elements of the open space in which they are placed – in the certainty that it is a mistake to concentrate on one dimension or the other (far removed both from hyper-absorbent residential machines and from the disappearance of architecture in favour of nature) and that only both dimensions together – the volume constructed and the open space around or inside – can engender correctly expressive architecture.

Looking back over a decade of activity and rereading the story that each of our projects expresses, we find ourselves today working on a city that we did not foresee ten years ago but that perhaps provides us with a great stimulus. The city of today, or at least the one close to us, seems to take shape increasingly as a succession at different distances of contexts of greater or lesser rarefaction, the result of a strange period of seventy years, sometimes so quickly as not to notice the effects of its own action but today, not least due to the slowness imposed by the crisis, in vital pursuit of quality in terms of settlement, environment, infrastructures and relations. Our projects have engaged in a dialogue with this geography of varying speeds and varying resistance to the inertia of rarefaction. They have seen places capable of organizing themselves around their centre and around the heart of their history, and helped them to structure a geometry of high-quality relational spaces, places capable of rediscovering the fabric of retail commerce, and helped them to support this with suitable policies of mobility and parking. They have seen places ready and willing to see the consumption of building land not as a non-critical consideration but as a condition to be accepted only in return for the greatest public benefit, and helped them to develop processes of cooperation with private concerns at a high level. Our projects have understood in time that the construction of urban phenomena of quality – sometimes located far from one another but in such a way as to underscore the existence of once consolidated contexts provided that they are well connected – may be the most stimulating and emergent geography on which to work. For this, we need planning instruments capable of involving implementation and its difficulties directly in the planning stage, and for this it is necessary to work around a design capable of expressing a vision and guiding it along a pathway of rules and standards to be constructed gradually as the implementation takes shape, a plan in progress of the kind discussed above and exemplified by our projects. Not everything we have done has been a success; not all of the projects have been carried all the way through: and not all the plans have been built as we conceived them. It is important for us to gather them together here, however, because they all speak about an ongoing process in the conviction that urban quality, the design of space and the form of residential settlements are the best expression of our way of being alive in this time.

Dialogue on the City

Marco Dellavalle You'll be happy now. See? Milan now has its skyscrapers too, and all in a group, not just one isolated as before, the poor old Pirelli that no one talks about any more. So many and all together, just as we like, as in the US.

Marco Facchinetti The effect is really good. Milan is a small city. You can see it all if you get high enough: the green of the Agricultural Park in the south, the Trade Fair complex in the north with its two crooked towers, Linate airport and San Siro in the west. In short, with such a limited extension, the skyscrapers are all right there in the middle. They give a scale, as though attracting all of the territory and making it seem more contained, more measurable. Of course, everything is bounded by the Alps and the Apennines, which make it clear that the possibility for growth of the urban areas starts and ends here on the plain.

MDV It is small, but the space over which its sphere of influence extends is not so limited if we consider the metropolitan area as a whole. The new skyscrapers can also be seen clearly from some outer areas, at least the highest spire of the bank tower. So even the Duomo's spire is overshadowed.

MF True, but the skyscrapers don't seem to have much to do with the metropolitan area. This is why I didn't answer when you said that I'd be happy. I can't be so one hundred percent. They are splendid, they look great from a distance and they give a sense of measure, like any "peg" stuck in a large expanse. But there is something that jars for me, and you've put your finger on it: the metropolitan area. How is an operation like the redevelopment of the Garibaldi and Repubblica district in Milan connected with the development of the metropolitan area? What dialogue does it establish with the very urgent need to rebalance the metropolis? Little or nothing. The skyscrapers are not a territorial point of reference in terms of functions, meaning and weight for the metropolitan area as a whole to the benefit both of Milan and of the neighbouring municipalities. No, not at all. They are the umpteenth instance of growth – albeit splendid, as I said – well inside the city boundaries. And this doesn't make me happy, because it means that we have failed this time too, in this series of transformations. We were not convinced that metropolitan coordination with the metropolitan region could work.

MDV We have seen, however, in our plans and our everyday experience that there is constant day-to-day reference in the activities of all the municipalities to the higher levels of the province and the region. These bodies are fully involved in the action of a municipality every day as regards rules, plans, constraints, incentives, references and authorizations. But we never manage to go beyond this. The province and the region seem to be light years away from the functioning of a municipality, while at the same time the problems of a municipality seem to be solvable only within the local context, so small and confined as to exclude even the neighbouring municipalities.

MF You therefore understand that in this way there will be no skyscrapers and no homogeneous development at the metropolitan scale if we are not convinced to the point of resolutely addressing this division and lack of coordination. And yet, you know, I still believe strongly in the need for an intermediate level of coordination. I believe that municipal planning – through its own territorial management plan, as it is called in Lombardy, or through any other tool for management of municipal plans – is very important and the responsibility of the municipality. I am also convinced, however, that it cannot develop ignoring the planning of the neighbouring municipalities and therefore of the territory as a whole, es-

Plan of the Martesana-Adda area. Province of Milan. Communicational and strategic map of the area

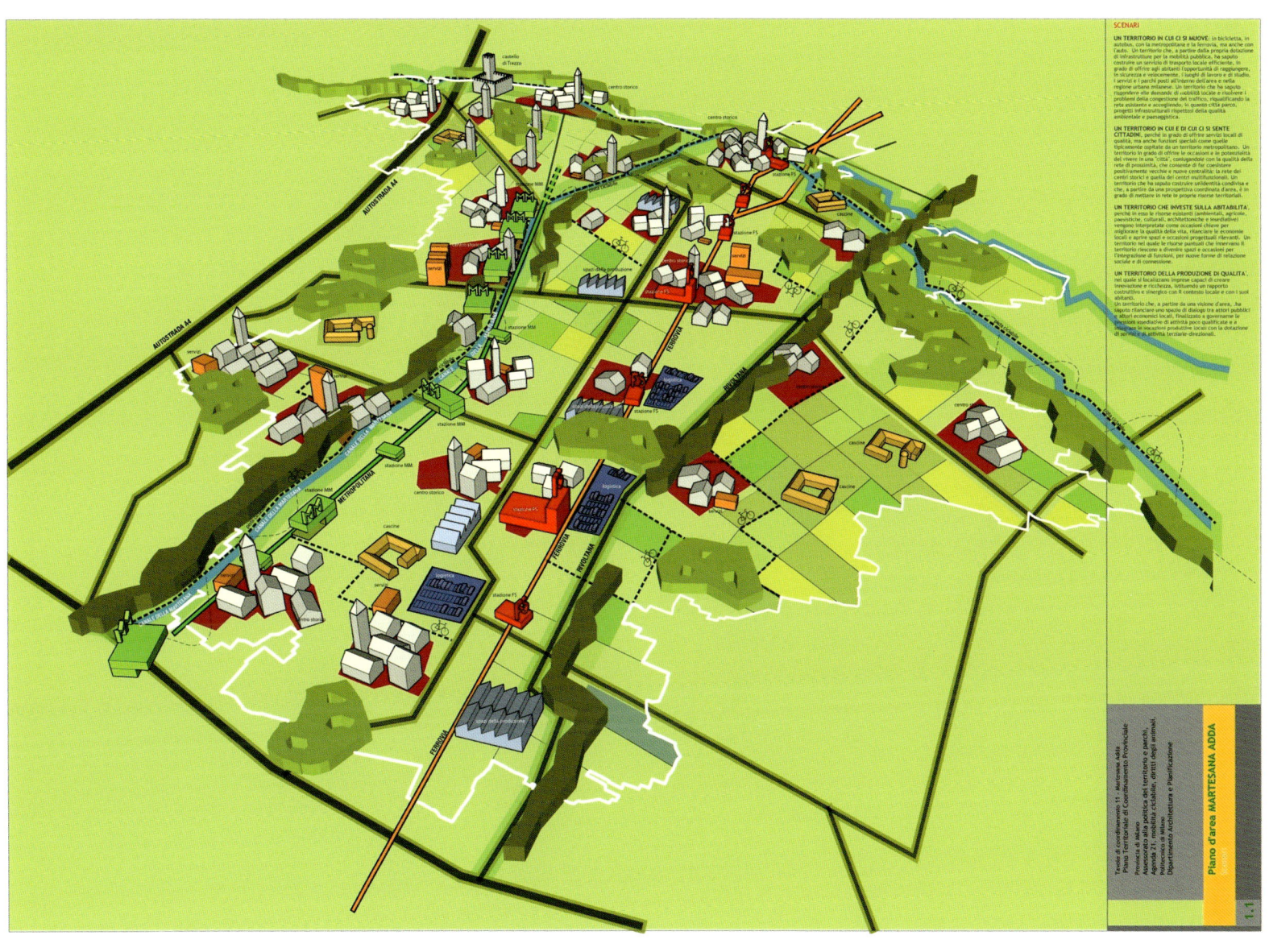

DIALOGUE ON THE CITY

Plan of the Martesana-Adda area. Province of Milan.
Map of project systems

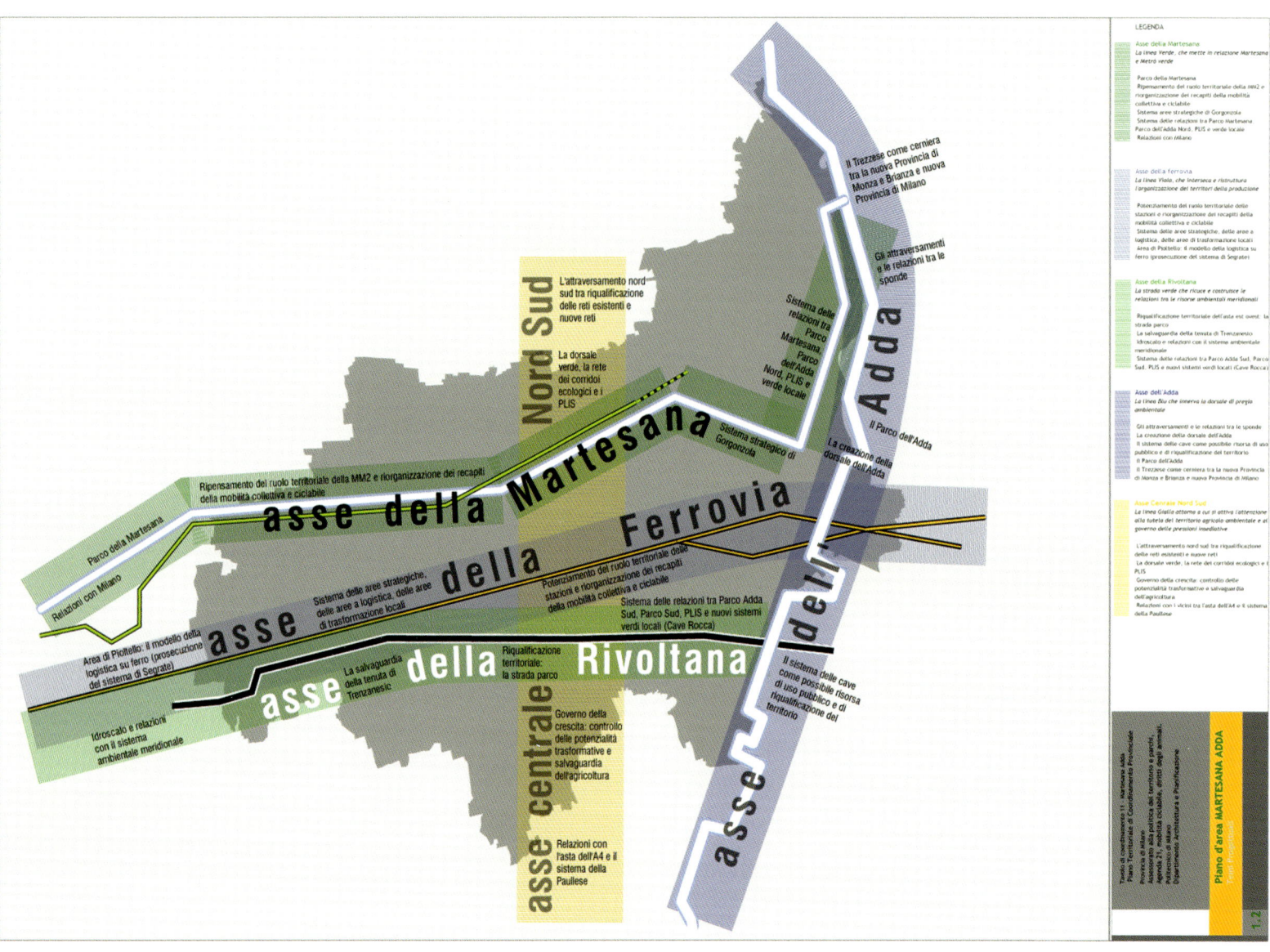

Plan of the Martesana-Adda area. Province of Milan.
Map of hierarchies and polarities

DIALOGUE ON THE CITY

Plan of the Martesana-Adda area. Province of Milan. Map of the transformational potentialities of the territory

pecially in such a dense and compact context as the Milanese. I don't know where the blame lies. Perhaps with the recent reform of urban planning, which did not have the courage, in handing over all responsibility to the regions, to tell them that the municipalities are not all the same, that the territories are not all structured in the same way, and that it is therefore not possible for there to be just one instrument, the same for all, large and small alike, in the hands of the municipality alone. If we add the attacks now made on the provinces from all sides, as though they alone were to blame for Italy's financial woes, you will understand that no intermediate level is justifiable in this atmosphere. It is a mistake. I will always maintain this and we have seen it for ourselves in our plans and our everyday experiences. The intermediate dimension is the only one that makes inter-municipal coordination and planning possible and the only one that makes it possible to hold the pieces of territorial design together. We showed this years ago. The experience of the plan for the Martesana Adda area, capable of bringing twenty-eight municipalities in the east of the province of Milan together around the same table and conceived as a tool for implementation of the territorial coordination plan, was unique and in some respects splendid. It even managed to produce a plan with three scenarios and associated special projects and strategic policies. Perfect. But what happened? Today, after all these years, nothing of that plan remains, because the law changed in the meantime and the procedure of the territorial management plan seemed so fast and unhampered by control that the very mayors who sat around the table all called us in to design their own little pieces or territory, their own back yard and vegetable patch of transformations.

MDV What should we have done? Not draw up those plans? Or do them differently?

MF I'm convinced that we were quite right to do them in that way, precisely because our experience of the area plan made us realize that no plan can exist by itself and no municipality can see itself as an island.

MDV That's true. In the plan for Vaprio d'Adda we addressed the entire question of the road system, the crossing of the Adda and the insertion of special functions in dialogue with the neighbouring municipalities and their expansionistic ambitions. In the plan for Grezzago we addressed together with Trezzo d'Adda the problem of the development of the plots of building land along the A4, then handled through a single office. And in the more recent plan for Verano Brianza we pushed for the municipality to coordinate its planning with the higher bodies and the neighbouring municipalities, first through integrated programmes and then through the traffic plan. But it was our plans that assumed the responsibility of addressing a question otherwise overlooked in the confusion of the province and its incapacity to understand the evolutionary phenomena of the territory.

MF And its failure to develop a tool of general coordination in urban planning capable of developing guidelines for economic and then territorial and social development. It is hard to understand why there should be such limited awareness of these questions. I have often wondered why. Local interest? Advantage? Laziness? The situation in other countries shows, however, that it is precisely coordination and joint action between a number of territorial bodies that can and do give birth to incredible experiences of development to the advantage of all the parties involved. Just think how many opportunities for development have been born in so many of the cities we like to visit, from Amsterdam and Hamburg to the United States. We have tried to work within this perspective in our plans, especially in drawing up the provincial plan of Novara, even though it was a short-lived experience. Territorial planning cannot but be concerned with development that is sustainable, balanced, social acceptable and not at the expense of components like the environment, land and all the finite resources. Without development no territory can hope to continue along its path. Incredible though it may appear, many plans are avowedly opposed to development because they see this solely in terms of increased building. While we have managed in these years to produce plans with little growth or a great deal of growth depending on the size of the municipality, the context and the conditions, we have always worked for plans that take development as their primary and central aim. I believe in this, as you know. Otherwise, the territory stops moving and dies. You too, with your experience in municipalities, mostly at the decisions' table, should know this and agree with me that a municipality comes to a halt when there is no development. Moreover, if a municipality intends to launch policies for the transformation or expansion of its built-up areas but fails to provide the right balance of economic development, it fails.

MDV Working in a municipality helps you understand which and how many difficulties the implementation process of a plan or project runs up against, starting with the plan's ability or otherwise to attract investors, rally forces and obtain consensus, if this does not happen in a context with an ongoing positive trend and dynamics of development. Why should investors work in a dead area that produces nothing? Why should they go on investing? The plan must drive the development and progress of the economic forces of a context, and this can only happen, for reasons of coordination and in order to try to do it even better, in an expanded context like the metropolitan area. If this happens, as it has in many of our municipalities thanks also to shrewd and intelligent mayors, it generates the dynamics of smart growth we have seen repeatedly in Rozzano, Missaglia and finally – we hope – in Cassano d'Adda, so strong as to produce new urban phenomena precisely in those somewhat scattered territories.

MF You have touched on a central point and one to which, as you know, I attach great importance, because I have seen constant mutation over these years of the areas where we live and have worked, both in Italy and in the United States. It is true that there has been a transformation of residential settlements, but I am very far from thinking simply that I have lived in an age of change. I believe that nothing more ingenuous could have been said during the 1980s about the end of expansion and the transition exclusively to an age of transformation. Many sites have indeed been transformed, many cities have changed the face of some of their most central areas, but the territories have gone on growing at the same time. The more evolved contexts have understood this and tried to stop or at least to govern this phenomenon, whereas others have done less and some nothing at all. The metropolitan areas have in fact increased in size. Many places have seen not only growth but also increased density, which we can this time attribute to the recent transformation of consolidated areas once underused. And so, while urban contexts grew on the outskirts, the volumes constructed increased inside them, and not necessarily in the centre, sometimes generating new episodes of centrality: new small phenomena in which the aim

PGT (Territorial Management Plan) for Verano Brianza (Monza and Brianza). Strategic framework of transformations for the San Giuseppe district

of the transformation project was to increase the urban sense of the area; replacing disused factories with a little catalogue of urban objects like squares, promenades, public buildings and places for relations. We were among the first to take an interest in New Urbanism and its ability to undertake precisely this kind of operation. I at least often found myself thinking that they were somewhat useless commercial operations, as they created neat little urban episodes – a bit flimsy, as happens in America – far away from the city centre, from the heart and the connections. Well, I've had to think again. Today I regret the slightly snobbish, old European attitude I had then. Though separated from one another, though isolated in a shapeless sprawl, episodes of urbanism do have an effect. They bring quality and they attract even only a small part not of the territory, which continues to be scattered, but of the people, the life and the exchanges present there. The territory is thus centralized and decentralized at different speeds. It finds episodes of aggregation and increased density but then returns to distance and rarefaction. This is what the city is now at the metropolitan level.

MDV Consider Milan. It's the same to some extent here too. The development of Assago, the areas of transformation following on from the era of urban redevelopment plans, and tomorrow the railway stations. While these are certainly not capable of redesigning the city completely, as the plans of expansion once succeeded in doing, but are able to increase the urban episodes or reduce the areas where there is nothing urban. This is what we tried to

Inzago (Milan). Project for the creation of a new cooperative social housing settlement. The central piazza, compositional fulcrum of the project and focal point of local relations

do with the transformation of the centre of Roncello. In a meaningless sea of residential buildings, erected all together and all in a hurry, the operation of transforming the historical centre with the construction of a new town hall was conceived in line with this philosophy and will lead one day, when completed, to a different view of the municipal territory, centralized and endowed with new meaning precisely in that point and around that particular sequence of functions.

MF How can we measure these effects? How can we now measure this proliferation of urban episodes? Or rather, what is it that make some transformations really new urban centralities and others banal instances of speculative reconstruction? I have thought a lot about this lately, because I really believe that this is the most interesting phenomenon to work on now, and the one upon which we have concentrated over in these years as planners and architects. I have very often thought that we should read with greater attention, not least between the lines, the studies of Peter Calthorpe or Andrés Duany, on the subject of the Transect, for example. We need to understand, for example, how to define a set of indicators serving to measure the manifestation of urban phenomena. I have thought of analyzing more closely the idea of a walking radius, which they estimate as about 800 meters, because we could identify the crowding of things and events within that radius so as to establish whether a urban phenomenon exists in that case. Or connect it with the presence of at least some functions that tells us whether there is a particular concentration, such as

Portland, Oregon, USA. Beaverton. Transit-oriented development of residential complexes around the public transport stop. Functional mix, volumetric concentration and compact composition of the constructed space

a café, tobacconist's or newsagent's. You know, if we managed to understand this more clearly, it would also help us to work on our plans and on the system of rules that we develop for documents and instruments required to address not only the consolidated, constructed and existing city (which we often do not know how to revitalize) but also the city to be transformed. For this, we must always have a clear vision of the position occupied by the area within the city's overall system and the system of functions and weights that can be embedded into it.

MDV You're right. I too believe that it is important to apply this reasoning not only to the areas of transformation. There has been a fairly clear shift of focus in the plans we have worked on over this period. Eight years ago, due also to the impetus of the reform of urban planning and the new regional law, we were all attracted by the different approach to the areas of transformation, thanks also in Lombardy to the transitory provisions for integrated action plans. Now that the areas of transformation have been conceived in some way, our attention must return to the historical centres, the already constructed contexts, the many central areas of now somewhat lifeless districts built in the 1950s and '60s. Many commercial enterprises have fled to shopping centres or closed down due to the lack of a future and an economy to support them. Many services no longer serve anyone. Thus it is that entire sections have lost their urban quality. We must, through the reasoning you have developed, try to restore this, albeit in the awareness that the city being built is different from before. We now have

DIALOGUE ON THE CITY

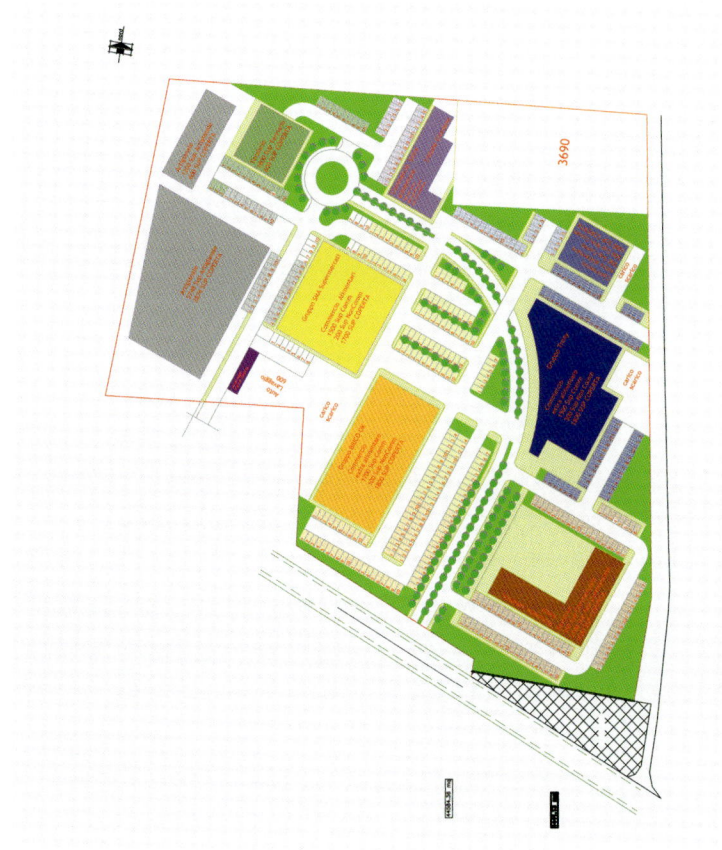

Trecate (Novara). Initial development for renovation of the Cascina Pellizzara complex. Layout of the central boulevard

a metropolitan region, inside which we will never have the same frequencies, the same distances, the same concentrations of things. We will have urban episodes of greater strength and relevance, and moments of less intensity and relevance. But we will have to be clever in ensuring that the urban phenomena are able also to attract the weaker parts round them, and that the softer and less active parts correspond increasingly to the environmental system.

MF And so you realize that the concept of metropolitan area changes a great deal. I don't know whether it is because we content ourselves with what has happened. I wouldn't like our attitude to appear defeatist with regard to any suggestions for reform or change, but I think I can say that the phenomenon referred to here is more or less what can be seen in all the consolidated cities, at least in the western world. How many times now in our travels have we realized that change has taken place and that these are the new images around which metropolitan areas are consolidated? How many times have we come across episodes of absolute urban quality far from a town or from the most consolidated districts of the city? In addition to recognizing this system, understanding that our metropolitan areas are structured in this way, and interpreting it in a positive way and to the benefit of our work, we must of course remember that we have a task to perform, one we have put into practice in our work over these years, namely to design. We must give form to these transformations. I am convinced, as you know, than our role is to design.

MDV It is very hard to think that design, as we understand it, should still be the essential part of our operations. Above all because many things push us in the opposite direction. Regulations, the need to work with instruments that do not accord primary importance to design, precise requirements and the great difficulty of getting concerns and institutions to think often cause us to relegate design, form and attention to composition to the lowest rungs of the ladder. Just think how many times this has happened in our urban-planning projects. Remember how many times we designed the multifunctional centre in Trecate? From the initial idea, from the curved boulevard capable of embracing all the buildings in a single sweep to the street that was then built by our client, always trying to save as much as possible. It was so hard to get him to understand that something more interesting could have been achieved through design.

MF I believe it's a mistake to think of design and implementation separately. If we go on thinking that the design serves to give form but in reality it is the instruments or phases of implementation that give substance and govern the process, we will go on making a mistake. In our work and in my studies, we have seen the master plan as a possible solution to this useless separation. Through the master plan we have shown our ability to develop a design giving precise formal answers that are clear, evident and above all legible. With this design, the master plan organizes its response to the primary question of the form to give to the transformation or the area we are working on. The master plan enables us to ask questions of the context, the people, the users, the actors and the operators, not about the process, dynamics or instruments but about the physical transformation that they may or may not like. It is about streets, squares, areas, green spaces and buildings that the master plan speaks. Parts are moved around and others are inserted solely in order to define a different arrangement or because they change the conditions inside the group called upon to carry out the operation, but it is understood that we always start from the physical point, from the arrangement of the parts. How many times have we dismantled and remade ours master plans? From Cassano d'Adda to Trezzo and Lainate: every time we have used the master plan to construct the process, control the response of the parties involved, understand and insert the needs of the end users, ensure compliance with the urban-planning regulations, from constraints to the application of environmental norms, without ever losing sight of the physical appearance and the formal result to be born out of it. It is an extraordinary instrument, one that belongs to us, that embodies most strongly our thinking on the city through its forms and its layout at the ground level and in elevation. The form guides the processes of decision-making and implementation. There have been cases where the design has triumphed, where many forces apparently opposed to it have been convinced of its correctness and given way. There have been cases where the design has had to yield, forced to change by particular requirements, constrains, rules or calculations. It is an instrument that has enabled us to obtain agreement, to fire the imaginations of the parties concerned, both professional and otherwise, about the transformation of a part of the city, that enables us finally to understand whether the rules we are drafting for a management plan or a set of regulations will work. How many times have we anticipated projects testing the working of the rules in our plans?

MDV We have used this type of instrument very often in our plans. Our focus on the formal transformation of the city, our desire always to include attention to form and to the "designed" end result in the planning perspective of the contexts in which we have worked, has made us realize that in actual fact the instruments at our disposal do not provide stimulus in this sense. You are right to say that for many years the wholly Italian dispute between advocates of the plan and advocates of the project was contrived and futile. The city is built through transformations and new things that follow one another, so let us find the best possible instrument to imagine, share and construct them. That's all. At the same time, however, working on this every day, I think that it is essential for a plan to anticipate questions of form and design within its framework. In our region at least, the existing instruments leave a great deal of space for the design of transformation to be regarded as the central phase around which to construct both the package of norms, rules and provisions to support the existence of that design and the path for its implementation.

MF We have worked in Italy and in other countries, above all the United States, over this period. We have realized how our cities are changing but above how much we love cities. I don't think I could live anywhere in the world other than in a city. It is the human creation that fascinates me most, to which I have devoted and will devote my entire life. I am deeply fascinated by every drawing and every image that speaks to me of the city, that tells me about the city and makes me dream of it. Living, working and teaching in New York, as well as completing my studies there, simply blew my mind. I remember, however, that even as a child I was always drawing houses and buildings. I think it is our duty, as architects and urban planners, to understand that the city has been the hub and the driving force of our way of life, of our culture and our civilization, for at least four thousand years. I don't like the arguments, which are admittedly heard only in Italy, between champions of the city and those who think we should all live as though the hills of Chianti were everywhere. The city has its own degree of anthropization, which is obviously at the highest level, but since I am very familiar with places like Tuscany, where we have worked and where I return very often, I can assure you that the city is a very strong presence also in the green hills of Chianti. Look at the aerial photographs and the growth projections for the Tuscan urban systems between Florence and Arezzo, along the Val di Chiana, between Florence and Lucca or along the coast south of La Spezia and see how many isolated green hills you find. In short, if we accept once and for all that it is the city that we must take into consideration, we will begin to understand the contexts in which we move a little better and also to have a more balanced view of the phenomena surrounding us.

MDV It is precisely the rational balance with which this subject is addressed in many north European countries that surprises me. Berlin and Hamburg are large and growing cities with very strong recent dynamics of development, and yet what is inside and what comes from outside appear to interweave very well indeed and with great equilibrium. Nobody talks about the advisability of maintaining and expanding the urban environmental system. It is taken for granted that urban biotopes, urban forests and green buffer areas exist. And nobody talks about the need to rebuild the city's disused central areas. Consider the transformation of Haven City in Hamburg and think about what we have had to hear day after day in connection with the redevelopment of the linen mill in Cassano d'Adda. Why don't we understand it here? Why don't we understand that the city is the driving force of our development and that what we must focus on with all our strength are urban phenomena from small to large, regardless of their scale?

MF You're quite right. I think that our work demonstrates precisely this. We have

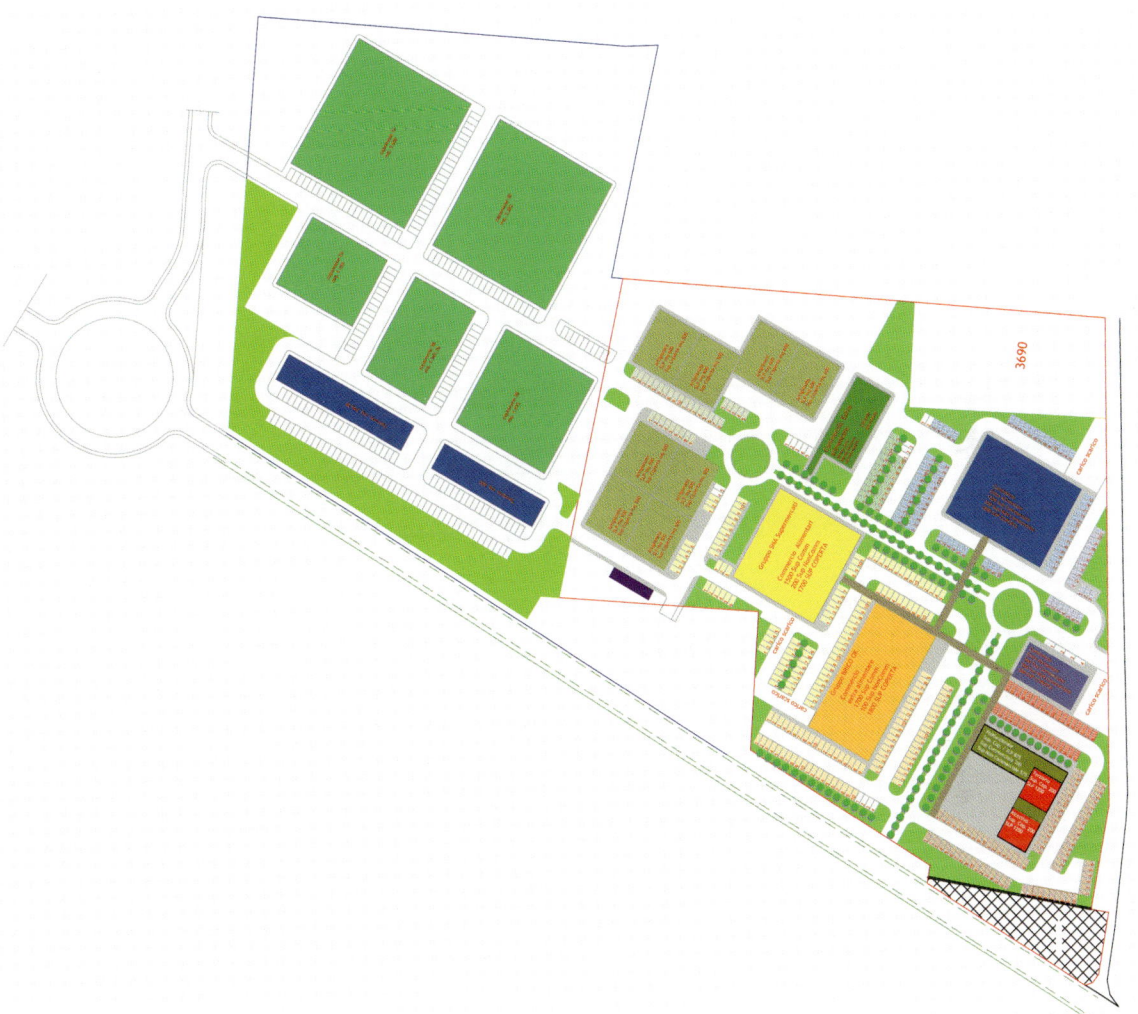

Trecate (Novara). Definitive development of the project for renovation of the Cascina Pellizzara complex. While the central boulevard organizes the less important spaces, the initial composition gives way to exploitation of the area and visibility from the road

championed the city. We have applied ourselves and worked so that every part of our activities, from plans and projects to policies and tools of implementation, even including our little works of interior design, can contribute to the virtuous production of quality. This is the point, and this is what I would like anyone reading and leafing through our anthology to understand. We have worked so that every project can contribute to the creation of a place in which quality is born out of the stimulation of relations between the local scale and the broader scale around it, between open spaces and built-up areas, between inside

Hamburg (Germany). Redevelopment of Hafencity areas. Building densities, spaces for relations, open spaces and environmental systems. A new urban environment constructed on the basis of types of consolidated spaces

and outside. The common feature of all our works is this: the stimulation of relations, contacts and exchanges between our focal point and what surrounds it. It is our duty to think that every time we work on a context, no matter how small and limited, we really have to address also what lies a few metres further on. The urban management plan of a small municipality or the traffic plan of limited urban area must in reality be part and parcel of the broader organization of the territory and help to improve the functioning of that extended slice of territory. Even though the instruments do not require it, even though the cultural context is awkward and little inclined towards such exchanges, this is what we have to do precisely because the creation of relations enables us to increase the opportunities for the creation of virtuous places where the quality of the design is spread over the quality of the intensity of these relations and contacts. This is the essence of the city. Even in our projects of interior design, every time we address a constructed environment we have gone on beyond the boundaries of inner and outer walls. Work on an apartment in a condominium designed and built by Luigi Moretti on Corso Italia in Milan meant addressing a special light and airy urban vantage point in what was a revolutionary context for the 1950s, where the evidently speculative operation left, however, an architectural masterpiece to be approached with the same courage as Moretti showed in proposing and build-

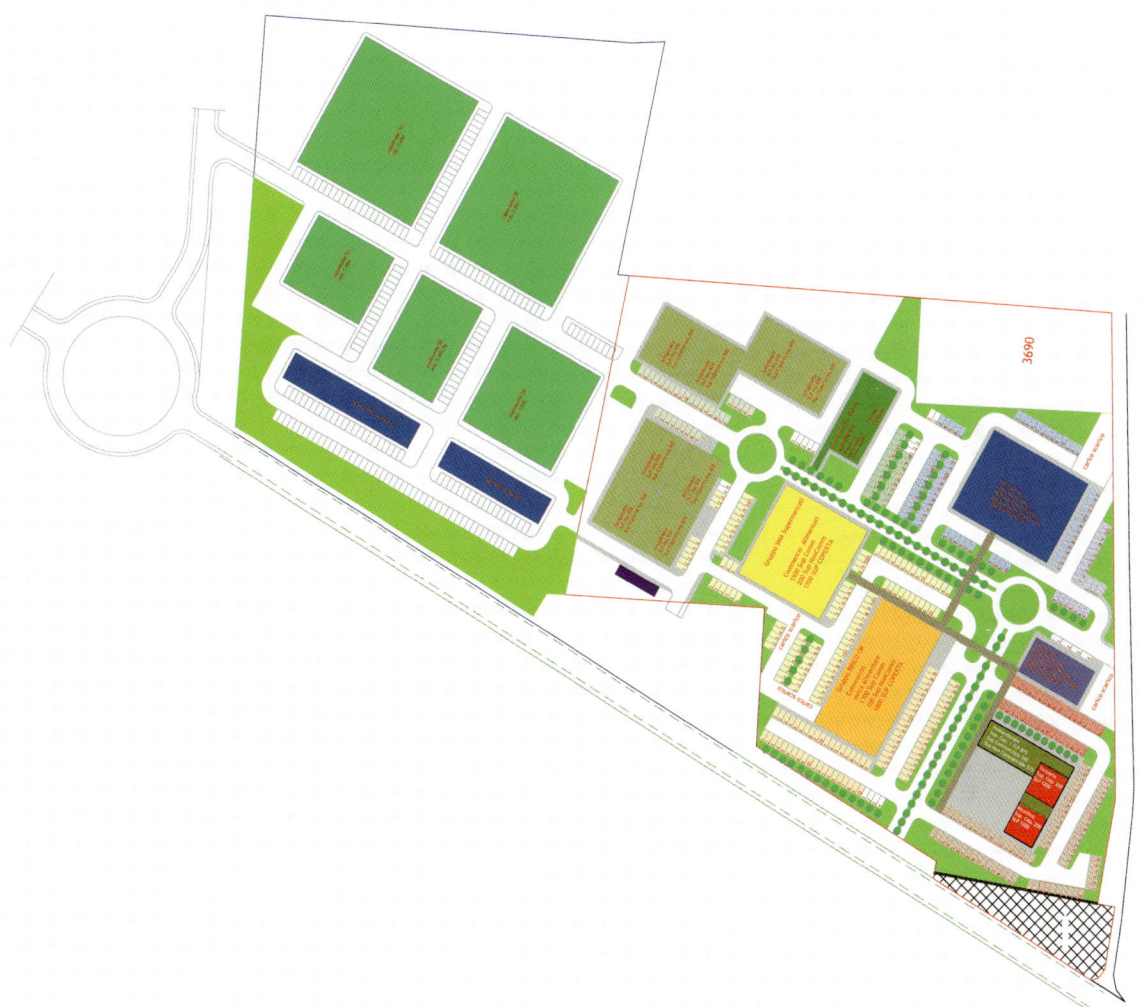

Cassano d'Adda (Milan). Redevelopment of the Linificio factory area. View of the internal boulevard

ing it. This is what our work is: constructing relations through design and supporting our ideas and proposals by securing them as much as possible to a concrete local system that legitimizes them, by respecting the rules and contexts that we find for what they are and what allows them to be altered in order to evolve. This process gives birth to quality. At the same time, we are far removed from those who attempt extreme and daring forms solely in order to shock and make an impression. No, what I would like is for our work to be seen precisely for what it is: a contribution to the day-by-day construction of virtuous relations and connections capable of producing new quality.

MDV Above all, my partner, let us not forget that our work has been and is the most interesting thing that we could have done and that we will go on doing, observing the city from above and below and always being sure that we are on its side.

Imagination and Design in Urban Planning

Urban planning is a very particular activity in Italy. It involves conviction that planning the development of residential settlements is a matter of paramount importance and that it is so both for the public administration of cities and for those who work in them. It involves working in particular contexts in the midst of forces that are not always friendly, speculative pressures and partisan interests, and generally in conditions where it is difficult to share the deeper meaning of planning action. Italian planning today is, however, the result of years of very important cultural interest and debate in relation both to the instruments used to manage the planning of cities and to the structure that cities and the territory in general should be given. Between pressures for growth as the result of private interests employed for the construction of settlements and attempts to impose approaches of greater breadth and public character, the discipline has now developed a particular vision in its everyday activities. It is evident that settlements, at least in most of Italy, can only be managed through the definition of a planning instrument and its implementation through tools of a more operative character serving to balance private transformations with public benefits or public use and advantage. It is, however, not equally evident how technical knowledge and knowledge of the channels through which planning must develop can drive both the public and the private sector to operate correctly. Not only in the negative terms of action by the public sector to restrain and limit the thrust of the private sector or by the private sector to bypass public constraints, but also and above all in the positive terms of understanding how the path of planning can in reality construct scenarios and visions, stimulate territorial production, increase the positive effects of every transformation for both the parties involved, and contribute to the balanced and sustainable evolution of settlements, their inhabitants and the environment. Our activities over the last ten years have taken place precisely in the midst of these opposing drives and in a panorama not necessarily informed and aware of the importance of the dissemination of technical knowledge.

As never before, but in actual fact confirming an anything but hidden or imperceptible trend, this very period has, however, seen recognition of the city as the most important form of the aggregation of people and their activities. In Italy, in Europe and still more in other countries, the city is again in the forefront and constitutes the key channel for phenomena of economic growth or decline (it is significant that the international crisis we have all lived through in recent years was born out of phenomena as incredibly earthly, urban and territorial as property speculation bubbles) and pressures for territorial transformation as well as expectations of growth and rebirth after the crisis. It is the city that retains the leading role as mankind's greatest invention to represent itself, its ability to imagine, invent and build, its urge to live together and create relations. It is the city that confirms itself as the most convincing image of the human way of living and that channels ideas, drives and reforms of collective life, above all as regards the sustainability of the urban framework itself, concerns about the excessive growth of some urban contexts and love for what cities preserve within them as bearing witness to the past. The city is therefore in the midst of a great many interests. For this reason, even in a context as difficult as the one we have had to face, the object of our work has always proved so interesting and important that it is precisely engagement in urban planning in this way that enables us to invest our efforts and ideas in the city and pay less attention to the associated difficulties and friction. Even in the particular period that cities have been going through in Italy but also elsewhere in Europe and the United States.

The city has been read and described for many years in terms of a model of constant and positive evolution in which, after the phases of post-war reconstruction and growth during the 1950s and '60s, it then began to transform itself, rebuilding settlements left free by the disappearance of various functions. This very period is witnessing a whole host of transformations of areas once extensively used for factories and production in general, replacing functions no longer in use and increasing the residential function as well as services for the inhabitants of urban areas. Everywhere in Europe and the United States, these areas of transformation have enabled cities to transform themselves, increasing their vocation as places of residence for people equipped with facilities, services and greenery. The evolution of the city and the description of this evolution have led to recognition of the phase we are living through as one of transformation, ongoing or nearing completion for the more evolved contexts and those that addressed this aspect with greater determination at the very outset.

What comes next? This is precisely the question that the activities of the last few years have considered in depth, not least as a result of taking place primarily in places affected by transformation and located in hybrid contexts between larger agglomerations and the less built-up areas within metropolitan areas of greater or lesser building density. These places seem to express with greater clarity the directions in which urban phenomena are moving. Both in the sharing of the terms and paradigms through which urban planning works and in the real, practical activity of planning, urban contexts are addressing the territorial dimension with greater investment after years of expansion in both larger and smaller nuclei, affected by the phenomena of urban expansion under way both in comparatively consolidated countries, like those of the west, and even more in countries of recent development. This is the territory that has in actual fact been affected by the emerging urban phenomena in the last few years, both because the central cities have increased in importance and scale, with increasing involvement of the surrounding area, and because of the more interesting fact that the smaller contexts historically providing the territory with support have grown and expanded in turn and taken on a different structure. We have worked on this subject in recent years in our activity as planners and identified two aspects of great importance in these areas. First, they are historical nodes of a polycentric but hierarchical organization of the territory with a very substantial agricultural and environmental heritage. Second, they have becomes contemporary nodes of a metropolitan structure that is still hard to interpret and in which the environmental heritage is not always recognizable.

Working as planners in these areas, we have been prompted to recognize this situation and focus on two primary aspects capable of structuring the territory as a whole in a more fruitful way: on the one hand, recognition that the recent transformations and ongoing evolution of these areas are capable of developing urban episodes of great importance even in contexts that are less urban than the major cities; on the other, reappraisal of the value of open spaces and investment in the possibility of preserving what remains with active functions of importance for human activities. Our plans have worked on these two aspects

Territorial Management Plan (PGT) for Liscate (Milan). Design of green systems and open space. Upgrading of areas of the South Milan Agricultural Park

with great attention. The production of urban places and the structuring of open space are two activities that make it possible to define the nodes of the territory with greater strength, both the towns with a long history and those of recent development, and the territory that surrounds them, not as negative – awaiting construction in order to become positive – but as an enlarged "plenum" rich in resources and potential if seen as the active connective tissue between the territorial nodes. The metropolitan dimension has been resolutely addressed through the instruments of urban planning as regards both provisions and their implementation. The territorial management plans in Lombardy and the instruments developed in other regional contexts or other countries have led to identification of transformations of territories as a way to increase their urban character precisely in pursuit of urbanization as an indispensable element for people to identify with that context, again in virtue of the initial consideration, namely recognition of the city as the major organizer of the spatial dimension of human relations. At the same time, the management plans and above all the supra-local tools have worked over this period to assign the free and less intensely urbanized territory the role of active connective tissue. Through provisions for infrastructures designed in more territorial and less engineering-oriented terms, the constitution of inter-municipal spheres for the preservation of open space, and a more active and sustainable vision of the territory, the plans produced have sought to assign once exclusively agricultural territory a role of connecting the built-up areas, reinterpreting it as a container not only for preservation but also for all the activities,

IMAGINATION AND DESIGN IN URBAN PLANNING

Roncello (Monza and Brianza). Redevelopment of central areas. The new town hall and central piazza

including those of a typically urban nature, that can be expressed through sports facilities, places for cultural activities, services and environmentally significant places like areas for the production of biotopes and spheres of environmental regeneration in an active vision of open space.

The plans developed have experimented on smaller urban spheres with the capacity to imagine different structures and geometries for their immediate future. Above all, they have addressed the transformation that the position and nature of these places can undergo in relation to the different role that the metropolitan territory can take on. Many of these contexts, e.g. satellite and dormitory towns around the city of Milan, have rediscovered historical, economic and social dignity as elements of a more deeply structured territory more intensely designed for relations. For this very reason, they have endeavoured through plans to imagine a different future with a more active role in relation to the territory and the ability to express centralities, functions and services created or susceptible in some highly urbanized settings. The plans and plans of implementation drawn up have thus made it possible in many cases to design new places capable of expressing a strongly urban character through the forms constructed, the organization of spaces, the relations

between the new and existing spaces, and the alternation of residential and service functions. In this way, they have given new meaning to the once lost centres of towns and begun to offer an alternative to repetitive urban spawl. The Inzago settlement of cooperative building thus addresses the idea of creating a new section of the municipality and imagines a new square capable of attracting buildings and stimulating new relations between inhabitants. The new design for the civic centre of Roncello considers the significance of a centre for a very small town that has grown over the years only through the addition of residential functions and envisages a succession of open spaces and spaces for relations of great breath. The perspectives and scenarios of the plan for Verano Brianza envisage a small centre for every district in such a way as to lend new meaning to the territory as a whole in opposition to the customary image of growth through sprawl. The new developments of territorial urbanization thus combat the monotony, repetition, anonymity and sprawl that have distinguished those territories until now. It is possible to reorganize functions and relations around these new territorial centres to the point of imagining a territory no longer attracted by a single major urban reality, as in the case of Milan and many other cities, but with a polycentric distribution of different urban elements connected with one another as in a single city, not rarefied but certainly discontinuous, not separated but certainly endowed with focal points of such intensity as to give meaning to the territorial system and make it even richer than the central city. The plans developed work for this reversal in line with the most recent views of the territory and the most recent proposals for the reorganization of areas of urban sprawl, which seems to have been the only future for too many western countries for too many years.

The territory plays a key role in this perspective. If the search for new urbanization is capable through plans and projects of producing new episodes of sufficient strength to refocus attention inside rather than outside contexts, it must also be capable of demonstrating that the alternative of rebalancing the weights is better than the current alternative of spreading construction all over the territory. Thus freed from the pressure of growth through sprawl, the territory can be seen once again not as a void to be filled but as central connectivity, active and capable of encapsulating more than function and meaning. The territory of the South Milan Agricultural Park around the municipality of Cassina de' Pecchi is seen by the Territorial Management Plan not only in terms of the protection and defence of a heritage that has miraculously escaped urban sprawl but also in active terms as a vast area available for the development of urban functions in green and open space. The old farmhouses thus become the centre of the town – a town that had no centre – and accommodate the civic centre and many other public activities. Some areas accommodate new sports centres and revitalize the system of hamlets scattered through the context of the park. The territory around the municipality of Inzago considers the creation of a local park of supra-municipal interest as a key objective not only of the Territorial Management Plan but also of the dialogue to be initiated with the neighbouring municipalities. This dialogue has already succeeded in obtaining agreement on a variant for the only existing road, thus demonstrating how an urban-planning instrument can enable towns with a traditionally parochial attitude to talk to one another and develop shared innovative visions of the overall territory.

A different organization of the territory is just a short step away. The plans drawn up over these years, the processes that these plans are designed to manage together with the parties involved, the objective attained and what has been proposed and constructed all show that a territory can be interpreted and planned in accordance with a different structural vision: no longer in negative terms with respect to the power of attraction of a single context but in positive terms, harnessing the forces and dynamics that the territory, independently of its major city, possesses and is able to express. The perspective is post-metropolitan. The sequence of distributed centralities makes it possible to inhabit a vast territory as though it were a city made up of episodes of concentration and parts of greater slowness and emptiness, a region studded with salient points in which functions and use generate systems of open spaces and vital spaces of relations, and relaxed in natural spheres of value that are used and protected. This is the image in which the work have invested and through which the plans and projects have endeavoured to secure an advance in urban planning.

The instruments available have of course been used, first and foremost the law

IMAGINATION AND DESIGN IN URBAN PLANNING

Cassina de' Pecchi (Milan). Design of Cascina Bindellera. Centre of municipal territory inserted into the South Milan Agricultural Park and new town centre

passed by the Lombardy Region in 2005 and implemented in the following years. Apparently, and with great courage at the beginning, the transition from a slow, long, restrictive and exclusively regulatory instrument to a set of more streamlined tools with shorter temporal horizons designed to accelerate decision-making procedures and the approval of urban planning provisions afforded a glimpse of the possibility of urban planning focusing primarily on the implementation of provisions, thus reducing the uncertainty that accompanied the old town planning scheme for years between the provision and what was actually put into effect. In actual fact, with the loss of the initial impetus, a continuous series of additions and modifications to the original framework of the law, and the general slowing down as regards planning and provisions undergone by urban contexts due to the general crisis, the reform of urban planning undertaken by Lombardy and other regions has also displayed some weaknesses. We have worked on these over the last few years, seeking to understand how the lack of expanded planning frameworks, not necessarily corresponding to a supra-local body (be it the province, the park agencies, the local communities or the region) but in line with the territorial realities identified (e.g. the metropolitan city), is one of the most important problems and capable of crippling the best possible planning through lack of coordination. We have thus equipped our plans not only with broader vision but also and above all with tools and opportunities to ensure that fruitful dialogue between municipalities and planners could be stimulated through the invention and inclusion in plans of projects capable of combining the interests of various bodies and institutions. In order to ensure coordination worthy of the name and concentrate it on the reality of a specific project, above all when based on perspectives of redevelopment, transformation and the creation of episodes of quality.

Secondly, we have focused on understanding another fundamental problem and equipping our production to provide help and stimulation in the search for a solution. The reform of the instruments of urban planning and the general reform that has taken place in urban planning over the last few years have slightly accelerated a general framework and an approach to urban planning that for so many years, even in the presence of changes, did nothing to alter the basic structure of planning. The accumulation of knowledge and practice in the bodies responsible for the planning (primarily municipalities and supra-local agencies in Italy) prevented the reform from instilling new technical skills and realization that a change in speed was indispensable. In addition to human resistance to change, the natural inertia of certain contexts led in many cases to failure to understand the renewal of instruments and the renewal of the perspectives within which they would operate, and above all to take a different approach to the city and its structural organization in relation to the territory. The plans and pro-

IMAGINATION AND DESIGN IN URBAN PLANNING

jects produced over these years have endeavoured to increase and disseminate technical knowledge of greater complexity in urban planning. Plans and projects have sought to broaden their spheres in an effort to understand the tools with which the technicians and those responsible for implementing their provisions would address them. In the same way, we have taken care to equip our plans and projects with a broader array of tools for regulation and implementation than actually requested in an attempt to create technical knowledge that is more widespread, more pervasive and more capable of conferring dignity on a discipline wonderfully made up of invention, the observation of reality and technical ability to handle the rules, consisting entirely as it does of the interweaving of the planning vision, projection towards the future, and the reality of the codes and norms of the present.

In the midst of all this, the use of master plans together with general planning tools is an important investment for us. Over these years and in the projects developed, we have shown great belief in the evocative capacity and anticipatory possibilities of the master plan, seen precisely because it is an intermediate instrument – midway between planning and architectural design – as a point in which a number of aspects could be forced to coexist: urban planning and architecture as well as the lightness of vision and the heaviness of rules. Both in plans of territorial management and in planning instruments in general, the master plan has been used to provide a framework for provisions for the transformation of an area or the vision of a system (made up of various areas and objects) and in order to anticipate verification of the functioning of the rules of the transformation. Two of the cornerstones of urban planning are ex-

Verano Brianza (Monza and Brianza). Urban Traffic Plan. Development of the central road, from an inter-municipal relief road to a vital boulevard

IMAGINATION AND DESIGN IN URBAN PLANNING

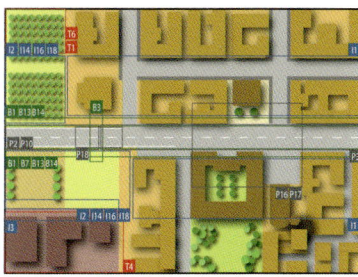

Puglia region. Guidelines for road design.
Urban sections and relations between roads, open spaces and spaces for relations

pressed through the master plan, namely design and rules.

We have assigned an increasingly predominant role to design over the years. It is through design that we have expressed our idea not only of space but also of spatial organization, of implementing provisions in order to regenerate it, of structuring functions and uses, of the alternation of spaces and so on. An urban-planning design expresses many things and many dimensions. It has been capable for us over the years of speaking about constructed space, open space and the space of relations, of expressing the form of the volumes of constructed space and the functions accommodated within it, and at the same time of planning the sequence of open spaces, both public and private, and outlining their ability to cohere in a system or remain uselessly separate. It has been capable of expressing relations and demonstrating links and connections between the various spaces. In short, it has been capable of envisaging and illustrating the extraordinary alternation of spaces of relations that makes urban contexts for us the human creation of greatest interest. The use of design has made it possible to discover connections and relations between the parts to the point of reading them as systems and discovering the most dynamic ways of giving form and substance to those systems in terms of rules and implementation. The design of systems and the design of the city in terms of systems enable us to structure urban spaces precisely with a view to the urban quality that we have seen give importance to settlements and their position in the territory.

It is also to design that we have assigned over the years the task of representing the overall form of the settlements addressed: a thorny question upon which a great deal has been said and written over the years, also recently, and one that apparently clashes with the vision of a territory consolidated over time as rarefaction and sprawl. It is, however, precisely the focusing of attention on the power that settlements can have in hosting new centralities that has made it possible to understand the renewed importance of the overall shape of the settlement. Not a precise, complete and closed form – because such an idea does not belong to our culture, to the structuring of the territory we inhabit or to the dynamics of the territory's evolution – but a relational form capable of defining the parts through which a settlement is structured in relation to the surrounding space, be it countryside, a park or other settlements. Only by designing relations is it possible to design the territory and to understand how it functions. The plans drawn up by the masters, from which all we have learned, often start precisely from the overall design in search of the completeness of their vision. Important and indeed historic plans are imprinted in our memory precisely through the image with which the overall design endowed their provisions. Thus it is today that the plans on which we have worked, e.g. the plans for Liscate and Verano Brianza, have succeeded in expressing an overall image capable of representing a project to be aimed at and that if put into effect, even in forms and periods other than those envisaged, is capable of defining different relations and a different organization of the settlement.

Rules give urban planning its structure and have been the object of a great deal of study over the years. Plans are made up of rules, but we have found ourselves operating in a particular cultural context where the rules have created suffering – legitimate or otherwise – in those who have approached the city, and where failure to obey them accounts for much of the history of Italian urban planning. The reform of urban planning shifted its focus on rules so radically as to lead in many regions even to a change in the name of the general instrument of planning so as to eliminate precisely its regulative connotation. The plans still speak about rules, however, and it is through rules that projects are put into effect. We have examined this question significantly over the years and realized that rules cannot be written by one party and obeyed by the other with the same ideas and respect. Those who lay down the rules and those who write them start from two different positions and have two different aims. The projects developed have sought to reverse the point of view and place the objective to be attained in the centre. Be it an envisaged transformation or an existing slice of city to be arranged, the final vision to be attained dictated the rules and the master plan used as a tool made it possible to try them out. Nor is it a question of rigid rules or flexible rules. The discourse based on this dichotomy all too often opens the door to tussles between those who seek to punish by imposing tough rules and those who seek to escape control by advocating weak ones. What is needed are rules of performance, capable of adapting to the conduct of the parties involved on condition that the end result is attained, rules connected with the design and the form to be pursued by means of a specific transformation, rules capable of adapting to the period and the ongoing dynamics as well as the dialogue established between the various parties. The absence of this dialogue is a possibility that affects the evolution of the rules, which must, however, remain as a fixed basis and ensure an equilibrium to be attained in any case.

Between design and rules, our plans and projects have thus worked over the years above all in search of urban quality, convinced as we are of the centrality of urban contexts both for their ability to offer mankind stimuli and relations, and for their

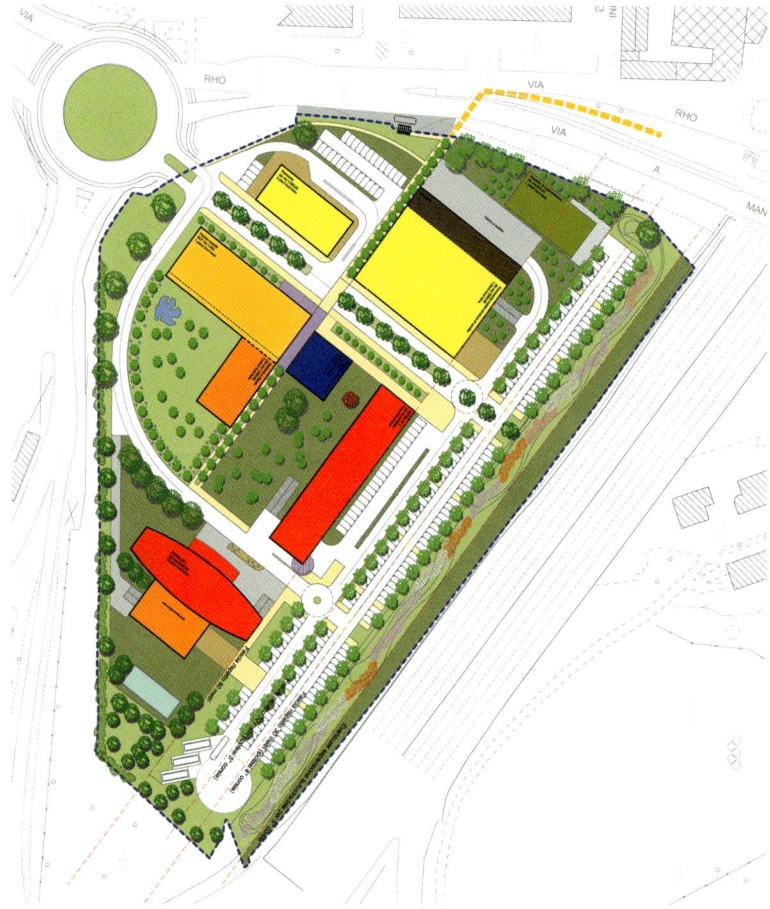

Lainate (Milan). Integrated Plan of Operations (PII) for areas along the motorway. General site plan

IMAGINATION AND DESIGN IN URBAN PLANNING

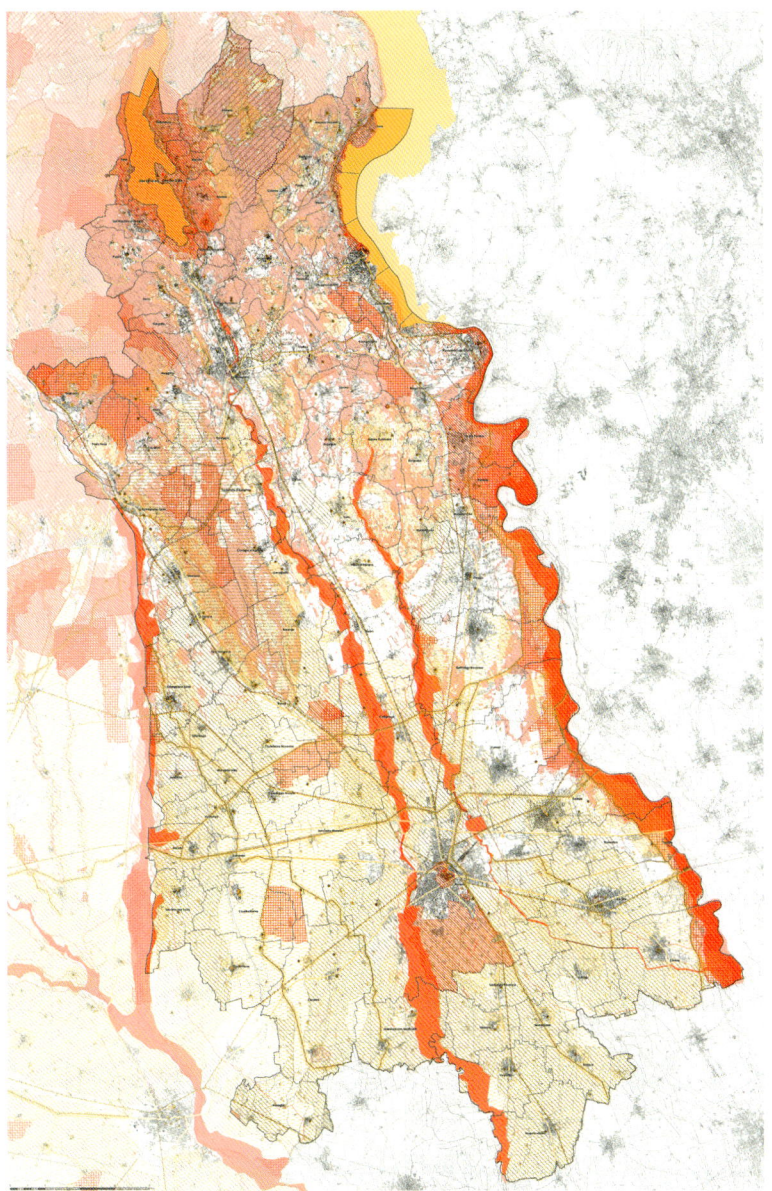

Revision of the Territorial Plan (PTP) of the province of Novara. Table of the degree of impact of constraints, norms and rules on local transformations and structure

"post-metropolitan" structuring in a broader dimension capable of finally embracing the territory and no longer constituting a destructive alternative for both sides. We have endeavoured in this way, albeit within the confined sphere of apparently local dimensions, to broaden our horizons and encompass the most recurrent themes in the dynamism displayed by urban contexts in the world. This dynamism and this confidence in the ability of urban contexts to act as the driving force of many economies and the point of reference of many societies are associated with the new dignity that their surrounding territory must assume in a finally sustainable balance between city and non-city, taking us out of the dichotomy, away from the image of urban sprawl of a few years back, and towards the construction of a polycentric territory rich in urban episodes and connected by a structured and respected environment.

37

Architectural Design and Construction

Giving birth to architectural projects directly out of experiences and processes of urban planning makes it possible to follow an idea from start to finish all the way through the difficulties of private or public decision making. Many of the projects we have developed over the years have been directly commissioned by clients involved in pathways of urban planning upon which we have worked, in addition to some public works designed and built in contexts where we were in any case familiar with the urban framework. For the attention that we have always focused on the process generating the transformations with which urban planning and architecture are concerned, this is a very fortunate, as it makes it possible to place the buildings planned on a different terrain made up of more stimuli and opportunities, as well perhaps as more problems. Direct knowledge of the rules makes it possible to apply them and use them correctly, not as constraints but as technical specifications serving as a starting point for design and creation. The terrain of urban planning in which we have embedded our buildings has sometimes been prepared by urban-planning instruments that we ourselves have drawn up, as in all the cases where we have gone on to design buildings envisaged by our plans. In these cases, the genesis of the building coincides with the genesis of the urban-planning provision and advantage is taken of the opportunity to derive the maximum benefit from the coordination of urban planning and architecture. The question of the freedom of architecture with respect to the constraints of planning or the legitimacy of planning with respect to the unruliness of architecture is perhaps as old as the world or in any case not much less. Its most recent form juxtaposes the correctness of developing planning pathways capable of regulating what is generated by the architect's pencil and the full validity of architectural projects justified by their internal rules of composition with no reference to an external normative framework. As stated, the debate is age-old and has resurfaced in history very often, also in recent times. It is perhaps always triggered by the same question of which should give shape to the city: architecture, which interprets by itself the natural rules and the requirements of the context in which it takes place, if correctly undertaken, or urban planning and those whose profession it is to draw up the rules and design the whole.

Over the years, since we began to work in planning and indeed since I was a child, I have always been convinced that the city is the human creation of greatest power. I am crazy about cities and cannot stand the thought of being far away from an urban context, from the wealth of things, people, events, opportunities, objects and relations that only an urban environment can offer. In time, and above all in relation to the changes and transformations of recent years, the city has asserted itself increasingly as practically the only form of human organization. Apart from villages and markedly rural or isolated contexts, the city is the form of organization towards which human groups of greater or lesser size tend. The countries that have taken the path of development focus on the construction of cities in order to invest in a different economy and make manifest their new power and spending capacity. The consolidated countries would never abandon their constellations of more or less interconnected cities, and even the countries that have suffered most from the beginning of the century until today (or rather yesterday) from urban phenomena markedly born in order to escape the compactness and proximity of the city (I refer to urban sprawl) are witnessing an ever-greater number of events and opportunities conducive to the construction of urban episodes. New transformations that involve operations of an urban character with squares and buildings closely grouped around open spaces all lead us to think that proximity and vicinity are indispensable elements for the correct and stimulating organization of human activities. The city thus again permeates the very places – such as suburbs – created in order to escape from the traditional city in accordance with different cultures and ideas (from the garden city on), and demonstrates its strength in being what the newly developed countries have assiduously striven to build ever since their wallets were filled to bulging. The city thus continues to be the central element around which we all recognize the validity of human organization. As clearly written in dozens of books and essays, the city continues to be the driving force of the economic, social, political and cultural development of the developed world. If this is so, and if we agree to speak about the city as the central expression of human construction (with apologies to isolated buildings and the countryside), then we must agree that the city is the stage upon which buildings appear: as soloists or members of the chorus but in any case on a stage. For this reason, I am firmly convinced that the expressive freedom of architecture can only be born in the context of the city, or its surroundings, and respect

Missaglia (Lecco). Integrated Plan of Operations (PII). I Platani. View of the central sunken road

for the same. The architecture we have undertaken and for which we have worked is markedly urban in its way of inserting itself respectfully into a context, establishing relations with the same (opening, closure or even neutrality), and necessarily creating opportunities for new relations to be generated, virtuous connections between built-up space, open space and the space serving for relations, as well as enrichment – albeit minimal, limited and circumscribed – for the entire urban system in which it is embedded. We have admittedly worked during these years precisely in contexts of a very marked urban character, either because they are already part of the city or because they are on their way towards the by now almost spontaneous concentration that many contexts are undergoing, as stated above, and in which we have been involved. We have therefore endeavoured to ensure that the architectural works we have designed and built can help – through a reading of the complex rules of the city, both urban-planning and otherwise – to construct another new piece of city full of relations and stimuli, in the awareness that the city we like most is precisely the one where different contributions made by different parties in different periods contribute to the construction of space and stimulation of relations between people, functions and spaces. Our architecture is born in this particular conceptual framework. While agreeing to be an expression of the rules of an urban environment, it is therefore rigorous in its formal expression. The formal rigour that distinguishes what we have conceived and created thus corresponds to the most correct interpretation of the rules, the norms and the context in which the architectural works are located while at the same time forging a simple and honest link with the tradition of Italian architecture, from Rationalism to the present, through the best works of the 1950s and '60s. In the awareness that precisely because we are rigorous and precisely because we are different from those who design buildings in accordance with a vision and compositional logic of their own, our role can only be that of contributing to the construction of the city in which we are located. Formal rigour is thus expressed through the adoption of a vocabulary already consolidated around us, made up of balanced volumes, rigour in composition and the distribution of façades and elevations, and the correspondence of function and form. It is rigour that respects the context in which the building is to stand.

While many contexts today are noisy, crowded, heterogeneous and chaotic, a din of voices all trying to shout the loudest, this is rigour that instead expresses itself in correct, composed and orderly language and seeks with its composition to make the best possible contribution to the city and the urban system in which it is situated. In concrete terms, it strives to stimulate innovative and virtuous relations between people, things, environments and nature.

In this way, our architecture can take a different approach to various themes. More serene in compositional choice and more honest in the solutions put forward, it can work with greater attention on the composition and organization of space as an expression of the functions to be performed inside the construction and of the people inhabiting it. The organization of space becomes a central theme upon which architectural design expresses itself. Pathways, lines of force and predominant directions work on the geometric composition of environments, on the canons and layout of environments, once again with the rigorous need for the organization of space to work as their starting point but with a few more degrees of freedom, giving rise also to innovative relations and configurations.

ARCHITECTURAL DESIGN AND CONSTRUCTION

Missaglia (Lecco). Sections of residential units

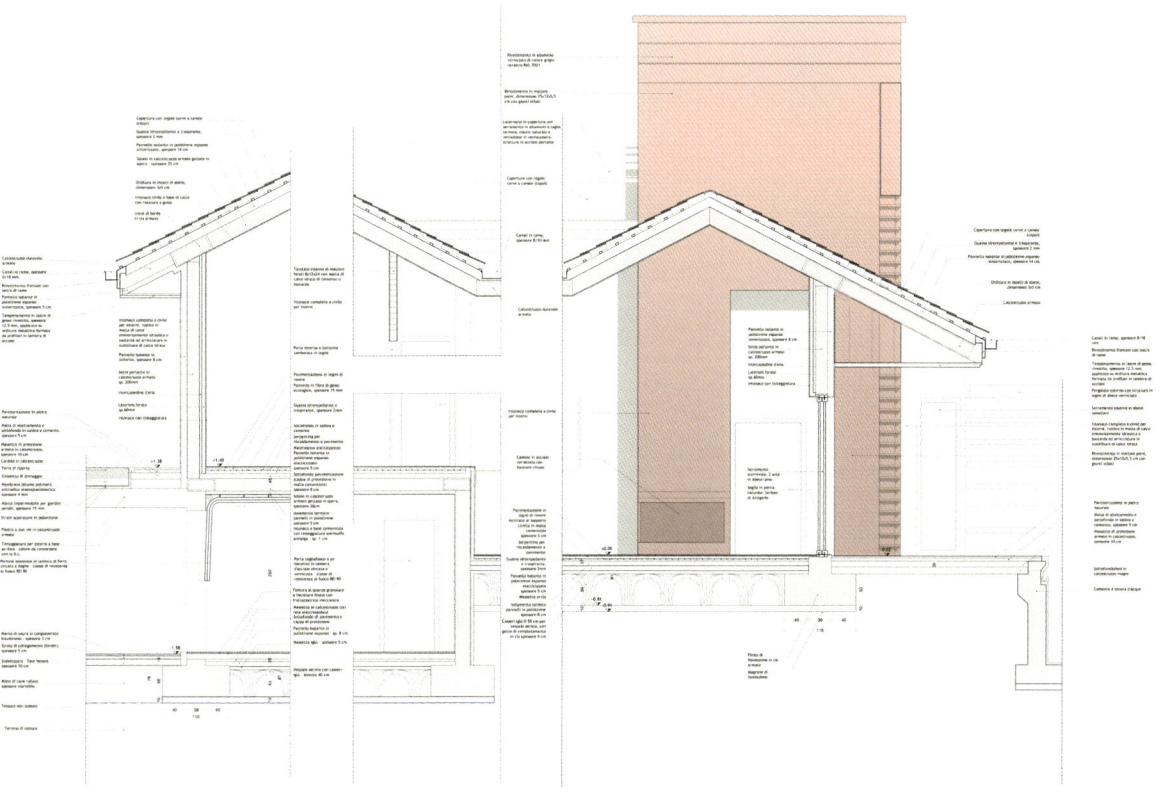

The homes in Missaglia revolve around the fulcrum of the central fireplace. While there is little new in this, modules of flexible space are placed at either end of the main living room to embody the functions that can be performed outside the home. Reworking the relationship between inside and outside, and using the composition of the constructed space to increase filtering, beyond the obvious use of the windows, the homes open up to the outside and pierce the ground, using differences in level to shift the floors and increase movement between rooms. The space thus organized gives shape to the building and – while always recalling the terrain of urban planning on which the works stand – designs the overall composition of the work, i.e. the master plan, on a larger scale. In this way, complete correspondence is attained between the individual dimension of architecture and the organic dimension of urban design as well as coordination between constructed space, open space, green space and the space of relations and exchange between the parts. The project for the transformation and redevelopment of the area of a linen mill constructs a network of connections with the exterior and surroundings. A modern extension of the historical centre of Cassano d'Adda, the project envisages pathways, cycle tracks and pedestrian areas as a vast network upon which the open spaces and constructed spaces converge at the same time to form architectural compositions, elements born out of the relationship between what is constructed and what is left open. The buildings thus interpret and give shape to architectural objects in which the constructed part, the architecture proper, is integrated with the design of open space precisely because the minimal object of the design is not the building but the urban relationship it creates, thereby taking up the concept of urban typology as the heart and nucleus of planning. Again in Cassano, the public street of shops presents a composition of volumes and arrangement of functions that combine to create precisely this urban type. The central composition between the redevelopment of the area of the old linen mill and the opening of new spaces connotes the composition of a public square for a settlement of markedly urban connotations. A far deeper investigation is thus carried out through architecture of the urban type and the value conferred on the project by the composition through the correct arrangement of urban types. The buildings are part of the type but are required to open up their layout and reflect their elevations in the urban space around them, because it is only through this interplay that the city can be constructed.

Many themes have been taken up and integrated into architectural design over these years. Reflection on the city as object and realization of its complexity necessitate answers that are complex, rich and not unambiguous despite arising from simple objects. The adoption of principles of sustainability, which is evident in most of the works, is thus combined with the adoption of criteria of their urban and economic sustainability in the conviction that the question of sustainability in terms of urban planning is far more complex because it involves the appraisal of viability, public advantage, the sustainability of costs and benefits, and many other variables. Sustainability has unquestionably guided the choice of building components in the architectural works developed and we have worked with great attention to the question of sustainability in choosing the materials, technologies and solutions required to ensure the best possible performance of the building in terms of energy. Efforts have also been made, however, to broaden the horizons and encompass the network of systems not of the building alone but of the planned complex as a whole: the water and waste disposal systems, automobile circulation and the layout of parking spaces as well as assessment of the urban weight of each building on its own and within the complex in which it is planned.

Albeit within the rigour of compliance with the expanded system of rules, the return to the essence of Rationalist architecture, attention to the context and what the context expresses, and the need to contribute to the construction of the urban system with an important urban episode, the architectural projects illustrated display their freedom in developing a creative response to the context of reference. Every completed architectural work is a creative response. To ensure that modification of the context takes place through the creativity of a stimulating solution, the projects seek to avoid banal compositions and customary interpretations of the site, which can be pierced or raised, and the surroundings, which are respected but enhanced through new forms. Above all, there is a focus on analyzing the relations that each project can establish with the context and making them part of the project. This is what the completed architectural works are: a contribution to the construction of urban episodes in particular spaces, not necessarily dense, compact or vibrant but capable of accommodating places of high urban value around which new significance can be given to more complex territorial systems. Our architectural works undertake to divest themselves of the complexity of particular compositional solutions so as to express to the utmost their nature as elements of more complex spaces, urban types made up of various things, designed to establish relations between things, people and functions, and capable of deriving the greatest opportunities from the relation between open space, constructed space and connective space. This has always been the objective: to create innovative fragments of urban space. We have asked architecture to submit to being part of more intense and complex creations in order to enhance the urbanization and proximity of things and relations and to offer difficult, fragmented and rarefied territories new points of connection and new significance in the certainty that the city of tomorrow can only be made up of many places with a strong urban vocation connected and organized within an increasingly rarefied territory.

ATLAS OF PROJECTS

1. URBAN PLANNING

1. Vaprio d'Adda (Milan): Municipal Territorial Management Plan (PGT) (2006–07)
2. Cologno al Serio (Bergamo): Municipal Territorial Management Plan (PGT) (2007–08)
3. Cambiago (Milan): Municipal Territorial Management Plan (PGT) (2007–09)
4. Vignate (Milan): Municipal Territorial Management Plan (PGT) (2007–09)
5. Inzago (Milan): Municipal Territorial Management Plan (PGT) (2008–10)
6. Liscate (Milan): Municipal Territorial Management Plan (PGT) (2008–12)
7. Novedrate (Como): Municipal Territorial Management Plan (PGT) (2008–12)
8. Canzo (Como): consultation on the drafting of the Municipal Territorial Management Plan (PGT) (2008–13)
9. Cassina de' Pecchi (Milan): Municipal Territorial Management Plan (PGT) (2008–13)
10. Verano Brianza (Monza and Brianza): Municipal Territorial Management Plan (PGT) (2009–12)
11. Basiglio (Milan): Municipal Territorial Management Plan (PGT) (2009–13)
12. Pognano (Bergamo): Variant of the Municipal Territorial Management Plan (PGT) (2010–13)
13. Gambassi Terme (Florence): Urban Traffic Management Plan (2007)
14. Gambassi Terme (Florence): project for redevelopment of the urban road system and Via Gramsci (2007)
15. Canegrate (Milan): Urban Traffic Management Plan (2009–12)
16. Inzago (Milan): Urban Traffic Management Plan (under way since 2010)
17. Melegnano (Milan): Urban Traffic Management Plan (under way since 2011)
18. Verano Brianza (Monza and Brianza): Urban Traffic Management Plan (under way since 2012)
19. Florence: feasibility study for the creation of an urban transformation agency for the Piagge area (2005–07)
20. Puglia: Territorial Landscape Plan. Guidelines for the landscaping and environmental quality of infrastructures (2009–10)
21. Inzago (Milan): Guidelines for plans for the re use of farmhouses (2011)
22. Novara: adaptation and updating of the Provincial Territorial Plan (2011–12)
23. Basiglio (Milan): Building Regulations (2013)
24. Verano Brianza (Monza and Brianza): project for area AT22 (under way since 2013)

URBAN PLANNING

1. Vaprio d'Adda (Milan): Municipal Territorial Management Plan (PGT) (2006–07)

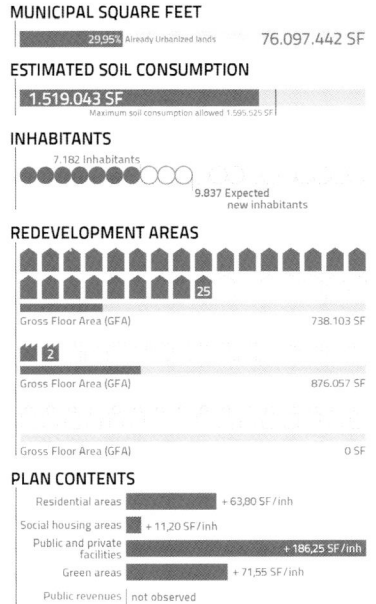

MUNICIPAL SQUARE FEET
29,95% Already Urbanized lands — 76.097.442 SF

ESTIMATED SOIL CONSUMPTION
1.519.043 SF
Maximum soil consumption allowed 1.595.525 SF

INHABITANTS
7.182 Inhabitants
9.837 Expected new inhabitants

REDEVELOPMENT AREAS
25
Gross Floor Area (GFA) — 738.103 SF
2
Gross Floor Area (GFA) — 876.057 SF

Gross Floor Area (GFA) — 0 SF

PLAN CONTENTS
Residential areas — + 63,80 SF/inh
Social housing areas — + 11,20 SF/inh
Public and private facilities — + 186,25 SF/inh
Green areas — + 71,55 SF/inh
Public revenues — not observed

Vaprio d'Adda is a municipality situated on the river Adda between Milan and Bergamo on the outskirts of the Milanese metropolitan area, far enough from Milan to be located in an environmentally characterized context but an integral part of the system of intense relations developed by the territory between Milan and Bergamo every day. One of the major traffic arteries passes through Vaprio, where it is possible to cross the Adda. The town has grown over the years to increase the density of its historical structure stretching along the riverside, confined between rural settlements and patrician villas, the structure of the modern city, with phenomena of attraction along the main artery and residential sprawl on the north-south axis connecting all the towns along the river. At the time of drawing up the plan, the territory was thus fairly compact along the two "backbones", parallel to and crossing the Adda, albeit with evident spreading into the agricultural area. At the same time, the industrial plant installed in the past in many of the municipalities of the hinterland was already disused or being closed down due to the shifting and reduction of production activities.
The municipality thus found itself faced with major infrastructural problems, the need for overall redefinition of its form and the desire to restore meaning to much of its territory, with an undervalued historical centre that was hard to redevelop and a still expanding settlement system inherited from past planning.
The Territorial Management Plan, one of the first drawn up in the province of Milan and the Lombardy region in general after regional law 12 of 2005 came into effect, addressed the questions posed by the territory, developing some strategic directions of overall redefinition. The two backbones were the target of a series of projects, directly contained in the plan, capable of giving new meaning to the strategic axis of the road running through the municipality, reshaping the boundary between town and country to the northwest, and establishing a new environmental relationship with the Adda. The first to try out the new regulations and instruments imposed by the law, the plan also sought to ensure the economic sustainability of the operations envisaged through a mechanism of urban compensation capable of supporting the many public works involved. Through the new plan, Vaprio hoped to transform its position on the edge of a territory centred elsewhere and construct new episodes capable of placing the town within the network of smaller centres and giving a sense to the parts constructed in the consolidated fabric, rediscovering its juxtaposition on two sides with the environmental systems of the Adda and the agricultural land.

Systems, provisions and rules. Atlas of the plan and elements of management for major territorial systems

URBAN PLANNING

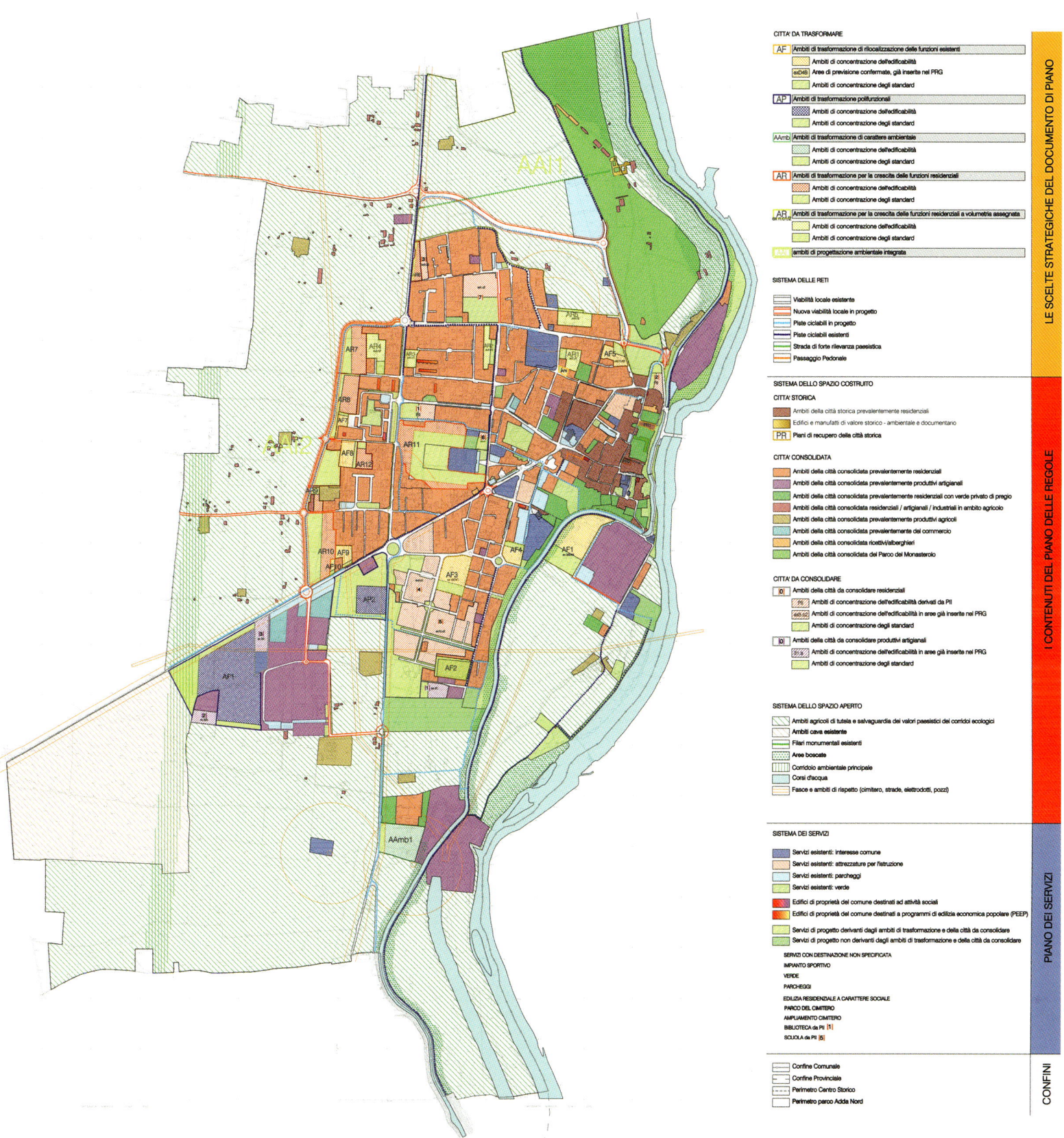

49

URBAN PLANNING

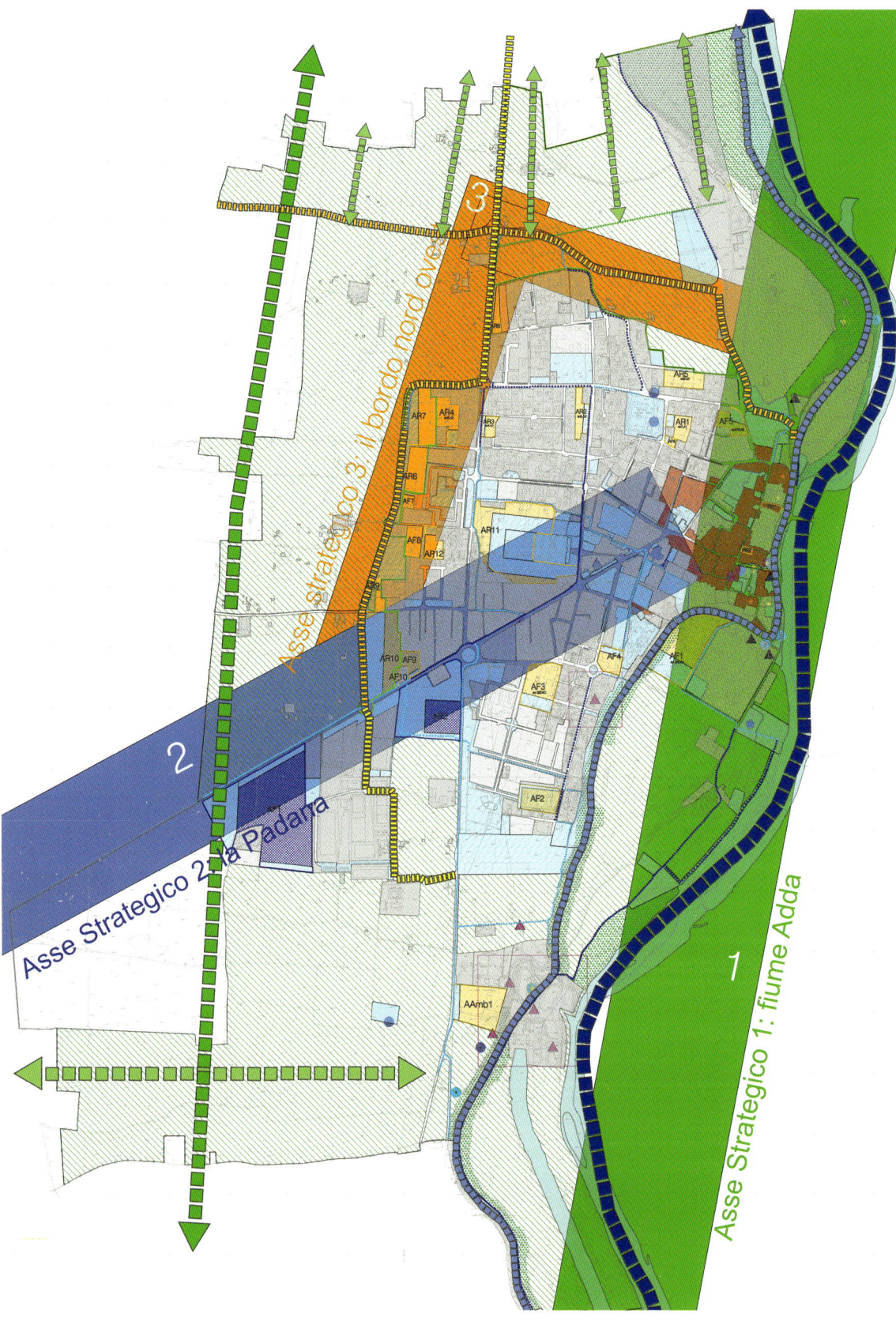

Strategic axes of territorial redefinition. The strategic choices are structured around three different territorial areas, identifying projects for each of them capable of redefining the relationship between the existing infrastructural, environmental and settlement elements

URBAN PLANNING

*Reconfiguration of relations with the river.
Specific planning criteria to re-establish correct
dialogue between the system of natural and historical
elements of the river Adda and the urbanized fabric
of Vaprio d'Adda*

CRITERI PROGETTUALI

A Parco del Monasterolo

Il Parco del Monasterolo costituisce una delle principali risorse ambientali di Vaprio d'Adda. Per salvaguardare e potenziare il valore ambientale di questa parte del territorio, il PGT07 prevede l'aumento della qualità ambientale, soprattutto in relazione alla necessità di collegare l'ambito alle reti ecologiche sovra locali e alle reti fruizionali (pedonali e ciclabili).

B Villa Castelbarco

Il patrimonio storico architettonico della Villa rappresenta uno dei beni di maggior pregio del sistema costruito.
Il piano delle regole identifica la normativa per la valorizzazione storico documentale del bene.
E' importante riconoscere la Villa come uno dei capisaldi dell'immagine di Vaprio e come uno dei simboli sui quali la stessa comunità si possa riconoscere.
E' altresì importante aumentare insieme ai gestori della Villa le attività pubbliche che vi si possono svolgere, affinchè diventi una delle porte del sistema parco della Valle dell'Adda.

C Le cartiere Binda

Il PGT07 mantiene la destinazione industriale produttiva per le cartiere Binda, dal momento che non è ancora dismessa alcuna attività. Tuttavia, vista la localizzazione degli impianti, è necessario mantenere un livello di produzione che non contrasti con la situazione ambientale di particolare pregio all'interno della quale sono inserite; pur non dimenticando il valore storico documentale dell'impianto produttivo, all'interno di un sistema di forte artificializzazione del corso del fiume, proprio a scopi produttivi.
Sarà necessario prevedere forti accorgimenti affinchè eventuali future trasformazioni non compromettano l'ambito naturalistico.

D Il Naviglio Martesana

Il PGT07 individua l'ambito del Naviglio come uno dei principali patrimonio storico ambientali di Vaprio. Per questa ragione, il PGT07 lo identifica all'interno dell'asse strategico dell'Adda, su questo concentra la riqualificazione delle sponde, la valorizzazione della percorrenza pedonale e ciclabile delle stesse (con la relativa messa a rete dei percorsi pedonali e ciclabili all'interno del sistema ciclo pedonale esistente e previsto per la zona) e l'aumento della concentrazione del verde e dei servizi.
Per ogni intervento, sia pubblico che privato, sarà necessario seguire le indicazioni del Master Plan dei Navigli, che identifica tutti i possibili interventi sia sullo spazio aperto che sullo spazio costruito.

E Il ponte tra Vaprio e Canonica

Il passaggio sul fiume, tra Vaprio e Canonica, è costituito dal ponte in cemento a livello della sponda di Canonica. A causa del forte traffico di attraversamento, e senza previsione nell'arco di validità del PGT07 di miglioramento significativo, il ponte rappresenta uno dei punti di maggiore criticità per il sistema. In attesa di interventi significativamente migliorativi, è necessario aumentare la sicurezza della pedonalità sul ponte e nelle strade limitrofe, anche attraverso operazioni di ridisegno della carreggiata del tratto di strada tra il ponte e l'attacco della variante a nord e di aumento dello spazio pedonale.
Può essere prevista in prossimità del ponte la realizzazione di punti panoramici o punti di approdo al letto del fiume, soprattutto in relazione alla fruizione estiva delle aree sull'acqua.

F Il centro storico di Vaprio

Il centro storico di Vaprio rappresenta un patrimonio per il territorio e per la comunità di Vaprio che il PGT07 decide di valorizzare, attraverso quanto previsto dal Piano delle Regole.
Strategicamente, deve essere massimizzata la riqualificazione dell'affaccio del sistema costruito e del sistema dello spazio aperto verso il fiume: in particolare devono essere recuperati, riqualificati e valorizzati i punti di affaccio a terrazza verso la valle dell'Adda. Inoltre, devono essere posti in rete i percorsi di collegamento tra il sistema delle piste ciclabili, il sistema delle aree pedonali, il sistema della fruizione degli spazi aperti del centro storico.
Il PGT07 da ultimo valorizza il sistema delle funzioni inserite nel centro storico, mantenendo il sistema dei servizi diffusi e ricercando politiche e strategie per aumentare la fruibilità turistica del patrimonio costruito e degli spazi aperti del centro.

G Il Cotonificio Visconti

Il PGT07 mantiene la destinazione industriale produttiva per il Cotonificio Visconti, ad eccezione della parte sulla quale è previsto il PII, dal momento che non è ancora dismessa alcuna attività. Tuttavia, vista la localizzazione degli impianti, è necessario mantenere un livello di produzione che non contrasti con la situazione ambientale di particolare pregio all'interno della quale sono inserite; pur non dimenticando il valore storico documentale dell'impianto produttivo, all'interno di un sistema di forte artificializzazione del corso del fiume, proprio a scopi produttivi.
Sarà necessario prevedere forti accorgimenti affinchè eventuali future trasformazioni non compromettano l'ambito naturalistico.

H Le aree agricole a sud

Le aree a sud del centro storico mantengono la propria funzione agricola di grande pregio paesaggistico e ambientale. Per queste aree, il PGT07 prevede il mantenimento della funzione, senza nessuna possibilità di trasformazione. Tale patrimonio di aree concorre a costruire il corridoio ambientale dell'Adda.

2. Cologno al Serio (Bergamo): Municipal Territorial Management Plan (PGT) (2007–08)

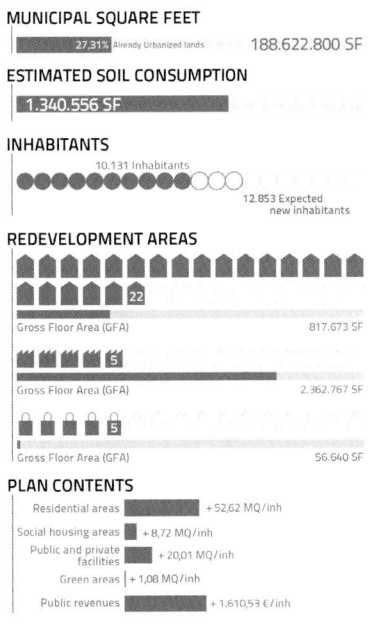

Located on the agricultural plain south of Bergamo, Cologno al Serio exemplifies the settlement dynamics of recent years in the areas of the Po Valley close to the large towns. Outside the historical centre, still perfectly recognizable and legible in the town's fabric with its form of a well-preserved stronghold, the settlement system has expanded through the construction of a closely packed town, a dense agglomeration of low-density buildings with little greenery due to the widespread practice of seeking the maximum financial benefit and avoiding the creation of services and green areas. The compact fabric has spread out in all directions around the historical centre as far as the main artery of communication in the north (the so called "Francesca" highway) to the point of forming a vertical strip along state highway 591 with the creation of a compact industrial district in accordance with the typical provisions made in the 1970s and '80s (through the Plan for Production Districts). Recent times have seen the strengthening of infrastructures envisaged in general for the areas connected with Corridor 5 and the associated provisions made by the provincial and regional authorities.

The construction of the new motorway between Milan and Brescia south of the municipal territory and the provision for one of the link roads envisaged in the Territorial Coordination Plan (PTCP) of the province of Bergamo as a corridor for automobiles and trams transformed the position of the municipal territory, which thus became central to one of the many territorial crossings envisaged by the new system. The plan operates in this context, seeking to obtain the maximum quality for the urban system, so compactly built as to prove slightly suffocated, and investing in some areas of transformation to construct new centralities and a stock of public areas and services, enclosing the provisions for growth within the boundaries of a new road system. Above all, however, it invests in the route of the new road built to connect the province. An area of transformation, which also solves the question of a disused and environmentally problematic agricultural area, is envisaged in connection with the new road and creates a link between the settlement territory and the infrastructural system. The plan establishes a new relationship with the open territory and invests in the resource of the river Serio, not least with the creation of supra-municipal park to preserve and protect the environmental heritage. In the same way, all of the south-eastern and western part of the territory is designated as an area for environmental protection and promotion of the agricultural activities that characterize the town's economic system.

The plan has been largely put into effect apart from the agricultural transformation area. Connected as this was to the construction of the new infrastructure, the strategic environmental assessment monitoring process deemed its *a priori* implementation incorrect within an ongoing process putting the plan's provisions into effect so as to observe the dynamics triggered and establish the strategic programme of operations piece by piece.

Strategic vision. Ideas of territorial development that intersect with transversal themes: new urban centralities, strengthening of the infrastructural system, policies of environmental protection and promotion

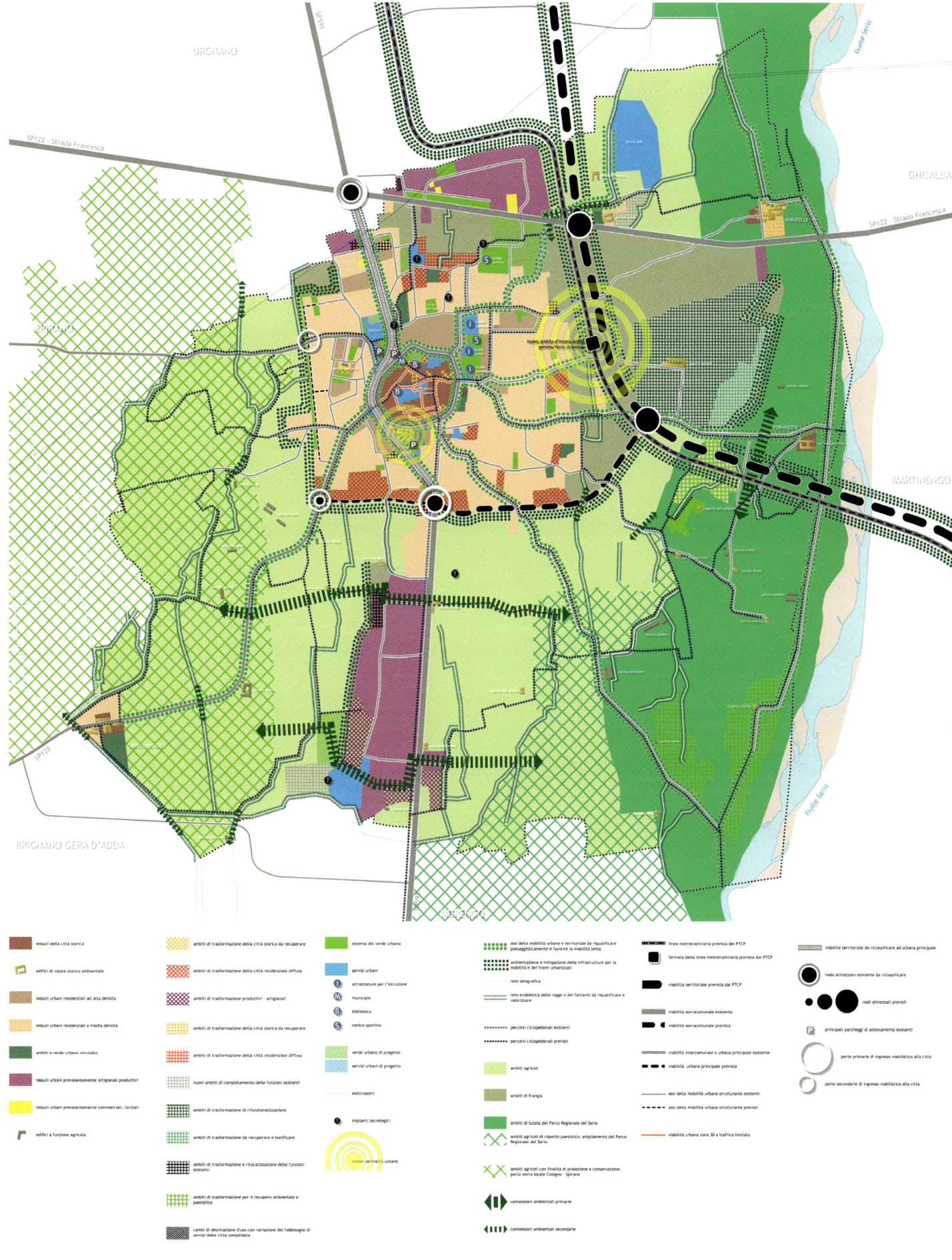

Quality of the urban system. Areas of urban transformation, new centralities, services and areas of public use for reorganization of the settlement fabric

Road system and utilisation of the town. Traffic decongestion and the strengthening of pathways of sustainable mobility inside the residential fabric

Opposite
Environmental connective system. Operations of environmental promotion and reconnection at the local scale as well as policies to safeguard the agricultural heritage for the creation of supra-local ecological networks

URBAN PLANNING

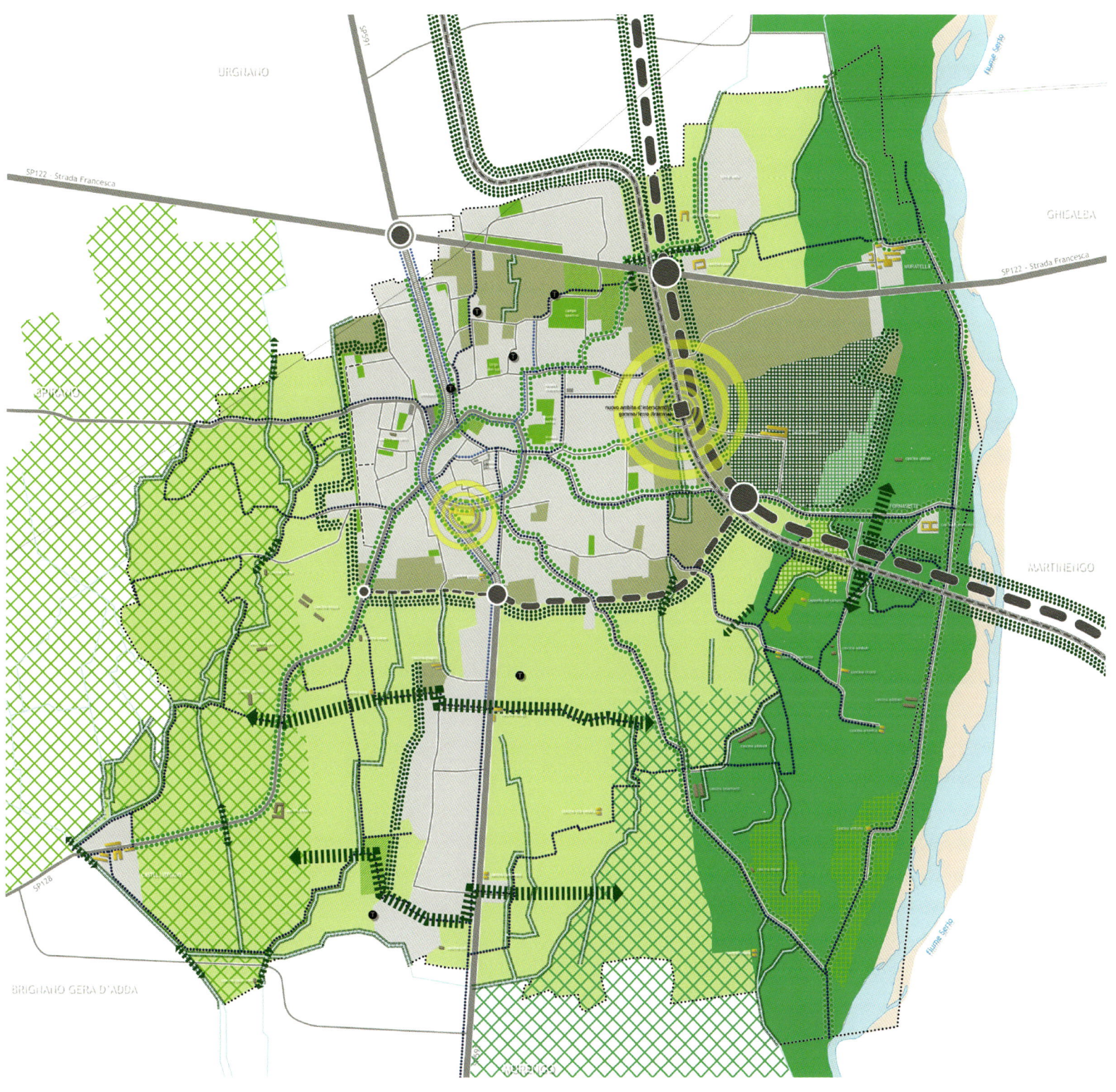

3. Cambiago (Milan): Municipal Territorial Management Plan (PGT) (2007–09)

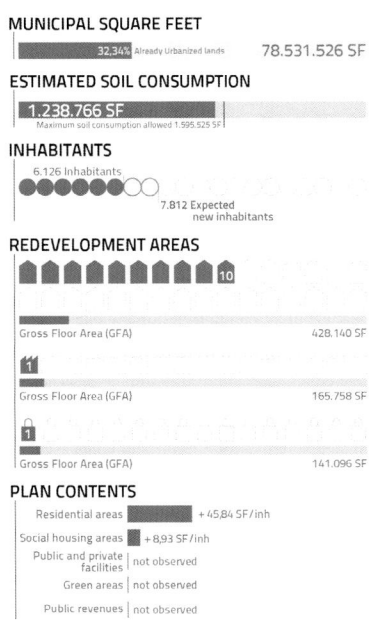

Together with the railway line for Venice, the construction of the A4 motorway constituted one of the first infrastructural corridors of North Italy and has worked in time to alter the relations existing in the agricultural area. Subsequent widening of the infrastructural strip has increased the division and created a rigid, impermeable and impenetrable element splitting the territory cleanly. Cambiago has a privileged location with respect to the accessibility offered by the motorway but is unquestionably invaded by the division, further emphasized by the consolidation of a production system that occupies sites looking onto the motorway so as to take advantage of the opportunity for visibility and leaves the municipality to cope with all problems regarding access by road. Moreover, the construction of the new bypass system for eastern part of the Milanese metropolitan area creates a further divide in the vicinity of the hamlet of Torrazza, which still preserves a historical architectural heritage of great importance. The plan thus sought to restore the connections broken by the infrastructural systems and ensure the compactness of the overall form of the territory. Its policies were designed to inject new dynamism into the built-up territory, transforming the available areas of building land within the boundaries as opportunities for the creation of small new centralities. If Cambiago enjoys a position of particular infrastructural advantage, it must avert the risk of attraction leading to invasion of the territory with new weights and new functions, and concentrate instead on the orderly incorporation of the new potential into the territory. The road that constitutes the western boundary was thus designed as a green bastion attenuating transition between the built-up area and the system of the agricultural territory, and the areas of transformation contained within it were called upon to define a more precise urban design. Through the policies of the plan, Cambiago can thus redefine its position in the territory and consolidate itself as a small new centrality built up around the key node of the motorway, strongly connected with the other systems running through the territory, and compactly contained within its own boundaries.

Strategies for the creation of a centrality. Policies, actions and priorities for the urban redefinition and management of the impact of major infrastructural arteries

URBAN PLANNING

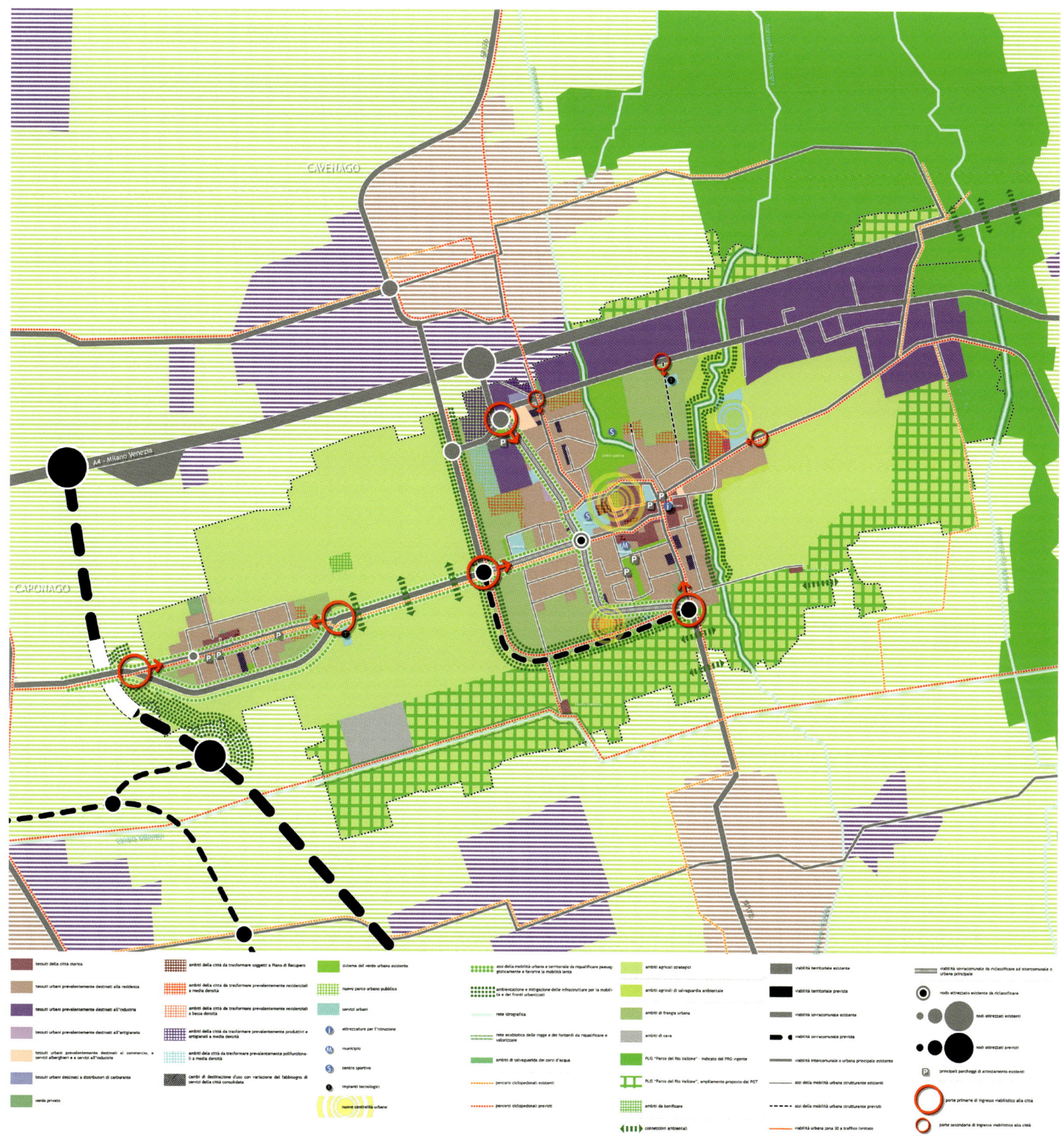

Objectives for the settlement system. The upgrading of existing assets and revitalization of rundown areas as well as sustainability and compactness of the urban form constitute the key principles of the planning strategies

Efficiency of the infrastructural network. Planning elements and actions for the construction of a efficient road system capable of establishing correct relations with the contexts traversed and restoring the relationship between urbanized fabrics and agricultural land

Promotion of the agricultural heritage. The plan identifies priority actions for greater use of natural areas of municipal territory, regarding the agricultural areas as fundamental economic and natural assets

Implementation of planning provisions. Feasibility study for the urban development of the ARm6 residential area of transformation

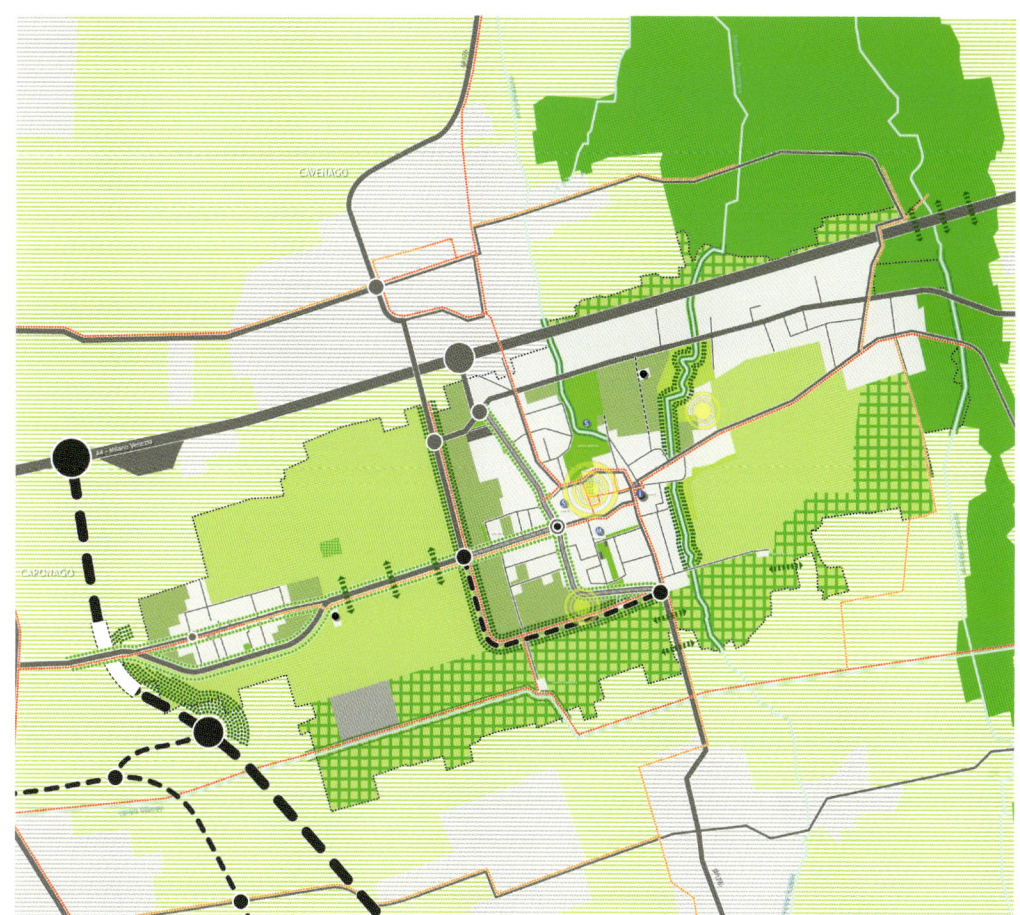

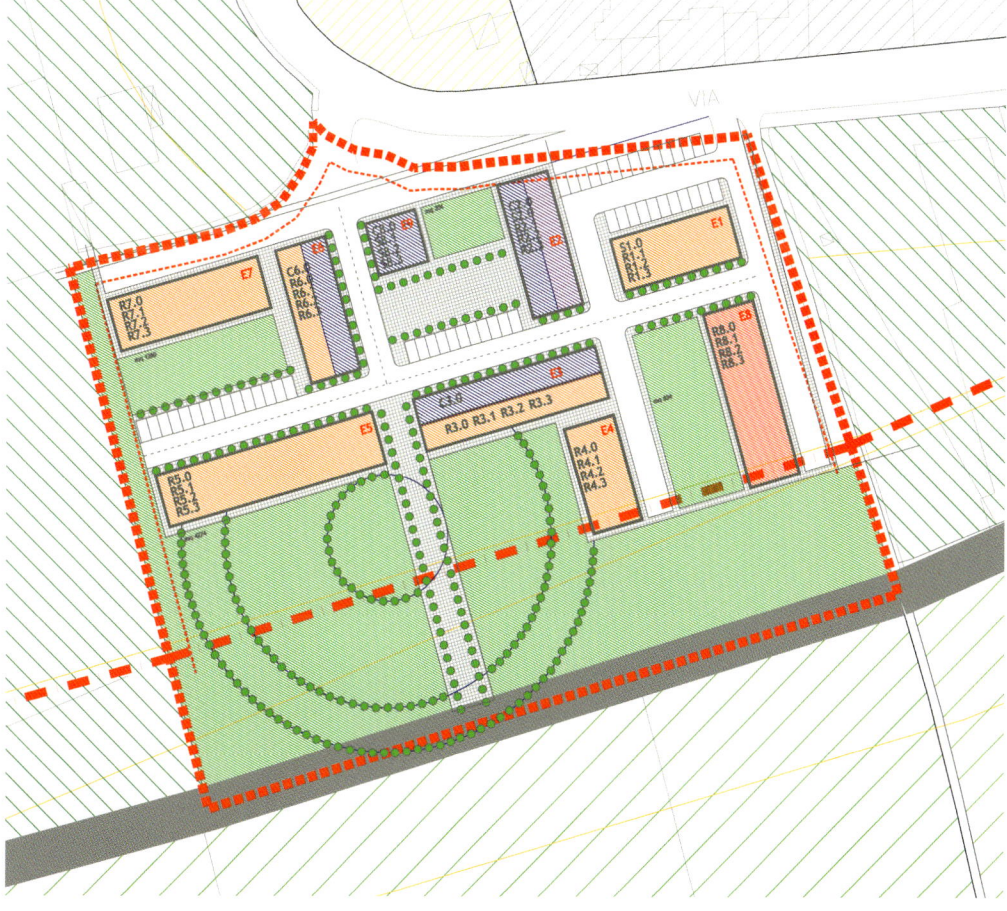

URBAN PLANNING

4. Vignate (Milan): Municipal Territorial Management Plan (PGT) (2007–09)

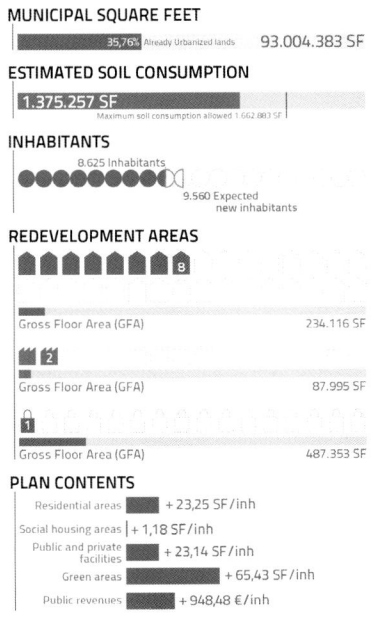

MUNICIPAL SQUARE FEET
35,76% Already Urbanized lands   93.004.383 SF

ESTIMATED SOIL CONSUMPTION
1.375.257 SF
Maximum soil consumption allowed 1.662.883 SF

INHABITANTS
8.625 Inhabitants
9.560 Expected new inhabitants

REDEVELOPMENT AREAS
8

Gross Floor Area (GFA)   234.116 SF

2
Gross Floor Area (GFA)   87.995 SF

1
Gross Floor Area (GFA)   487.353 SF

PLAN CONTENTS
Residential areas   + 23,25 SF/inh
Social housing areas   + 1,18 SF/inh
Public and private facilities   + 23,14 SF/inh
Green areas   + 65,43 SF/inh
Public revenues   + 948,48 €/inh

The Municipal Territorial Management Plan for Vignate was drawn up at the same time as a set of actions and operations contributing to modification of the territorial context. The major infrastructural upgrading to which the eastern sector of the province of Milan has been subjected is evident in the municipal territory of Vignate.
The strengthening of the Cassanese and Rivoltana highways, respectively north and south of the municipal territory, and the railway system with the construction of the new high-speed Milan-Venice line have in fact served to consolidate the east-west infrastructural corridor, part of the broader policy of strengthening the connections forming part of the European Community's Corridor 5. As one of the many settlement sytems involved, Vignate is thus called upon to sacrifice much of its equilibrium and part of the compactness of its environmental system in favour of infrastructural flow on a larger and broader scale. The plan drawn up focuses on the overall form of the settlement in an effort to rebalance the east-west flow, parallel to the infrastructural systems, with the creation of an environmental road system capable of closing the territory on two sides and avoiding further expansion. The two north-south axes permit a different relationship with the high-quality environmental system. Traversed by major flows, the town opens up to the heritage of its environmental system. As in other plans subsequently developed for neighbouring municipalities, the riches of the South Milan Agricultural Park are drawn upon to confer meaning on the town as a whole, harnessing the valuable green area and opening its use to the adjoining towns, one of which is Vignate. The Municipal Territorial Management Plan seeks to create a special gateway to the park by providing for an area of transformation and services capable of counterbalancing the weight of the commercial centre previously built on the Cassanese highway, and to identify some services of municipal interest precisely in the area of the park.
Unanimously approved by the majority and minority of the local government, the plan harnesses the regulatory framework already tried out in some latest-generation schemes by the reformist school of urban planning, recognizing the need for different rules for the historical city, the consolidated city, the city to be consolidated and the agricultural spheres, and seeking to include tried and tested rules in the new set of planning tools.

Settlement system and urban structure. Criticalities and potentialities identified and addressed through various policies of protection and promotion with an effective impact on the dialogue between open and built-up spaces

System design. Actions for contextualization of the primary projects of reinforcement and new infrastructures of supra-local character as well as operations to rationalize and buffer the local system

URBAN PLANNING

Policies for harnessing the environmental heritage.
Planning guidelines to foster the use and promotion of the South Milan Agricultural Park

Opposite
The constructed city: strategies for the Zoning Plan.
Objectives and guidelines for correct management of the physical components of constructed and open space

URBAN PLANNING

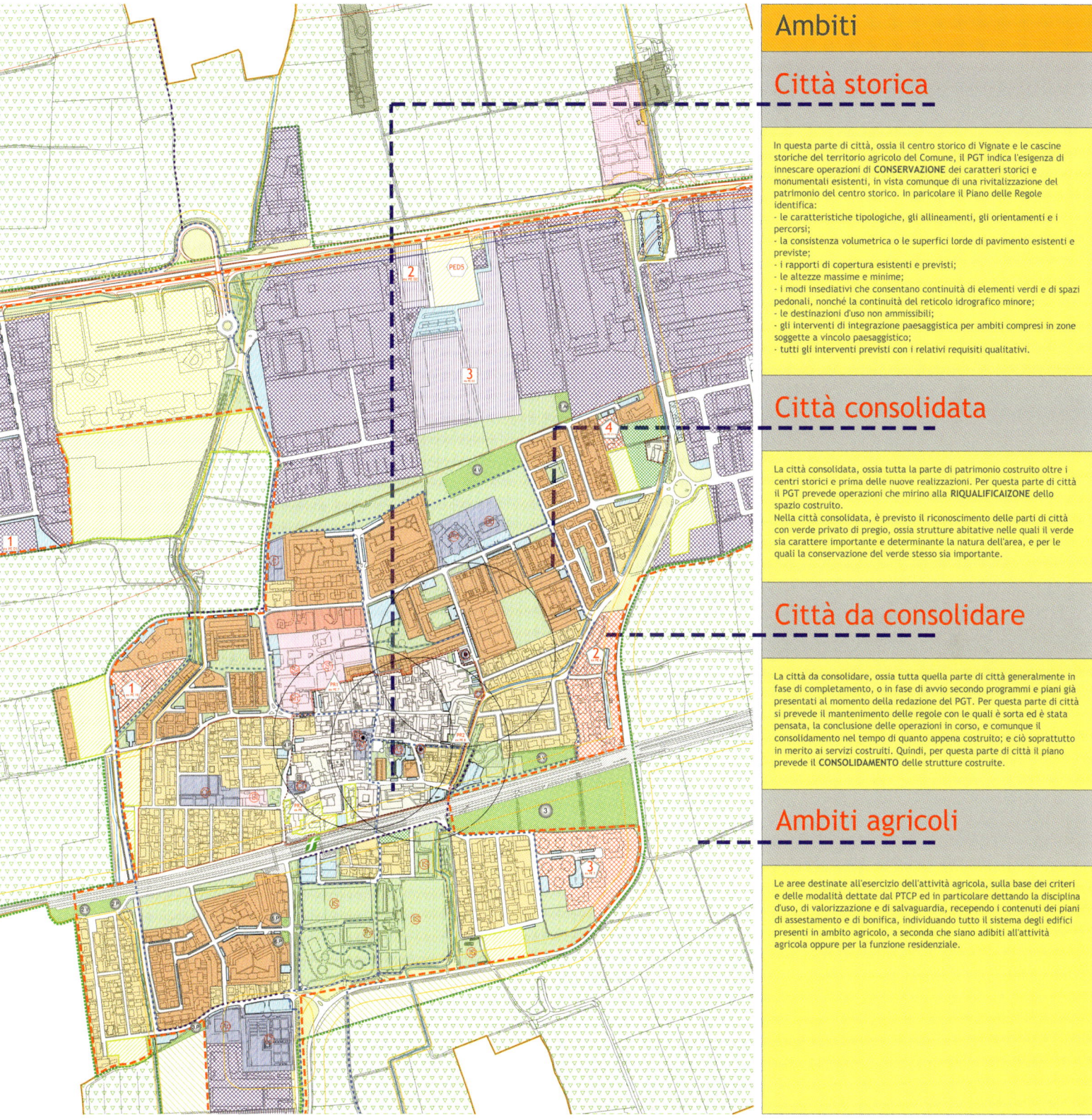

Ambiti

Città storica

In questa parte di città, ossia il centro storico di Vignate e le cascine storiche del territorio agricolo del Comune, il PGT indica l'esigenza di innescare operazioni di **CONSERVAZIONE** dei caratteri storici e monumentali esistenti, in vista comunque di una rivitalizzazione del patrimonio del centro storico. In paricolare il Piano delle Regole identifica:
- le caratteristiche tipologiche, gli allineamenti, gli orientamenti e i percorsi;
- la consistenza volumetrica o le superfici lorde di pavimento esistenti e previste;
- i rapporti di copertura esistenti e previsti;
- le altezze massime e minime;
- i modi insediativi che consentano continuità di elementi verdi e di spazi pedonali, nonché la continuità del reticolo idrografico minore;
- le destinazioni d'uso non ammissibili;
- gli interventi di integrazione paesaggistica per ambiti compresi in zone soggette a vincolo paesaggistico;
- tutti gli interventi previsti con i relativi requisiti qualitativi.

Città consolidata

La città consolidata, ossia tutta la parte di patrimonio costruito oltre i centri storici e prima delle nuove realizzazioni. Per questa parte di città il PGT prevede operazioni che mirino alla **RIQUALIFICAIZONE** dello spazio costruito.
Nella città consolidata, è previsto il riconoscimento delle parti di città con verde privato di pregio, ossia strutture abitative nelle quali il verde sia carattere importante e determinante la natura dell'area, e per le quali la conservazione del verde stesso sia importante.

Città da consolidare

La città da consolidare, ossia tutta quella parte di città generalmente in fase di completamento, o in fase di avvio secondo programmi e piani già presentati al momento della redazione del PGT. Per questa parte di città si prevede il mantenimento delle regole con le quali è sorta ed è stata pensata, la conclusione delle operazioni in corso, e comunque il consolidamento nel tempo di quanto appena costruito; e ciò soprattutto in merito ai servizi costruiti. Quindi, per questa parte di città il piano prevede il **CONSOLIDAMENTO** delle strutture costruite.

Ambiti agricoli

Le aree destinate all'esercizio dell'attività agricola, sulla base dei criteri e delle modalità dettate dal PTCP ed in particolare dettando la disciplina d'uso, di valorizzazione e di salvaguardia, recependo i contenuti dei piani di assestamento e di bonifica, individuando tutto il sistema degli edifici presenti in ambito agricolo, a seconda che siano adibiti all'attività agricola oppure per la funzione residenziale.

URBAN PLANNING

5. Inzago (Milan): Municipal Territorial Management Plan (PGT) (2008–10)

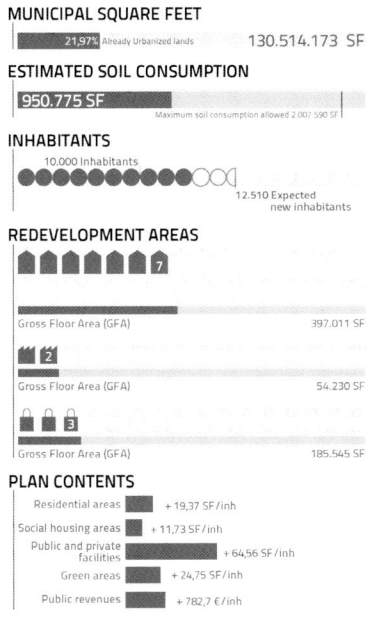

MUNICIPAL SQUARE FEET
21,97% Already Urbanized lands   130.514.173 SF

ESTIMATED SOIL CONSUMPTION
950.775 SF
Maximum soil consumption allowed 2.007.590 SF

INHABITANTS
10.000 Inhabitants
12.510 Expected new inhabitants

REDEVELOPMENT AREAS

Gross Floor Area (GFA)   397.011 SF

Gross Floor Area (GFA)   54.230 SF

Gross Floor Area (GFA)   185.545 SF

PLAN CONTENTS
Residential areas   + 19,37 SF/inh
Social housing areas   + 11,73 SF/inh
Public and private facilities   + 64,56 SF/inh
Green areas   + 24,75 SF/inh
Public revenues   + 782,7 €/inh

The plan for Inzago addressed significant questions characteristic of the territory in which the town is located. Situated just outside the most densely urbanized section of the Milanese metropolitan area, Inzago is representative of the environmental and historical richness of the eastern part of the province of Milan. Crossed by the Martesana canal and possessing a considerable amount of green agricultural land, Inzago has succeeded in preserving its image of quality despite the major phenomena of growth affecting it. It is this factor of quality – both settlement quality and environmental quality – that the plan seeks to exploit, envisaging policies and actions capable of endowing the municipal territory as a whole with high quality through episodes of virtuous territorial production. From the construction of a new urban section around the square, the redevelopment of a large refuse dump as a natural green area and reconnection of the central municipal territory with the offshoots in the south to major infrastructures, Inzago focuses on making its fabric compact, intensively redeveloping all the parts of the historical centre and improving the settlement quality of the residential village to the south in order to demonstrate the inviolability of the open agricultural territory. To this end, the plan even envisages the granting of a large area of land (about 8 million m^2) to constitute the central nucleus of a local park of supra-local interest, inside which it is planned to salvage and preserve a very rich settlement heritage of farmhouses. We thus have a close dialogue between built-up areas and agricultural land in which the canal serves as a "blue thread" capable of connecting all the contexts from the historical town centre to the countryside.

The plan thus takes shape through the three instruments envisaged by the regional law while at the same time channelling a great deal of energy into the construction of a major territorial information system connected with all the sources of territorial and municipal data. This important undertaking has made it possible to streamline the flow of territorial knowledge and disseminate information drawn from the bodies responsible for management of the territory.

Planning vision: strategies of the Structural Plan. Elements of environmental protection, lines of expansion, nodes of the road system and policies for upgrading of the built-up area so as to improve dialogue between settlement territory and agricultural context

URBAN PLANNING

URBAN PLANNING

The constructed city and open spaces: strategies of the Zoning Plan. Actions, guidelines and rules for management of the built-up area and upgrading of the system of open spaces

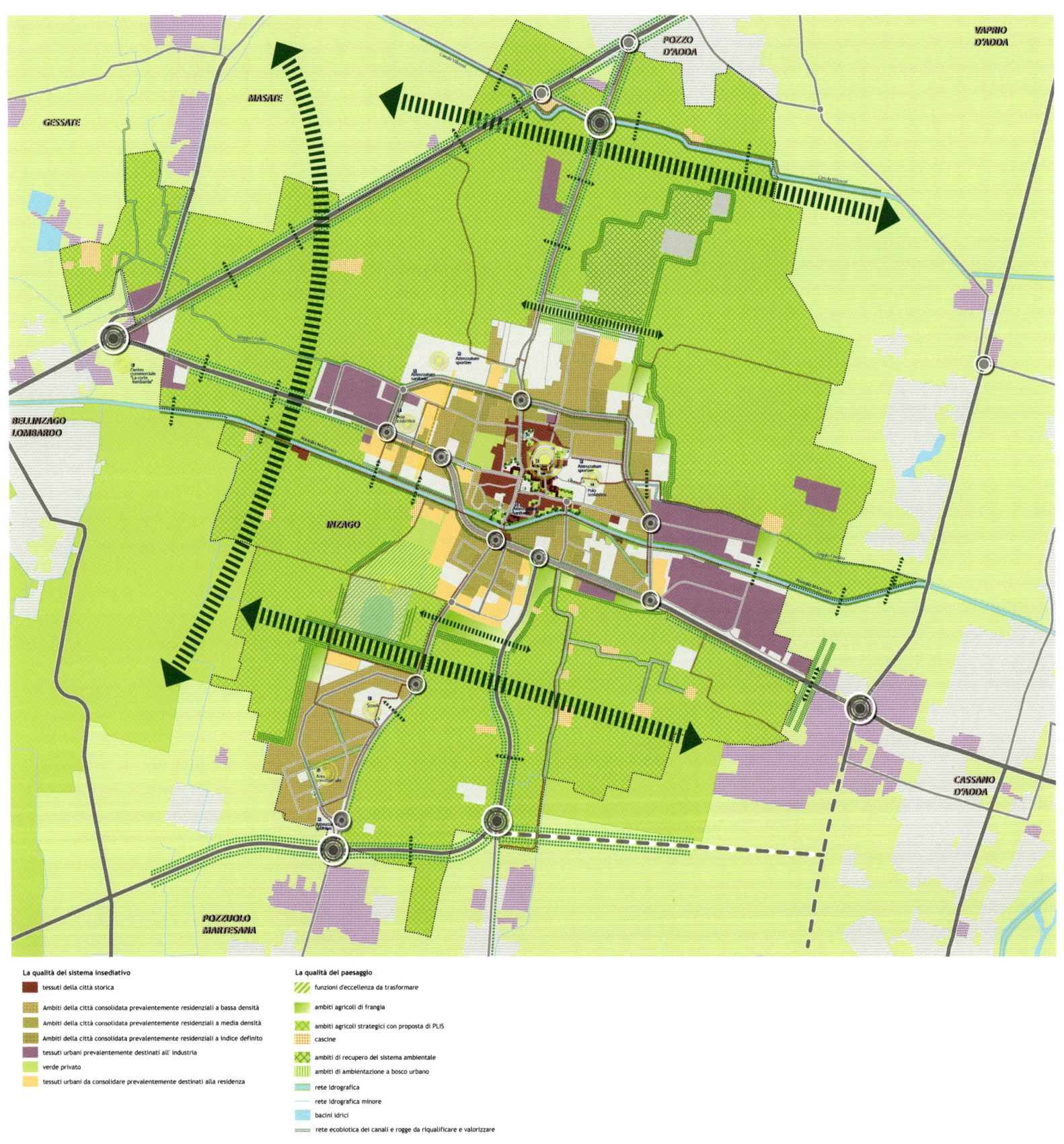

The public city: strategies of the Public Facilities Plan. Objectives and actions for redefinition of the existing and planned public city: provision of services, efficiency of the road system and quality of pedestrian pathways

URBAN PLANNING

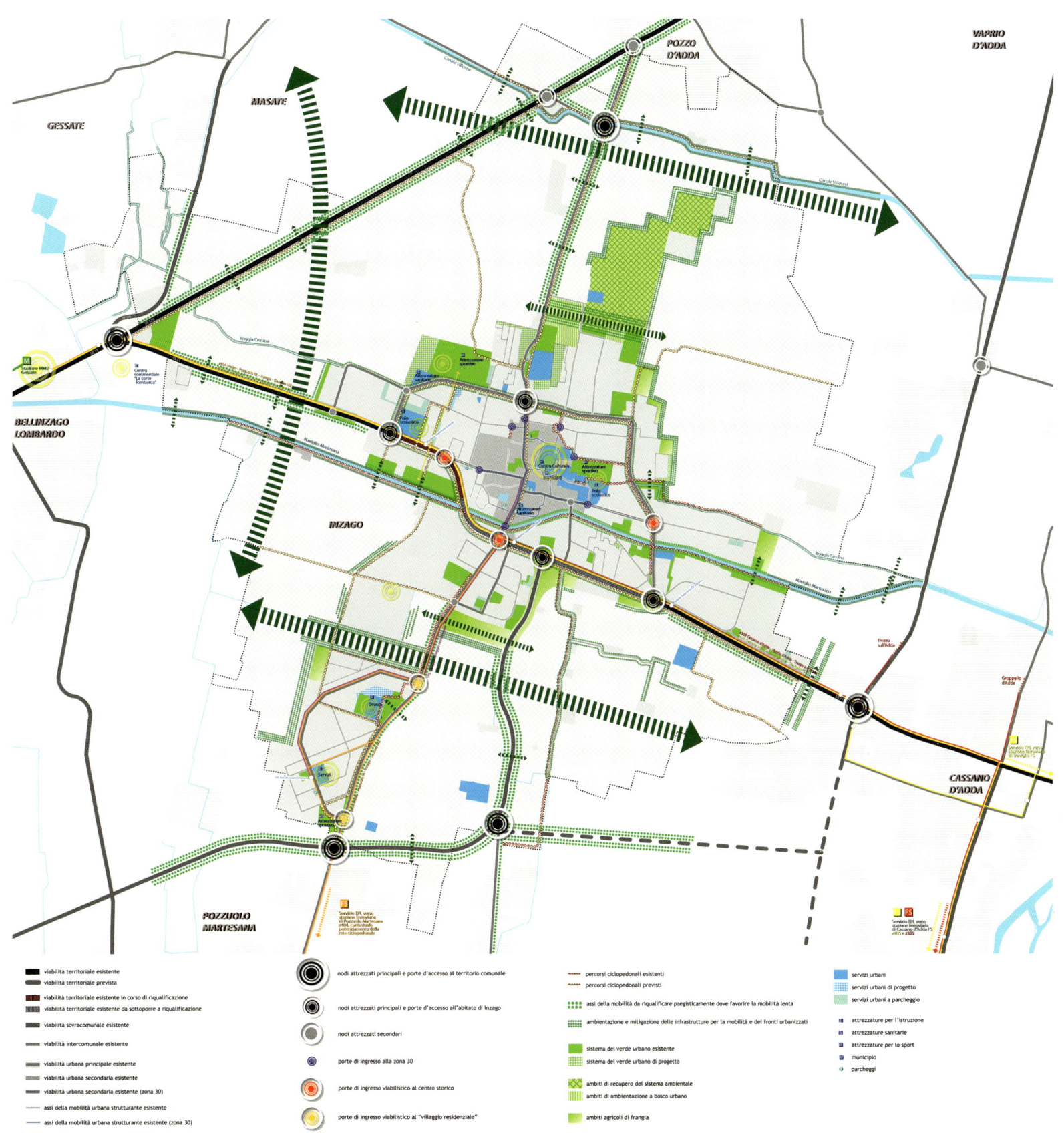

URBAN PLANNING

6. Liscate (Milan): Municipal Territorial Management Plan (PGT) (2008–12)

The plan for Liscate addresses a number of questions arising in similar territorial situations. The presence of the South Milan Agricultural Park as a tool for the preservation of agricultural territory makes it necessary for the municipalities concerned to comply with the park's territorial plan of coordination. Now somewhat dated, this imposes a vision of planning that is hardly in keeping with the dynamics to which the territory has been subjected. As in many other municipalities, infrastructures constitute a key factor here too, as Liscate is affected by the construction of Eastern new beltway, a new motorway link serving the eastern section of the Milanese metropolitan area. At the same time, the presence of the tollgate for access to this new highway system, connected with the redevelopment of the Rivoltana highway, has prompted provisions for a variant to the south, which actually separates the municipal territory from the park. In addition, some provisions for expansion of the territory contained in the old plan have proved incompatible with the plan of the park. For these reasons, the plan drawn up addressed the subject of relations with supra-local and sectoral planning through a number of specific projects, developed also by means of master plans, for the following: reorganization of the area south of the town, between the urbanized territory and the Rivoltana variant; organization of the major production centre in the north of the territory; attenuation of the impact of infrastructures in general; and the creation of new centralities within the municipal territory. *Five petals* are used as a slogan and image for the policies through which the plan takes concrete shape, both in strategic terms and by addressing the question of communicating the contents of the plan to the citizens and bodies concerned. Great attention is focused on mechanisms for the implementation of provisions, through the use of reward schemes, capable of guiding work on the various spheres of transformation and governing operations on the existing urban structure through mechanisms providing incentives and reducing obligations so as to highlight the need to invest in the compact and concentrated development of the existing territory.

It is in this plan that the concept of economic sustainability was rigorously introduced, yoking provisions to the operation of the ordinary, everyday management of the territory by local government and including taxes and obligations within feasibility simulations of the individual transformations involved in the plan.

Planning strategies: the five petals. The five strategic objectives constitute the five "petals" around which the plan develops its vision, boosting the territory's potential and providing a strong channel of communication with the citizens and parties affected by the plan

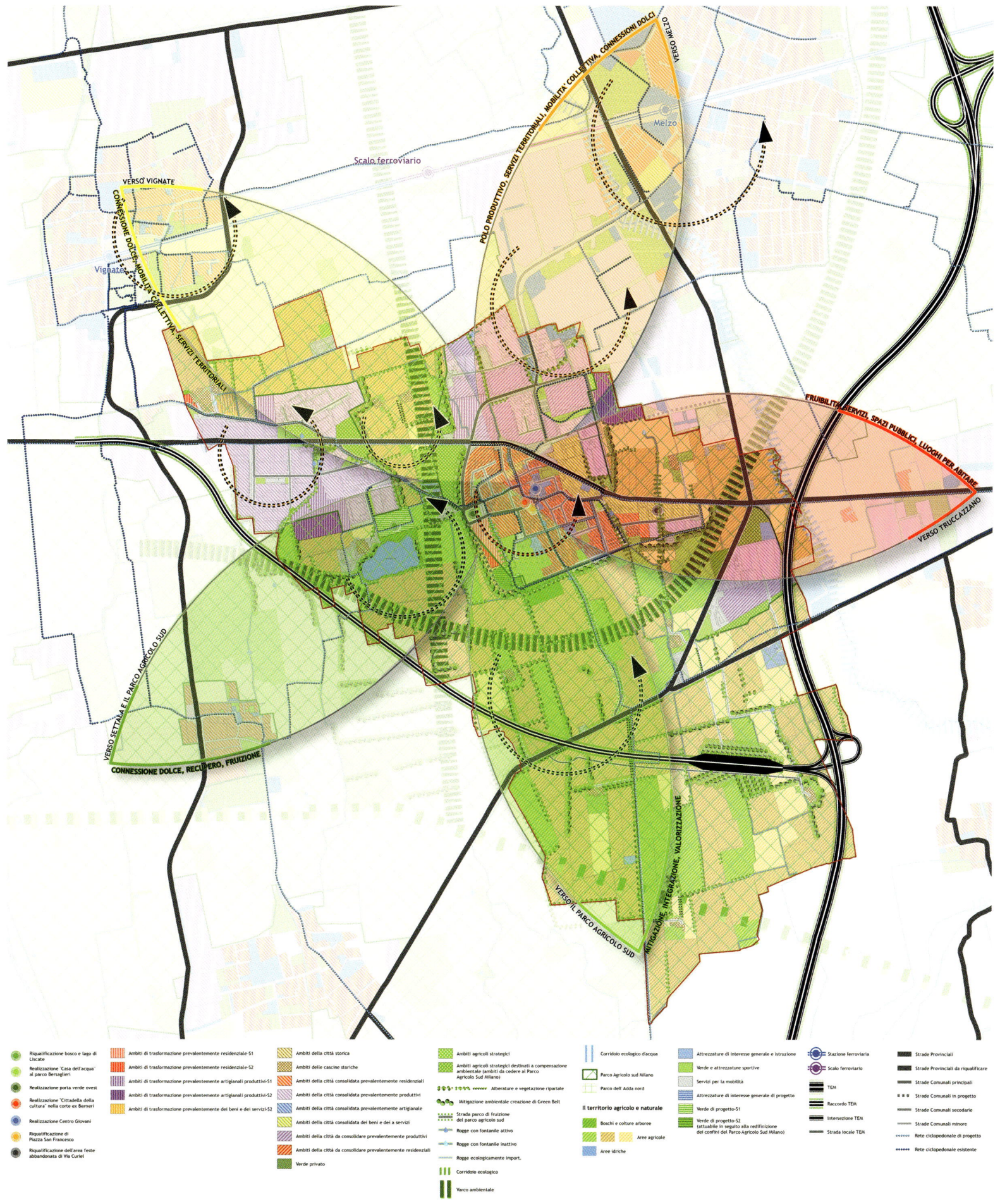

URBAN PLANNING

Redevelopment of the town as a place to live. In-depth development of the five planning objectives through a system of actions accorded priority for the territory and concrete suggestions for their implementation

URBAN PLANNING

Rules for the historical nucleus and the system of farmhouses. Analysis, modalities of operation and Guidebook Chart of the operations on the territory's historical architectural heritage

Bottom
Five objectives for Liscate. Strategic lines of the plan

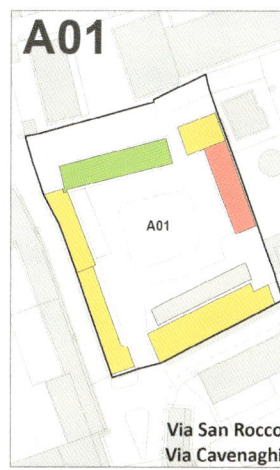

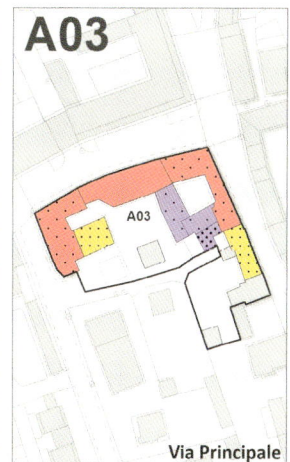
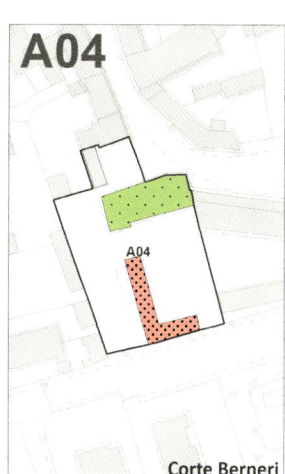

INDIVIDUAZIONE DEI POLI TERRITORIALI

Rafforzando i legami dei sistemi territoriali urbani di Vignate e Melzo. Costituendo il distretto produttivo Liscate-Melzo e Liscate-Vignate.

L_1

RECUPERO DELLA CITTÀ COME LUOGHI PER ABITARE

Recuperando i parchi urbani, creando la cittadella della cultura e riprogettando lo spazio pubblico dei principali luoghi di aggregazione

L_2

MITIGAZIONE AMBIENTALE DELLA TEM/BREBEMI E VARIANTE DI LISCATE

Realizzazione della mitigazione ambientale lungo il tracciato della TEM

L_3

REALIZZAZIONE DELLA CINTURA VERDE A OVEST

Rafforzando il corridoio ecologico nord-sud e recuperando il lago di Liscate

L_4

RIDEFINIZIONE DEI CONFINI DEL PARCO

Cedendo aree da includere nel parco e acquisendo altre aree da inserire come ambiti di trasformazione

L_5

7. Novedrate (Como): Municipal Territorial Management Plan (PGT) (2008–12)

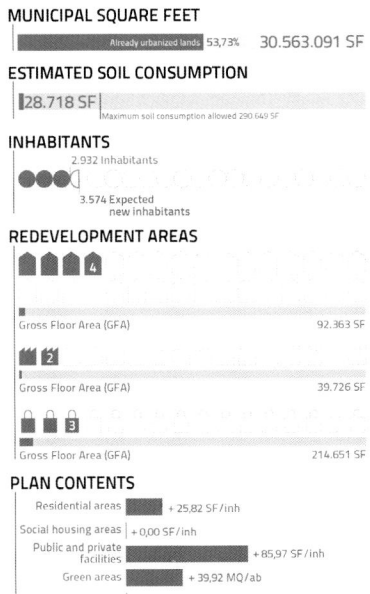

MUNICIPAL SQUARE FEET
Already urbanized lands 53,73%   30.563.091 SF

ESTIMATED SOIL CONSUMPTION
28.718 SF
Maximum soil consumption allowed 290.649 SF

INHABITANTS
2.932 Inhabitants
3.574 Expected new inhabitants

REDEVELOPMENT AREAS
Gross Floor Area (GFA)   92.363 SF
Gross Floor Area (GFA)   39.726 SF
Gross Floor Area (GFA)   214.651 SF

PLAN CONTENTS
Residential areas   + 25,82 SF/inh
Social housing areas   + 0,00 SF/inh
Public and private facilities   + 85,97 SF/inh
Green areas   + 39,92 MQ/ab
Public revenues   non conteggiati

The territory of Novedrate is particular. It is bounded to the west by a major environmental system that constitutes an interruption of the plain. The historical centre facing this system is particularly confined and overlooked by the rapid expansion that has taken place on the once agricultural plain, both residential in the vicinity of the historical centre and – still more evidently – industrial towards the infrastructural corridor of the provincial highway. It is an intermediate territory, capable of expressing both the environmental quality of the Brianza highland and the more consolidated dynamics of the plain. Attention is thus focused not on design, for which there is no space in a territory with such a structure, but on the regulatory procedure of the plan. Though small in size, the areas of transformation are addressed using specific technical dossiers in an attempt to include prescriptions in a process of implementation that provides for no prescriptive mechanisms in the plan.
The parts of the consolidated town are addressed with criteria of negotiated planning. Mechanisms for the sale and monetization of areas for services are taken into consideration and the relationship between the private and public sectors is probed through mechanisms for negotiation and reaching agreements. The challenge is considerable. At a time of crisis, reduced investment in territorial transformation and general reassessment of the value of investments in construction, the plan bases the mechanisms of its implementation on the relationship between private investors and public authorities, rediscovering the key role that the private sector must play in the construction of the city not least through mechanisms like the "*borsino volumetrico*" making it possible to exchange property rights in the residential areas. In this connection, the plan rediscovers important mechanisms, such as the transfer of volumes from one area to another, and innovates the same through an effort to determine the existence of parts of the settlement fabric requiring greater or lesser density. Importance attaches to the mechanism for implementation of the plan, which necessarily obeys this logic, because it must be able to ensure close scrutiny of the functioning and development of such transfers. At the same time, the strategic environmental assessment procedure plays a key role precisely as a tool for monitoring the implementation of the plan and the transformation of the territory.

Objectives of the Structural Plan. The nine objectives identified by the plan exceed the temporal validity of the planning document, developing on medium/long-term temporal lines and involving different resources and parties in their concrete implementation

URBAN PLANNING

URBAN PLANNING

URBAN PLANNING

perequazione   *decollo*   *atterraggio*

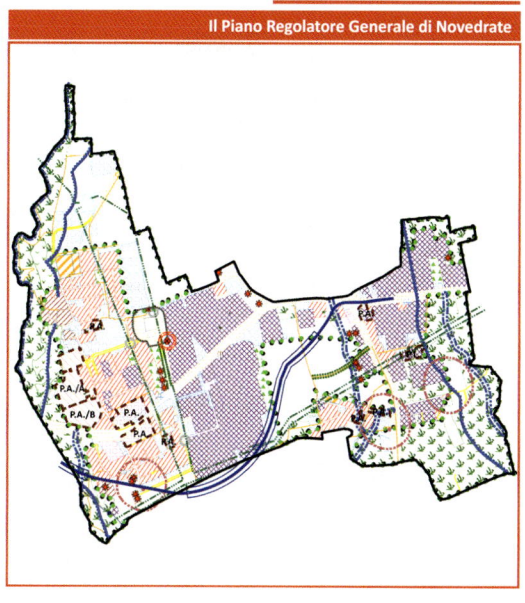
Il Piano Regolatore Generale di Novedrate

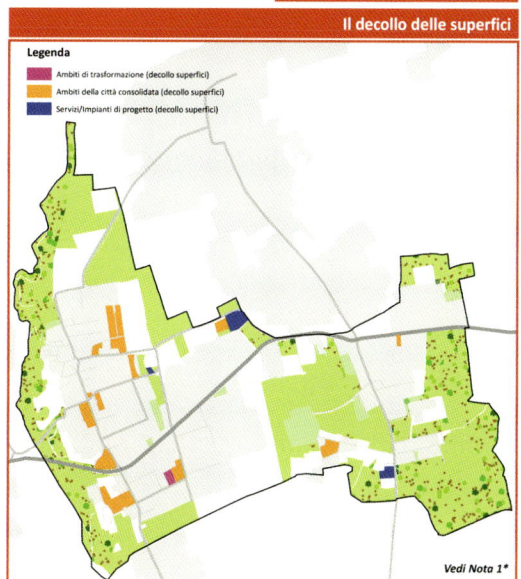
Il decollo delle superfici

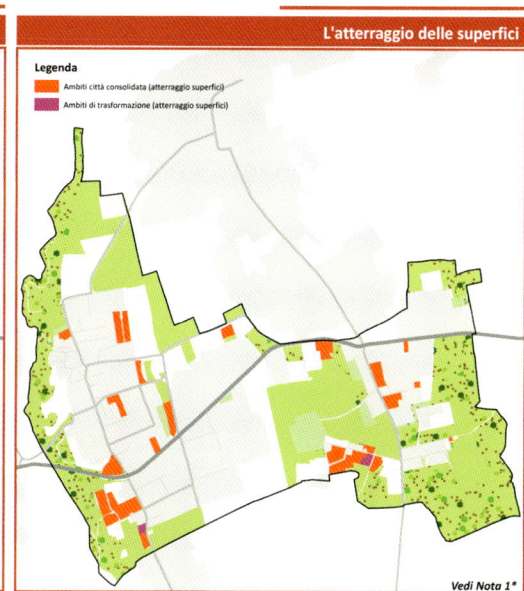
L'atterraggio delle superfici

Opposite
"*Borsino delle superfici*": a mechanism for the exchange of building rights in residential sections that constitutes a crucial tool to permit the use of residual areas of the consolidated fabric often regarded as marginal from the planning standpoint

"*Areas in flight*": method. The residual areas of "takeoff" scattered over the territory – involving both the consolidated fabric and the project areas of transformation and services – are redistributed within "landing" areas capable of absorbing additions due to their urban-planning characteristics

URBAN PLANNING

8. Canzo (Como): consultation on the drafting of the Municipal Territorial Government Plan (PGT) (2008–13)

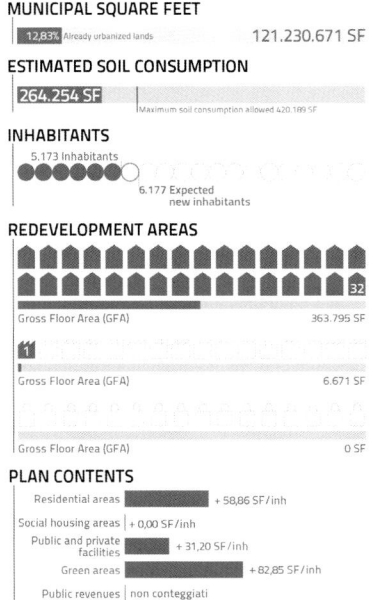

MUNICIPAL SQUARE FEET
12,83% Already urbanized lands   121.230.671 SF

ESTIMATED SOIL CONSUMPTION
264.254 SF
Maximum soil consumption allowed 420.189 SF

INHABITANTS
5.173 Inhabitants
6.177 Expected new inhabitants

REDEVELOPMENT AREAS
32
Gross Floor Area (GFA)   363.795 SF
11
Gross Floor Area (GFA)   6.671 SF
Gross Floor Area (GFA)   0 SF

PLAN CONTENTS
Residential areas   + 58,86 SF/inh
Social housing areas   + 0,00 SF/inh
Public and private facilities   + 31,20 SF/inh
Green areas   + 82,85 SF/inh
Public revenues   non conteggiati

Advising the town of Canzo, located in a pre-Alpine valley between the two branches of Lake Como, on the planning of its territory meant addressing particular issues for a very particular context. The last stop on a direct railway line from Milan, the town constitutes a bridgehead for the system of relations of the plain and the key point of reference for the entire valley. Canzo has played various roles over the years: as an industrial town hosting some activities of a very particular character but connected in some way to the nature of the territory (e.g. the production of bottled drinking water); as a holiday resort hosting an important system of high-quality villas for the industrial middle class of Milan and Brianza; and as a small residential town within an important environmental system. As the plan has discovered, all these systems, key points of reference in the past, are weaker today and the associated parts of the territory are in difficulty.

The industrial system is hit by problems of connections and accessibility with the rest of the productive territory and some of its activities have been discontinued (including the bottled water plant). The villas are run-down or even abandoned and have unquestionably failed to develop as a network and establish relations with the rest of the town. The environmental system has come under attack from recent development but can still boast areas of great importance like the ecosystem of Lake Segrino. The plan requires an understanding of the scenario to be designed for such a context driven by different dynamics: the defence of micro-transformations on the small scale; maximization of the private benefits of some transformations of disused areas on the intermediate urban scale; and the potential broader, knock-on effects of the 2015 Expo in terms of transformation of the territory on the large scale. The plan thus invests in the quality of the existing territory, initiating micro-actions to boost the quality of the settlement system (starting with the historical centre) and policies to safeguard the substantial environmental heritage, choosing to work on its provisions in the short term and wait for the external tensions to take concrete shape as impetus for transformation of the territory. Until this happens, the plan will act as an authentic tool of management, with no particular visions that the local context cannot support, in the form of a strategic map of actions that can be undertaken in the everyday course of running the territory. It thus works actively on the capacity of its provisions to ensure that the existing territory works efficiently, eschewing recourse to particular events and relying on the ability of the territory as it is to generate virtuous micro-processes of quality.

The adoption of a short-term planning perspective also makes it possible to keep the situation under observation and avoid undertaking actions that cannot be implemented within the set period.

Strategic analysis: the longitudinal axis. The central backbone on which the system of services and green space is concentrated. The plan develops a single pathway of projects for the municipal areas along this axis so as to endow the public city with a concrete and perceptible structure

URBAN PLANNING

Gli ambiti

2 La valorizzazione patrimonio ambientale
L'ambito del torrente Ravella è l'elemento di congiuntura fra l'asse centrale e l'asse longitudinale ne quale rappresenta il principale elemento di connessione. Il Ravella costituisce un elemento essenziale per il raccordo dei vari sistemi.
Rappresenta un corridoio importante che permette di collegare il sistema centrale agli ambiti naturali esterni.

5 La spina dei servizi
L'ambito dei servizi si struttura lungo tutto il sistema seguendo l'andamento della strada provinciale e del torrente Ravella. L'estensione dei servizi su questo asse può essere stata indotta dalla facile accessibilità (ambito ovest) dovuta sia alla stazione ferroviaria di Canzo che alla vicinanza delle due strade provinciali che, seguendo le valli, collegano Canzo alla pianura lombarda.

L'ambito della stazione ferroviaria di Canzo Centro è un elemento importante, sia come polo della mobilità che come centralità dello spazio pubblico. L'ambito si pone al centro del tessuto abitato, in posizione baricentrica fra il nucleo storico e l'area dei servizi.

3 La valorizzazione del patrimonio storico-culturale
L'ambito del centro storico viene incluso completamente nel sistema dell'asse longitudinale dove rappresenta il fulcro centrale, all'opposto è contenuto per poco meno della metà della sua globale estensione nell'asse centrale. Anche questo risulta un passaggio significativo in quanto il sistema dell'asse centrale, con il ruolo di ossatura fondamentale della città pubblica che gli è stato attribuito, entra e si distribuisce all'interno del centro di Canzo.

3 La valorizzazione del patrimonio storico-culturale
L'ambito delle ville storiche costituisce una fascia a sud dell'abitato di Canzo dando luogo, assieme al torrente Ravella, al Parco Rizzoli, ai giardini, ai parchi urbani dell'area di recupero ed al campo di Miro, ad una green belt con sfumature mutevoli che arricchisce notevolmente il valore paesaggistico del comune.

Politiche ed interventi

2 La valorizzazione patrimonio ambientale
Agevolare i collegamenti tra le due parti di città specialmente a riguardo della mobilità debole. In questa occasione l'asse centrale interseca l'asse longitudinale caratterizzato dalla presenza di servizi, che devono essere raggiunti in sicurezza. Devono essere previsti accessi al sistema dei percorsi pedo ciclabili longitudinali da realizzare sull'argine del Ravella, sia per la fruizione funzionale che per la fruizione ambientale. La fascia verde tra il torrente Ravella ed il centro storico vedrà il recupero di Parco Barni. Attribuire valore urbano alla sezione stradale che dovrà ospitare spazi pedonali per stare, per andare, pista ciclabile per la fruizione più urbana della strada.

5 La spina dei servizi
L'obiettivo è l'integrazione e connessione a sistema di tutti i servizi e gli spazi pubblici presenti con la costruzione di percorsi protetti attraversando contesti di pregio. Elemento essenziale del sistema dei servizi è la svolta del fronte verso il sistema fluviale. Il sistema longitudinale trova un importante elemento nel corridoio est - ovest costituito da via Roma che dovrà assumere una valenza prevalentemente urbana, dunque la sua sezione dovrà essere adeguata per ospitare e mettere in sicurezza i vari utenti in modo da poterla definire la "strada pubblica dei servizi".

4 Il potenziamento del sistema infrastrutturale
Realizzazione e consolidamento dei percorsi della mobilità debole che si diramano dalla stazione ferroviaria di Canzo Centro, anche tramite la riqualificazione a "strada urbana" dell'asse dei servizi. Assicurare la presenza di spazi pedonali per stare, per andare e piste ciclabili per la connessione in sicurezza delle utenze deboli. Riqualificazione dello spazio pubblico adiacente alla stazione e consolidare il corridoio est - ovest (stazione - verde - municipio - centro storico).

3 La valorizzazione del patrimonio storico-culturale
Sono necessarie azioni e politiche che permettano di aumentare le numerose potenzialità esistenti del centro storico di Canzo e d'altra parte è necessario porre in essere strategie che riducano o eliminino le criticità presenti. Grande attenzione dovrà essere posta per migliorare non solo le singole residenze dei cittadini residenti, ma la qualità della vita di tutta la comunità, rilanciando la politica del commercio.

3 La valorizzazione del patrimonio storico-culturale
Valorizzazione dell'ambito delle ville storiche che costituiscono, assieme agli altri elementi naturali, un importante patrimonio territoriale. Valorizzare questi elementi vuol dire sviluppare il sistema Canzo nella sua complessità. Si devono investire risorse sulla fruibilità delle ville creando percorsi tematici. Riconfigurazione degli affacci delle ville sulla strada, messa a sistema dei percorsi pubblici assieme ai corridoi verdi delle ville.

URBAN PLANNING

Strategic analysis: the central axis. The primary vector of the existing and future public city is the territorial area, which makes it possible to relate two major polarities and develop the relationship between the settlement system and infrastructural axes to the full

Gli ambiti

1 La valorizzazione dell'ambito della stazione
La stazione di Canzo-Asso è l'elemento terminale della ferrovia proveniente da Milano, la principale porta d'accesso del comune e del Triangolo Lariano in quanto fulcro del trasporto pubblico locale.
L'ambito della stazione rappresenta la testa nord dell'asse centrale, quell'asse che ha come principale obiettivo la "ricucitura" del tessuto della città pubblica da nord a sud. Quindi la valorizzazione dell'ambito della stazione rappresenta un perno fondamentale del sistema dell'asse centrale e dell'azione che questo vuole perseguire.

2 La valorizzazione patrimonio ambientale
L'ambito del fiume Lambro ricopre un ruolo fondamentale all'interno del sistema ambientale del territorio comunale, ponendosi come asta principale di connessione ambientale. In particolare si devono tutelare e valorizzare le aree di pianura adiacenti al fiume con scopo naturalistico - ambientale.

2 La valorizzazione patrimonio ambientale
L'ambito del Parco di Villa Rizzoli si inserisce in questo sistema come prezioso contributo ambientale, costituendo assieme al Lambro un'armatura verde di considerevole valore. Rendere fruibile il polo della villa storica con il suo parco vorrebbe dire incrementare il valore complessivo del territorio. Inoltre si rende necessario il ripristino del corridoio verde e pedonale verso est interessando l'area di recupero a nord del centro storico.
L'ambito della testata del parco di Villa Rizzoli rappresenta un nodo fondamentale in quanto costituisce la parte conclusiva della grande area verde che, attraverso il recupero dell'ambito di trasformazione 15a e 16, entra nell'abitato.

3 La valorizzazione del patrimonio storico-culturale
L'ambito del centro storico viene incluso completamente nel sistema dell'asse longitudinale dove rappresenta il fulcro centrale, all'opposto è contenuto per poco meno della metà della sua globale estensione nell'asse centrale. Anche questo risulta un passaggio significativo in quanto il sistema dell'asse centrale, con il ruolo di ossatura fondamentale della città pubblica che gli è stato attribuito, entra e si distribuisce all'interno del centro di Canzo.

4 Il potenziamento del sistema infrastrutturale
L'ambito della stazione ferroviaria di Canzo Centro è un elemento importante, sia come polo della mobilità sia come centralità dello spazio pubblico. L'ambito si pone al centro del tessuto abitato, in posizione baricentrica fra il nucleo storico e l'area dei servizi.

2 La valorizzazione patrimonio ambientale
L'ambito del torrente Ravella è l'elemento di congiuntura fra l'asse centrale e l'asse longitudinale ne quale rappresenta il principale elemento di connessione. Il Ravella costituisce un elemento essenziale per il raccordo dei vari sistemi.
Rappresenta un corridoio importante che permette di collegare il sistema centrale agli ambiti naturali esterni.

3 La valorizzazione del patrimonio storico-culturale
L'ambito delle ville storiche costituisce una fascia a sud dell'abitato di Canzo dando luogo, assieme al torrente Ravella, al Parco Rizzoli, ai giardini, ai parchi urbani dell'area di recupero ed al campo di Miro, ad una green belt con sfumature mutevoli che arricchisce notevolmente il valore paesaggistico del comune.

Politiche ed interventi

1 La valorizzazione dell'ambito della stazione
L'ambito della stazione ferroviaria offre l'occasione per un complessivo ripensamento dell'area, il miglioramento dell'accessibilità, l'integrazione con il contesto e la creazione di un nodo di interscambio.
L'ambito della stazione oltre a essere la testa nord dell'asse centrale si configurarsi anche come elemento di connessione fra il sistema costruito e l'ambito naturale del Lambro.

2 La valorizzazione patrimonio ambientale
Valorizzazione del sistema fluviale sia in termini di fruizione per il tempo libero che per il consolidamento della rete ecologica.
Mantenere, valorizzare e mettere a rete i percorsi, osservare attente politiche di tutela sulle aree limitrofe al corso d'acqua rimaste libere.

2 La valorizzazione patrimonio ambientale
Valorizzazione delle potenzialità attrattive del polo di Villa Rizzoli che costituisce una importante realtà da valorizzare a favore della comunità.
L'obiettivo è quello di integrare il parco e le realtà della Villa storica con il verde urbano ed il sistema dello spazio pubblico recuperato con la riorganizzazione dell'area dismessa a nord del centro storico. Contestualmente deve essere riqualificazione della sezione stradale con la messa in sicurezza degli attraversamenti. Facilitare il collegamento tra le due parti di città: il Parco di Villa Rizzoli e l'area verde verso il centro città

3 La valorizzazione del patrimonio storico-culturale
Sono necessarie azioni e politiche che permettano di aumentare le numerose potenzialità esistenti del centro storico di Canzo e d'altra parte è necessario porre in essere strategie che riducano o eliminino le criticità presenti. Grande attenzione dovrà essere posta per migliorare non solo le singole residenze dei cittadini residenti, ma la qualità della vita di tutta la comunità, rilanciando la politica del commercio.

4 Il potenziamento del sistema infrastrutturale
Realizzazione e consolidamento dei percorsi della mobilità debole che si diramano dalla stazione ferroviaria di Canzo Centro, anche tramite la riqualificazione a "strada urbana" dell'asse dei servizi. Assicurare la presenza di spazi pedonali per stare, per andare e piste ciclabili per la connessione in sicurezza delle utenze deboli. Riqualificazione dello spazio pubblico adiacente alla stazione e consolidare il corridoio est - ovest (stazione - verde - municipio - centro storico).

2 La valorizzazione patrimonio ambientale
Agevolare i collegamenti tra le due parti di città specialmente a riguardo della mobilità debole. In questa occasione l'asse centrale interseca l'asse longitudinale caratterizzato dalla presenza di servizi, che devono essere raggiunti in sicurezza. Devono essere previsti accessi al sistema dei percorsi pedo ciclabili longitudinali da realizzare sull'argine del Ravella, sia per la fruizione funzionale che per la fruizione ambientale. La fascia verde tra il torrente Ravella ed il centro storico vedrà il recupero di Parco Barni. Attribuire valore urbano alla sezione stradale che dovrà ospitare spazi pedonali per stare, per andare, pista ciclabile per la fruizione più urbana della strada.

3 La valorizzazione del patrimonio storico-culturale
Valorizzazione dell'ambito delle ville storiche che costituiscono, assieme agli altri elementi naturali, un importante patrimonio territoriale. Valorizzare questi elementi vuol dire sviluppare il sistema Canzo nella sua complessità. Si devono investire risorse sulla fruibilità delle ville creando percorsi tematici. Riconfigurazione degli affacci delle ville sulla strada, messa a sistema dei percorsi pubblici assieme ai corridoi verdi delle ville.

2 La valorizzazione patrimonio ambientale
L'ambito del lago del Segrino costituisce un polo importante che tenta di ricucire la distanza tra il lago e l'abitato. A tal fine è fondamentale riqualificare l'asse viabilistico centrale. La posizione strategica, quale porta urbana del sistema insediativo canzese, è sottolineata dalla presenza del lago anche in relazione al patrimonio ambientale attualmente adeguatamente valorizzato e gestito.

2 La valorizzazione patrimonio ambientale
Assicurare la presenza di spazi pedonali per stare, per andare, pista ciclabile per la connessione in sicurezza delle utenze deboli. Per la fruizione ciclabile è individuabile anche un percorso in parte svincolato dalla strada e che corre parallelamente alla stessa ad est. I percorsi ciclopedonali si congiungeranno alla realtà ambientale del lago del Segrino a sud e da questa al lago ed ai percorsi attorno ad esso. La strada dunque avrà la funzione fondamentale di avvicinare il lago al paese e viceversa il paese al lago coprendo la distanza di 2000 metri.

URBAN PLANNING

Gli ambiti

2 La valorizzazione patrimonio ambientale
L'ambito del torrente Ravella è l'elemento di congiuntura fra l'asse centrale e l'asse longitudinale ne quale rappresenta il principale elemento di connessione. Il Ravella costituisce un elemento essenziale per il raccordo dei vari sistemi.
Rappresenta un corridoio importante che permette di collegare il sistema centrale agli ambiti naturali esterni.

5 L'spina dei servizi
L'ambito dei servizi si struttura lungo tutto il sistema seguendo l'andamento della strada provinciale e del torrente Ravella. L'estensione dei servizi su questo asse può essere stata indotta dalla facile accessibilità (ambito ovest) dovuta sia alla stazione ferroviaria di Canzo che alla vicinanza delle due strade provinciali che, seguendo le valli, collegano Canzo alla pianura lombarda.

L'ambito della stazione ferroviaria di Canzo Centro è un elemento importante, sia come polo della mobilità che come centralità dello spazio pubblico. L'ambito si pone al centro del tessuto abitato, in posizione baricentrica fra il nucleo storico e l'area dei servizi.

3 La valorizzazione del patrimonio storico-culturale
L'ambito del centro storico viene incluso completamente nel sistema dell'asse longitudinale dove rappresenta il fulcro centrale, all'opposto è contenuto per poco meno della metà della sua globale estensione nell'asse centrale. Anche questo risulta un passaggio significativo in quanto il sistema dell'asse centrale, con il ruolo di ossatura fondamentale della città pubblica che gli è stato attribuito, entra e si distribuisce all'interno del centro di Canzo.

3 La valorizzazione del patrimonio storico-culturale
L'ambito delle ville storiche costituisce una fascia a sud dell'abitato di Canzo dando luogo, assieme al torrente Ravella, al Parco Rizzoli, ai giardini, ai parchi urbani dell'area di recupero ed al campo di Miro, ad una green belt con sfumature mutevoli che arricchisce notevolmente il valore paesaggistico del comune.

Politiche ed interventi

2 La valorizzazione patrimonio ambientale
Agevolare i collegamenti tra le due parti di città specialmente a riguardo della mobilità debole. In questa occasione l'asse centrale interseca l'asse longitudinale caratterizzato dalla presenza di servizi, che devono essere raggiunti in sicurezza. Devono essere previsti accessi al sistema dei percorsi pedo ciclabili longitudinali da realizzare sull'argine del Ravella, sia per la fruizione funzionale che per la fruizione ambientale. La fascia verde tra il torrente Ravella ed il centro storico vedrà il recupero di Parco Barni. Attribuire valore urbano alla sezione stradale che dovrà ospitare spazi pedonali per stare, per andare, pista ciclabile per la fruizione più urbana della strada.

3 La spina dei servizi
L'obiettivo è l'integrazione e connessione a sistema di tutti i servizi e gli spazi pubblici presenti con la costruzione di percorsi protetti attraversando contesti di pregio. Elemento essenziale del sistema dei servizi è la svolta del fronte verso il sistema fluviale. Il sistema longitudinale trova un importante elemento nel corridoio est - ovest costituito da via Roma che dovrà assumere una valenza prevalentemente urbana, dunque la sua sezione dovrà essere adeguata per ospitare in sicurezza i vari utenti in modo da poterla definire la "strada pubblica dei servizi".

4 Il potenziamento del sistema infrastrutturale
Realizzazione e consolidamento dei percorsi della mobilità debole che si diramano dalla stazione ferroviaria di Canzo Centro, anche tramite la riqualificazione a "strada urbana" dell'asse dei servizi. Assicurare la presenza di spazi pedonali per stare, per andare e piste ciclabili per la connessione in sicurezza delle utenze deboli. Riqualificazione dello spazio pubblico adiacente alla stazione e consolidare il corridoio est - ovest (stazione - verde - municipio - centro storico).

3 La valorizzazione del patrimonio storico-culturale
Sono necessarie azioni e politiche che permettano di aumentare le numerose potenzialità esistenti del centro storico di Canzo e d'altra parte è necessario porre in essere strategie che riducano o eliminino le criticità presenti. Grande attenzione dovrà essere posta per migliorare non solo le singole residenze dei cittadini residenti, ma la qualità della vita di tutta la comunità, rilanciando la politica del commercio.

3 La valorizzazione del patrimonio storico-culturale
Valorizzazione dell'ambito delle ville storiche che costituiscono, assieme agli altri elementi naturali, un importante patrimonio territoriale. Valorizzare questi elementi vuol dire sviluppare il sistema Canzo nella sua complessità. Si devono investire risorse sulla fruibilità delle ville creando percorsi tematici. Riconfigurazione degli affacci delle ville sulla strada, messa a sistema dei percorsi pubblici assieme ai corridoi verdi delle ville.

URBAN PLANNING

Strategic analysis: the central axis. The primary vector of the existing and future public city is the territorial area, which makes it possible to relate two major polarities and develop the relationship between the settlement system and infrastructural axes to the full

Gli ambiti

1 La valorizzazione dell'ambito della stazione
La stazione di Canzo-Asso è l'elemento terminale della ferrovia proveniente da Milano, la principale porta d'accesso del comune e del Triangolo Lariano in quanto fulcro del trasporto pubblico locale.
L'ambito della stazione rappresenta la testa nord dell'asse centrale, quell'asse che ha come principale obiettivo la "ricucitura" del tessuto della città pubblica da nord a sud. Quindi la valorizzazione dell'ambito della stazione rappresenta un perno fondamentale del sistema dell'asse centrale e dell'azione che questo vuole perseguire.

2 La valorizzazione patrimonio ambientale
L'ambito del fiume Lambro ricopre un ruolo fondamentale all'interno del sistema ambientale del territorio comunale, ponendosi come asta principale di connessione ambientale. In particolare si devono tutelare e valorizzare le aree di pianura adiacenti al fiume con scopo naturalistico - ambientale.

2 La valorizzazione patrimonio ambientale
L'ambito del Parco di Villa Rizzoli si inserisce in questo sistema come prezioso contributo ambientale, costituendo assieme al Lambro un'armatura verde di considerevole valore. Rendere fruibile il polo della villa storica con il suo parco vorrebbe dire incrementare il valore complessivo del territorio. Inoltre si rende necessario il ripristino del corridoio verde e pedonale verso est interessando l'area di recupero a nord del centro storico.
L'ambito della testata del parco di Villa Rizzoli rappresenta un nodo fondamentale in quanto costituisce la parte conclusiva della grande area verde che, attraverso il recupero dell'ambito di trasformazione 15a e 16, entra nell'abitato.

3 La valorizzazione del patrimonio storico-culturale
L'ambito del centro storico viene incluso completamente nel sistema dell'asse longitudinale dove rappresenta il fulcro centrale, all'opposto è contenuto per poco meno della metà della sua globale estensione nell'asse centrale. Anche questo risulta un passaggio significativo in quanto il sistema dell'asse centrale, con il ruolo di ossatura fondamentale della città pubblica che gli è stato attribuito, entra e si distribuisce all'interno del centro di Canzo.

4 Il potenziamento del sistema infrastrutturale
L'ambito della stazione ferroviaria di Canzo Centro è un elemento importante, sia come polo della mobilità che come centralità dello spazio pubblico. L'ambito si pone al centro del tessuto abitato, in posizione baricentrica fra il nucleo storico e l'area dei servizi.

2 La valorizzazione patrimonio ambientale
L'ambito del torrente Ravella è l'elemento di congiuntura fra l'asse centrale e l'asse longitudinale ne quale rappresenta il principale elemento di connessione. Il Ravella costituisce un elemento essenziale per il raccordo dei vari sistemi.
Rappresenta un corridoio importante che permette di collegare il sistema centrale agli ambiti naturali esterni.

3 La valorizzazione del patrimonio storico-culturale
L'ambito delle ville storiche costituisce una fascia a sud dell'abitato di Canzo dando luogo, assieme al torrente Ravella, al Parco Rizzoli, ai giardini, ai parchi urbani dell'area di recupero ed al campo di Miro, ad una green belt con sfumature mutevoli che arricchisce notevolmente il valore paesaggistico del comune.

2 La valorizzazione patrimonio ambientale
L'ambito del lago del Segrino costituisce un polo importante che tenta di ricucire la distanza tra il lago e l'abitato. A tal fine è fondamentale riqualificare l'asse viabilistico centrale. La posizione strategica, quale porta urbana del sistema insediativo canzese, è sottolineata dalla presenza del lago anche in relazione al patrimonio ambientale attualmente adeguatamente valorizzato e gestito.

Politiche ed interventi

1 La valorizzazione dell'ambito della stazione
L'ambito della stazione ferroviaria offre l'occasione per un complessivo ripensamento dell'area, il miglioramento dell'accessibilità, l'integrazione con il contesto e la creazione di un nodo di interscambio.
L'ambito della stazione oltre a essere la testa nord dell'asse centrale si configurarsi anche come elemento di connessione fra il sistema costruito e l'ambito naturale del Lambro.

2 La valorizzazione patrimonio ambientale
Valorizzazione del sistema fluviale sia in termini di fruizione per il tempo libero che per il consolidamento della rete ecologica.
Mantenere, valorizzare e mettere a rete i percorsi, osservare attente politiche di tutela sulle aree limitrofe al corso d'acqua rimaste libere.

2 La valorizzazione patrimonio ambientale
Valorizzazione delle potenzialità attrattive del polo di Villa Rizzoli che costituisce una importante realtà da valorizzare a favore della comunità.
L'obiettivo è quello di integrare il parco e le realtà della Villa storica con il verde urbano ed il sistema dello spazio pubblico recuperato con la riorganizzazione dell'area dismessa a nord del centro storico. Contestualmente deve essere riqualificazione della sezione stradale con la messa in sicurezza degli attraversamenti. Facilitare il collegamento tra le due parti di città: il Parco di Villa Rizzoli e l'area verde verso il centro città

3 La valorizzazione del patrimonio storico-culturale
Sono necessarie azioni e politiche che permettano di aumentare le numerose potenzialità esistenti del centro storico di Canzo e d'altra parte è necessario porre in essere strategie che riducano o eliminino le criticità presenti. Grande attenzione dovrà essere posta per migliorare non solo le singole residenze dei cittadini residenti, ma alla qualità della vita di tutta la comunità, rilanciando la politica del commercio.

4 Il potenziamento del sistema infrastrutturale
Realizzazione e consolidamento dei percorsi della mobilità debole che si diramano dalla stazione ferroviaria di Canzo Centro, anche tramite la riqualificazione a "strada urbana" dell'asse dei servizi. Assicurare la presenza di spazi pedonali per stare, per andare e piste ciclabili per la connessione in sicurezza delle utenze deboli. Riqualificazione dello spazio pubblico adiacente alla stazione e consolidare il corridoio est - ovest (stazione - verde - municipio - centro storico).

2 La valorizzazione patrimonio ambientale
Agevolare i collegamenti tra le due parti di città specialmente a riguardo della mobilità debole. In questa occasione l'asse centrale interseca l'asse longitudinale caratterizzato dalla presenza di servizi, che devono essere raggiunti in sicurezza. Devono essere previsti accessi al sistema dei percorsi pedo ciclabili longitudinali da realizzare sull'argine del Ravella, sia per la fruizione funzionale che per la fruizione ambientale. La fascia verde tra il torrente Ravella ed il centro storico vedrà il recupero di Parco Barni. Attribuire valore urbano alla sezione stradale che dovrà ospitare spazi pedonali per stare, per andare, pista ciclabile per la fruizione più urbana della strada.

3 La valorizzazione del patrimonio storico-culturale
Valorizzazione dell'ambito delle ville storiche che costituiscono, assieme agli altri elementi naturali, un importante patrimonio territoriale. Valorizzare questi elementi vuol dire sviluppare il sistema Canzo nella sua complessità. Si devono investire risorse sulla fruibilità delle ville creando percorsi tematici. Riconfigurazione degli affacci delle ville sulla strada, messa a sistema dei percorsi pubblici assieme ai corridoi verdi delle ville.

2 La valorizzazione patrimonio ambientale
Assicurare la presenza di spazi pedonali per stare, per andare, pista ciclabile per la connessione in sicurezza delle utenze deboli. Per la fruizione ciclabile è individuabile anche un percorso in parte svincolato dalla strada e che corre parallelamente alla stessa ad est. I percorsi ciclopedonali si congiungeranno alla realtà ambientale del lago del Segrino a sud e da questa al lago ed ai percorsi attorno ad esso. La strada dunque avrà la funzione fondamentale di avvicinare il lago al paese e viceversa il paese al lago coprendo la distanza di 2000 metri.

The system of the historical centre. Analysis of the settlement morphologies, open spaces and architectural values of the historical nucleus in order to guide the norms of protection and promotion of the Zoning Plan

URBAN PLANNING

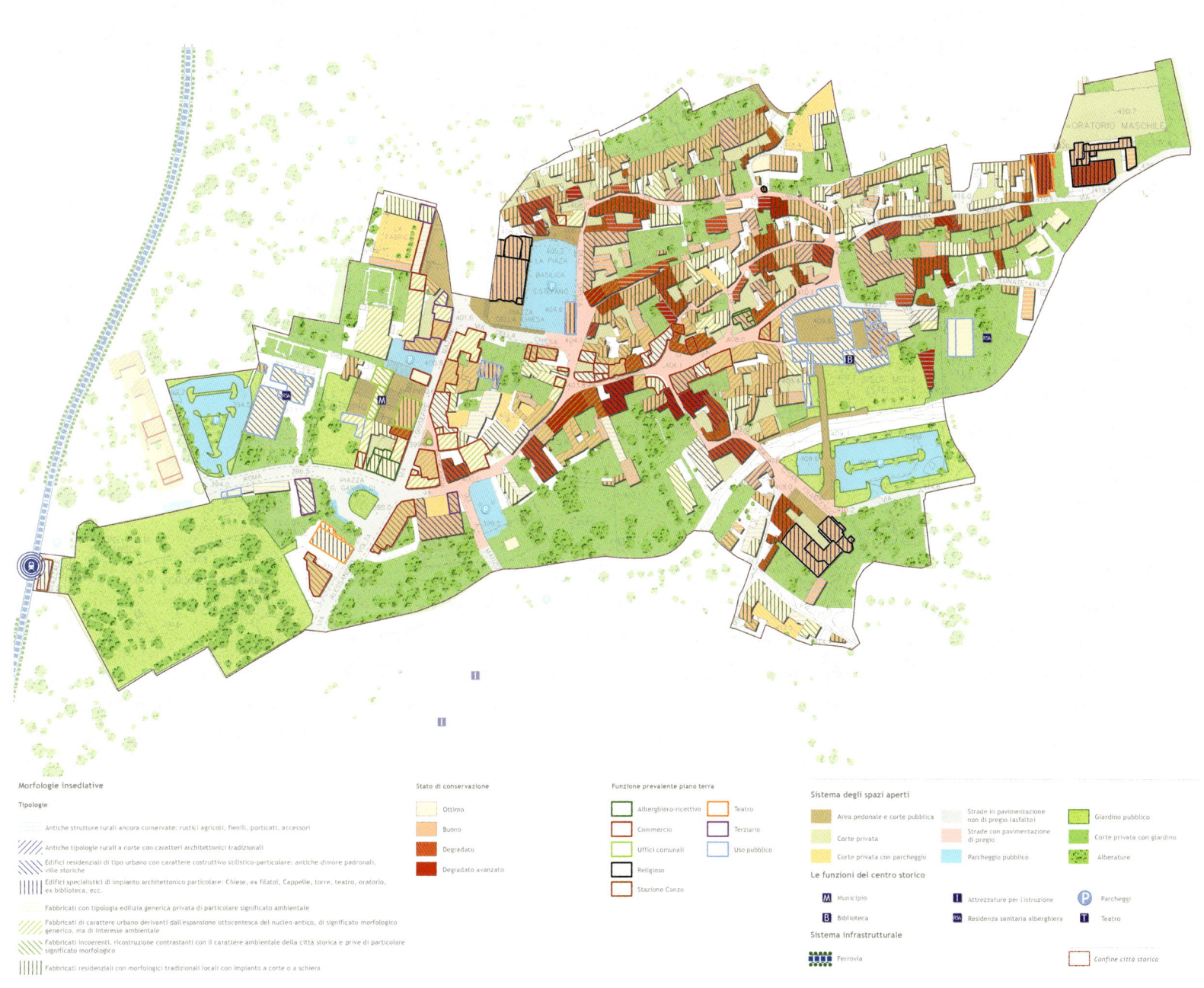

9. Cassina de' Pecchi (Milan): Municipal Territorial Management Plan (PGT) (2008–13)

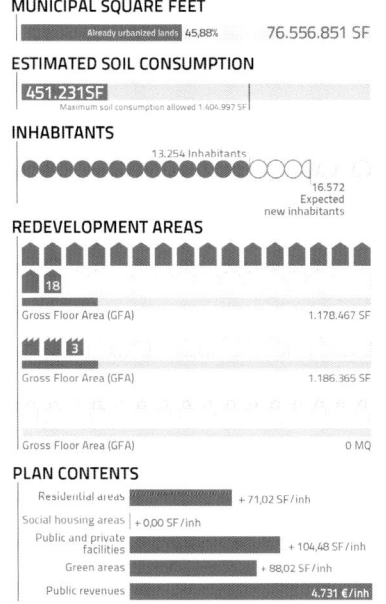

The protracted work for Cassina de' Pecchi demonstrates that also a tool built for speed like the Municipal Territorial Management Plan can develop on location through differentiated timing. The plan's actions are focused on the creation of some central places for the territory in full awareness of its nature as a very particular municipality that initially fell victim to the great wave of speculation in the 1950s and '60s and then saw intense building growth over the next two decades prompted by the metropolitan railway. With very high density in the central part and low densities in those of more recent construction, it is a typically metropolitan area with major territorial axes generating important relations between Cassina and its surroundings. The presence of the Martesana canal, the metropolitan railway and no fewer than three provincial highways (the Padana Superiore, Cassanese and Cerca) make the question of infrastructural connections central to the plan, above all in relation to the policy in place for development of these systems and to the problems expressed by a saturated territory precisely in the vicinity of the same. The plan invests in quality for all its components and focuses primarily on the construction of new centralities in order to modify the position of Cassina de' Pecchi within the metropolitan territory. The municipality has a great many opportunities to attain centrality, including redevelopment of the canal, the area of the station and the town centre, the creation of public services and sports facilities in connection with the South Milan Agricultural Park, and the transformation of a farmhouse into a new centre in order to rejoin the two parts of the town, all initiatives that constitute specific projects of the plan. Use is made of a master plan to examine the viability and ascertain the feasibility of these projects and secure the benefits that their implementation would mean for the territory as a whole. Through design, the plan identifies a different role for Cassina, not least in relation to the deeper dynamics connected with use of the constructed parts of the town, both devoted to public services and private, non-residential structures. It is a long and evolving plan, constructed more as a process than a snapshot of the town's future, in which design plays a strategic role in guiding the process under way and implementing the planning provisions over time.

URBAN PLANNING

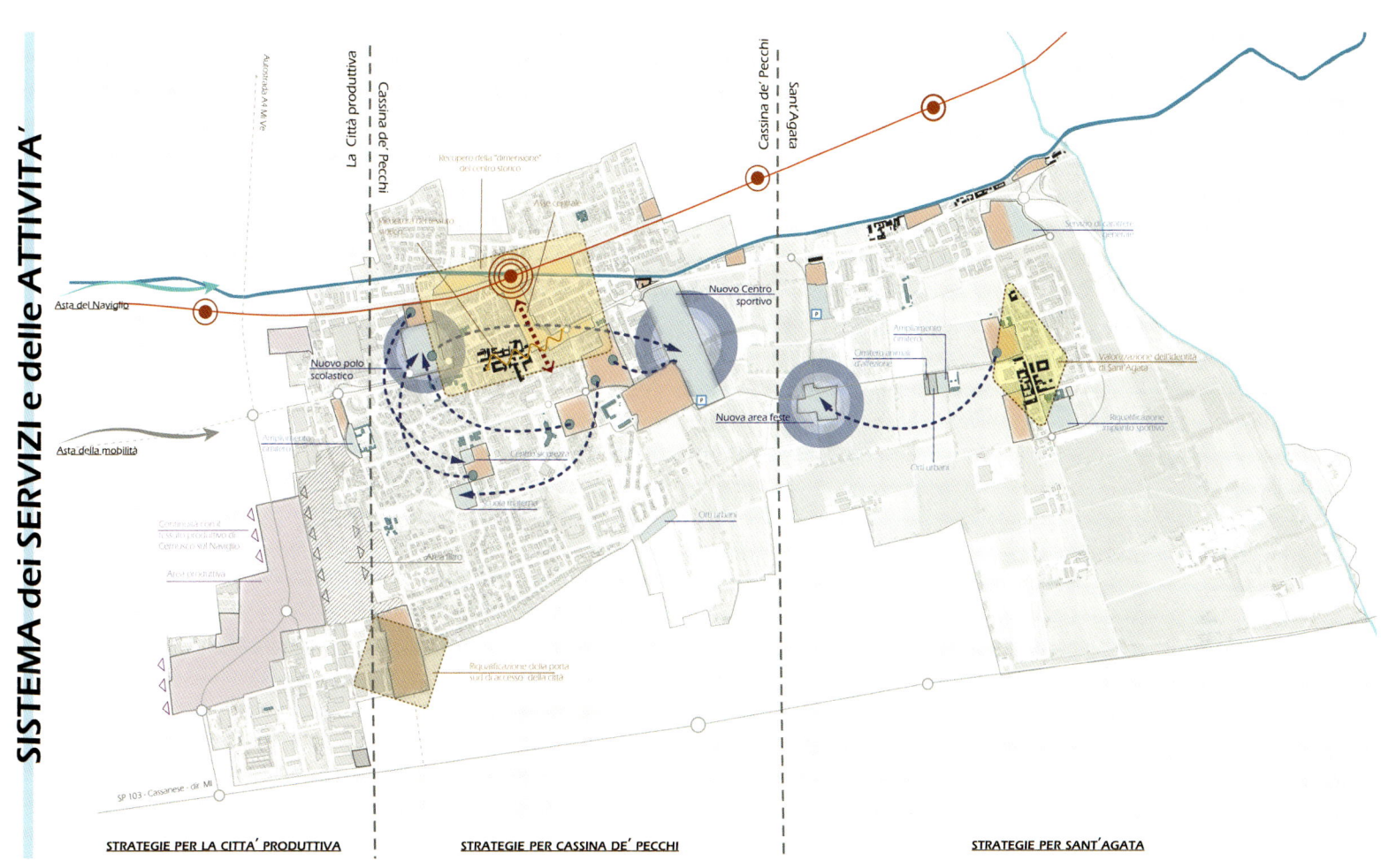

The system of services and activities. The primary objective of rationalization and reinforcement of the public city is achieved through a complex mechanism of alienation of areas that ensures the urban and economic sustainability of the plan as a whole

URBAN PLANNING

The mobility system. Redefinition of the infrastructural system takes shape through a series of mobility policies and works of different territorial and economic weight that act in synergy to ensure an increase in the urban quality of the territory as a whole

The environmental system. Identification of the primary existing and planned ecological and environmental connections in favour of complete upgrading of the South Milan Agricultural Park

URBAN PLANNING

Planning indications for implementation. The detailed dossiers developed for every area of transformation furnish important indications to orient implementation towards planning with close attention to the territory

Procedures of implementation. The economic and urban sustainability of the transformations is highlighted in the detailed dossiers of the transformation areas through diagrams that illustrate the specific mechanisms of implementation of the planning decisions

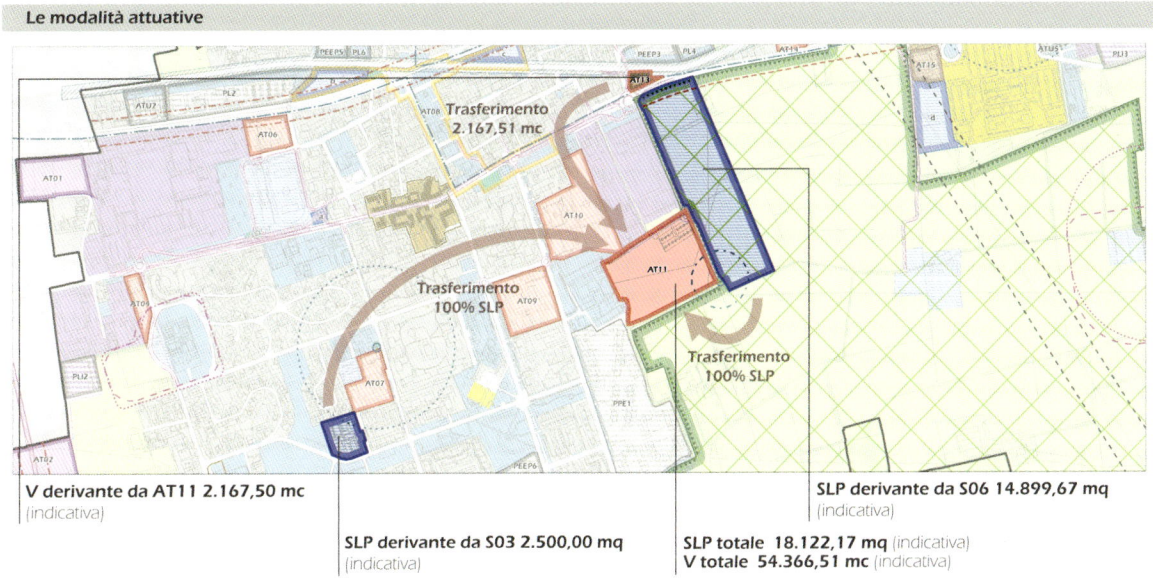

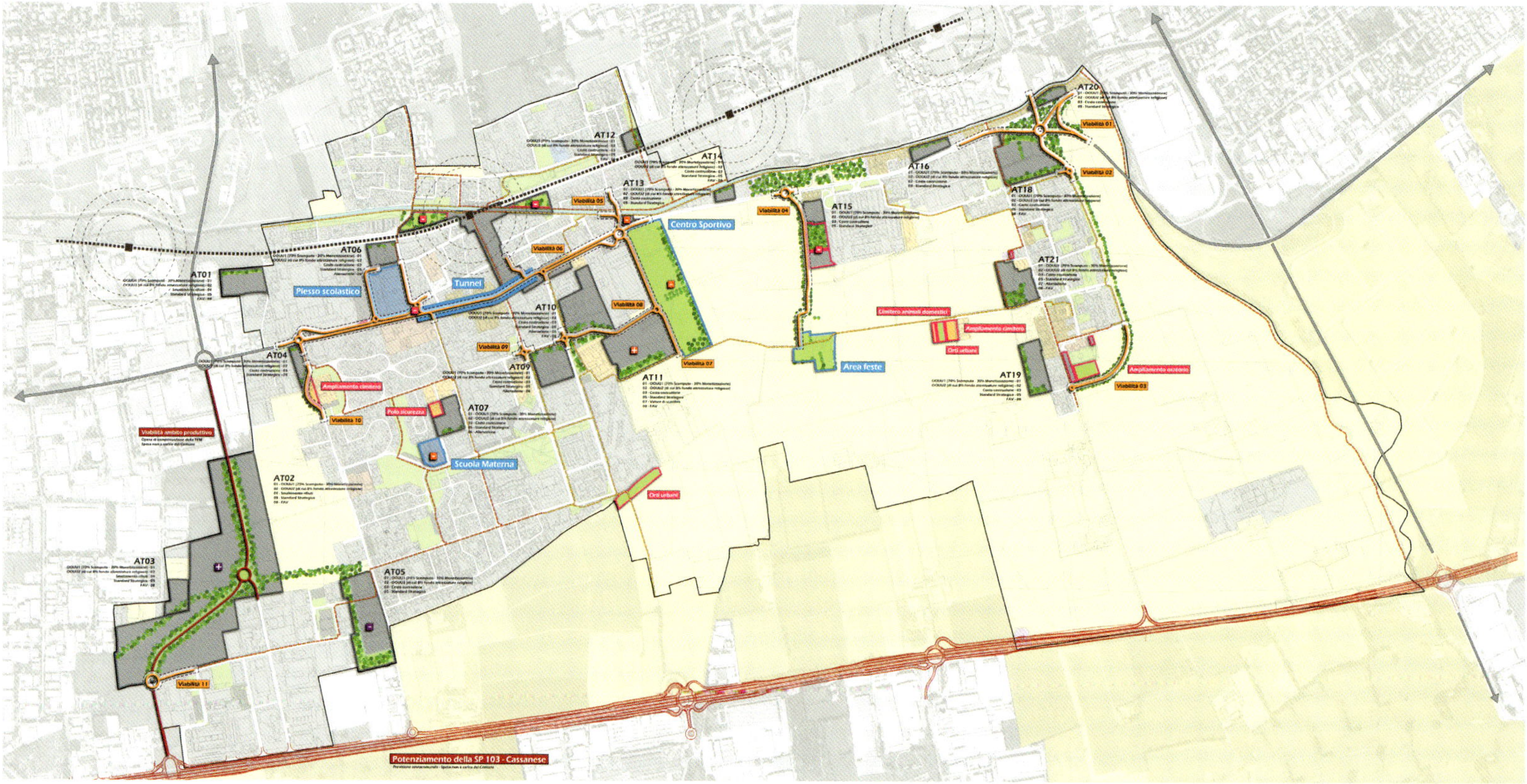

AT01
AT02
AT03
AT04
AT05
AT06
AT07
AT09
AT10
AT11
AT12
AT13
AT14
AT15
AT16
AT18
AT19
AT20
AT21
Tunnel
Centro Sportivo
Plesso scolastico
Scuola Materna
Area feste
Orti urbani
Polo sicurezza
Cimitero animali domestici
Ampliamento cimitero
Ampliamento oratorio
Viabilità settore produttivo
Viabilità 01
Viabilità 02
Viabilità 03
Viabilità 04
Viabilità 05
Viabilità 06
Viabilità 07
Viabilità 08
Viabilità 09
Viabilità 10
Viabilità 11
Potenziamento della SP 103 - Cassanese

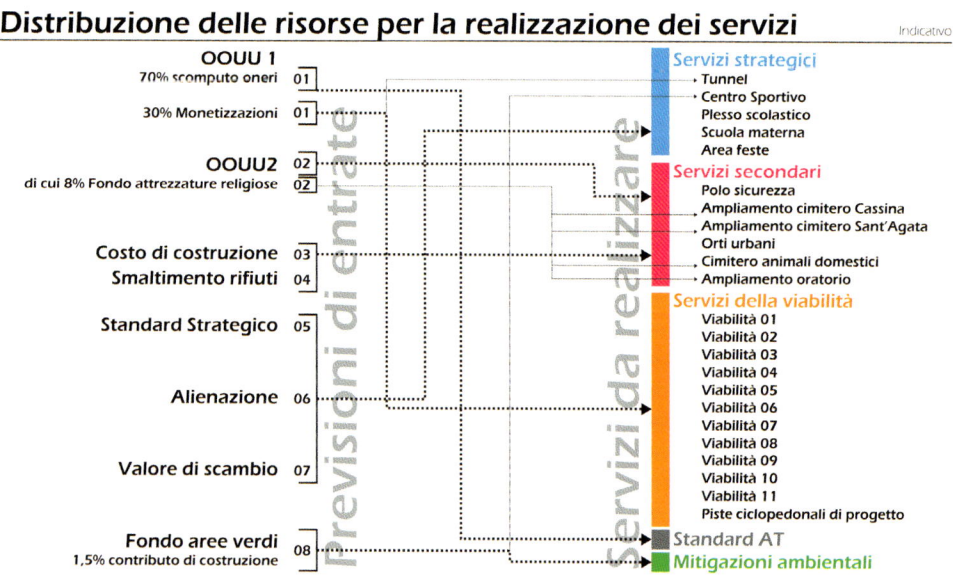

Distribuzione delle risorse per la realizzazione dei servizi

Indicativo

OOUU 1
70% scomputo oneri 01
30% Monetizzazioni 01
OOUU2 02
di cui 8% Fondo attrezzature religiose 02
Costo di costruzione 03
Smaltimento rifiuti 04
Standard Strategico 05
Alienazione 06
Valore di scambio 07
Fondo aree verdi 08
1,5% contributo di costruzione
Previsioni di entrate
Servizi da realizzare
Servizi strategici
Tunnel
Centro Sportivo
Plesso scolastico
Scuola materna
Area feste
Servizi secondari
Polo sicurezza
Ampliamento cimitero Cassina
Ampliamento cimitero Sant'Agata
Orti urbani
Cimitero animali domestici
Ampliamento oratorio
Servizi della viabilità
Viabilità 01
Viabilità 02
Viabilità 03
Viabilità 04
Viabilità 05
Viabilità 06
Viabilità 07
Viabilità 08
Viabilità 09
Viabilità 10
Viabilità 11
Piste ciclopedonali di progetto
Standard AT
Mitigazioni ambientali

Economic sustainability of the plan. This key element of the Public Facilities Plan provides the economic framework in support of the planning provisions, indicating the revenues and expenditure generated by the transformations and the redistribution of resources for an upgrading of the public city

Resources for the public city. Estimate of the economic resources generated by implementation of the plan and provisions for an upgrading of the public city

URBAN PLANNING

Planned services: sports centre. Planning indications and suggestions and guidelines of contextual insertion for the creation of the new municipal sports centre

Planned services: the events area. Planning indications and suggestions and guidelines of contextual insertion for the creation of the new municipal area for events

10. Verano Brianza (Monza and Brianza): Municipal Territorial Management Plan (PGT) (2009–12)

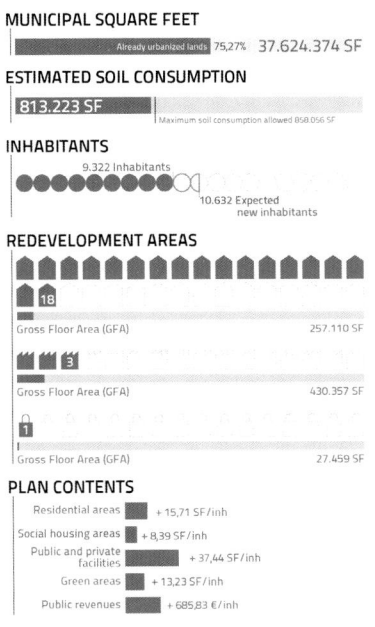

MUNICIPAL SQUARE FEET
Already urbanized lands 75,27% 37.624.374 SF

ESTIMATED SOIL CONSUMPTION
813.223 SF
Maximum soil consumption allowed 858.056 SF

INHABITANTS
9.322 Inhabitants
10.632 Expected new inhabitants

REDEVELOPMENT AREAS
18
Gross Floor Area (GFA) 257.110 SF
3
Gross Floor Area (GFA) 430.357 SF
1
Gross Floor Area (GFA) 27.459 SF

PLAN CONTENTS
Residential areas + 15,71 SF/inh
Social housing areas + 8,39 SF/inh
Public and private facilities + 37,44 SF/inh
Green areas + 13,23 SF/inh
Public revenues + 685,83 €/inh

The Municipal Territorial Management Plan for Verano Brianza addresses a very particular territory generated by the intense urbanization of central Brianza, completely joined to the neighbouring municipalities and traversed by a major road artery but endowed at the same time with unexpected environmental value along the valley of the river Lambro, and presenting residential settlements and industrial areas that bear eloquent witness to its long process of urbanization. The territory thus appears to present the typical problems of similar contexts: traffic, a host of disused industrial structures, failure to make the most of the historical centre and external building on a larger scale threatening the minute fabric of both residential and commercial functions. In examining this situation, the plan is developed primarily as a tool for painstaking investigation of the territory, interpretation of the underlying dynamics and observation of the inhabitants' quality of life. The existence of different speeds is thus discovered: on the one hand, transformations to be carried out on areas ripe for redevelopment for everyday use; on the other, micro-operations on existing fabrics in pursuit of a level of residential quality not detectable at first. The plan is therefore developed as a hybrid instrument made up of different actions in different phases. A master plan is used to anticipate (through the tool of the integrated programme of intervention) the vision, rules and benefits of the transformation of some disused structures, then incorporating into the plan the design and the benefits to be obtained by the town as a whole in terms of standards and works. Maps of policies and actions are created for the districts into which the territory is divided in order to increase the sense of belonging to a circumscribed context (thus combating the sense of disorientation engendered by settlement sprawl). The possible and envisaged operations are spread out not only in the transformative capacities of the plan but also through the combined development of further instruments, like the plan for the management of traffic and parking system. The plan thus takes shape both as an authentic road map for the management of processes under way and susceptible of stimulation by its provisions and as a tool to keep the transformations and the results of the implementation under observation through sound use of the strategic environmental assessment procedure. Each of these aspects is strongly informed by design. From the reorganization of the areas of transformation incorporated into the plan through the anticipation of projects to the overall restructuring of the districts and the minute level of the traffic plan, design expresses the pursuit of quality for a hybrid, in-between territory not accustomed or inclined to see public space as a great resource for the overall quality of the living. It thus expresses a structure while at the same time governing the dynamics and policies required for its attainment.

URBAN PLANNING

A sun for Verano Brianza: the strategic framework.
The planning strategies are born out of a particular reading of the territory in terms of "districts", territorial areas recognizable and recognized at the local level that make it possible to instil a sense of belonging and participation in the population

UN SOLE PER VERANO BRIANZA

87

URBAN PLANNING

The Valle Lambro district: master plan. The Valle Lambro district constitutes the territorial area in which the plan concentrates the primary elements of environmental upgrading and refurbishment of the historical architectural heritage

URBAN PLANNING

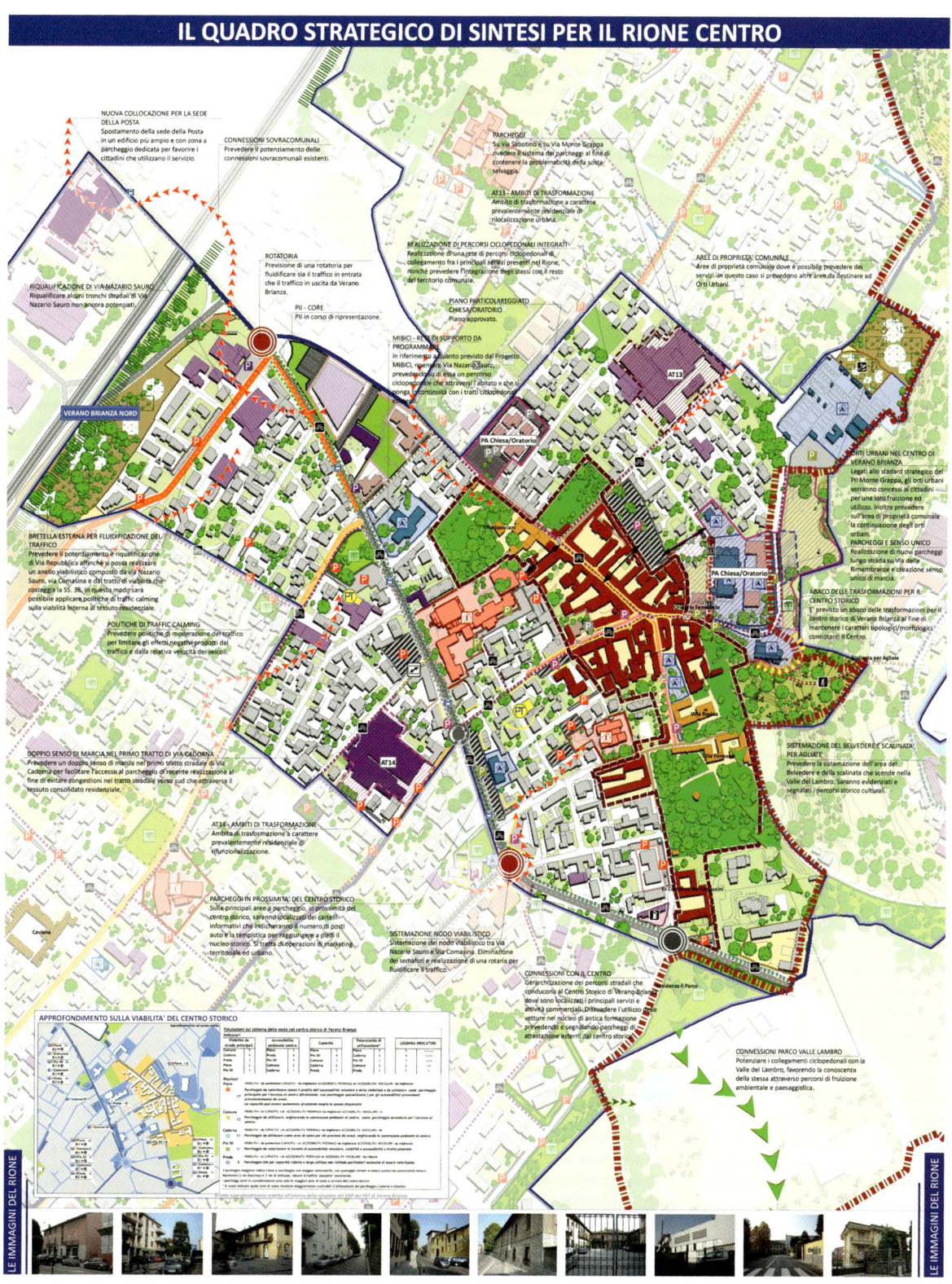

The Centre district: master plan. The heart of the municipal territory and the fulcrum of initiatives to upgrade the existing buildings and actions to improve the accessibility system

URBAN PLANNING

The Madonnina district: master plan. Consisting primarily of recent, low-density residential building, the Madonnina district is characterized by a certain number of public structures and the major infrastructural axis running longitudinally through it

Opposite

SWOT analysis: Centre district. Analysis of the opportunities and criticalities in each territorial area permits a synoptic vision of the elements on which the plan intends to work in order to obtain a major improvement in the existing level of urban quality. The analysis also paves the way for the Strategic Environmental Assessment process

Objectives, rules and prescriptions. The master plans developed for each district envision the identification of a set of fundamental rules and prescriptions to regulate the areas of transformation, the fabrics of the built-up system and the open spaces and the areas of the public city, providing indications of prescriptive value for correct management of the territory

URBAN PLANNING

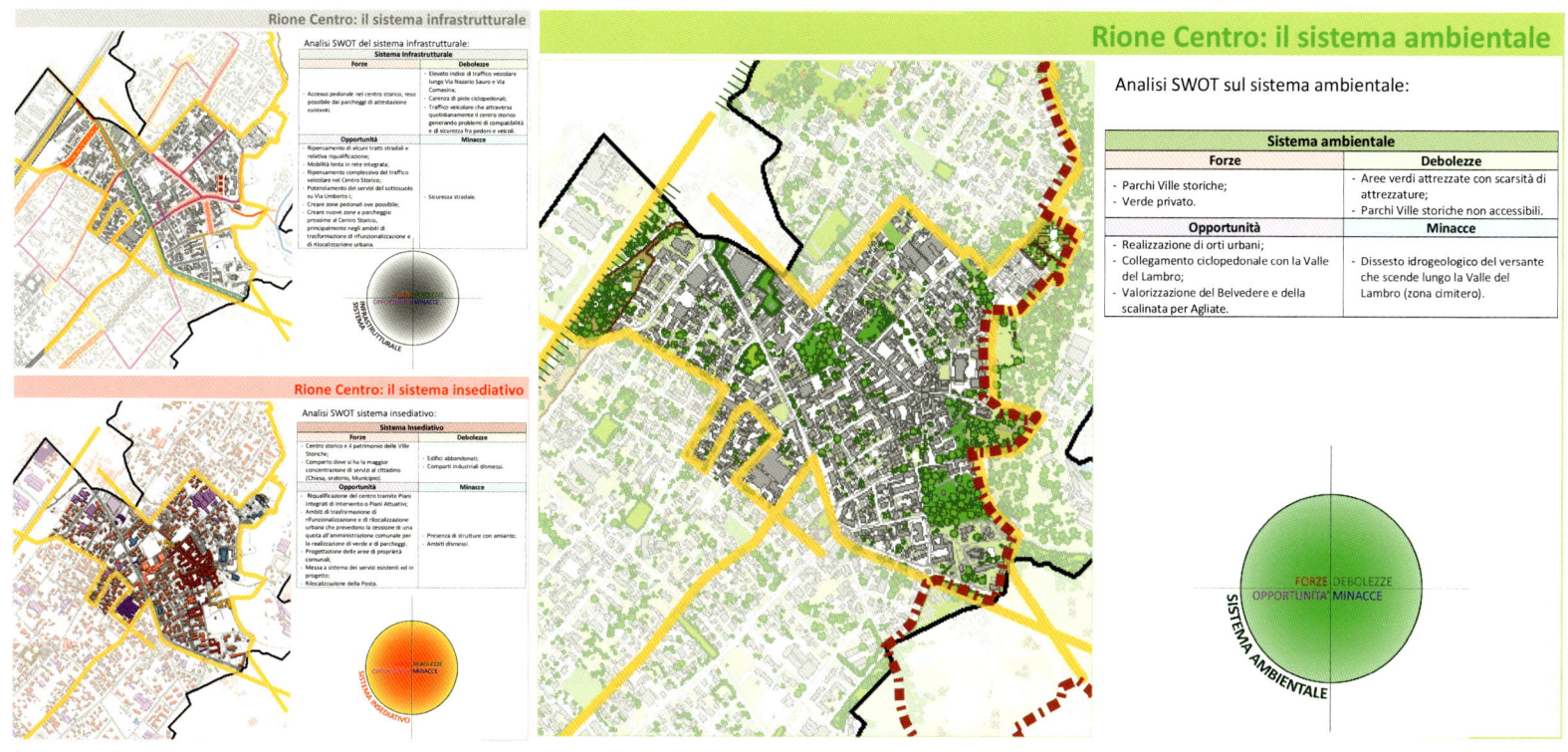

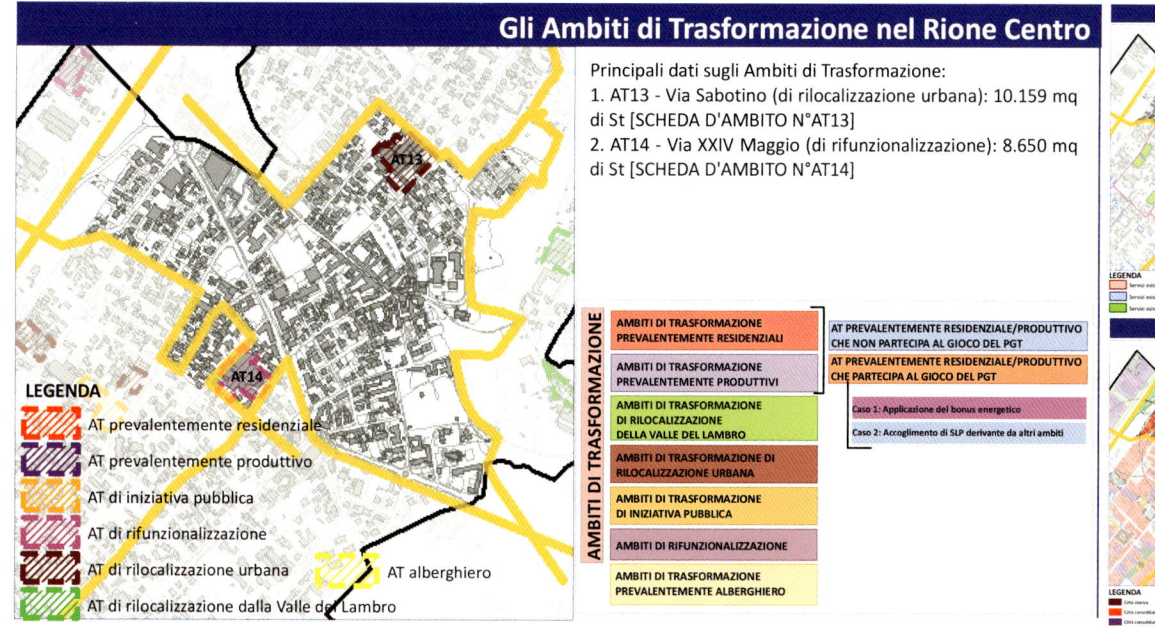

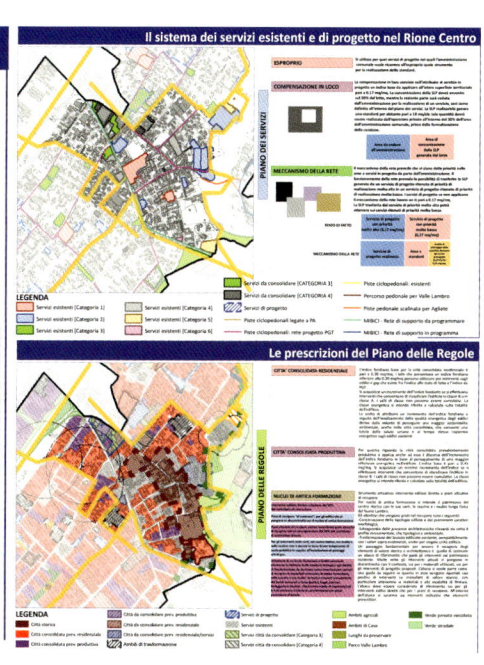

URBAN PLANNING

Historical nucleus: permitted modalities of operation.
Regulation of the operations permitted for
refurbishment and upgrading of the historical centre
on the basis of the knowledge obtained in the
preliminary analytical phase

Historical nucleus: significant elements for planning.
Elements, materials, connections and indications for
harmonious refurbishment of the historical centre

URBAN PLANNING

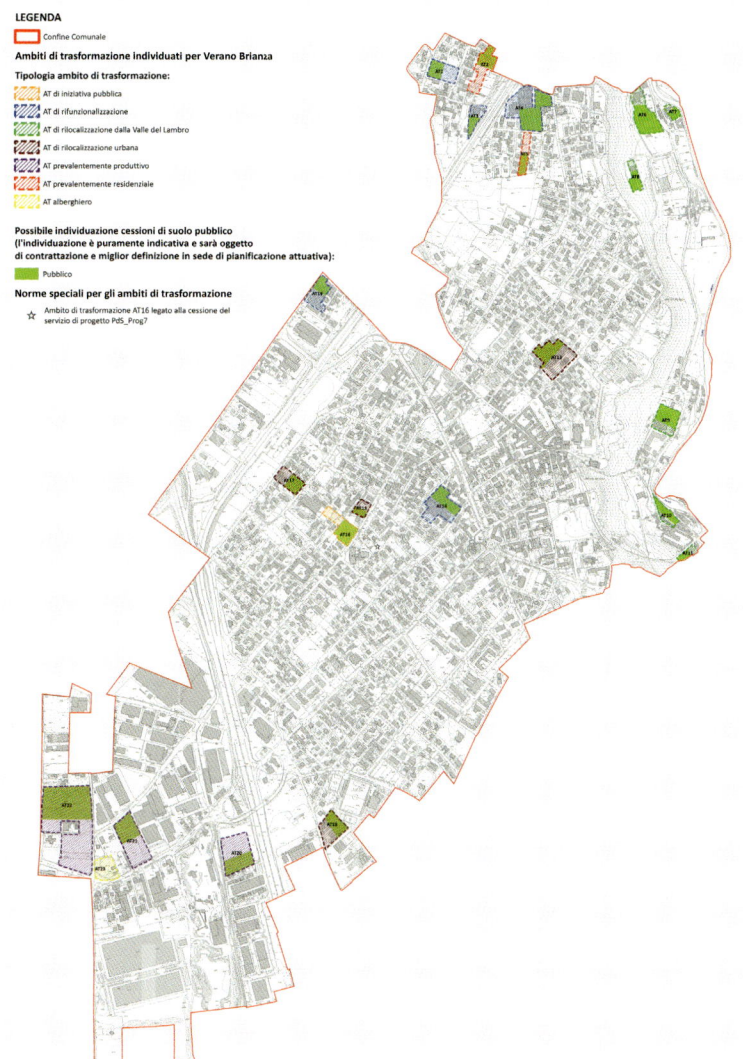

Areas of transformation of the Territorial Government Plan (PGT). The areas of transformation identified by the PGT in its strategic apparatus are divided by functional category with non-definitive indications of the areas to be sold

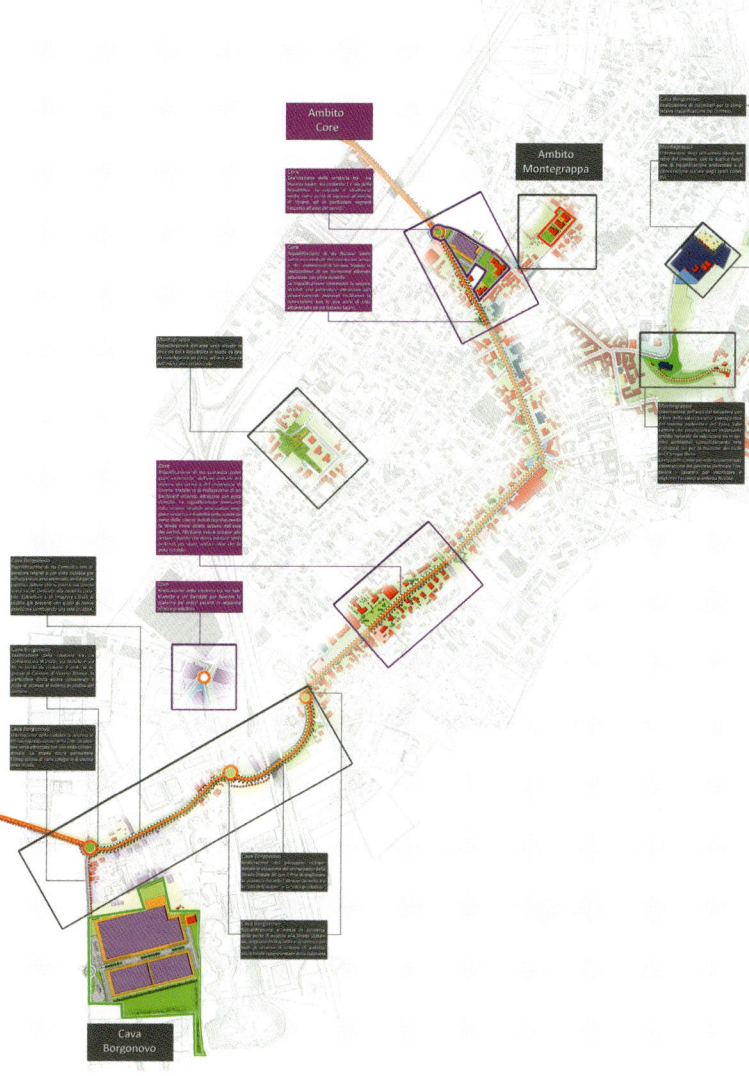

Areas of transformation and planning indications. Rules and planning indications to guide implementation and ensure that each operation is correctly embedded in the municipal territory

11. Basiglio (Milan): Municipal Territorial Management Plan (PGT) (2009–13)

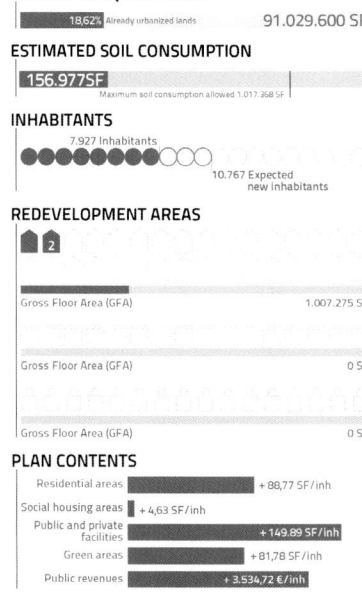

MUNICIPAL SQUARE FEET
18,62% Already urbanized lands 91.029.600 SF

ESTIMATED SOIL CONSUMPTION
156.977 SF
Maximum soil consumption allowed 1.017.368 SF

INHABITANTS
7.927 Inhabitants
10.767 Expected new inhabitants

REDEVELOPMENT AREAS
2

Gross Floor Area (GFA) 1.007.275 SF
Gross Floor Area (GFA) 0 SF
Gross Floor Area (GFA) 0 SF

PLAN CONTENTS
Residential areas +88,77 SF/inh
Social housing areas +4,63 SF/inh
Public and private facilities +149,89 SF/inh
Green areas +81,78 SF/inh
Public revenues +3.534,72 €/inh

Basiglio is a particular town. Within the vast territory of the South Milan Agricultural Park, the historical nucleus of the municipality is small and clearly agricultural in structure, consolidated only with some recent residential additions. At the same time, the predominantly residential area of Milano 3 has been built north of this nucleus on the northern borders of the municipal territory, initially as a green alternative to the traditional city and now a residential district of considerable size with some service functions and some major problems in terms of structure and organization. The plan thus addresses a territory that is unbalanced if observed exclusively within the municipal borders. For this reason, the horizons are immediately expanded to encompass both the broader nature of the system of the Agricultural Park and the rationale of Milano 3. The need is realized straight away for the territory to redefine its position and the conception of its being structured in this way. While in past decades the settlement of Milan 3 constituted the alternative both as a model (the garden city in place of the traditional city) and in terms of functioning (immersed in the green and connected by some public means of road transport), it now constitutes an enclave of greenery and construction in close contact with the park but richly endowed with other functions that are not necessarily confined to serving its inhabitants. A potential component of the post-metropolitan territory that appears to be undergoing consolidation precisely on the territorial axis of Milan 3 with the strengthening of services offered by the Humanitas hospital and the changes under way along the main highway to Milan, therefore rich in potential and possibilities in the aggregation of some new centralities around the consolidated structure of Milano 3 so as to transform the image from a garden city on the outskirts to the central urban pole of a broader territory including the boundaries of the neighbouring towns. Through the plan's investment in some areas of transformation and its provisions for strengthening the supply of services, Milano 3 can abandon the outskirts and place itself at the centre of its surrounding territory, offering facilities, services and public spaces worthy of an urban centre. With the mechanism of compensatory implementation and the granting of transformation rights only in return for marked public benefit, the plan makes it possible to solve precise and private problems (e.g. the financial contribution to be asked of condominiums for an improved supply of energy in line with the town's environmental sustainability targets), to make good the infrastructural failings of non-residential functions (by increasing the parking space and designing a more efficient road system), and above all to create a centre of services of broader interest capable of repositioning the nucleus of Milano 3 and enhancing its urban potential.

URBAN PLANNING

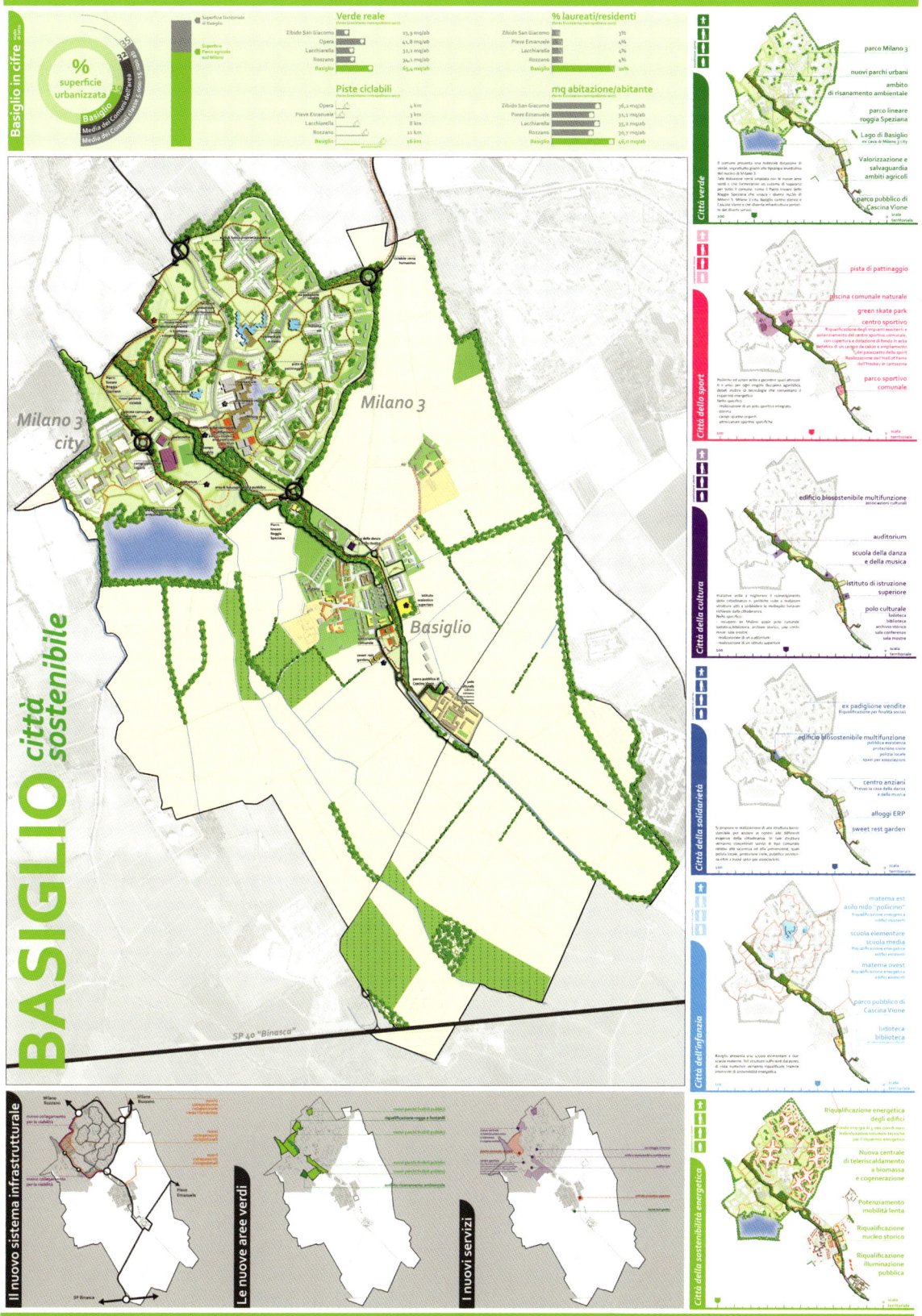

Basiglio, the sustainable town: Poster Plan.
The Structural Plan develops its strategic vision around themes of sustainability considered not only with respect to environmental issues but also and above all to more complex matters such as sociality and solidarity

URBAN PLANNING

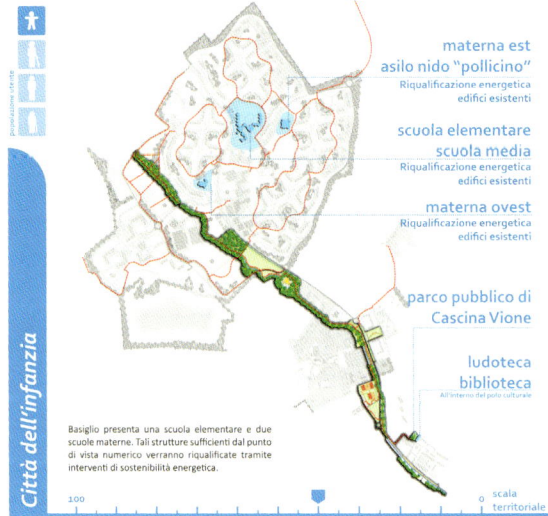

The six towns. The plan identifies six key themes closely linked to the territory:
– the green town, which includes elements of the existing and planned environmental system;
– the town of sport, for which the plan identifies policies and actions to strengthen the existing facilities;
– the town of culture, identifying a series of structures for the community;
– the town of children, aimed exclusively at the upgrading of education services;
– the town of solidarity, regarding structures for safety and accident prevention;
– the town of environmental sustainability, which sets the primary planning target of improving the energy efficiency of buildings and developing policies to reduce energy consumption

Opposite
Roggia Speziana environmental project. The Roggia Speziana, a watercourse running through the agricultural, residential and service areas of the municipal territory as a whole, is the backbone of a broader environmental project for the creation of a Linear Park of supra-local importance to take effective action on deteriorated environmental elements of rich potential

URBAN PLANNING

URBAN PLANNING

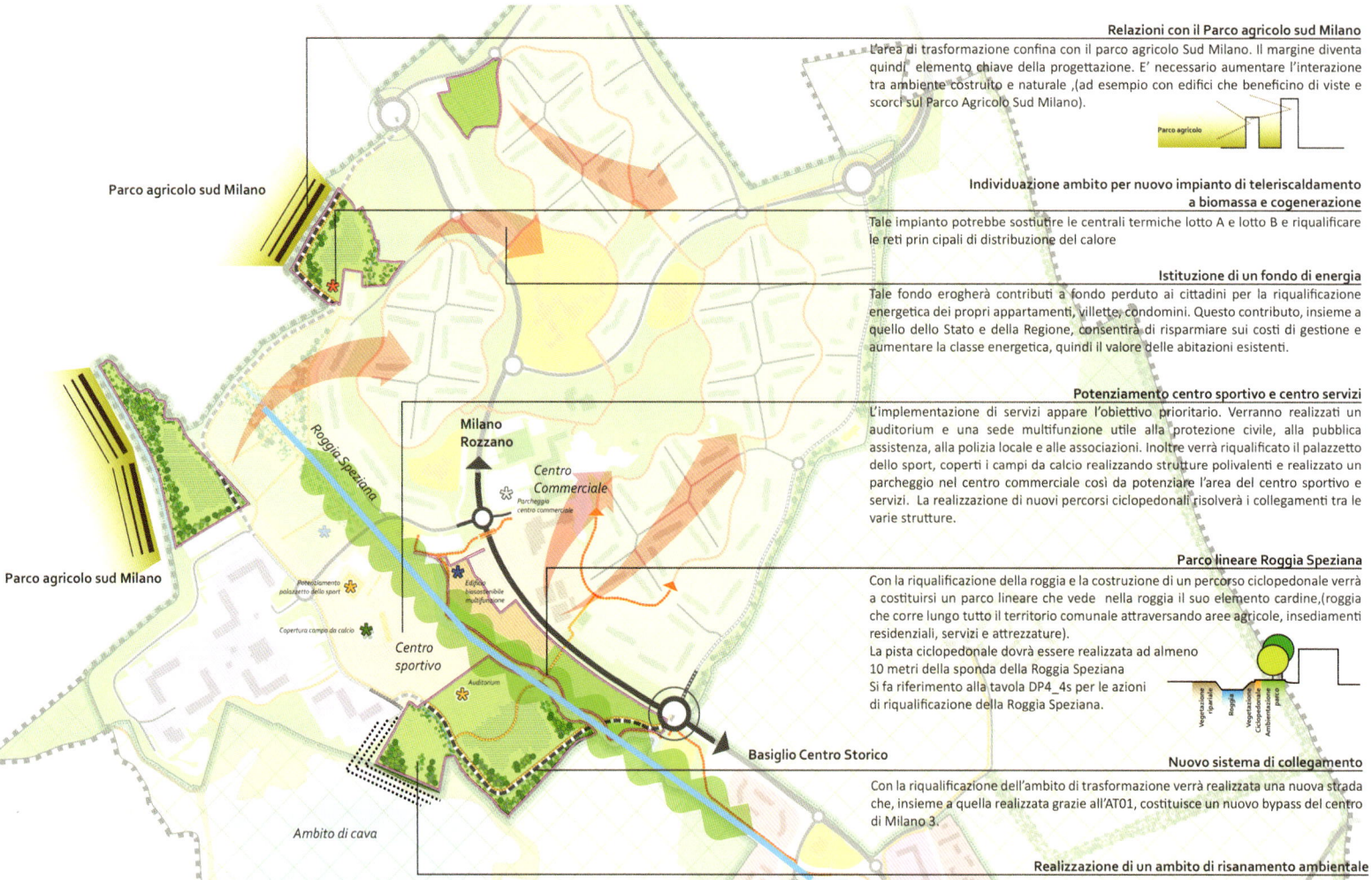

Areas of transformation: the system of relations.
The detailed dossiers on the areas of transformation provide a set of planning indications capable of guiding the phase of implementation towards correct integration of the operation in the context, regarding the territorial peculiarities as the primary existing resources for sound planning

URBAN PLANNING

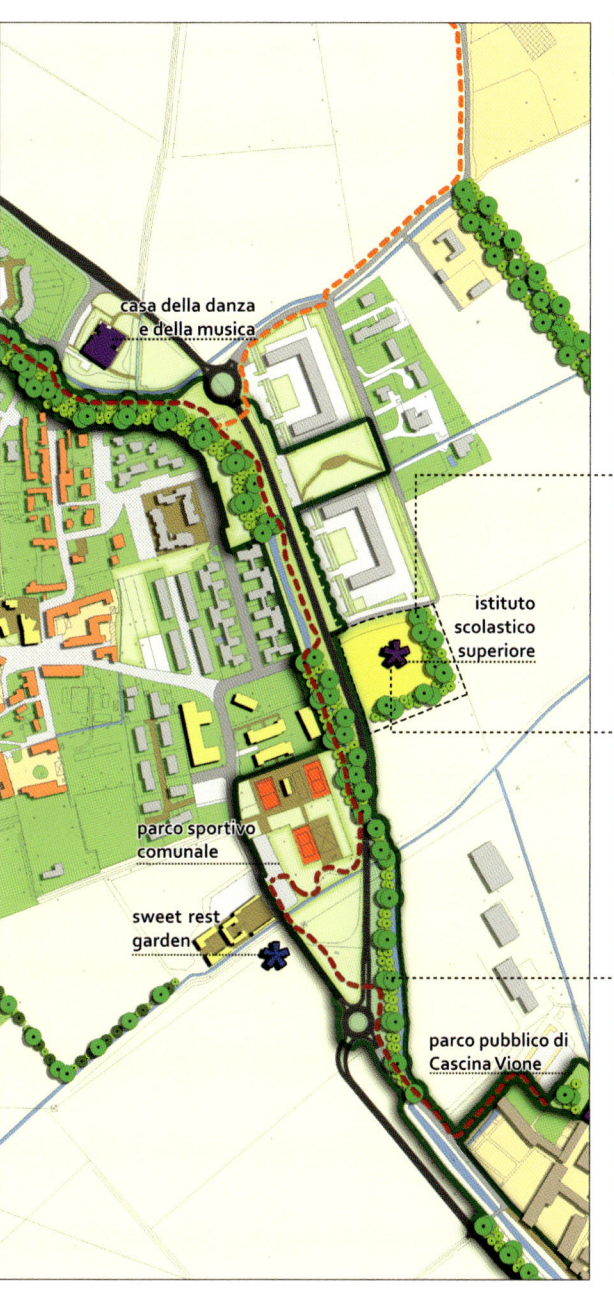

Strategie progettuali

Città della cultura
La realizzazione dell'istituto di istruzione superiore è una delle misure strategiche per la costituzione della città della cultura, per la quale sono comprese iniziative volte a migliorare il coinvolgimento della cittadinanza e, politiche volte a realizzare strutture utili a soddisfare le molteplici funzioni richieste dalla cittadinanza, tra cui il recupero del Mulino quale polo culturale (ludoteca, biblioteca, archivio storico, sala conferenze, sala mostre) e la realizzazione di un auditorium (a carico di AT02).

Fasce di mitigazione
Si prevede la realizzazione di fasce di mitigazione sul perimetro confinante con il Parco Agricolo e le aree agricole adiacenti. La vegetazione dovrà essere autoctona del luogo. Per la progettazione e la realizzazione di queste si fa riferimento al Repertorio B del PTCP della Provincia di Milano.

Strutture sostenibili
Dovranno essere utilizzati materiali di costruzione ecocompatibili, all'interno del loro ciclo di vita.
Si suggerisce che le strutture vengano realizzate con tecniche di costruzione che evitino la dispersione termica o che necessitino di un ridotto apporto energetico.
Dovranno essere intraprese misure per il riciclo delle acque. Inoltre dovrà essere valutata la possibilità di dotare le strutture realizzate di impianti di produzione di energia da fonti rinnovabili.

Parco lineare della Roggia Speziana
Con la riqualificazione della roggia e la costruzione di un percorso ciclopedonale verrà a costituirsi un parco lineare che vede nella roggia il suo elemento cardine, (roggia che corre lungo tutto il territorio comunale attraversando aree agricole, insediamenti residenziali, servizi e attrezzature). La pista ciclopedonale dovrà essere realizzata ad almeno 10 metri della sponda della Roggia Speziana.
Si fa riferimento alla tavola DP4_4s per le azioni di riqualificazione della Roggia Speziana.

RECUPERO EDILIZIO E FUNZIONALE
AMMESSO IN NUCLEO STORICO
(ART PR 12, comma 1 e 14)

AMPLIAMENTO EDIFICI
NON AMMESSO IN NUCLEO STORICO
(ART PR 12, comma 4, 5, 11 e 14)

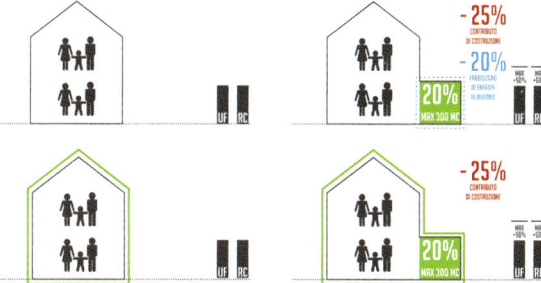

DEMOLIZIONE E RICOSTRUZIONE
(ART PR 12, comma 7, 8, 9 e 11)

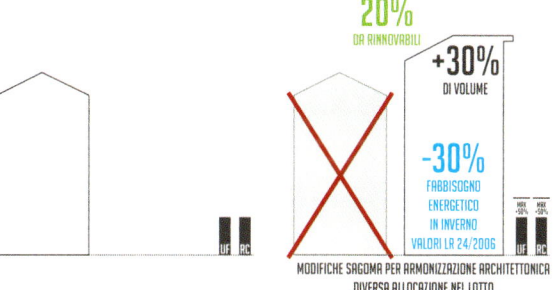

Planned services: guidelines for implementation.
The set of public structures envisaged by the plan is governed by the Public Facilities Plan through specific in-depth treatment that defines their operational characteristics and insertion in the municipal context

Management of the built-up area. The framework encompasses the mechanisms for management of the existing buildings and highlights the possibilities offered by the Zoning Plan: reductions on construction taxes, incentive mechanisms and regulation of the building density ratio subject to the attainment of set energy-efficiency standards

12. Pognano (Bergamo): Variant of the Municipal Territorial Management Plan (PGT) (2010–13)

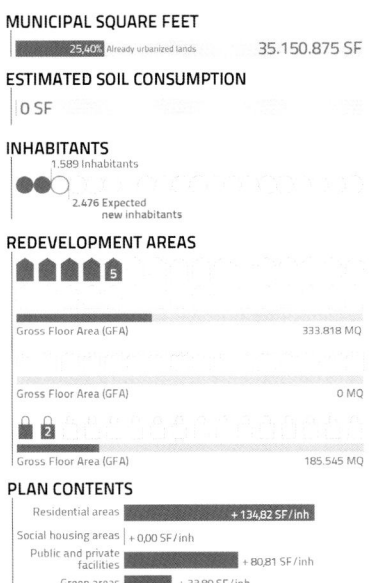

A cluster of houses around a small historical centre of agricultural appearance and a few firms along the main highway linking up with the rest of the province, Pognano stands in the centre of a section of the agricultural and industrial plain. The first question regards the advisability of planning for a territory of this size without reference to the surrounding contexts and the nature of a Municipal Territorial Management Plan for a context structured in this way. In the absence of actions and instruments more suitable to address the proximity of small towns and territories with low settlement density, the possibility emerges of provisions and actions that are not confined to the specific context of the town in connection with certain issues. The impossibility of broader and more fruitful planning scenarios is compensated for by the stimulus of working on themes that can involve other contexts. The road system and the imbalance between the level of service that the provincial highway can provide for the industrial sphere and its negative impact on the town's residential system are central themes precisely in this dual perspective of action to solve small problems of local circulation and the observation of phenomena on a broader scale. The safeguarding of the agricultural production system makes it possible for the concerns established on the territory to continue their activities without the threat of particular transformations but also raises the question of connections between the agricultural spheres of different territories and municipalities.

The plan thus adopts a broad-scale approach even to the problems of such a small context while working in operative terms as an authentic tool for action at the territorial level. Two key issues connected with this broader perspective are addressed in detail, namely redevelopment of the historical centre (where the proportion of disused buildings is very high, not least as a result of separation from the agricultural context by recent residential expansion) and the construction of a ring road to bypass the settlement system. Combining operative rules and procedures for the redevelopment of original structures in the historical centre and provisions for the completion and reorganization of the road system, the plan lays down a schedule of operations and mechanisms for identifying both the required sources of funds and the parties to be involved in the direct implementation of provisions.

Demonstrating that a plan can operate correctly if it embeds its operations in a scenario of supra-local legitimization, whatever the local reality may be, it then addresses them technically in depth to ensure their implementation within its temporal horizons.

Operational effectiveness: Poster Plan. The strategic choices are structured on effective and concrete operative elements such as to generate complete rethinking of the existing public city through a complex system of actions on the infrastructural system and direct specific norms for refurbishment of the historical nucleus. If correctly harnessed, these territorial invariants can lead to an optimal level of quality also in the smaller local areas

URBAN PLANNING

13. Gambassi Terme (Florence): Urban Traffic Plan (2007)

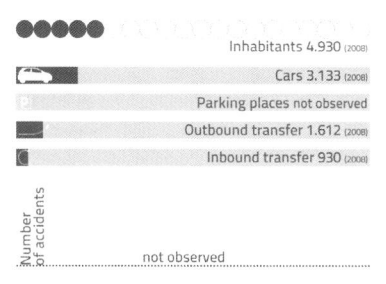

Inhabitants 4.930 (2008)
Cars 3.133 (2008)
Parking places not observed
Outbound transfer 1.612 (2008)
Inbound transfer 930 (2008)

Number of accidents: not observed

PLAN STATISTICS
- Traffic survey
- Parking survey
- Public areas detailed survey
- Traffic management
- Traffic calming crossroads
- Traffic calming crosswalks
- Traffic calming vulnerable targets
- Bike paths enhancements
- Controlled traffic zones projects
- Pedestrian areas projects
- Woonerf zones projects
- Parking management
- Public areas enhancement
- Enviromental area protection

Located in an area of great environmental beauty midway between the provinces of Siena and Florence, Gambassi Terme displays a particular infrastructural situation. With the Volterrana road running right through its historical centre, it developed historically in continuous strips along either side in a similar way to many other Tuscan towns. The particular geomorphology of the territory involves a slope down to the town's main square, which is also a tourist attraction due to the presence of a spa. After a tragic accident, this situation was regarded as incompatible with the level of road traffic and an external variant was constructed for supra-local circulation.

The town thus had an opportunity to rethink its system of streets and open and public spaces as a whole through a general traffic plan, a particular instrument framed by law and equipped with a series of tools for implementation of its provisions. In the plans drawn up over the years, the infrastructural component, upon which the provisions traditionally focus, are always considered on a par with the urban-planning component, giving the need to address the efficiency and rationalization of circulation and parking on the one hand while redeveloping as many spaces as possible for public use and ensuring their quality on the other. For this reason, the plans drawn up always focus on design of the layout as a tool capable of combining the engineering and urban-planning components alike with the due attention to implementation.

The plan drawn up for Gambassi focuses in particular on imparting hierarchical structure and form to the functioning of a territory with a marked infrastructural presence in which connections between the network and the settlement system prove weak and fragmentary. Through careful work on the system of access, parking and circulation, it seeks to restore correct perceptions and the most appropriate behaviour patterns so as to foster its integration into the town's urban system.

Give the complex situation to be addressed, the plan is thus given a character and a role identical to those of a strategic plan. It identifies operations to manage not only specific aspects of traffic and mobility but also aspects regarding the urban fabric, identifying the key points of the system and possible areas of cooperation between the public and private sectors to put its provisions into effect.

The general urban traffic plan thus hinges on two specific instruments. The first is the urban plan of mobility and movements, which establishes structural points for the organization of local mobility, pinpointing sensitive areas that require precise projects capable of modifying the existing space and its layout. The second is the urban redevelopment plan for open space and space for relations, which makes it possible to identify the overall scenario of reference including the physical reorganization of public spaces and mobility systems, thus acting upon the habits and behaviour patterns of the local inhabitants and the users of the functions the town provides.

Short-term planning scenario. The short-term scenario involves the identification of external gateways, reorganization of the Torrino area, recognition of Via Gramsci as the southern axis of penetration, management of through traffic and upgrading of the central section

URBAN PLANNING

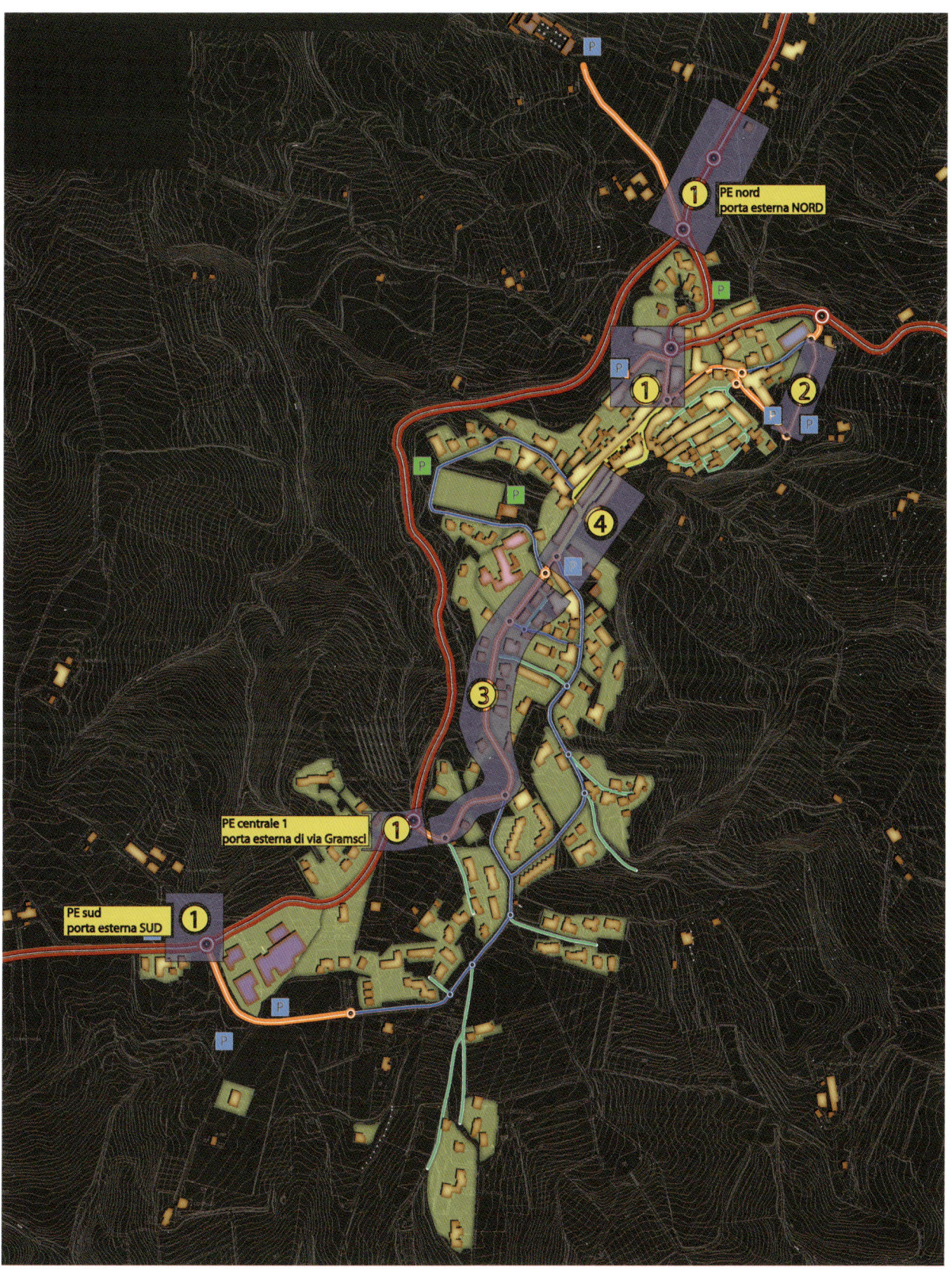

URBAN PLANNING

Overall planning scenario. On the basis of an important existing infrastructure, the plan of mobility and movement redefines the functional model of the road system, identifying an overall planning scenario of reference with four component parts: the road system, the system of gateways and nodes, the system of parking places and the system of strategic operations

Operations on the local road system. Reconstruction of the local road system with the road axes, points of access and system of parking places organized on rational and hierarchical lines. The road system is organized on the basis of primary functions in relation to territorial role and speed of service, and the gateways in relation to the presence of environmental islands and 30 kph areas. The system of parking spaces is divided on the basis of the primary existing and planned types recurrent in the municipal territory

Opposite
Analysis of provisions, potentialities and criticalities of the system. The major potentialities and criticalities of the system as a whole are examined and reconstructed on the basis of the four structural components identified by the strategic planning scenario

URBAN PLANNING

14. Gambassi Terme (Florence): project for redevelopment of the urban road system and Via Gramsci (2007)

PROJECT
Demolished sidewalk — 2.754 SF
Scarified road pavement — 10.964 SF
New pedestrian pavement — 10.114 SF
New roads pavement — 10.760 SF
Parking areas — 1.399 SF

PLAN STATISTICS
☐ Traffic survey
■ Parking survey
☐ Public areas detailed survey
■ Traffic management
■ Traffic calming crossroads
■ Traffic calming crosswalks
■ Traffic calming vulnerable targets
☐ Bike paths enhancements
☐ Controlled traffic zones projects
■ Pedestrian areas projects
☐ Woonerf zones projects
■ Parking management
■ Public areas enhancement
☐ Enviromental area protection

BUSINESS PLAN
266.000 €

Subsequent to formulation of the urban traffic plan for Gambassi Terme, the actions and policies envisaged were tried and tested through implementation in a project for the redevelopment of Via Gramsci. The restructuring of this axis pursues the aim of improving the conditions of road safety and circulation, focusing on the quality of the space involved in the knowledge that an increase in the design quality of road space prompts a change in behaviour on the part of its users and a friendlier perception of road space in general. The project thus focused on ensuring the safety of the routes devoted to slower forms of mobility and the resolution of conflict generated between this and traffic by redesigning vehicle access points and regulating traffic management while adapting its architecture to the rules of the highway code, which are certainly not oriented towards the creation of a high-quality system.

It is through the architecture of the road system that the project develops the urban design. The choice of materials, furnishings, lighting and environmental structures maximizes the embedding of the road in its context. As this is a public work and obviously subject to financial constraints, the design philosophy is not to present the redeveloped road as a separate construction but to construct through it and its surroundings a complete urban system, an entire urban typology and an object whose design is controlled by the project from the ground level to the elevation of the buildings. In this way, the project not only shapes the road but also helps to remould the urban surroundings and pursue the specificity and uniqueness of a single artefact made up of the road and the surrounding fabric of buildings, harmonizing use by road users and urban use, and regulating the impact of the road system in an attempt to create a single commonly used plateau for the human activities of the area, all gathered together and concentrated in a single redeveloped space.

URBAN PLANNING

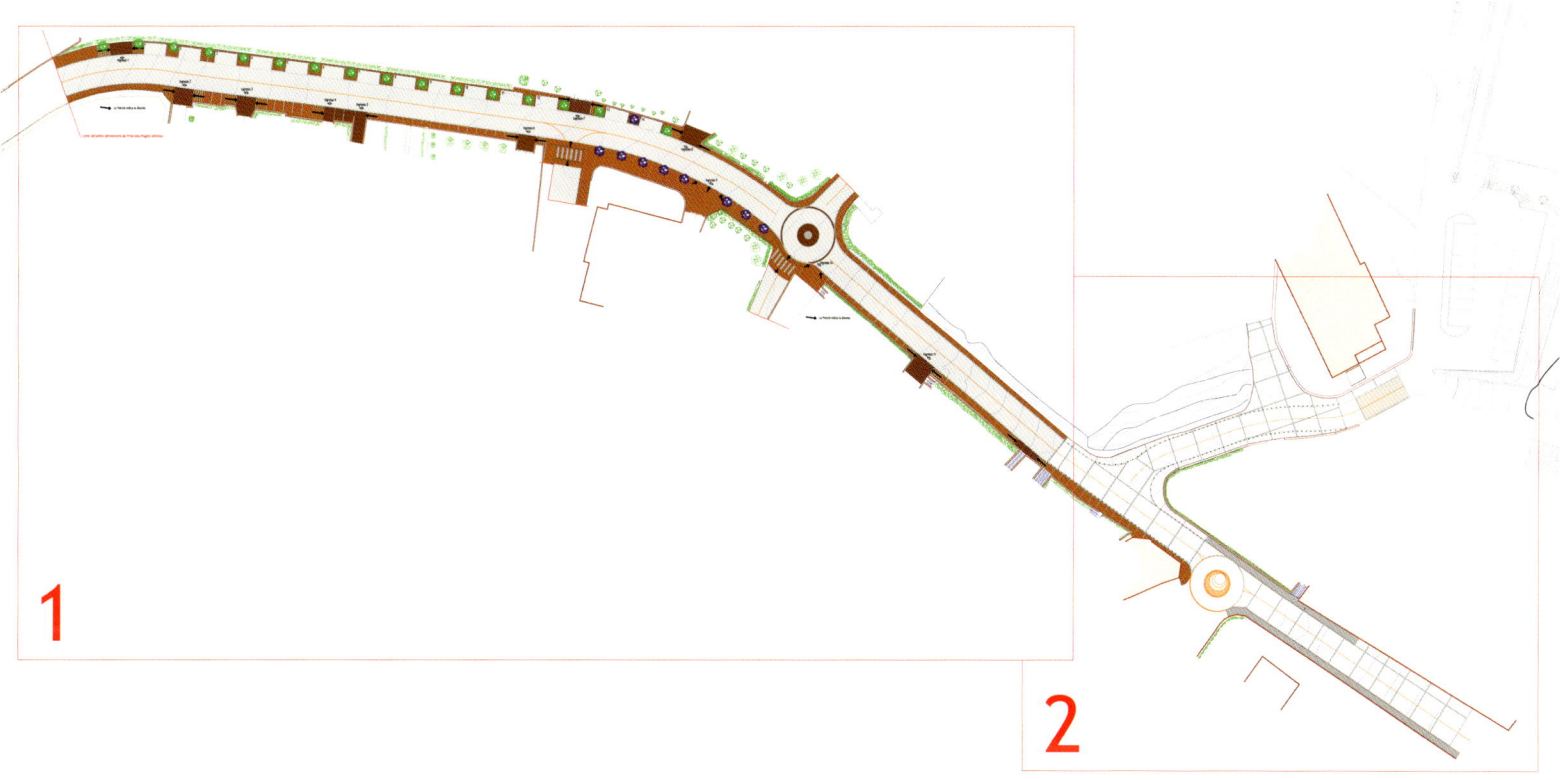

Areas of operation for the definitive project.
The project envisages the construction of a safe and continuous pedestrian system, the reorganization of access points and vehicle passageways, and the regulation of access traffic

URBAN PLANNING

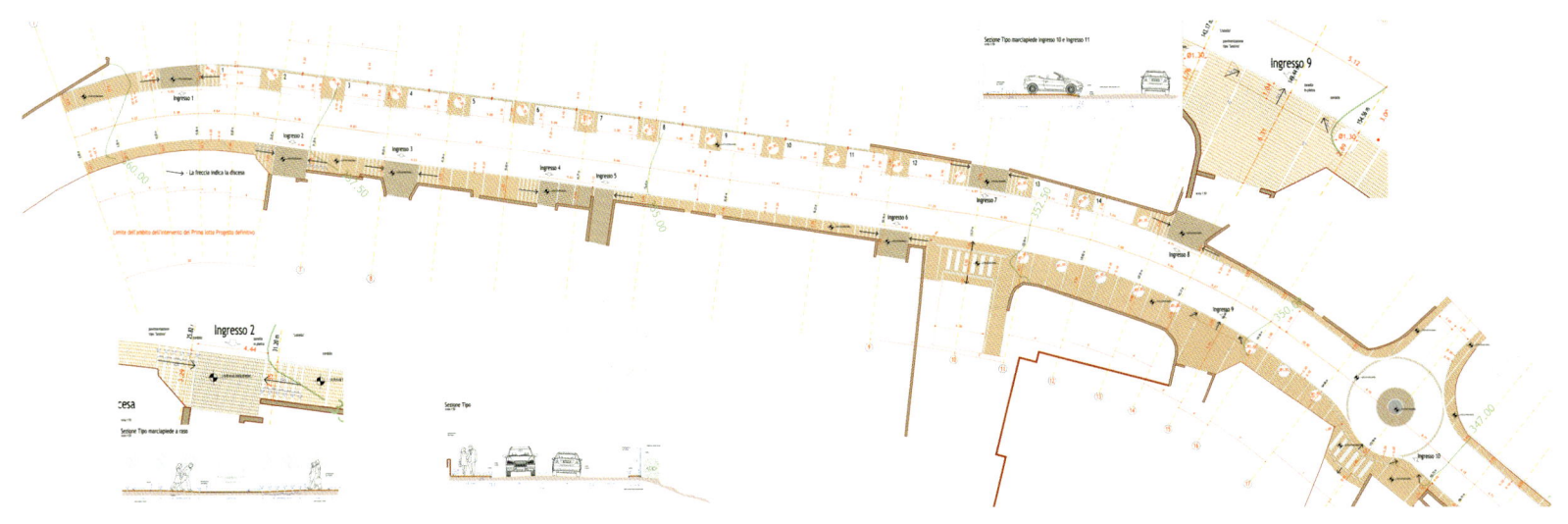

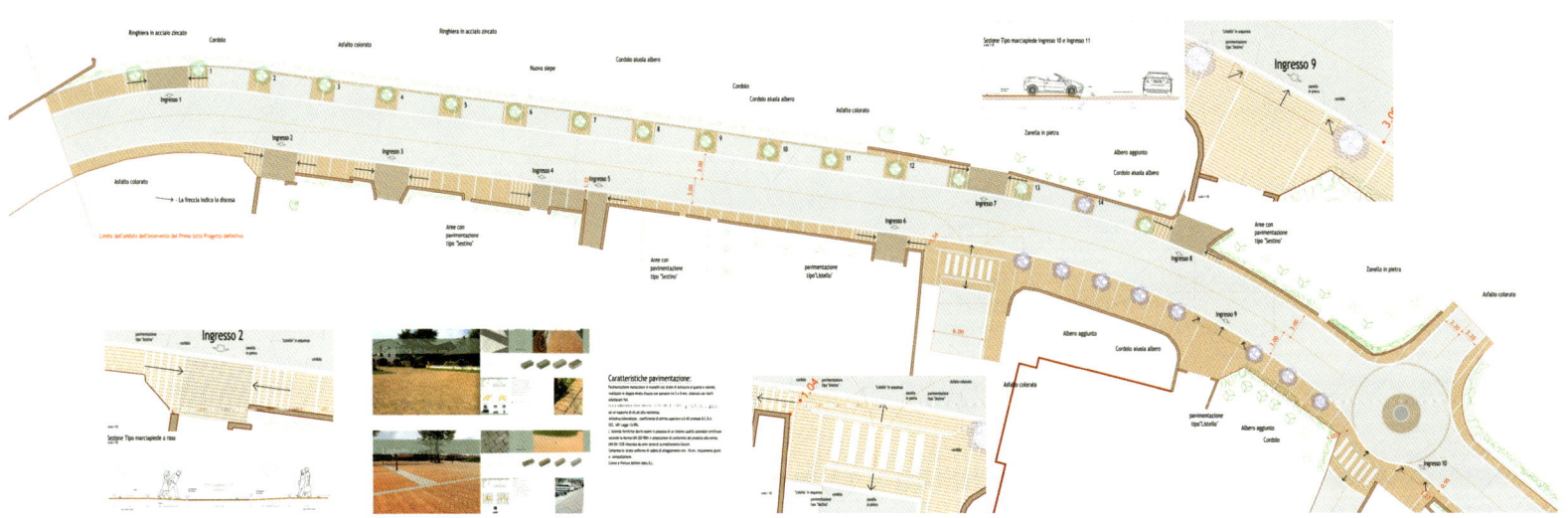

Project details. Materials, sections and paving

URBAN PLANNING

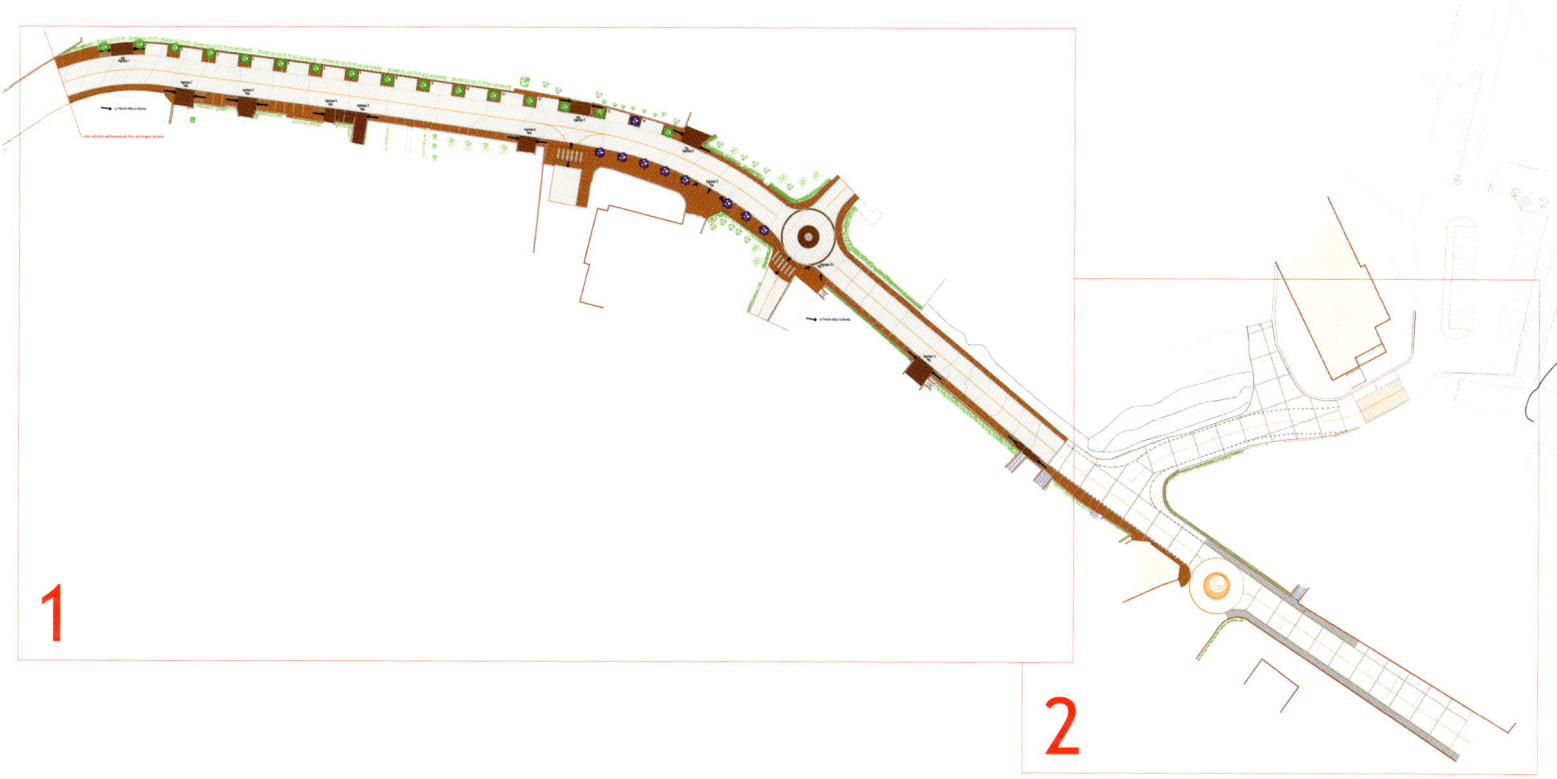

Areas of operation for the definitive project.
The project envisages the construction of a safe and continuous pedestrian system, the reorganization of access points and vehicle passageways, and the regulation of access traffic

URBAN PLANNING

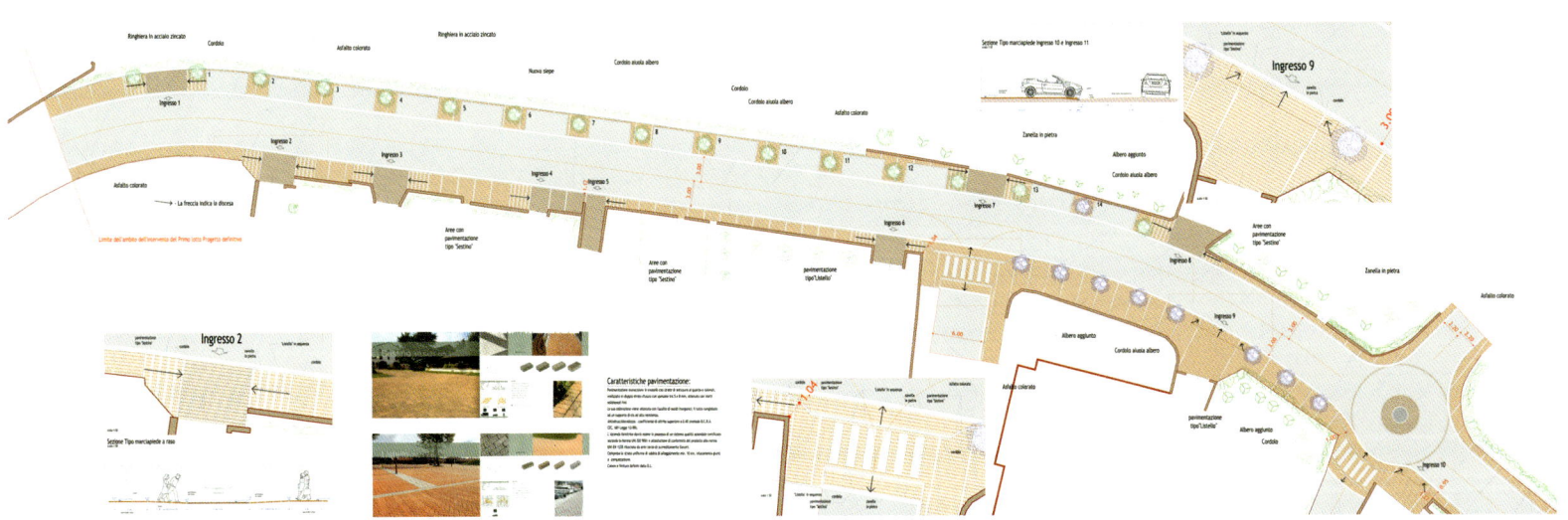

Project details. Materials, sections and paving

URBAN PLANNING

Elements of quality. Attention to detail and the use of quality materials make it possible to highlight key planning elements. The use of Sestino-type paving gives greater visibility to the sensitive points of the pedestrian pathway, such as crossings and intersections, while also contributing to the visual continuity of the pathway as a whole. Through correct use of the materials of urban furniture, the planned pedestrian system is embedded in the context so as to create harmony and urban quality

URBAN PLANNING

15. Canegrate (Milan): Urban Traffic Plan (2009–12)

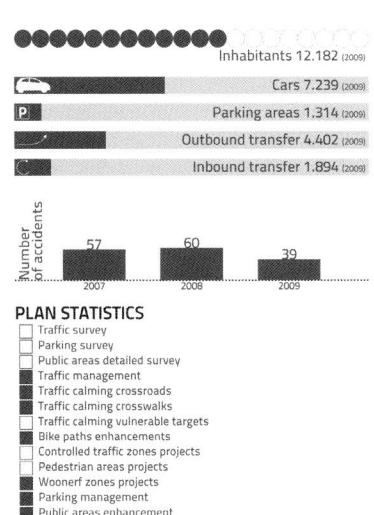

PLAN STATISTICS
- Traffic survey
- Parking survey
- Public areas detailed survey
- Traffic management
- Traffic calming crossroads
- Traffic calming crosswalks
- Traffic calming vulnerable targets
- Bike paths enhancements
- Controlled traffic zones projects
- Pedestrian areas projects
- Woonerf zones projects
- Parking management
- Public areas enhancement
- Enviromental area protection

The territory of Canegrate is typical of the contexts developed north of Milan. With no separation from the built-up areas of its neighbouring towns, the centre of Canegrate is no more than the small historical centre on the main north-south highway. The town as a whole is defined by the growth of the last thirty years, devoid of careful planning and developed through constant, small-scale additions with the creation of plans of implementation and individual property units. At the same time, while lacking an important industrial fabric of any great size, the municipal territory is crossed by flows of heavy vehicles from neighbouring towns. The only decidedly positive aspect as regards mobility is the presence of the railway line connecting the town with the rest of the metropolitan area and Milan as well as the plans now under way to strengthen and reorganize the rail system.

The traffic plan had first of all to examine, analyze and understand the nature of the municipal and neighbouring territory. As in every other plan drawn up over these years, a broader horizon was adopted, using this as an opportunity to drawn up an instrument with a strong territorial and therefore not only specialized character capable of putting forward solutions to a precise problem through a proposal for regional planning of greater breadth.

The resulting plan fully grasps the nature of the territory. The growth of past years has resulted in a dense territory, albeit of low-density construction, served by a limited, inadequate, non-hierarchical network devoid of urban episodes or efficient services for the built-up areas. The plan identifies the different parts of the territory to isolate the parts that can only be separated from the territorial network, which must be provided with a bypass system on the outskirts of the town. This focus on the existing structures makes it possible to redevelop the historical centre in the design of spaces and micro-systems of relations. The existing and consolidated fabric generated by the zoning plans of previous years is regarded as an area to be protected through the creation of woonerfs and environmental islands with access and use restricted exclusively to residents. A bypass system is designed for heavy traffic and circulation in the centre of the town is reorganized. The result pursued by the plan is overall reorganization of the road system and above all general territorial restructuring capable of generating new spaces for relations, new opportunities for quality and an urban system superior to the existing one. Since the plan cannot be put into effect all at once, a system of guidelines and tools is defined covering point by point all the solutions to be adopted in order to redesign the road system in territorial terms with a view to increasing local technical knowledge and ensuring implementation of the plan in sections by the public and private sectors.

Poster Plan. A key element in the definition of planning actions, the Poster Plan makes all the constituent aspects of the territory of Canegrate visible and legible. It highlights the parts of the territory in need of protection and upgrading, thus laying the foundations for the strategic vision of the plan

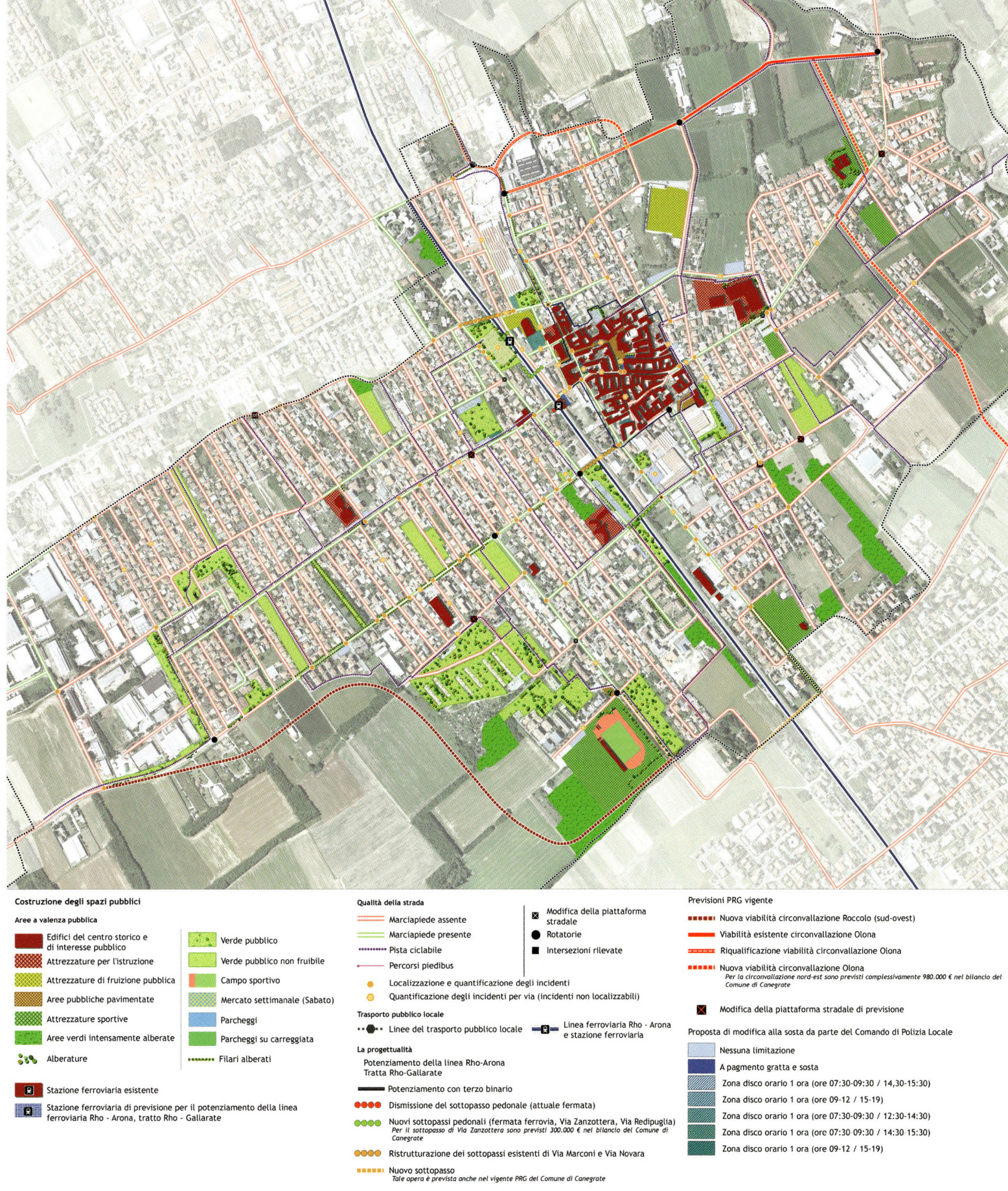

The medium-term planning scenario. With a view to correct implementation of the plan, the actions identified are divided into consecutive phases. The medium-term scenario accords priority to the limitation of vehicle speed in the most sensitive areas and redevelopment of the primary stretches of the road system

The long-term planning scenario. The last phase of implementation completes the trajectory developed in the previous phases, giving birth to overall reorganization of the road system. The actions envisaged in this last step regard management of the extra-urban road system so as to keep through traffic out of the urban fabric

Roads Typologies Chart. The images show the forms of treatment of the road sections, identifying the types present in the Canegrate system, defining the characteristics of the existing situation and developing a pathway that first applies the basic constructive norms and then arrives at an implemented definition that raises the quality of the axis through redefinition of functions and spaces, identifying sections devoted to specific users, like means of public transport, and designing spaces for parking and pedestrian and public areas

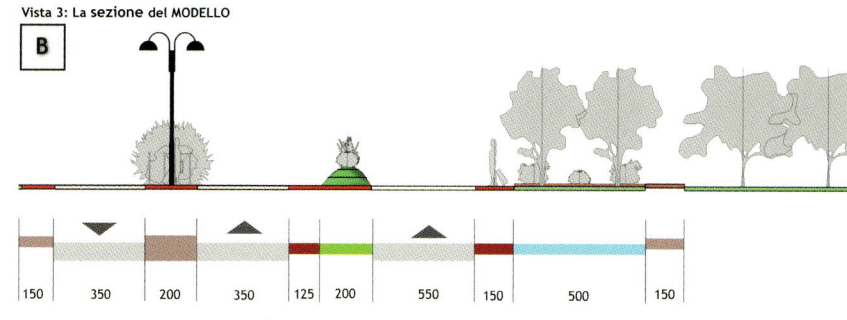

Vista 3: La **sezione** del MODELLO

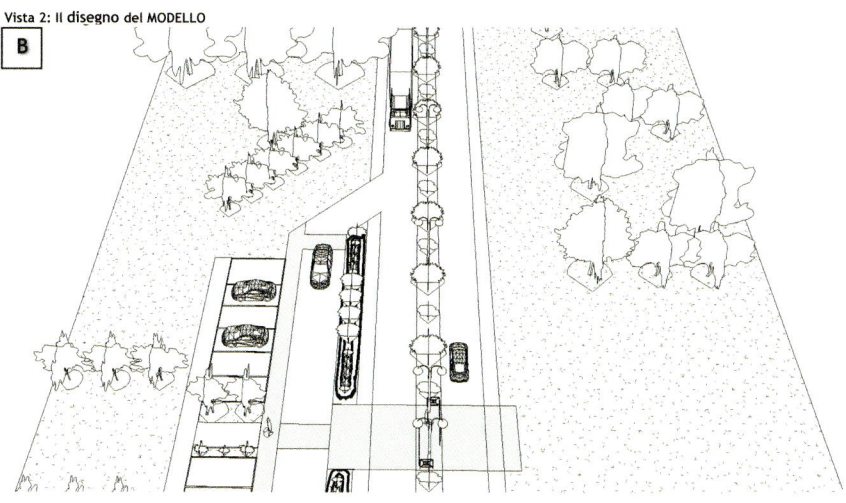

Vista 2: Il **disegno** del MODELLO

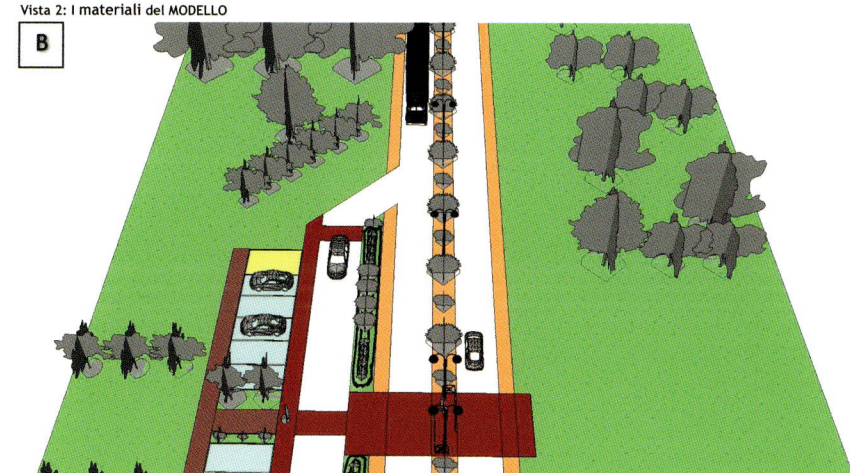

Vista 2: I **materiali** del MODELLO

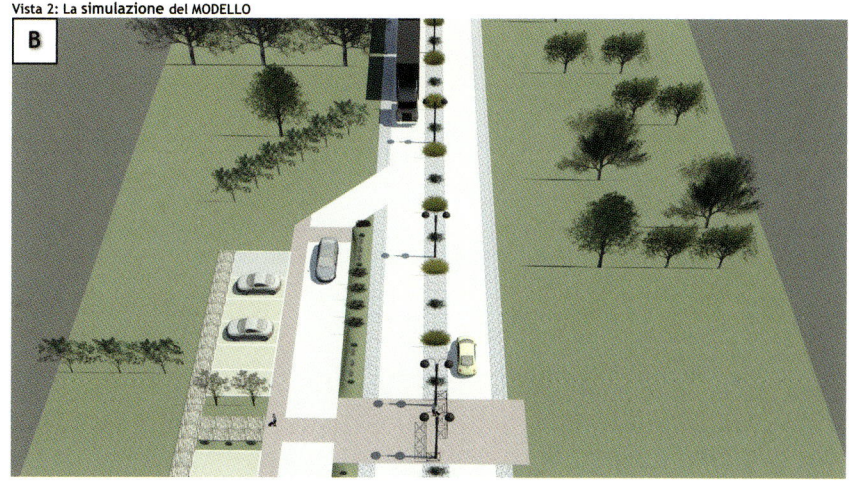

Vista 2: La **simulazione** del MODELLO

16. Inzago (Milan): Urban Traffic Plan (under way since 2010)

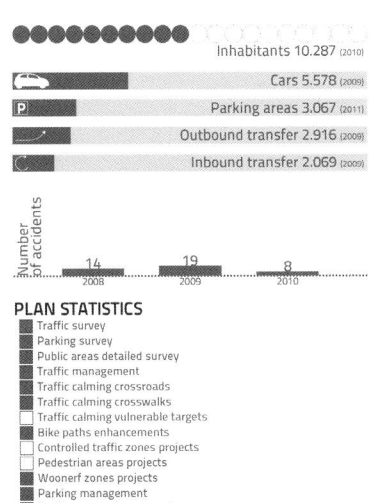

PLAN STATISTICS
- Traffic survey
- Parking survey
- Public areas detailed survey
- Traffic management
- Traffic calming crossroads
- Traffic calming crosswalks
- Traffic calming vulnerable targets
- Bike paths enhancements
- Controlled traffic zones projects
- Pedestrian areas projects
- Woonerf zones projects
- Parking management
- Public areas enhancement
- Enviromental area protection

The overall framework of planning at Inzago reached completion with the Urban Traffic Plan for overall regulation of the functioning of the territory's road system.

As elsewhere, the plan for Inzago expands its sphere of responsibility to observe the town's territorial organization, in this case with the support of the management plan drawn up shortly before. The traffic plan analyzes the various systems identified and addressed by the Territorial Management Plan. From the canal system to the historical centre, the municipal territory presents a rational structure upon which the plan works with a view not only to the creation of a functional road system but also to the identification of territorial units in the various parts of the town, investing in the pursuit of environmental and settlement quality. Taking stock of the decision not to create any alternative to the existing road system, preserving the agricultural territory already protected by the management plan with the creation of a local park of supra-municipal interest, and seeking in any case to eliminate traffic from the historical centre, the plan thus focuses on the presence of a bypass north of the town capable, despite its wholly urban structure, of siphoning off the east-west through traffic and lightening as much as possible the flow of traffic along the Padana highway, already the object of redevelopment. It is thus possible to rejoin the two parts of the town situated north (the larger) and south of the highway through the reduction of traffic and the handling of the primary link with a new urban design. The plan is put to the test by the north-south crossing, which proves to be of territorial importance as a quick way between the northern and southern parts of the eastern Milanese plain passing precisely through Inzago. Recognizing that the town's fine historical centre and urban fabric cannot be subjected to the traffic of an entire metropolitan area, the plan submits to the attention of the local inhabitants, primary actors and stakeholders various scenarios for the closure of the historical centre to circulation and through traffic so as to improve the liveability and quality of the municipal territory by deviating flows that form no part of it. The resulting open discussion has shown how difficult it is to reconcile different attitudes and points of view, not least the defence of personal interests and failure to understand that urban quality and settlement quality are two objectives whose attainment can enhance the economic, social, environmental and human value of an already rich and valid context like that of Inzago.

Poster Plan. Drawing its fundamentals from investigation of the territory of Inzago, built up also through the territorial management plan, the Poster Plan bases the definition of strategies on recognized territorial systems and reinforces the characteristics of territorial units

URBAN PLANNING

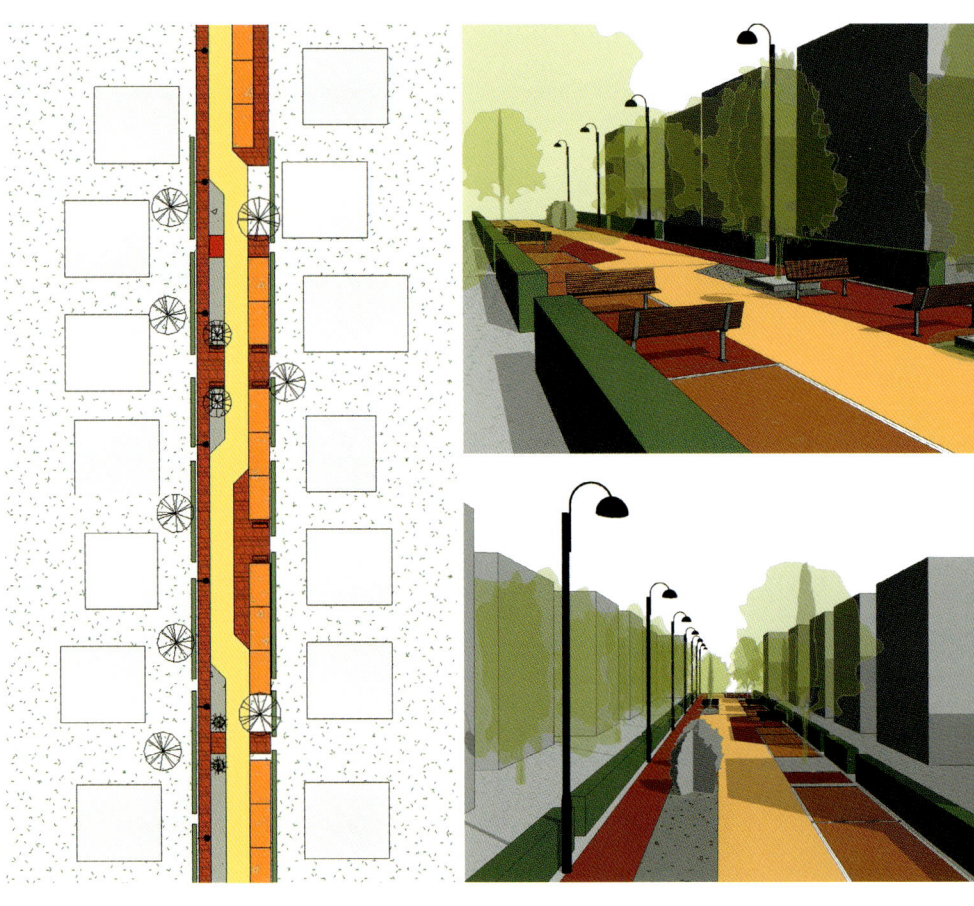

Roads Typologies Chart. The images provide a specific vision of the characteristics of the road system in this area with a view to improving the quality of the roadway and better insertion into the context.
In specific terms, the project regards the road system along the canal, where priority is given to public space and slow mobility

The project: overall view. This key element of the plan encompasses all of the identified planning actions. A fundamental role in the new infrastructural system is assigned to the central north-south axis, the object of various policies to limit crossing. Collateral actions include the overall strengthening, redevelopment and redefinition of the local road system

Specific actions for intersections. The reorganization of the road system includes specific operations on the intersections, including the creation of a surmountable rotunda, a new system of rights-of-way and redrawing the lines of consolidation to as to ensure the continuity of cycle and pedestrian pathways also through the institution of an alternate one-way system

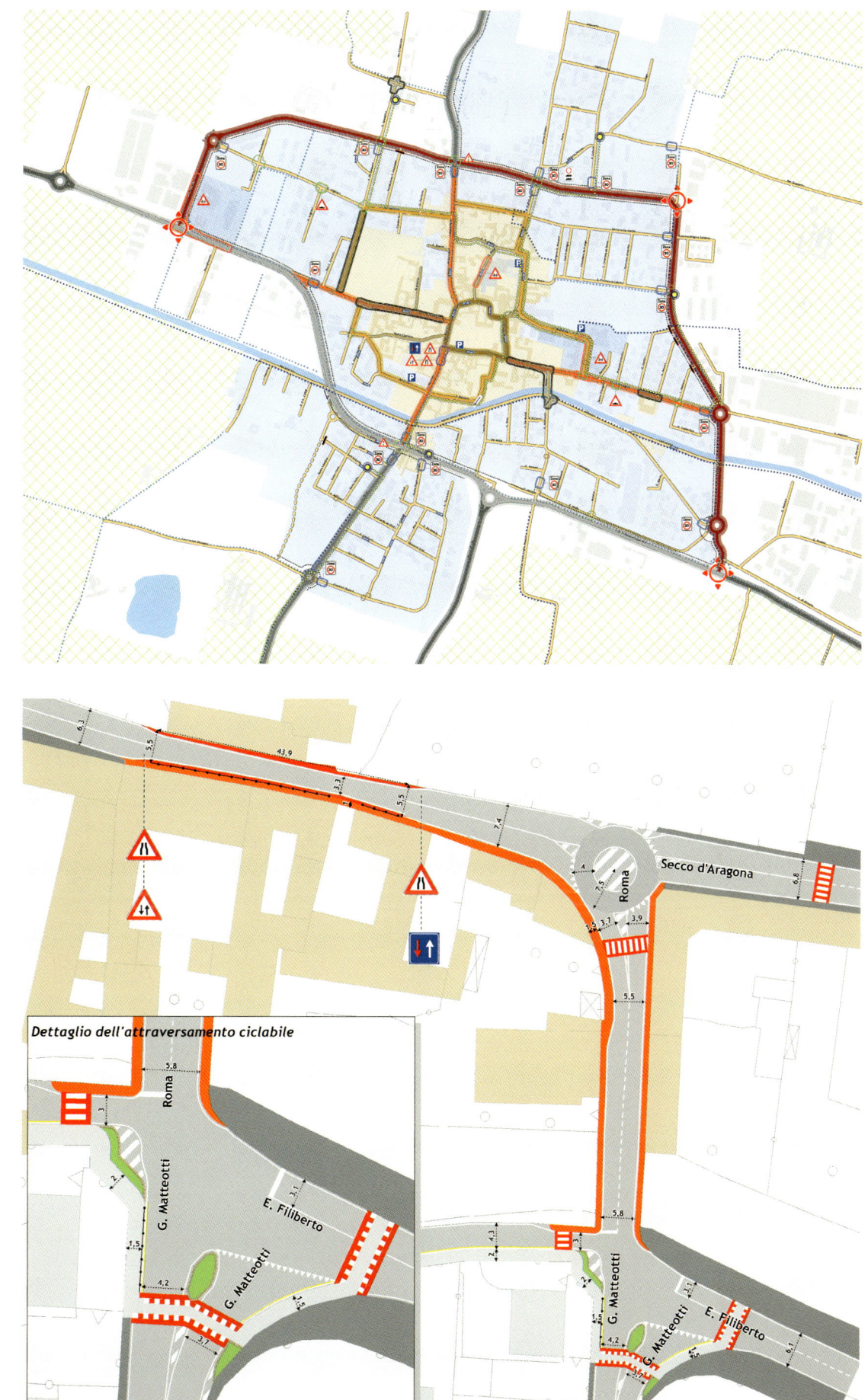

URBAN PLANNING

17. Melegnano (Milan): Urban Traffic Plan (under way since 2011)

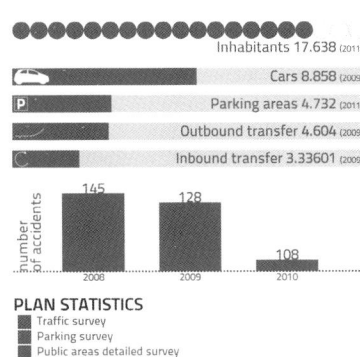

PLAN STATISTICS
- Traffic survey
- Parking survey
- Public areas detailed survey
- Traffic management
- Traffic calming crossroads
- Traffic calming crosswalks
- Traffic calming vulnerable targets
- Bike paths enhancements
- Controlled traffic zones projects
- Pedestrian areas projects
- Woonerf zones projects
- Parking management
- Public areas enhancement
- Enviromental area protection

The drafting of the Urban Traffic Plan for Melegnano made it possible to observe and study the infrastructural dynamics currently affecting the Milanese metropolitan area through a dense, consolidated territory rich in relations. The construction of the east bypass, the completion of work to strengthen the rail system and the general restructuring of the provincial road system of connection and access to both of these have modified the role and position of the municipal territory, which forms part of a territorial system of greater breadth.
Called upon to address some of the problems created by metropolitan congestion, the plan therefore focuses on the metropolitan dimension and makes it possible for the town council to take part with greater strength and competence in discussions regarding local structures and the local repercussions of major works.
It thus emerges that plans, even when sectoral in character, have a further fundamental strategic role to play if they prove capable of stimulating debate and the exchange of ideas at the various levels of analysis and observation of the consequences of all the choices. At the same time, the plan cannot avoid focusing its attention on the interior of the municipal territory, thus discovering the vitality and the overall attractiveness of the services and the commercial and residential systems of Melegnano. Far more than a satellite town of the Milanese metropolitan area,

Melegnano has the potential to organize itself as a centrality with strong and marked urban characteristics precisely through pursuit of the concentration around nodes and polarities that the outspread and largely built-up territory can now undertake.
The plan identifies the historical centre as the major driving force of the town's development and urban connotations, and thus realizes that the rationalization of traffic in and around the centre is indispensable. With a system of circuits around the most historical and dense nucleus, the reorganization acts like a huge turbine to involve all the surrounding districts, thus identifying environmental islands and areas to be safeguarded.
If carried out in this way, rationalization makes it possible to increase the spaces earmarked for urban and settlement quality. Reorganization of the fortnightly market, completion of work on the station area, overall revision of the parking plan and the proposal for gateways of access between external and internal systems, with supporting policies such as ensuring the greater usability of parking spaces through the provisions of precise information in real time, regulation of the times of access to the more sensitive areas with the flexible use of environmental islands and zones of limited traffic, thus recovering an ever-greater number of spaces and areas of the urban fabric.

Poster Plan. Backbones and areas are the cornerstones of the Poster Plan, which encompasses all of the elements brought out by broad and detailed analysis, translating the plan's strategic objectives into images and identifying specificities of treatment, points for attention, resources and potentialities

URBAN PLANNING

119

Opposite
Central area. Identified and addressed in detail in both the analytical and the strategic phases, the central area of Melegnano is redefined and reorganized by taking into consideration not only the different uses to which it is put but also and above all the characteristics and geometry of the street system

Short-term planning scenario. The project develops in the three temporal spans of the short, medium and long term. The short-term scenario identifies the actions for immediate implementation, as regards both their technical and economic feasibility and the need to resolve the most critical situations. It envisages, for example, hierarchical organization of the street system and the application of marketing principles to parking

Long-term planning scenario. In the long term, the plans for the municipal system are combined with the supra-local provisions for Milan East Bypass, which makes it possible through the collateral works envisaged to redefine the system of municipal crossing and assign them a new urban role

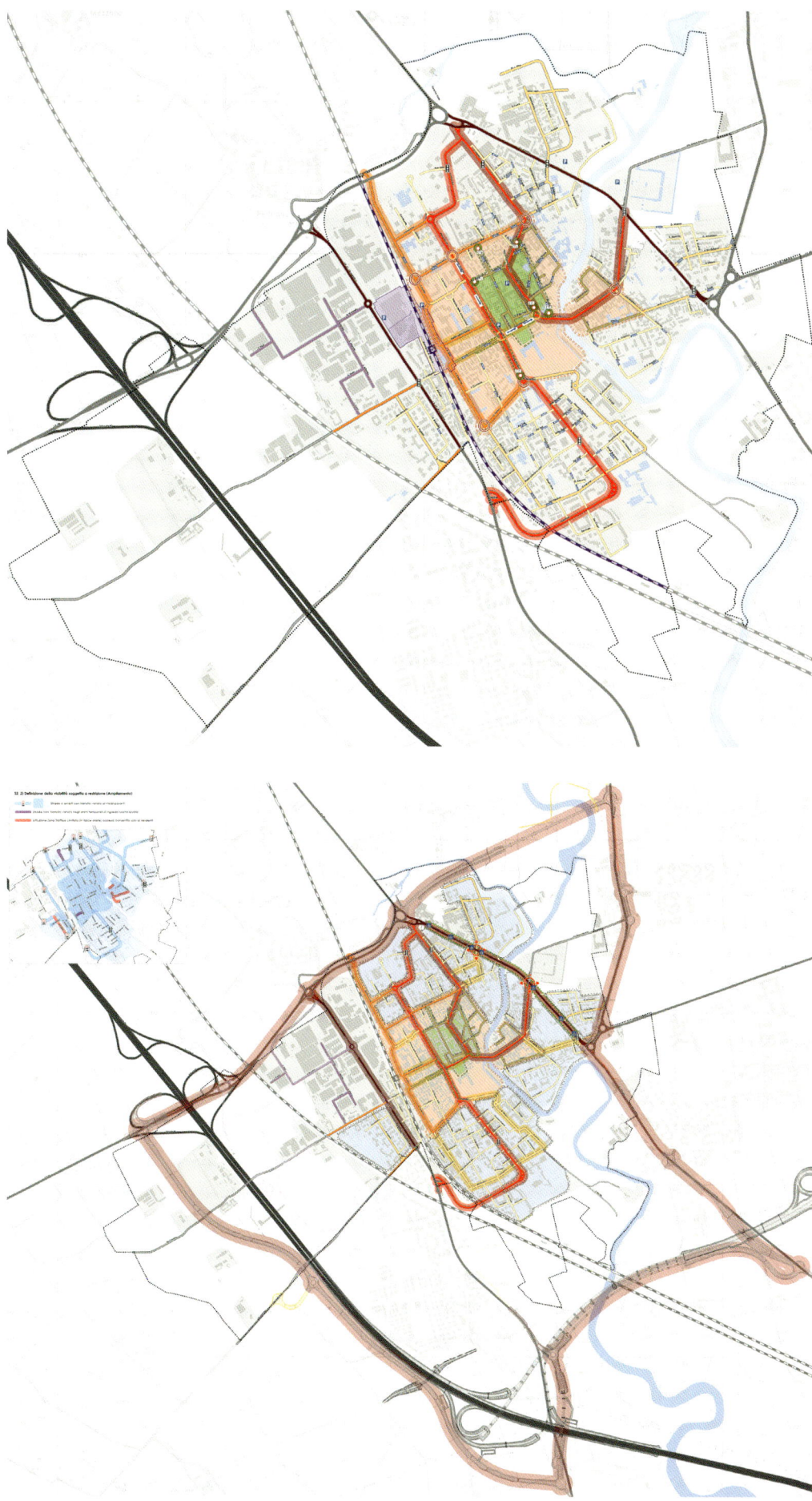

Limited traffic zone (LTZ) and town market.
The identification of an LTZ in connection with the town market becomes a key element for the management of municipal traffic, as the market constitutes a strong attraction at the supra-local level capable of generating major flows of traffic that the plan is designed to manage

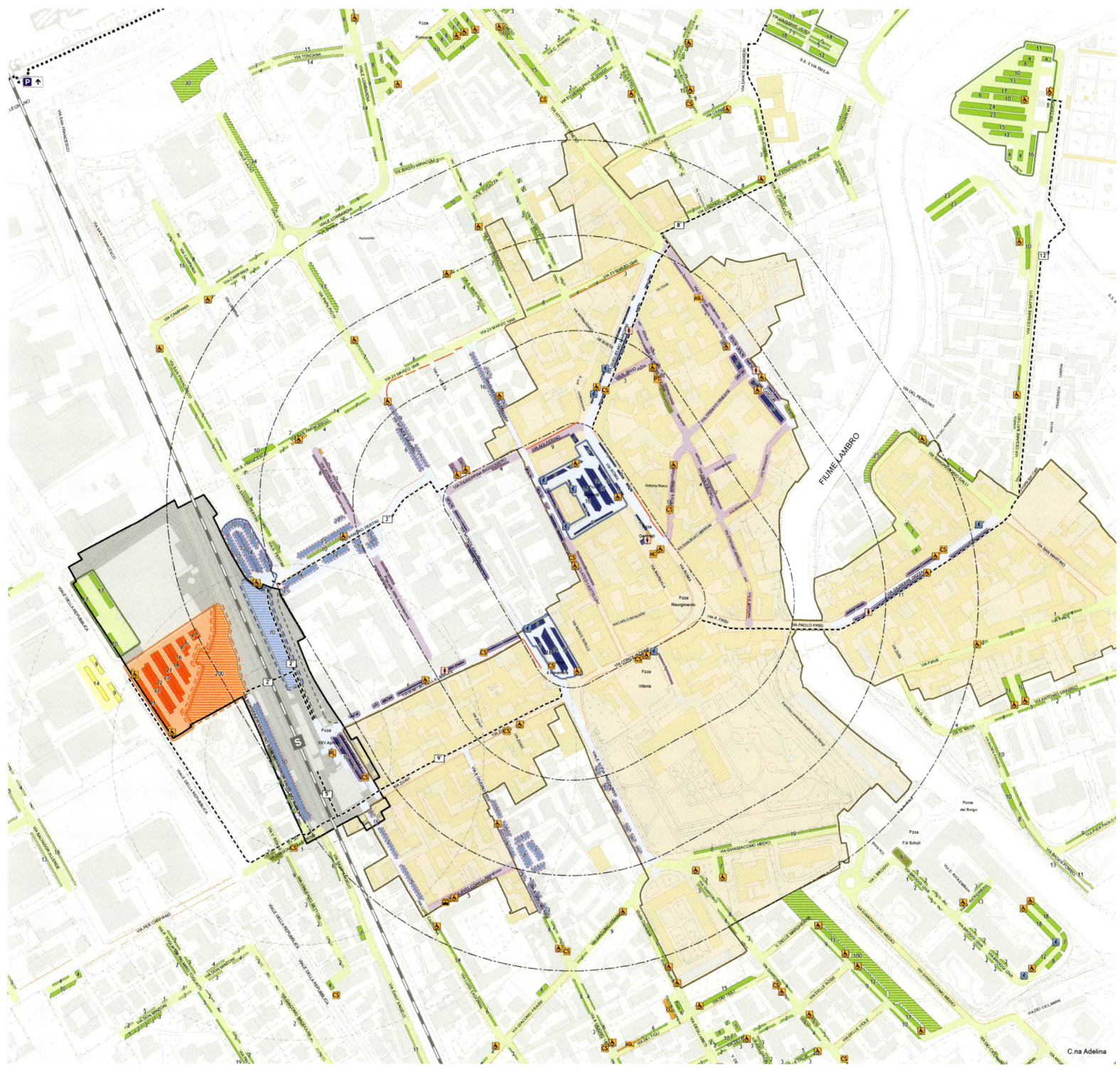

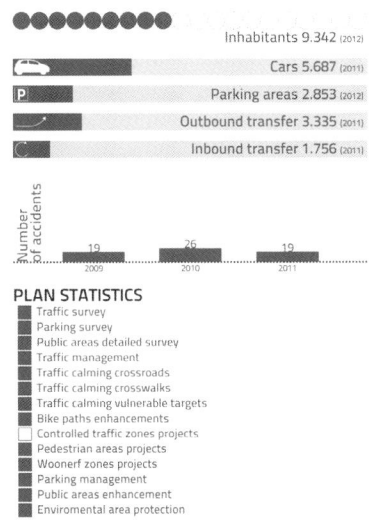

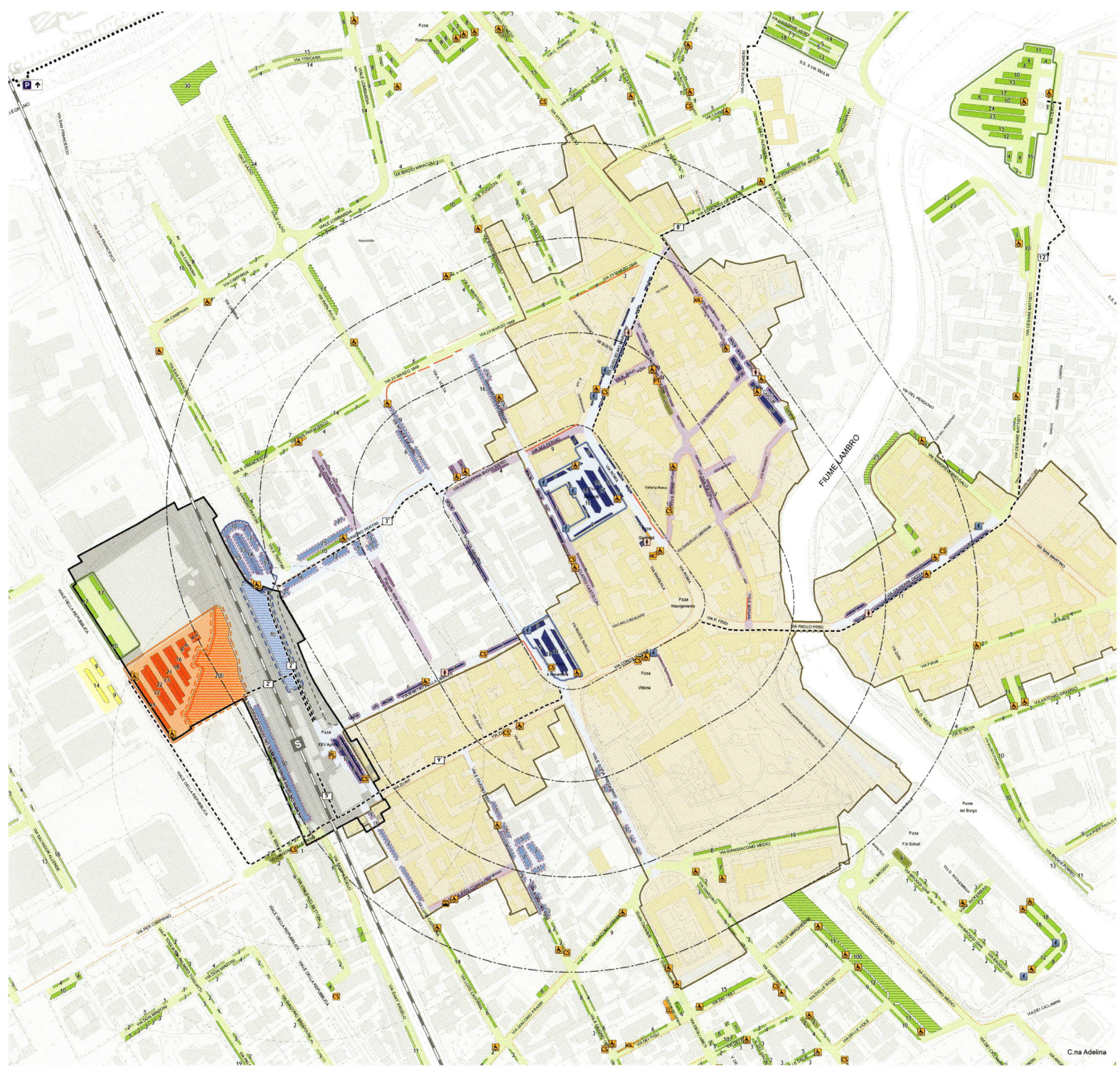

Plans for the parking scenario. Rethinking and managing the traffic in the central area of Melegnano means taking direct action on the parking system. The plan thus identifies differentiated levels of payment for parking in relation to proximity to the historical centre and recognizes the importance of parking areas to serve the railway station

URBAN PLANNING

18. Verano Brianza (Monza and Brianza): Urban Traffic Plan
(under way since 2012)

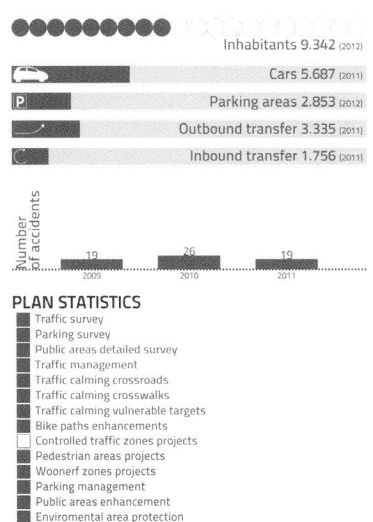

PLAN STATISTICS
- Traffic survey
- Parking survey
- Public areas detailed survey
- Traffic management
- Traffic calming crossroads
- Traffic calming crosswalks
- Traffic calming vulnerable targets
- Bike paths enhancements
- Controlled traffic zones projects
- Pedestrian areas projects
- Woonerf zones projects
- Parking management
- Public areas enhancement
- Enviromental area protection

As in other contexts, the drawing up of the Territorial Management Plan for Verano Brianza was followed by the Urban Traffic Plan, thus identifying the tool to give concrete shape to the provisions for reorganization of the town's urban spheres and to pursue objectives of urban quality. The major artery of the provincial highway runs by Verano, touching its settlement fabric on the west and north sides. No fewer than two access points make it possible to use this artery also for north-south movements and avoid going through the municipal fabric, but this does not happen. The main road, classed as a priority provincial highway before the construction of the bypass, runs through the most consolidated territory, passes close to the historical centre, and touches upon all of the town's major services. It could be seen as a vital backbone of support for the town's strategic activities, but this is prevented by the interference of too many demands expressed by too many users. The road along the valley of the river Lambro could be a green artery for use of the valley, but this is prevented by the presence of a factory whose heavy lorries are a plague on the road. The plan works on all these potentialities, discovering that the quick but short-lived development experienced by many of these contexts has not even resulted in a road system of sufficient geometric breadth to accommodate functions, uses and users in ever greater numbers with increasingly specialized and differentiated requirements. Working on the overall geometry of the network and its precise design, the plan immediately identifies a hierarchy making it possible to take full advantage of the characteristics of all the roads. On the one hand, it envisages strengthening the two access points to the major traffic artery, thus favouring its use also for internal purposes. On the other, the main road is seen as vital and capable of supporting the town's strategic functions while providing access to the various sectors into which it is divided. The road is redesigned, rethought and reshaped as a central backbone, traffic is regulated but not eliminated, and the system of the functions is made accessible with greater rationality. Greater attention can thus be focused on pedestrian use of the historical centre, freed from the weight of some through traffic that the main road can instead absorb. The plan has also been used as a tool to resolve the incompatibility of the presence of a factory on the road by the river Lambro. Since the aim is to enhance the environmental value of the axis of the river, fostering the integration of green areas with the previous industrial and agricultural settlement system, a series of traffic-calming measures are envisaged with policies to mediate between the presence of a factory and the municipal desire to use the artery in a different way so as to ensure maximization of the area's environmental value. The plan thus serves as a channel of dialogue and mediation between different parties, illustrating alternative scenarios, building up consensus on the solutions, and taking responsibility for their implementation.

Poster Plan. Construction of the Poster Plan constitutes the key phase of the planning process in that it makes it possible to outline synoptically the priority objectives and strategies identified also through the development of an in-depth analytical phase, pinpointing the initial indications for reorganization of the infrastructural system

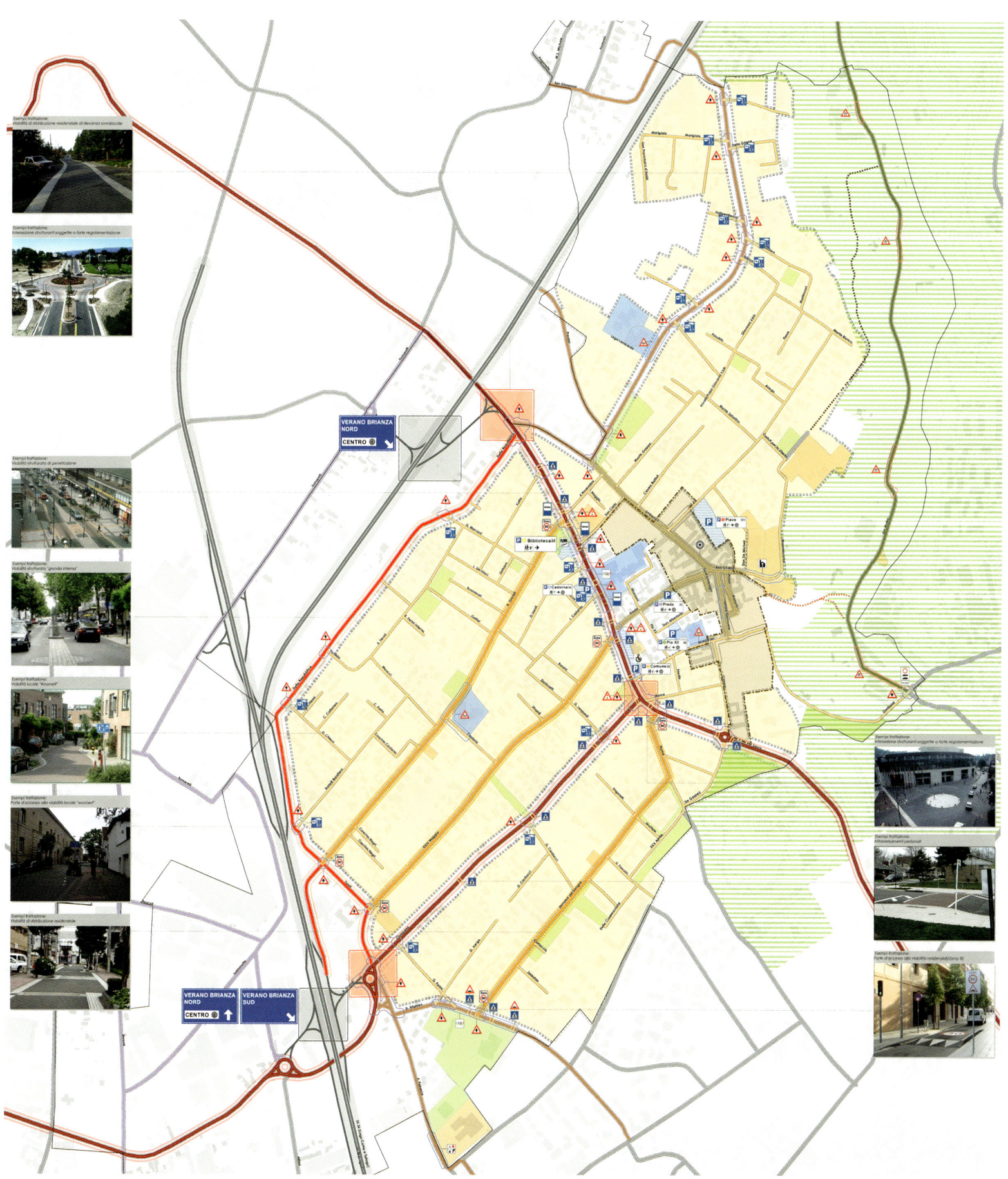

URBAN PLANNING

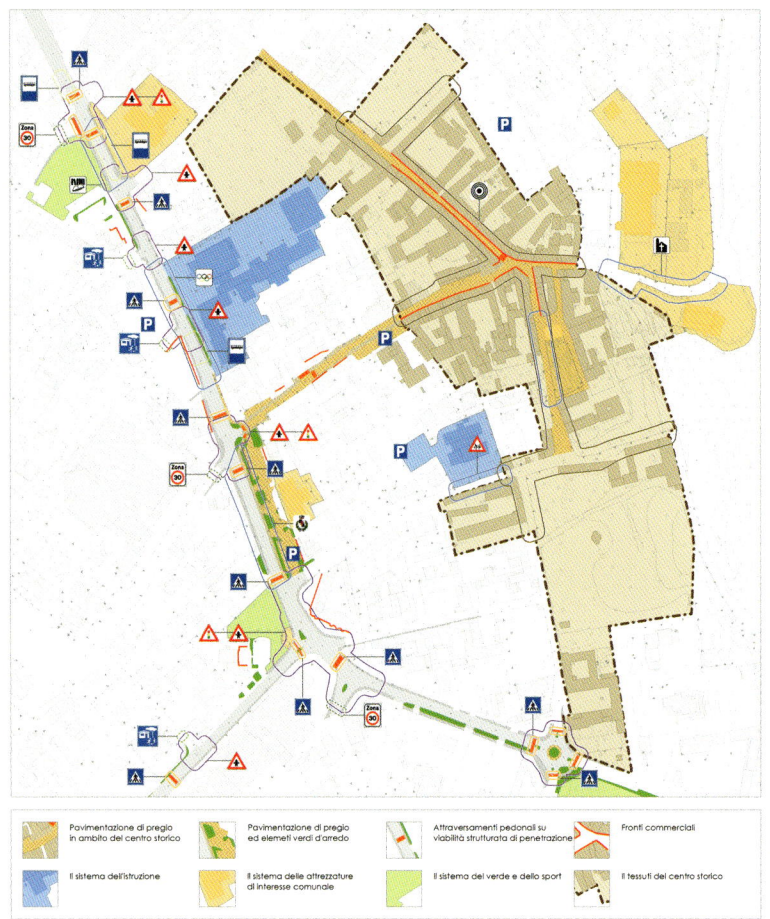

Central axis. Identifying the critical aspects and territorial potentialities, the plan pinpoints the fulcrum of the infrastructural and settlement system of Verano Brianza as the heart of specific operations aimed at upgrading and protecting the existing historical structures and the structure of the public city, which are often affected by different uses and users

Short-term planning scenario. The short-term scenario focuses on improving the accessibility of the central area by strengthening the cycle tracks and pedestrian pathways and creating an initial ring devoted entirely to slow mobility. At the same time, it involves action to organize and ensure the safety of crossings and intersections

URBAN PLANNING

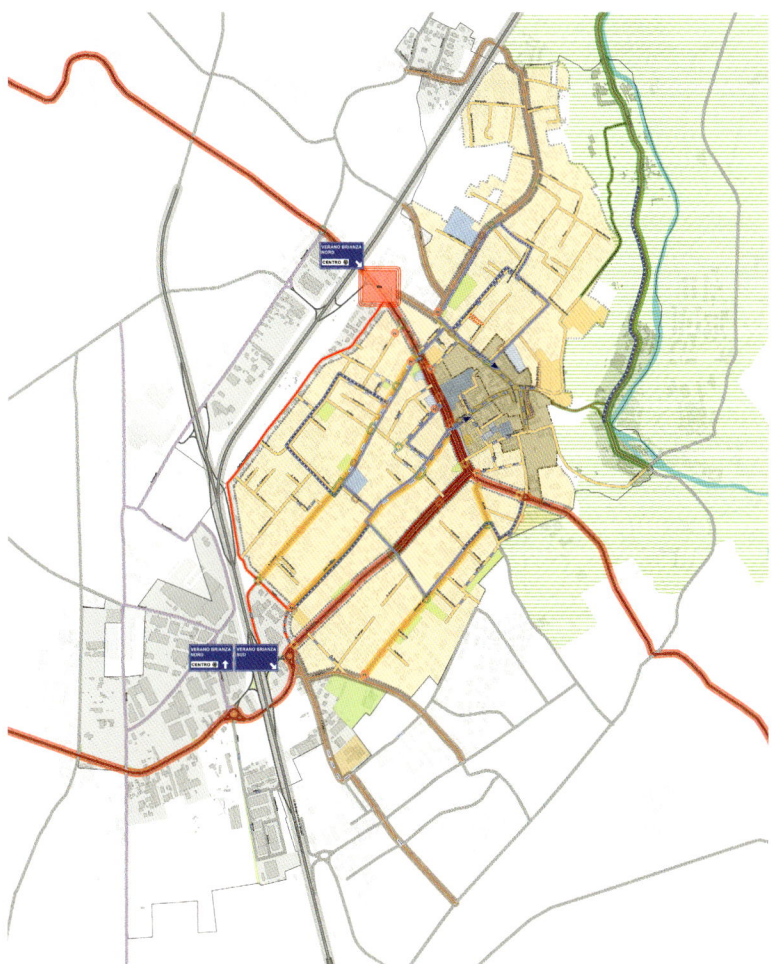

Medium-term planning scenario. The second phase of implementation identifies the most sensitive areas for which protective policies are required, including the historical centre and residential fabrics. The major points of municipal access and the areas requiring the creation of 30 kph zones are therefore identified. The system of cycle tracks expands into new areas of the city and a solution is proposed for one of the most problematic intersections

Long-term planning scenario. The most distant phase in temporal terms envisages operations of greater technical and economic complexity, like upgrading the main thoroughfares and restructuring some important intersections. The system of cycle tracks is completed through the definitive creation of a safe and continuous network all through the municipal territory

URBAN PLANNING

19. Florence: feasibility study for the creation of an urban transformation agency for the Piagge area (2005–07)

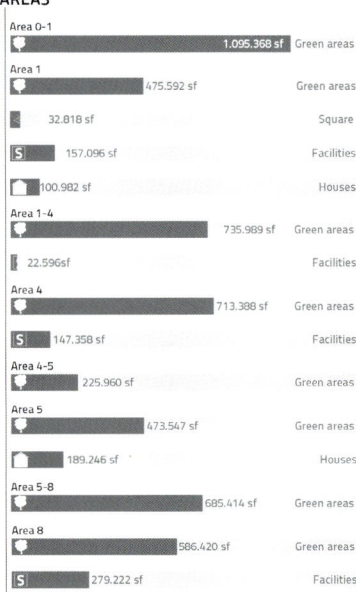

AREAS

Area 0-1	1.095.368 sf	Green areas
Area 1	475.592 sf	Green areas
	32.818 sf	Square
	157.096 sf	Facilities
	100.982 sf	Houses
Area 1-4	735.989 sf	Green areas
	22.596 sf	Facilities
Area 4	713.388 sf	Green areas
	147.358 sf	Facilities
Area 4-5	225.960 sf	Green areas
Area 5	473.547 sf	Green areas
	189.246 sf	Houses
Area 5-8	685.414 sf	Green areas
Area 8	586.420 sf	Green areas
	279.222 sf	Facilities

Located on the outskirts of Florence on the way to Pistoia, the Piagge district consists mainly of large public housing complexes with structures and services for commerce and small businesses. The area is characterized by a rigid framework of hydrological and geological constraints and problems connected with underground pollution due to the presence of unsupervised rubbish dumps.
The composite cross-section of the population resident in the district has made demands over the years for a marked increase in public space and incentives to foster the participation of private concerns in the process of urban redevelopment.
The Florence city council ordered a feasibility study for the planning, creation and management of redevelopment operations in the district. The Guiding Project for Redevelopment of the Piagge District, drawn up by the architect Giancarlo De Carlo, the Strategic Plan of the Florentine Metropolitan Area and the Structural Plan of the City of Florence constitute the organic frame of reference for the feasibility study.
The study focused on implementation of the provisions of the Guiding Project and the identification of innovative and experimental models of intervention capable of joining the various levels of the planning now under way.
The Guiding Project envisages both "rationalization operations" for the district and "target operations" for the city of Florence as a whole. The two types of operation are characterized by very different levels of complexity and feasibility, which the study interpreted and measured.
The cornerstones of the Guiding Project are reinforcement of the transversal systems that connect the residential area with the banks of the river Arno, the creation of a longitudinal system of vehicular connection parallel to the river and to the Pistoiese highway, and gathering the free areas together in one large urban park.
The study interprets this system of proposals as a device for the regulation of urban transformation and experiments with the use of the plan and the design for the management of an intense Guiding Project expanded to encompass many different territorial realities and themes. To this end, it maximizes its strategic nature and capacity to generate precise and specific actions on the territory.

General plan of operations and green systems

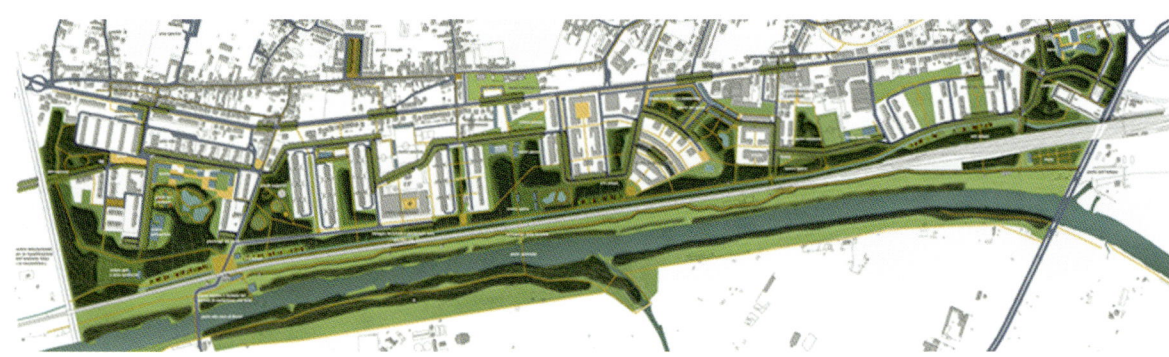

Project axes and actions

Polarities and services

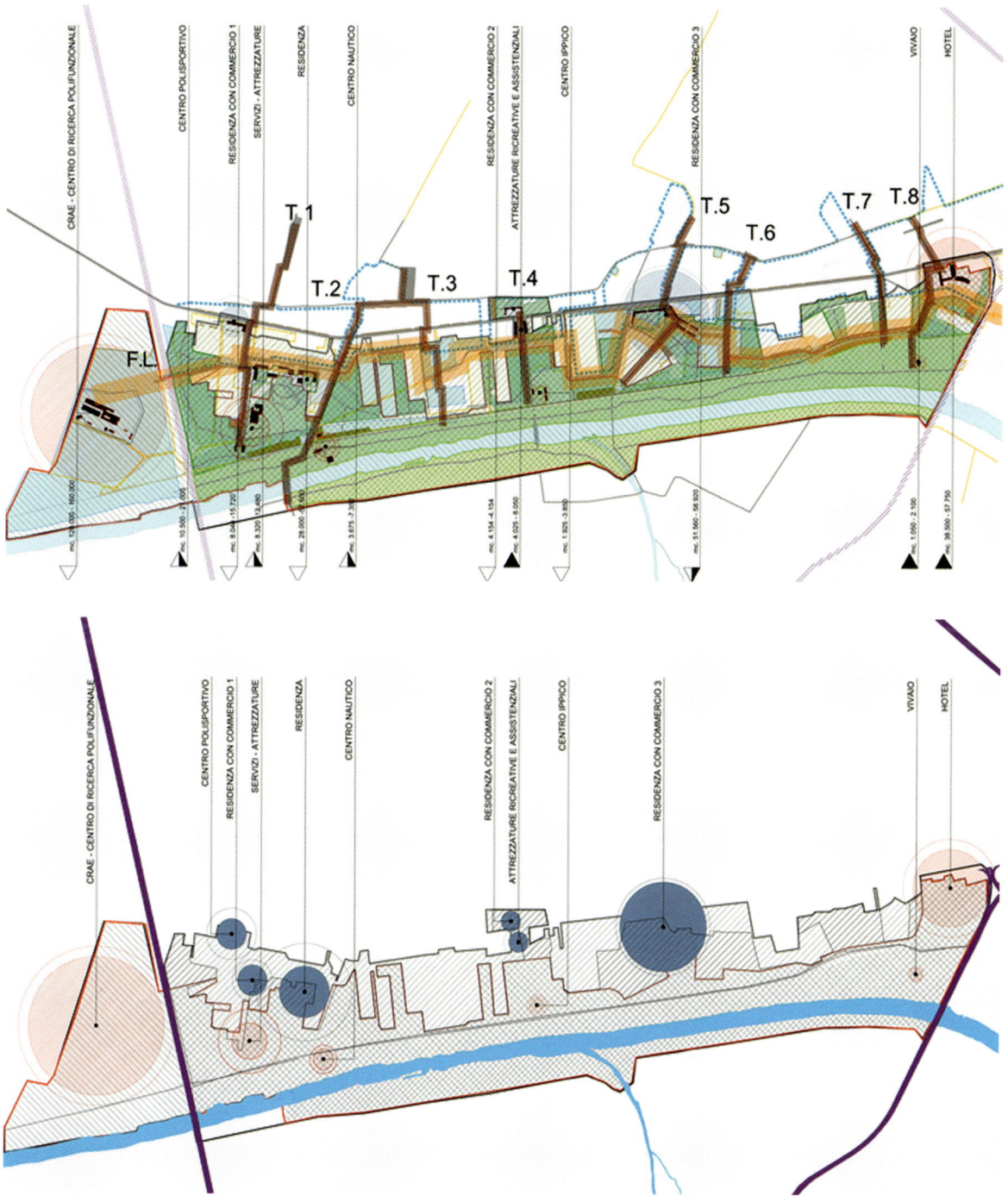

20. Puglia: Territorial Landscape Plan. Guidelines for the landscaping and environmental quality of infrastructures (2009-10)

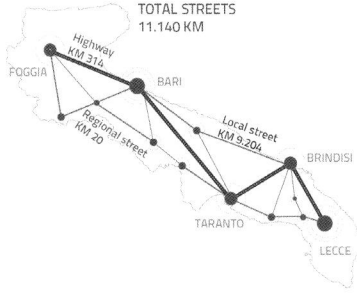

The guidelines drawn up constitute a manual of operations to improve the landscaping and environmental quality of infrastructures in the Puglia region in connection with the drafting of its Territorial Landscape Plan (TLP).

The purpose of the guidelines is to give the TLP a guiding role for the tools of implementation hierarchically subordinate to it, identifying all the actions and components that should be taken into consideration in order to endow the region's existing and planned infrastructures with landscaping and environmental quality. The project decided to maximize the planning and operative component of the guidelines. The risk of supra-ordinate instruments is failure to make sufficient impact on the territory and thus be disregarded in small-scale, everyday operations through distraction caused by an excess of problems or local influences. For this reason, and in order to draw attention to the instrument produced, the plan provides a wealth of instructions, suggestions for planning, designs and solutions for local contexts to use directly in the construction of roads. Above all, it expands the project's sphere with provisions, schemes and designs that also affect the territory surrounding the infrastructures, thus shifting attention from the individual road to the composition of the territory around it, and working on the composition of territorial typologies as a specific object of the project.

The project thus envisages two systems of reading. The first, Infrastructural Typologies, regards the identification of ten infrastructural categories capable of interpreting the historical, cultural, residential, morphological, environmental and settlement characteristics of the contexts involved as well as the objectives of quality to be attained in the work of upgrading. The second, Territorial Morphologies, regards recurrent and recognizable systems of networks, settlements and environments characterizing the various parts of the landscape of the Puglia region.

The territorial interpretation thus defined made it possible to draw up guidelines, actions, operations and projects for deployment point by point on the individual functional landscape profiles recognized or jointly all along the infrastructural axis.

The toolkit offered makes it possible to provide an active instrument of support for territorial planning decisions of use in the dissemination on the territory and in territorial practices of a synoptic planning technique capable of enhancing the landscape and rethinking the connective role of infrastructures in territorial systems.

Coastal road of natural beauty. The types identified run through coastal areas of high environmental value along coastal morphotypes of quality connecting important historical and cultural elements, seaside resorts, parks and nature reserves. The planning is oriented towards protection of quality views, preservation of the natural order of territories largely untouched by anthropization, the refurbishment of building complexes and the use of natural areas through substantial work to embed the infrastructure in the environment

Environmental corridor. The roads that run alongside or through transversal or longitudinal elements of ecological connection (greenhouses, ridges, marshland, rivers and streams) are addressed on criteria designed to reduce the impact of infrastructures on ecosystems and especially as regards their effect as a barrier to the movement of animal species and a source of acoustic, luminous and atmospheric pollution. Infrastructures upgraded in this way become key elements to establish and strengthen environmental network functions within the territory

STRADA COSTIERA PAESAGGISTICA

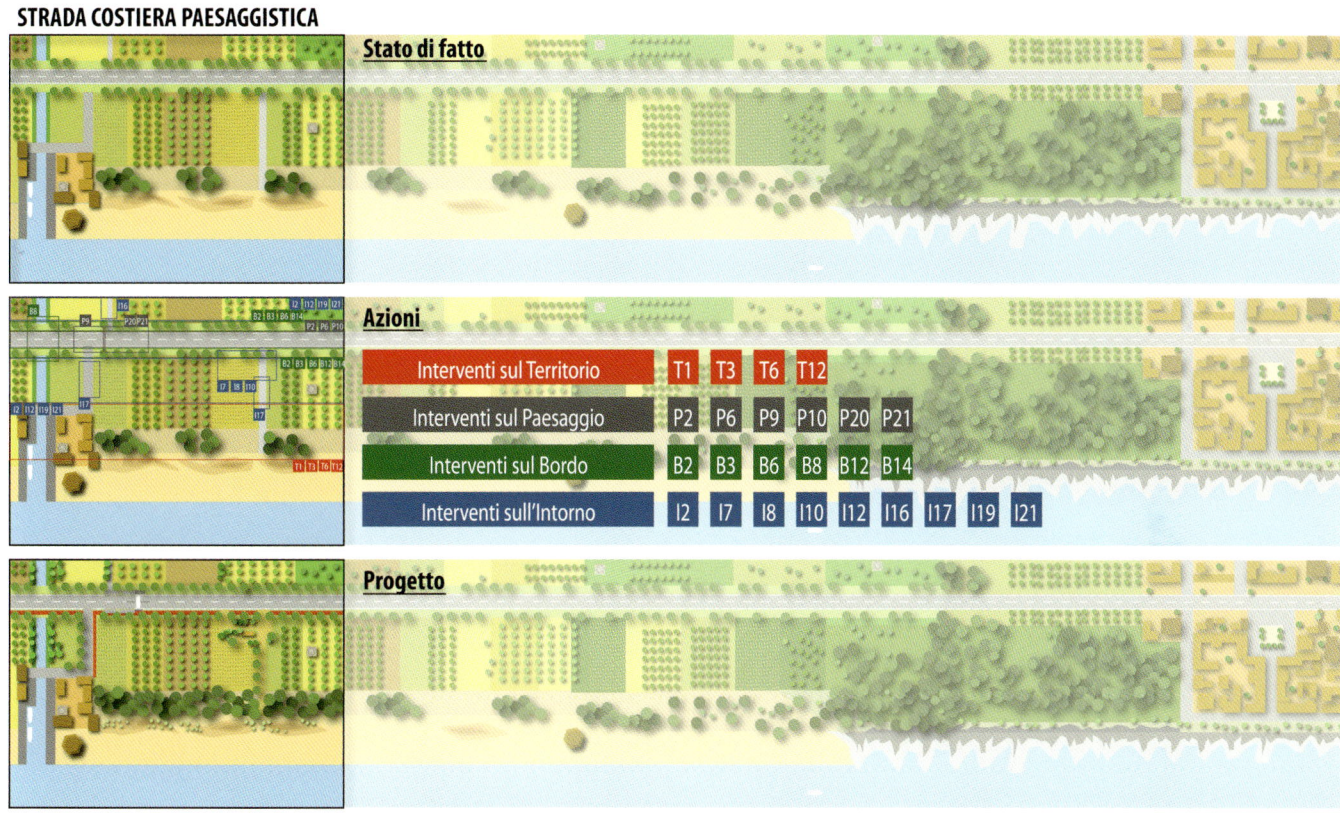

STRADA CORRIDOIO ECOLOGICO

URBAN PLANNING

STRADA MERCATO PRODUTTIVA LINEARE

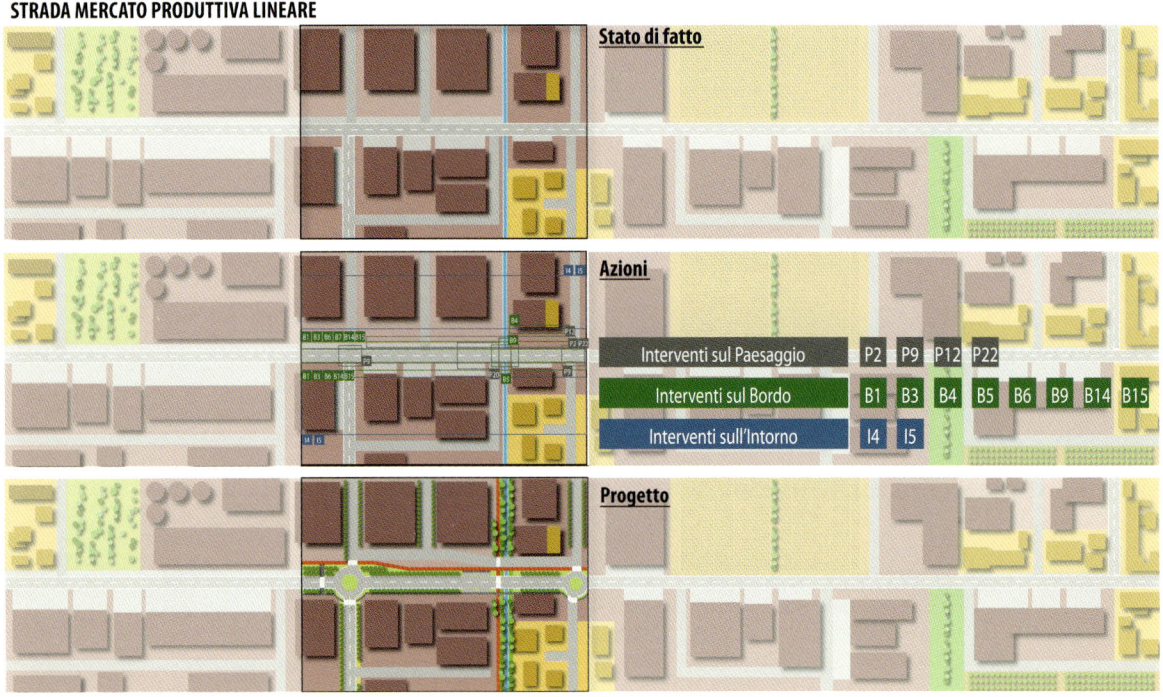

STRADA COSTIERA DA RIQUALIFICARE

Linear production/market road. The type of road identified runs through low-quality production areas. Upgrading involves the planting of trees, which work on the one hand to mark the structure of the existing landscape and make its morphologic characteristics visible, and on the other to create a screen for buildings and open production areas

Upgrading of a coastal road. The road in question runs through densely built-up areas of low urban quality largely devoid of public services and facilities. The project seeks to create public spaces for parking and public transport. Trees and safe pedestrian crossings are used to upgrade points of access to the sea and make them recognizable. There are also provisions for the restoration and maintenance of the morphological features of the landscape

Historical access road. The primary axes of urban penetration, characterized by the presence of physical or visual elements marking the entrance to the town, such as tree-lined avenues and panoramic views, are taken into consideration. The planning criteria for the type indicated are oriented towards the protection and enhancement of the integrity and recognizability of urban gateways and fronts through direct action to redefine margins, halt the processes of urban sprawl and spread, and reduce impact

Road of environmental interest. The road runs through rural contexts of natural interest. Its upgrading involves both the creation of views of important morphologic elements and the planting of trees to screen low-quality industrial and agricultural buildings

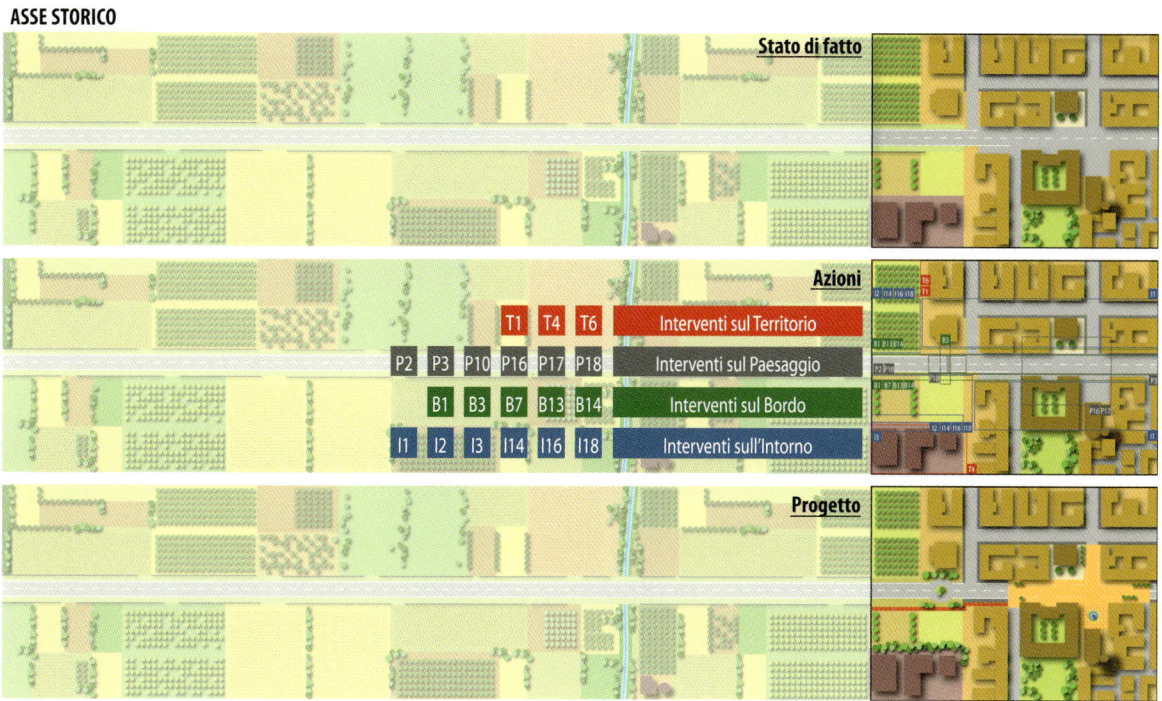

URBAN PLANNING

STRADA PAESAGGIO AGRARIO INFRASTRUTTURATO

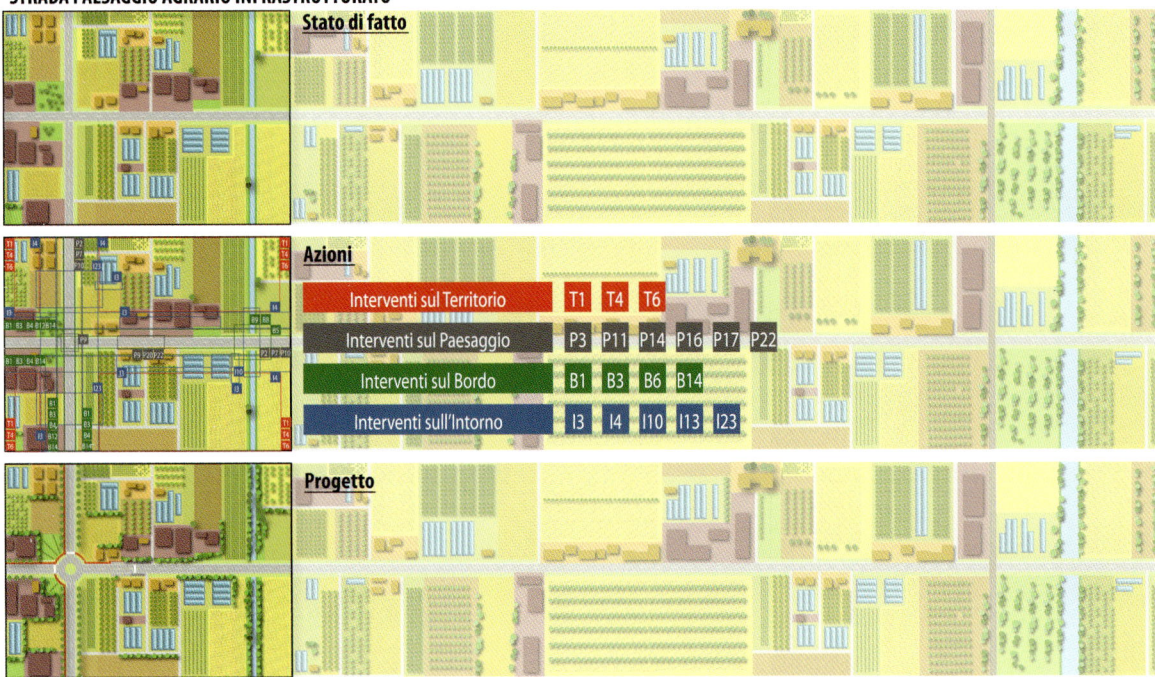

Road through a rural landscape with infrastructures. The road in question runs through rural areas of mixed urbanization. The upgrading involves the planting of trees to conceal industrial buildings and areas as well as agricultural areas occupied by temporary greenhouses. It is planned to strengthen weak mobility in the residential fabric through the creation of pedestrian crossings in the vicinity of bus stops. Rows of trees are to be planted where possible to mark out the road system

STRADA PARCO

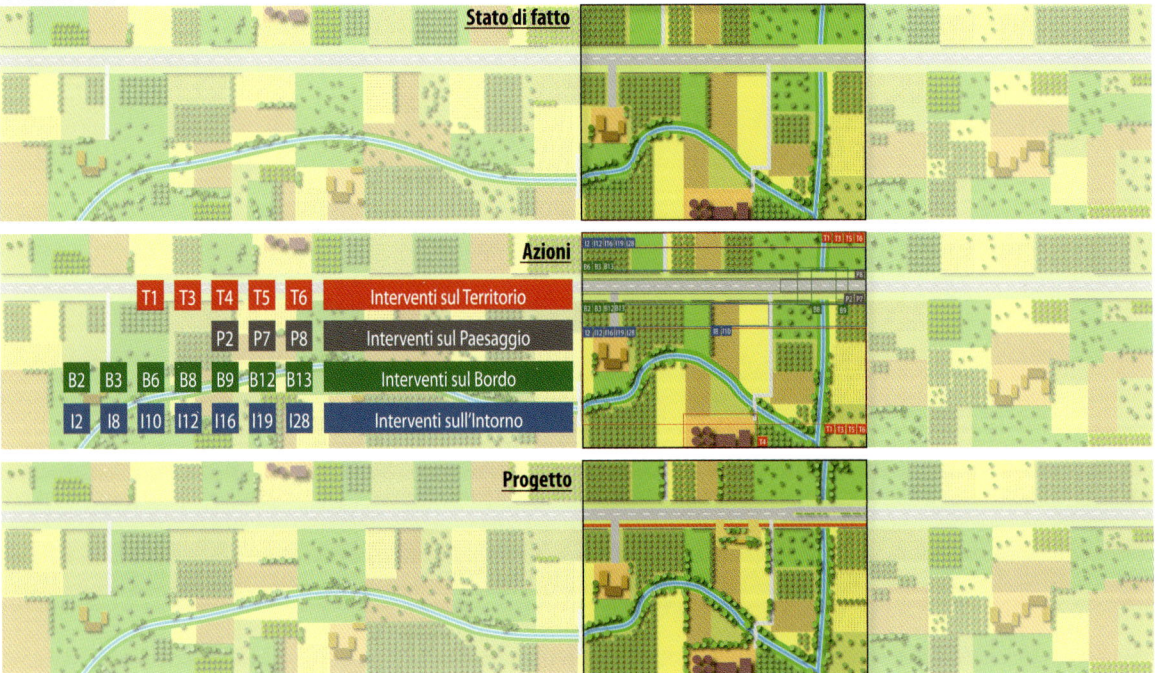

Park road. The upgrading of this particular road, which runs through landscape areas of considerable interest, involves division of the roadway so as to improve safety at critical points or emphasize views of the landscape. Wherever the park road runs through small towns, provision is made for systems of deceleration such as raising the roadway with the insertion of green areas and elements of urban furniture

Road of linear settlement fabrics. Roads that run through continuous linear settlements of a predominantly residential character, contexts characterized by low density in which agricultural connotations have given way to elements typical of the urban outskirts. The upgrading involves operations to reduce the joining of neighbouring towns through the redevelopment of interstitial agricultural areas and work on the roadside

Pendulum road. This type of road system includes links between towns in the hinterland and the coast road. The upgrading involves strengthening the pathways of slow mobility and reinforcing the nodes between orthogonal roads through the insertion of green roundabouts, pedestrian crossing systems and panoramic piazzas

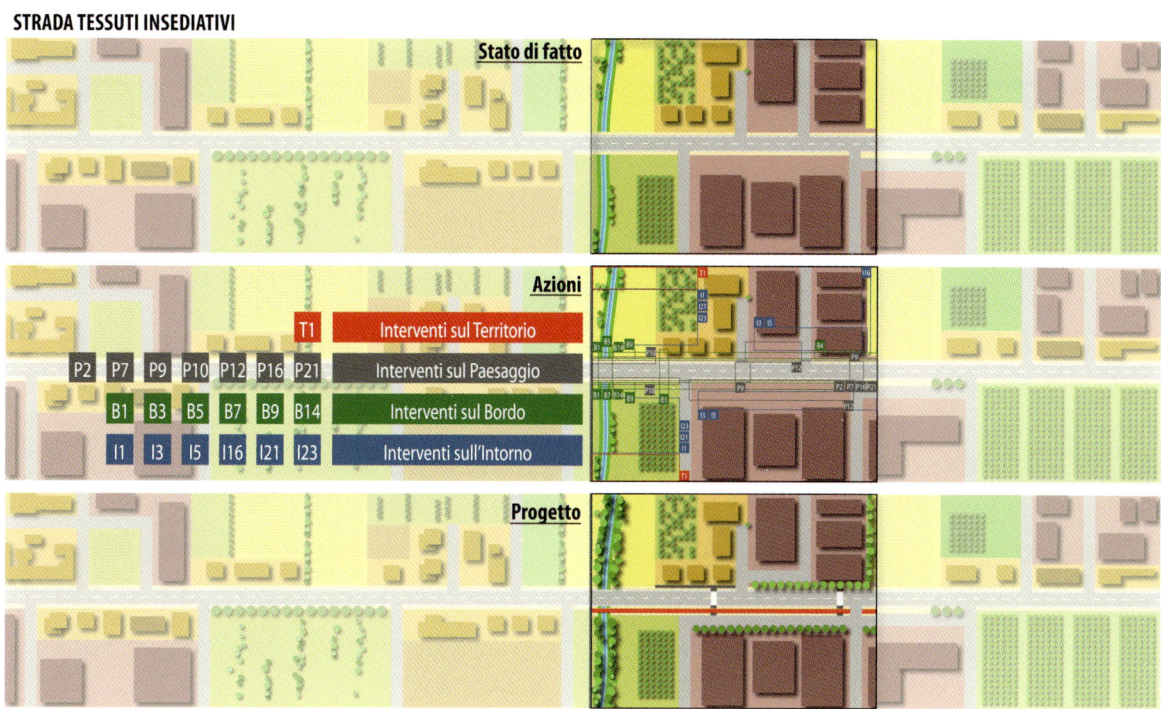

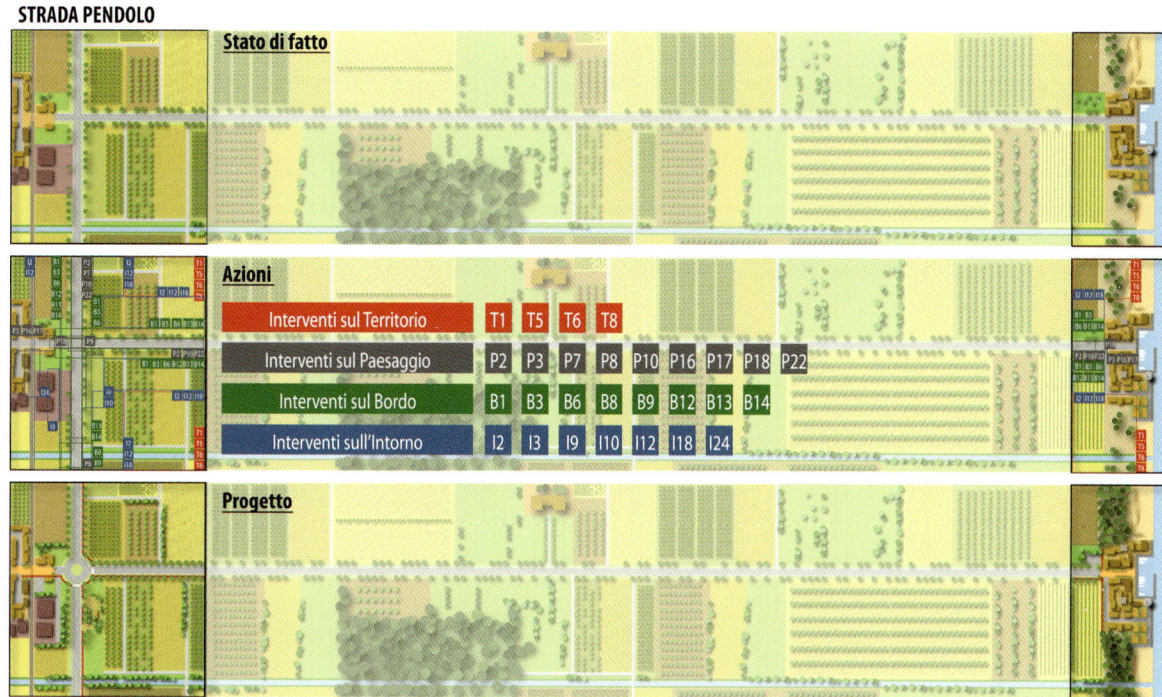

URBAN PLANNING

21. Inzago (Milan): Guidelines for plans for the re use of farmhouses (2011)

The territory of Inzago has a large stock of farmhouses and agricultural structures within a vast system of green, free and cultivated areas, many of which are included in the local park of supra-municipal interest proposed by the Management Plan. The policies formulated by the plan are designed to maintain the vitality of the fabric of farmhouses, both with natural functions of support for agricultural activities and through conversion for residential purposes, thus offering a different type of settlement pattern and interrupting the tendency towards urban sprawl with high consumption of building land.

The guidelines are drawn up as a intentionally hybrid instrument made up both of rules derived directly from the management plan (such as the urban planning rules on indices, covered surfaces, spheres of transfer and standards) and of morphological rules to guide the projects of implementation to be drawn up for every structure. The particular nature of the instrument prompted the use of preliminary architectural drawings in order to anticipate the appraisals that every detailed project will then have to undertake and in order to ascertain the viability of the urban planning rules derived from the plan.

Every farmhouse is analyzed in terms of its existing structure and assessed as regards typological and geometric consistency. Its historical composition is examined in order to distinguish the original nucleus from worthless additions and its typological functioning as evaluated with a view to understanding and suggesting how and where to supplement the existing structures not only with new ones but also with new functions they can host together with all the associated residential services and activities.

The interest of the instrument lies precisely in its particular nature as investigation, anticipation, simulation and provision, confirming once again the great strategic value of design in order to envisage transformations and govern the quality they can contribute to the context. The broad use of nomograms defines the materials and solutions admitted and excluded in accordance with a logic of overall design and attention to the context of the farmhouse that the renovation project will necessarily have to respect. Many of the tables included were constructed also with the purpose of providing back-up material in the search for financial support or aid in a logic of overall service of the design and the instrument produced.

General analysis of the complex. The preliminary phase involved application of an in-depth analytical method designed to develop a general reconstruction of every complex involved and examine its primary functions and typological structure

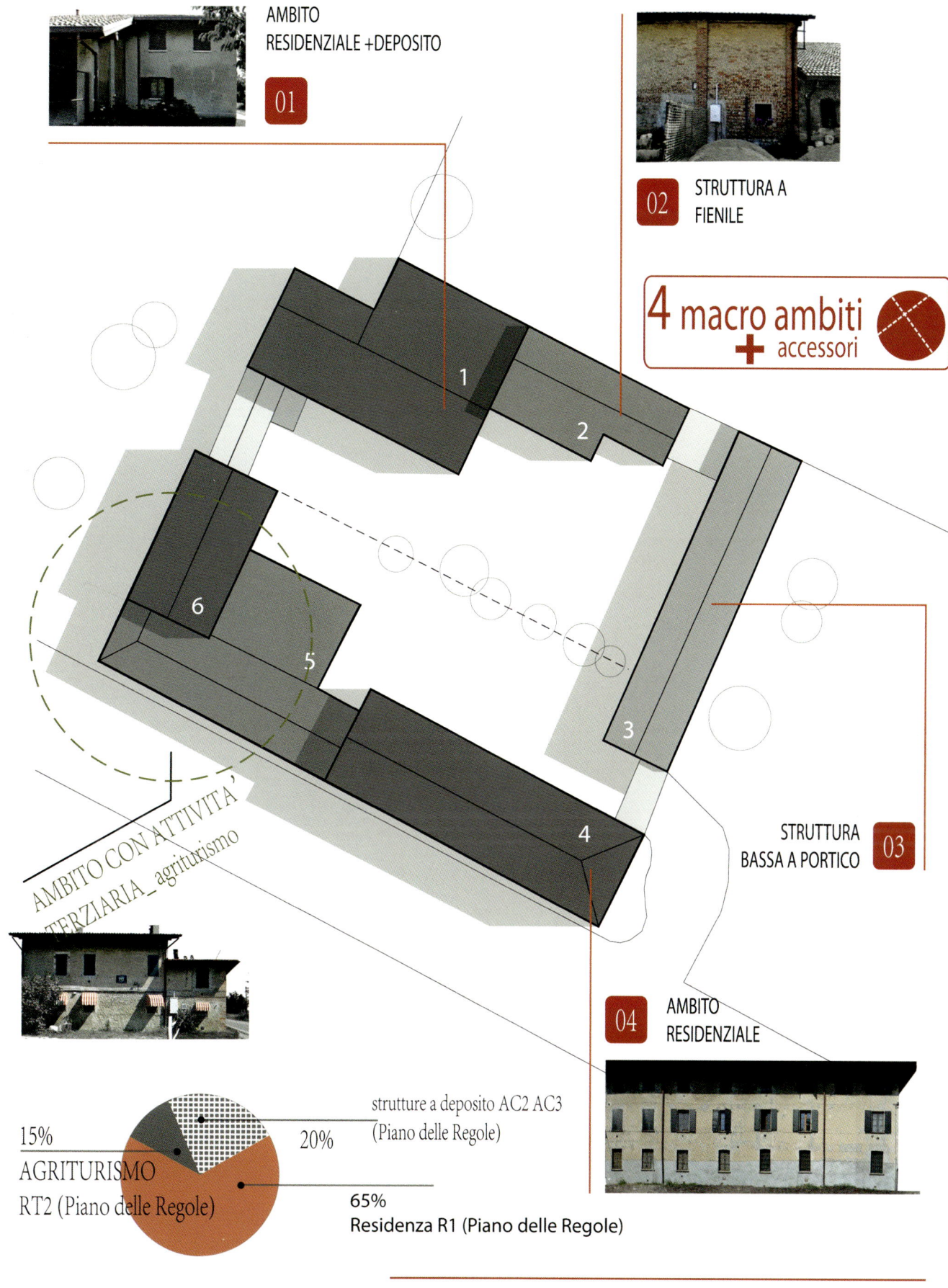

la struttura tipologica a corte

URBAN PLANNING

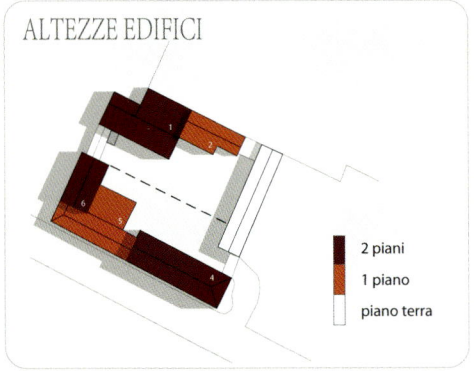
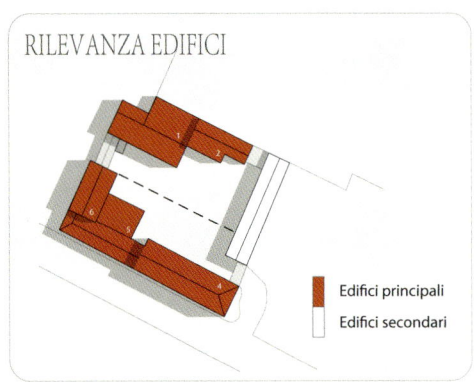
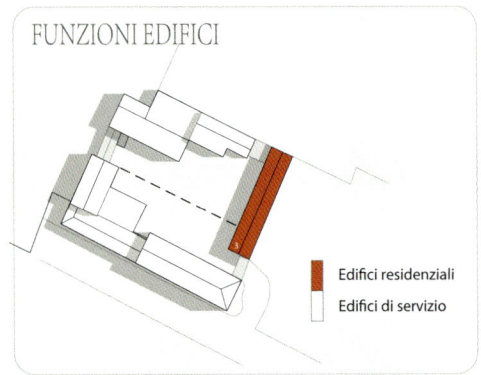

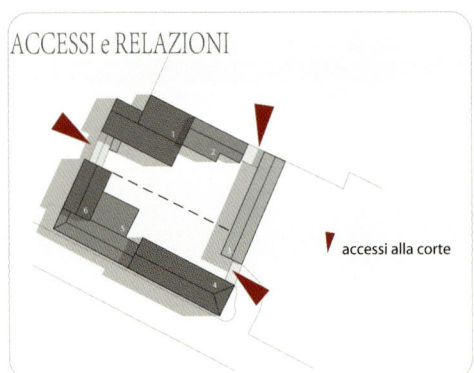

Present state and relationship with context. Every rural complex was broken down in terms of the major parameters of analytical investigation to provide information on its state of preservation, architectural value, system of access and relations with open space, which are crucial to guide the planning phase

Opposite
Photographic reconstruction of façades. Direct surveying of every rural complex led to detailed recording and photographic reconstruction of the façades of the buildings, thus providing crucial material for developing the guidelines. The specific functional divisions of the structures were thus identified as well as the existing additions and accessories

URBAN PLANNING

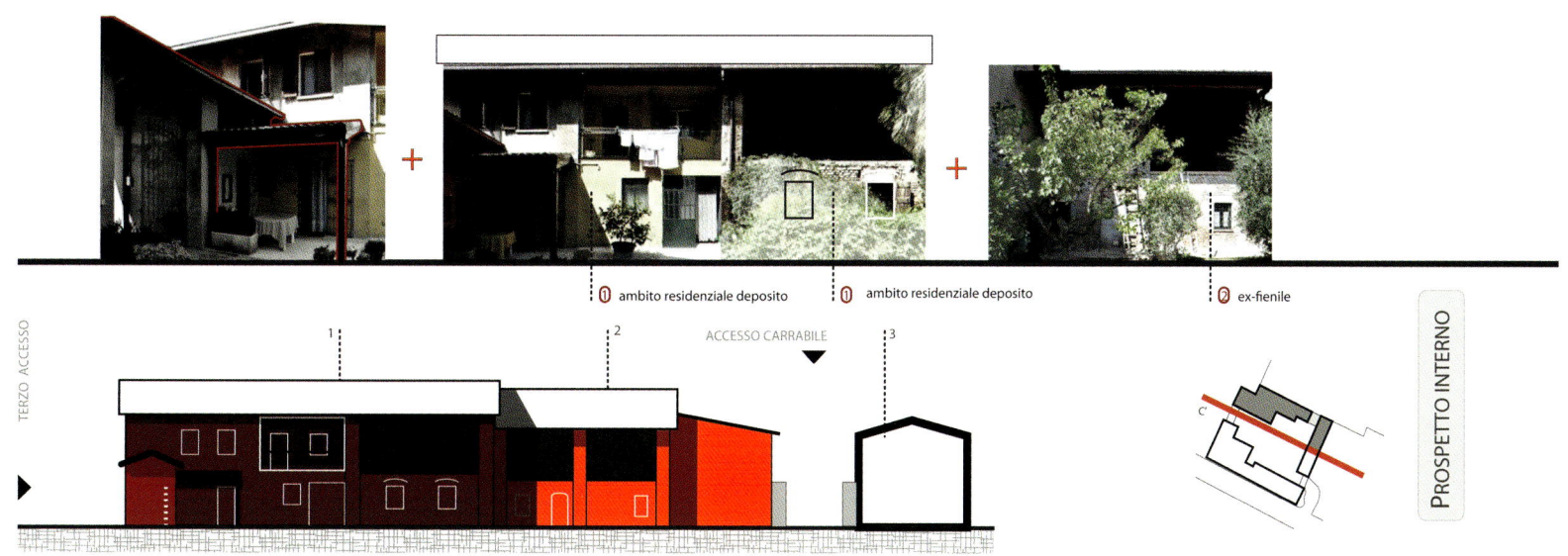

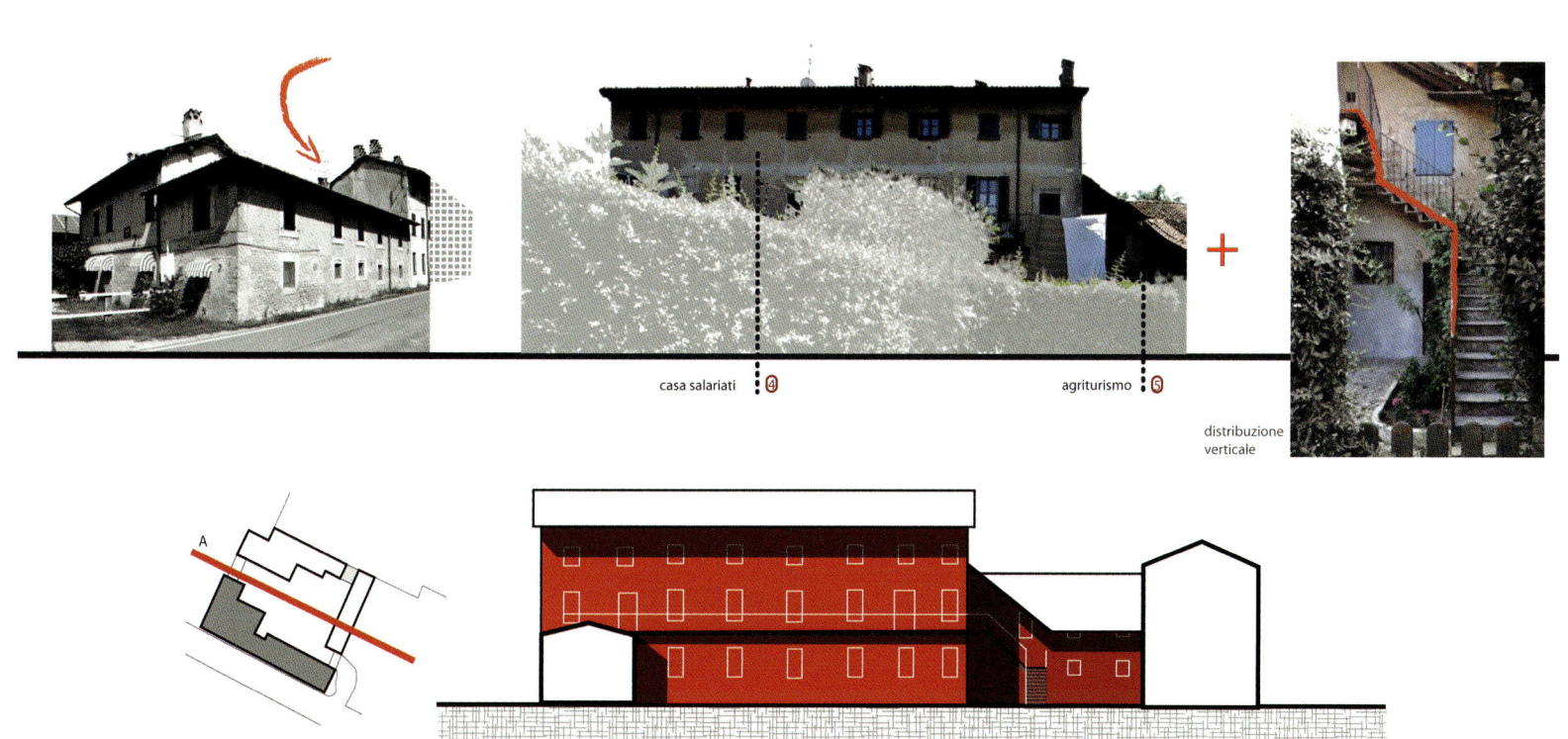

URBAN PLANNING

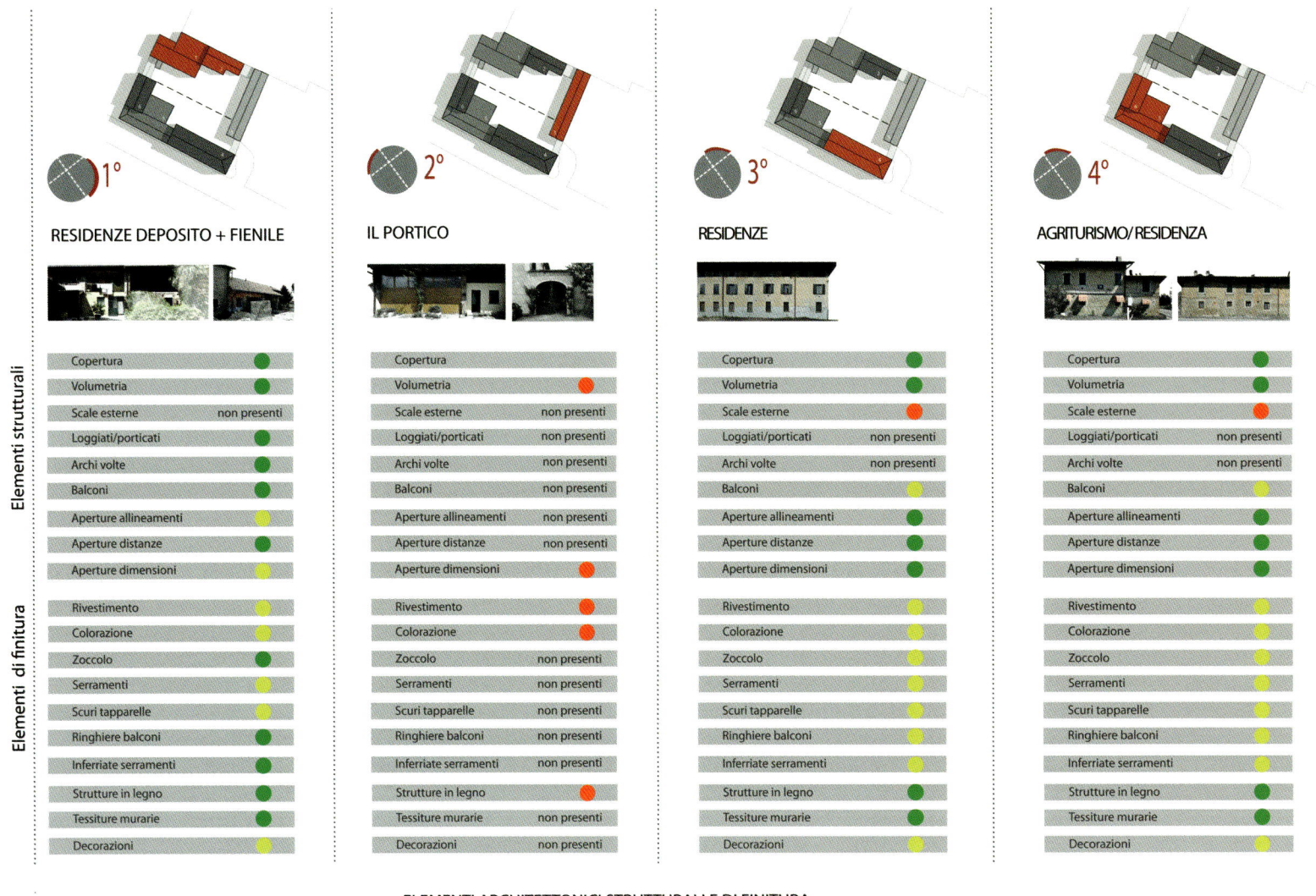

Qualitative appraisal of architectural elements.
The matrix summarizes a qualitative appraisal of the architectural elements of each farmhouse and establishes the level of coherence with respect to the historical rural context involved

URBAN PLANNING

SPAZI CON FUNZIONI DA MANTENERE

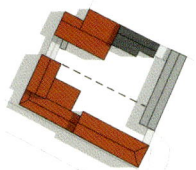

▮ da mantenere

Gli edifici evidenziati sono destinati principalmente ad uso residenziale
e presentano strutture compatibili con questa funzione

SPAZI CON FUNZIONI DA CONVERTIRE

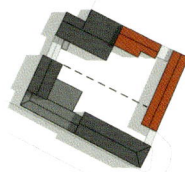

▮ possibili funzioni da convertire

Gli edifici evidenziati ed analizzati precedentemente appaiono
destinati a funzioni prevalentemente di deposito con spazi
in parte abbandonati convertibili in spazi residenziali
con alcune limitazioni e ristrutturazioni necessarie

SPAZI CON FUNZIONI DA INSERIRE

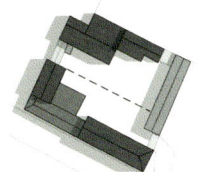

▮ possibili funzioni da inserire in nuove volumetrie

EL. ARCHITETTONICI DA SALVAGUARDARE

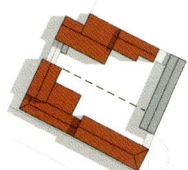

▮ spazi con elementi architettonici da mantenere

Gli edifici evidenziati presentano strutture con elementi
architettonici prevalentemente di pregio, e alcuni elementi
di finitura da recuperare

EL. ARCHITETTONICI DA TRASFORMARE e DA RECUPERARE

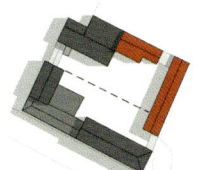

▮ spazi con el. arch. da recuperare e in parte da modificare

Gli edifici presentano elementi di pregio da mantenere e recuperare
(materiali di finitura)e , al tempo stesso, materiali e soluzioni
da trasformare poichè incoerenti (come da analisi)

  PILASTRI

SUPERFETTAZIONI/ divisioni DA DEMOLIRE

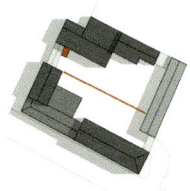

▮ possibile modifica

Gli edifici presentano scarsi/nulli elementi architettonici di pregio,
nonchè elementi estranei ed incoerenti con l'ambito

 SUPERFETTAZIONI

Meta-planning phase: preliminary criteria of operation. The information obtained in the fact-finding phase was used to develop the first guidelines for action on the farmhouses concerned, identifying in each case the elements to be preserved and enhanced, the spaces to be converted or refurbished, and the structures to be demolished

	1°	2°	3°	4°
Piano terra MQ (slp stima)	A_ 94 mq (senza portico) B_ 62 mq	83 mq	129 mq	A_ 180 mq B_ 105 mq (portico escluso) C_ 80 mq (portico escluso)
Piano terra funzioni	A_ Residenziale/ deposito R1 B_ fienile / deposito AC1 AC3	deposito AC1 AC3	deposito AC1 AC3	A_ residenziale/deposito R1 AC1 AC3 B_ ricettivo agriturismo residenza R1 RT2 C_ ricettivo agriturismo residenza R1 RT2
Piano primo MQ (slp stima)	A_ 94 mq B_ 45 mq	83 mq	non presente	A_ 180 mq B_ 105 mq (portico escluso) C_ 80 mq (portico escluso)
Piano primo funzioni	A_ Residenziale/ deposito R1 B_ fienile / deposito AC1 AC3	deposito AC1 AC3	non presente	A_ residenziale/deposito R1 B_ ricettivo agriturismo residenza R1 RT2 C_ ricettivo agriturismo residenza R1 RT2
Piano secondo MQ (slp stima)	non presente	non presente	non presente	non presente
Piano secondo funzioni	non presente	non presente	non presente	non presente
Totale MQ (slp stima) 1.337 mq	**312 mq circa**	**166 mq circa**	**129 mq circa**	**730 mq circa**
Da segnalare	La struttura ospita funzioni miste: residenze, depositi, locali servizi.		La struttura su un solo livello ha subito vari interventi di tamponamento incoerenti. E' necessario ricostruire l'unità del fronte.	La struttura ospita la funzione terziaria di agriturismo. La struttura al piano terra non ospita residenze, ma locali usati come magazzini (da recuperare)

	1°	2°	3°	4°
Piano terra MQ (slp stima)	A_ 94 mq (senza portico) B_ 62 mq	83 mq	129 mq	A_ 180 mq B_ 105 mq (portico escluso) C_ 80 mq (portico escluso)
Piano terra funzioni	A_ Residenziale/ deposito R1 B_ fienile / deposito AC1 AC3	deposito AC1 AC3	deposito AC1 AC3	A_ residenziale R1 B_ ricettivo agriturismo residenza R1 RT2 C_ ricettivo agriturismo residenza R1 RT2
Piano primo MQ (slp stima)	A_ 94 mq B_ 45 mq	83 mq	non presente	A_ 180 mq B_ 105 mq (portico escluso) C_ 80 mq (portico escluso)
Piano primo funzioni	A_ Residenziale/ deposito R1 B_ Residenziale R1	B_ Residenziale R1	non presente	A_ residenziale R1 B_ ricettivo agriturismo residenza R1 RT2 C_ ricettivo agriturismo residenza R1 RT2
Piano secondo MQ (slp stima)	non presente	non presente	non presente	non presente
Piano secondo funzioni	non presente	non presente	non presente	non presente
Totale MQ (slp stima) 1.337 mq	**312 mq circa**	**166 mq circa**	**129 mq circa**	**730 mq circa**
Da segnalare	Da Recuperare edificio A e conversione edificio B	Conversione funzionale del fienile B (slp su un solo livello)		Adeguamento a residenza del piano terreno (attualmente deposito)

Functional division: initial state. Functional division of the rural complex in its initial state

Criteria of functional and structural redefinition. The matrix identifies specific planning indications and pinpoints areas for renovation and functional conversion with respect to the present state

Opposite
Planning phase. Planning elements and functional reorganization of the rural complex

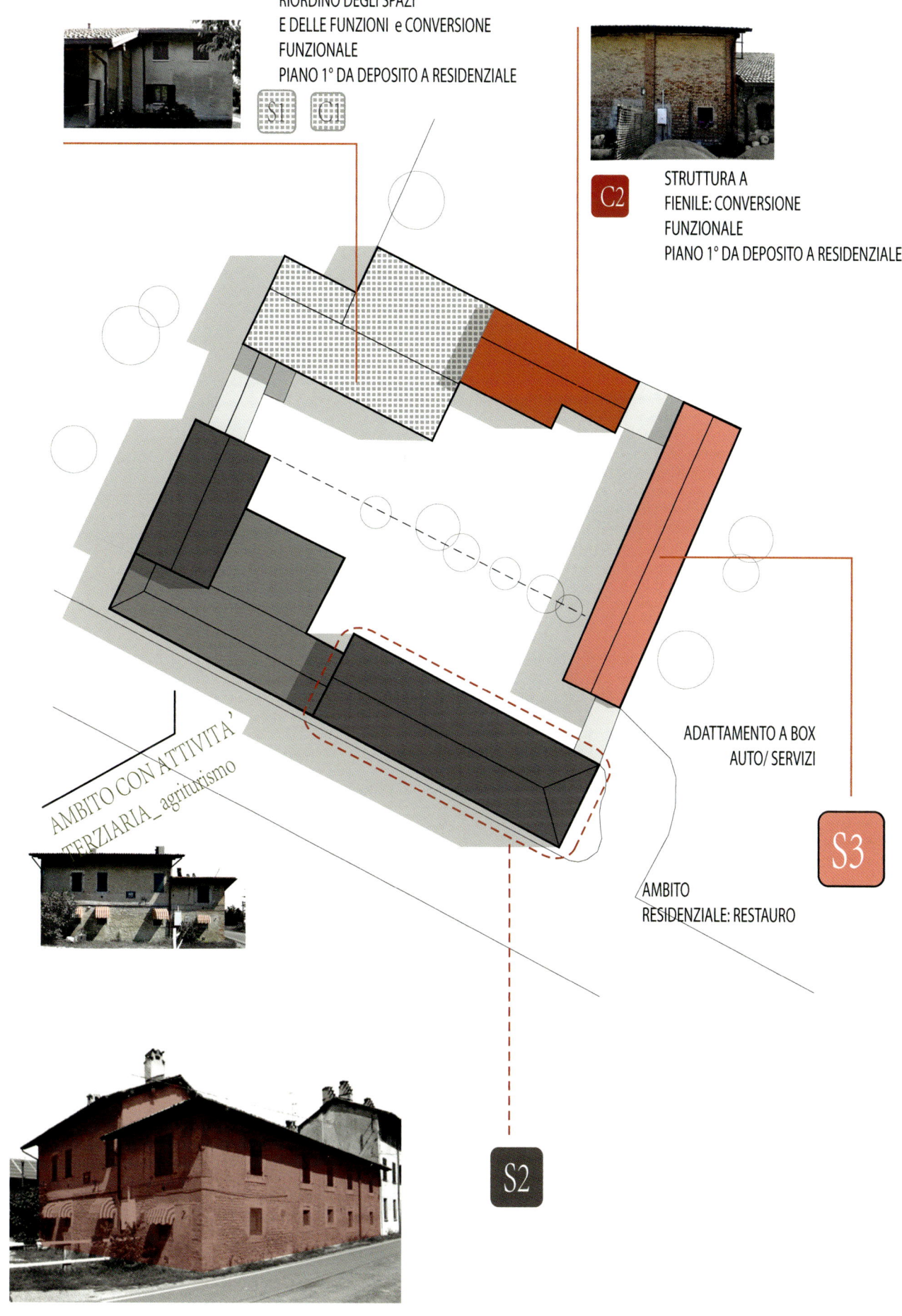

URBAN PLANNING

▶ TAMPONAMENTI ESTERNI_ MATERIALI

Survey of materials. Materials and finishes to orient the operations of functional renovation and refurbishment

TIPO_1 MURATURA IN LATERIZIO [M1]

(più comune) Disposizione per corsi orizzontali senza ordine nella posa delle teste/ dorso del mattone. Faccia a vista.

[M2] TIPO_2 MURATURA MISTA

Disposizione per corsi orizzontali senza ordine del laterizio, con integrazioni di pietre di piccola-media dimensione.

SOLUZIONE NON COERENTE

Rivestimento esterno in intonaco

▶ TAMPONAMENTI ESTERNI_ FINESTRE

Le aperture, realizzate in fase con il tamponamento sono solitamente di dimensioni ridotte (essendo rivolte verso l'esterno della cascina).
Non prevedono telai in pietra. Le inferiate sono in ferro battuto.

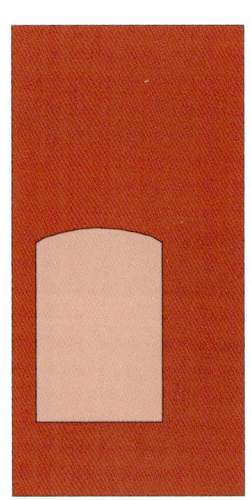

PER GLI INTERVENTI DI RISISTEMAZIONE DELLE APERTURE SUSSISTE L'OBBLIGO DI MANTENIMENTO DEL RAPPORTO TRA PIENI E VUOTI, E DI UTILIZZO DEI MATERIALI TRADIZIONALI.

Sound practices. Solutions advised and operations permitted for harmonious renovation of rural complexes

COPERTURA E FALDE

MANTO DI COPERTURA

INTERVENTI DI MODIFICA DELLA FALDA AMMESSI

22. Novara: adaptation and updating of the Provincial Territorial Plan (2011–12)

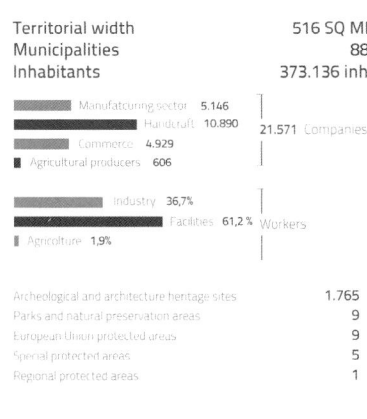

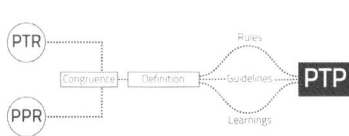

The definition of an adequate strategic framework on the territorial scale necessarily entails the creation of a cogent fact-finding component capable of capturing and representing the essential peculiarities of a territory. The drafting of the latter is in fact, and above all in the territorial planning of a vast area, a fundamental and indispensable step for the identification of planning themes with the strength and capacity to express an objective and a clear and unequivocal strategy for a territory of provincial scale.

Based on this principle, the updating of the fact-finding component of the Provincial Territorial Plan of the province of Novara involved a precise reading of the territory making it easy to understand and manage its peculiar characteristics. All the constituent elements were observed in detail, not only in physical terms but also from the social, economic and normative viewpoints. From the regional and interregional scale down to the provincial level, the various norms that discipline the management of territory were reconstructed together with the characteristics of the infrastructural system in all its components, defining their hierarchical order, the components of the environmental system, identifying in detail all the environmental constraints and assets that constitute the natural structure of the province, and the peculiarities of the socio-economic and settlement structure, all with a view to constructing a global and all-inclusive analytical and fact-finding framework of support in devising suitable strategies of territorial development.

Great strategic importance attaches to the upgrading of maps. The adaptation of the territorial plan is based on a strong and direct relationship with the municipalities in a territory where the implementation of provisions proves very difficult precisely due to the existence of various levels of rules and regulations. The instrument produced is thus designed as a map of action in close contact with the activity of ordinary municipal planning and of support for the coordination that only the large scale can exercise. The design of the tables thus assumes a strongly strategic character, capable in the completeness of the information found and presented of selecting themes and viable projects ready for use around which it is possible to build up agreement amongst the parties involved. Only in this way is the potential of the tool expressed and evident. At the very moment when the role of the province seems to be unclear, the instrument has been developed to give renewed strength to the components of design, order and management of phenomena that coordination can provide in a particular region like Piedmont, where the framework of planning and instrumentation dates from different periods and no longer corresponds to the present-day conformation of the territory. In addition, the strength and courage of the instrument as regards the coordination of planning and decision making for the territory are clearly evident.

Analysis of the Regional Landscape Plan (PPR).
The natural, environmental, historical and cultural components identified by the PPR are summarized in the knowledge base with respect to the prescriptive level assigned by its normative framework: guidelines, directives and prescriptions

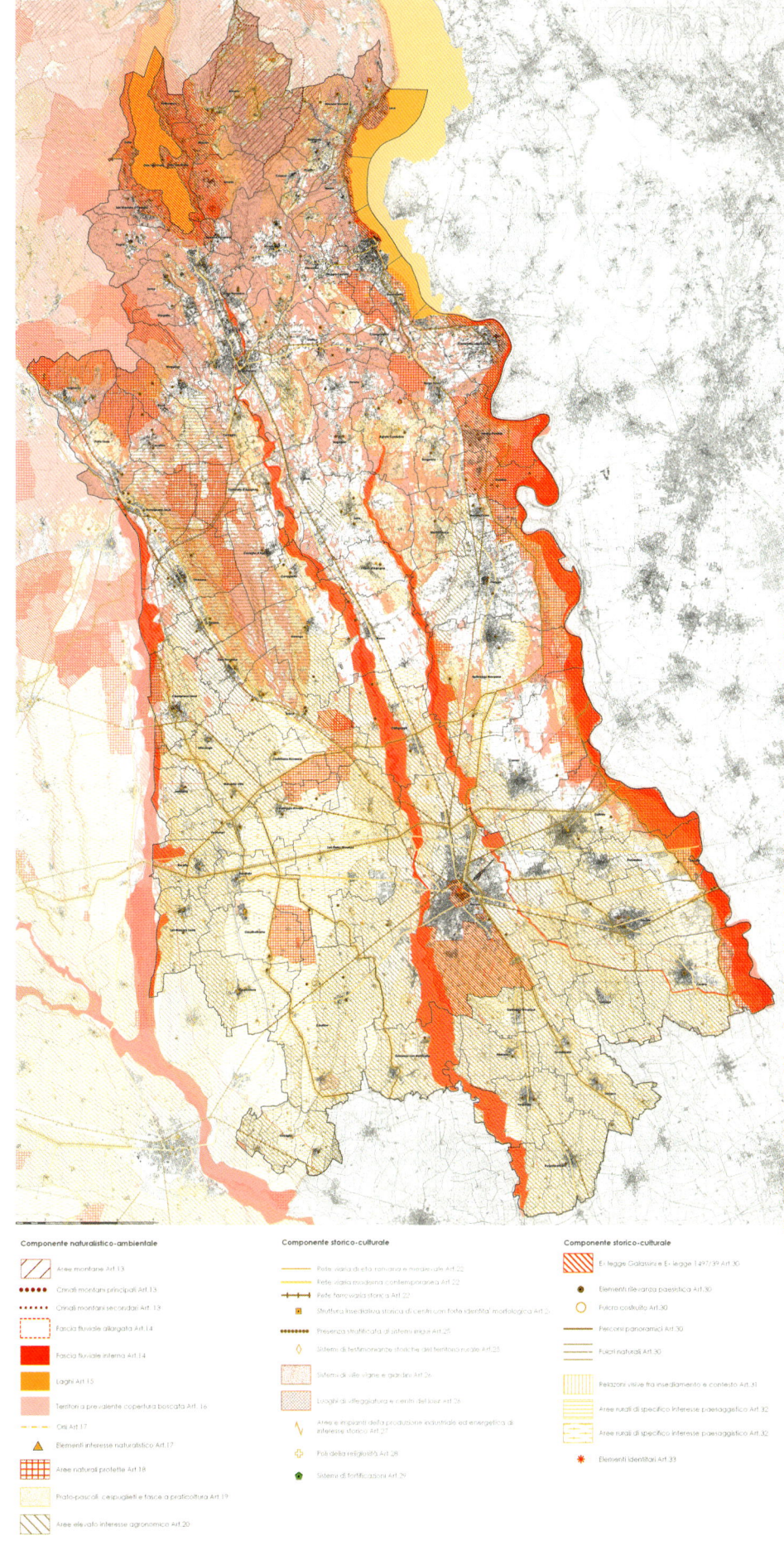

The infrastructural system. The knowledge base reconstructs the structure of the provincial road system and identifies its functional hierarchy with respect to the rules of highway code, taking into consideration the elements of the railway system and connections in the regional and interregional context

Analysis of the Regional Landscape Plan (PPR).
The natural, environmental, historical and cultural components identified by the PPR are summarized in the knowledge base with respect to the prescriptive level assigned by its normative framework: guidelines, directives and prescriptions

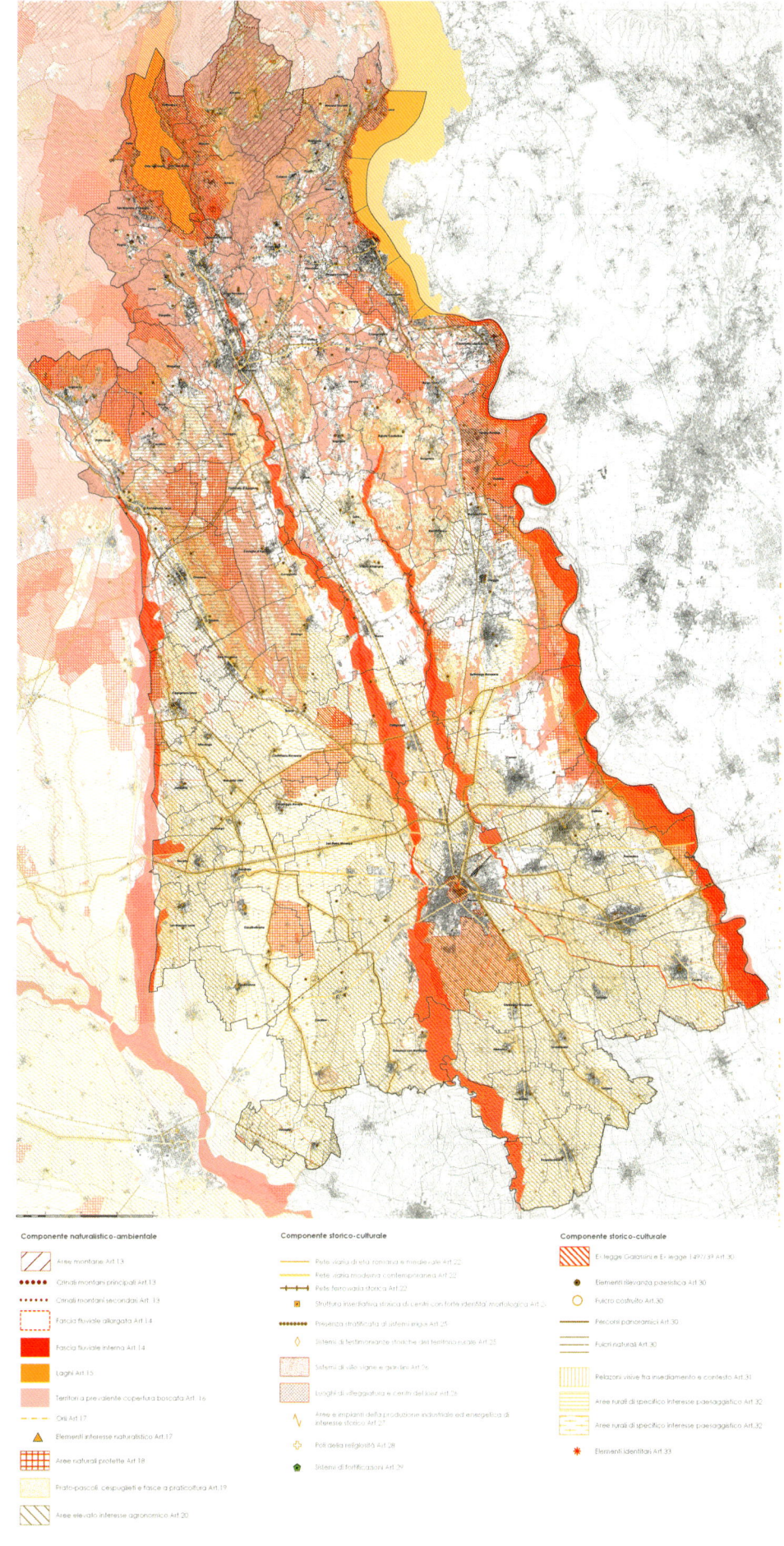

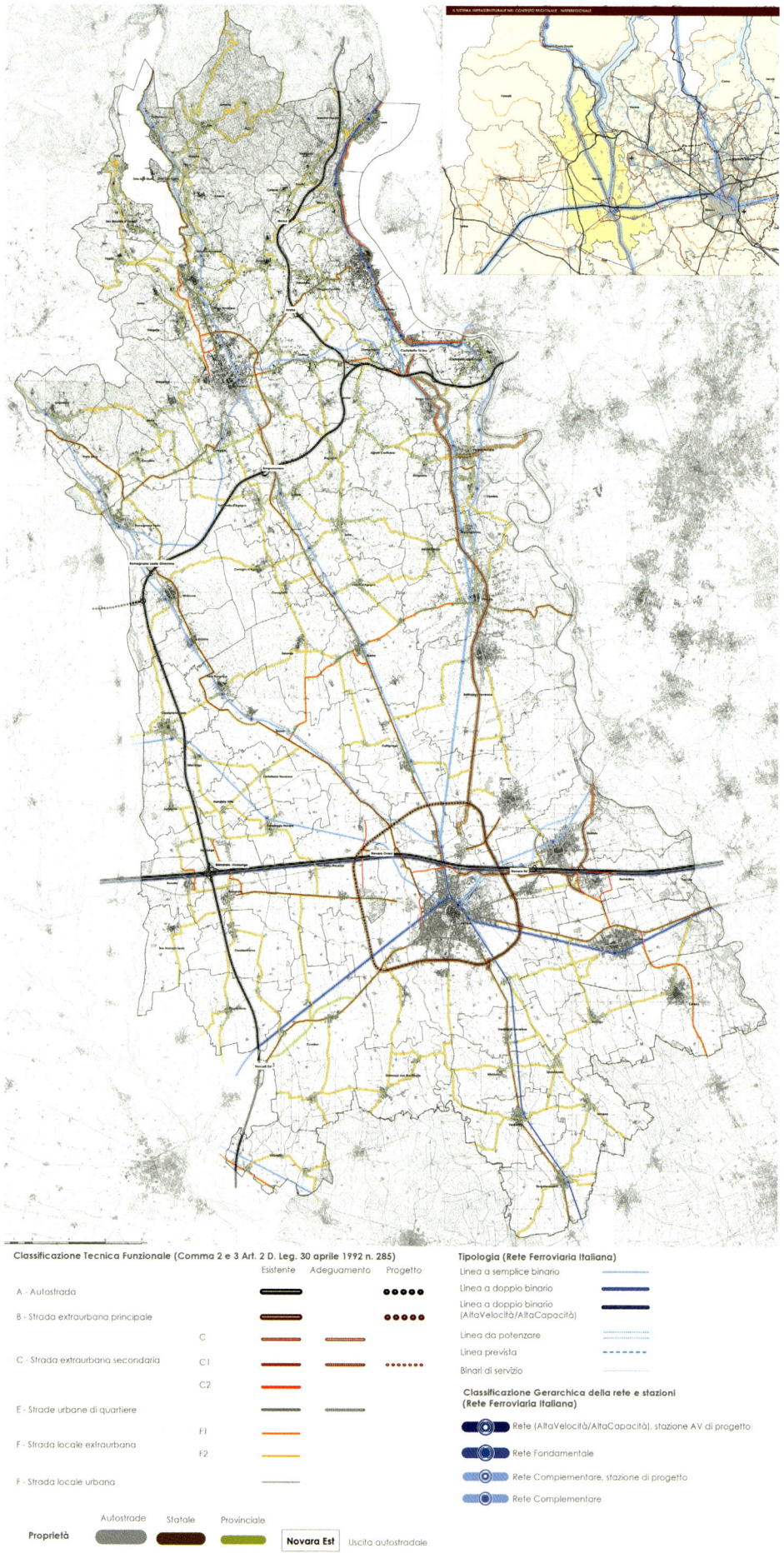

The infrastructural system. The knowledge base reconstructs the structure of the provincial road system and identifies its functional hierarchy with respect to the rules of highway code, taking into consideration the elements of the railway system and connections in the regional and interregional context

Environmental system of the Regional Landscape Plan (PPR). The investigation identifies the key structural elements of the regional environmental system, pinpointing the project areas and the planned zones of environmental upgrading as well as the existing large areas of environmental support

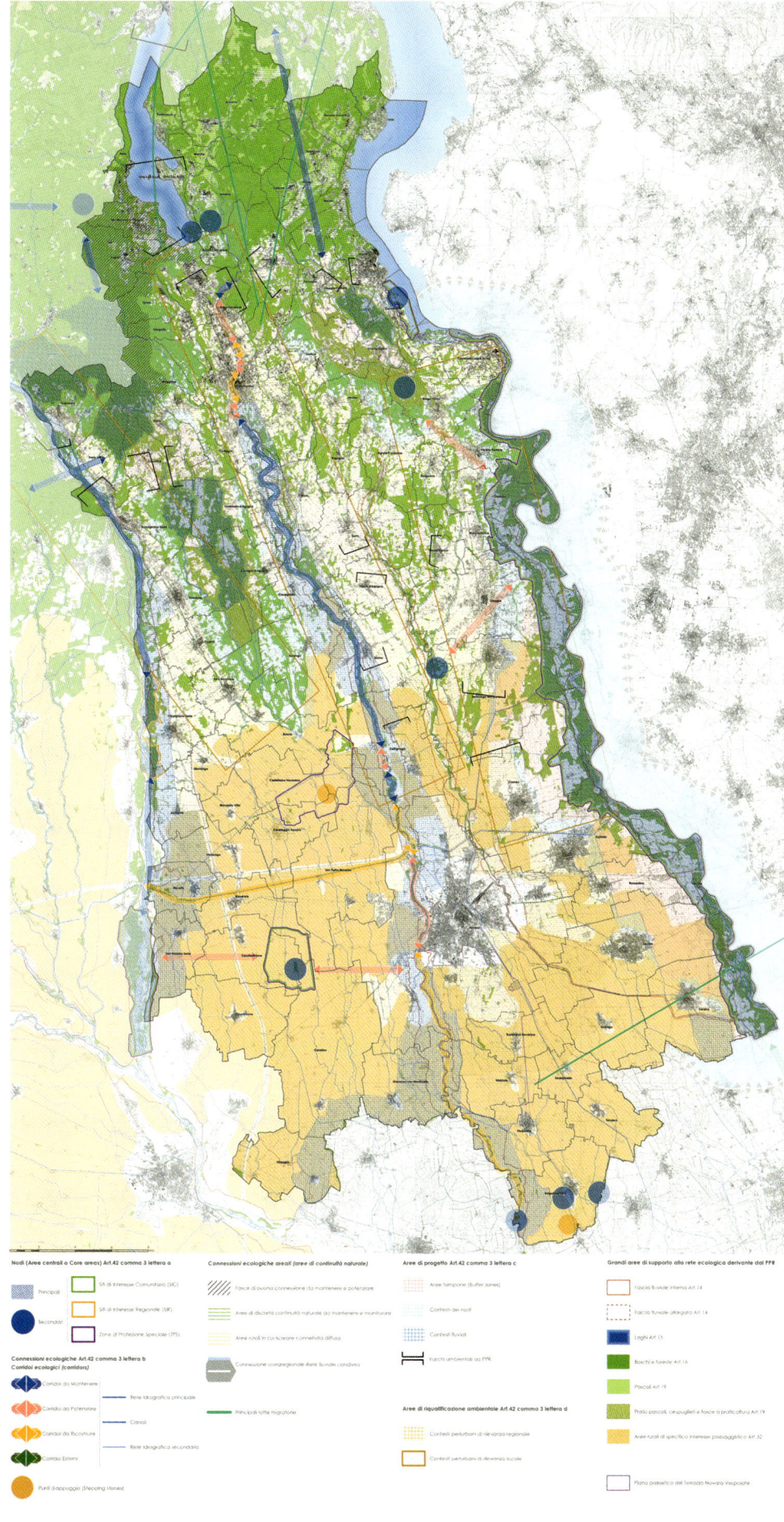

URBAN PLANNING

23. Basiglio (Milan): Building Regulations (2013)

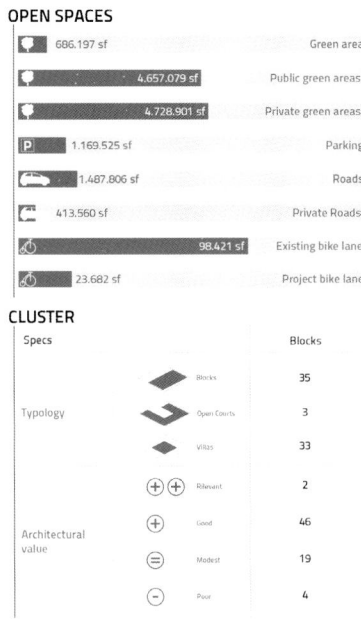

Subsequent to approval of the Territorial Management Plan, the municipal administration of Basiglio decided to have new building regulations drawn up.
These are divided into three sections, the first devoted to the set of subjects taking part in building initiatives, the second to the key administrative processes and procedures, and the third to identifying the primary technical and aesthetic parameters that govern actual building.
A large part of the building regulations is also devoted to the description and identification of specific actions as regards improving the energy efficiency of the existing buildings. This is essential in order to give concrete effect to the idea of a sustainable town promoted by the municipal administration and developed by the regulations through prescriptive norms, advice and good practices capable of governing and guiding the operations of new building as well as the renovation and maintenance of existing edifices.
The question of energy efficiency is addressed on the basis of specific study of the numerous international and national experiments with sustainable districts and sustainability, thus providing concrete examples that can serve as a stimulus for sound planning. The regulations are not, however, oriented exclusively towards the rules of sustainable construction. They also define the working of the energy fund mechanism provided for by the Territorial Management Plan, with separate rewards for operative procedures, the use of environmentally compatible materials, improvements on the minimum qualitative values identified and the integration of different solutions. Finally, they establish criteria for the transformation and planning of public and private space and the ratio of built-up areas to open space. Basiglio, and the Milano 3 district in particular, by virtue of its morphology, composition of green areas, and unified, recognizable buildings, require operations that respect their present-day peculiarities so as to avoid losing the features that characterize them and make them recognizable.

Intero edifici, unità immobiliari indipendenti	
Finanziamento intervento singolo 10%	**Incidenza**
Installazione per la diffusione della luce naturale	+1
Installazione schermature contro il soleggiamento	+1
Riduzione del consumo di acqua potabile	+1
Installazione sistemi di regolazione autonoma del riscaldamento	+1
Installazione dispositivi per la contabilizzazione energetica	+1
Azioni per efficientamento degli impianti elettrici luminosi	+1
Azioni per la riduzione dell'inquinamento elettromagnetico	+1
Finanziamento intervento singolo 20%	**Incidenza**
Interventi per l'isolamento delle coperture	+3
Installazione sistemi solari passivi	+3
Correzione dei ponti termici	+3
Installazione dispositivi ventilazione meccanica controllata	+3
Recupero delle acque piovane	+3
Installazione impianti per la produzione di energia elettrica rinnovabile	+3
Installazione impianti termici ad alto rendimento	+3
Installazione impianti termici autonomi con impianti centralizzati	+3
Installazione impianti a bassa temperatura	+3
Finanziamento intervento singolo 45%	**Incidenza**
Interventi per l'isolamento di strutture verticali opache	+5
Interventi per la realizzazione dei tetti verdi	+5
Interventi per la realizzazione di pareti verdi	+5
Sostituzione infissi e serramenti	+5
Recupero acque reflue domestiche	+5
Azione per la riduzione dell'inquinamento da radon	+5
Istallazione impianto solare termico	+5
Installazione impianti per la produzione di calore rinnovabile	+5
Utilizzo materiale ecocompatibile	**incidenza**
+ 10% sul costo del prodotto utilizzato	+0,5 Per ogni materiale max 3 materiali
Superamento dei valori minimi richiesti	**incidenza**
+ 10% del costo del singolo intervento	+1 Per ogni intervento
Integrazione	**TOT incidenza**
+ 2% sul totale degli interventi	8 - 9
+ 5% sul totale degli interventi	10 - 12
+ 10% sul totale degli interventi	≥ 13

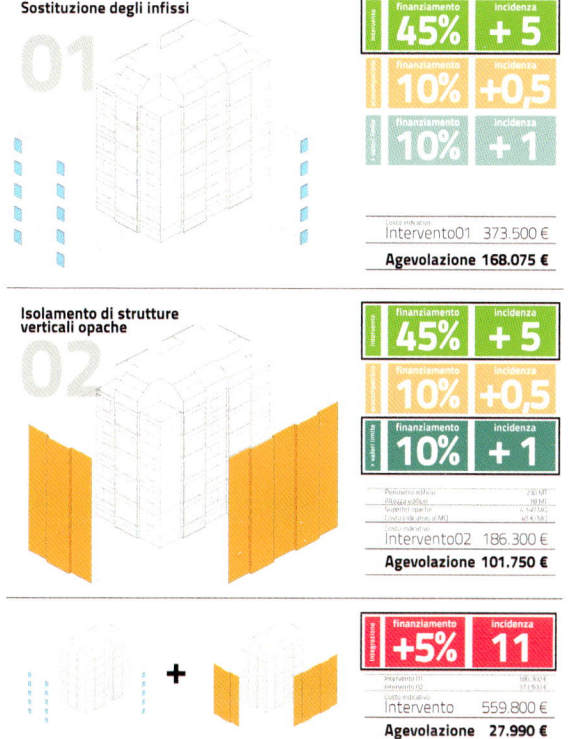

Incentive mechanisms. The schema shows the modalities of allocation of the Energy Fund introduced by the Territorial Management Plan (PGT) and the mechanism of access to incentives on the basis of the envisaged modes of operation, use of environmentally compatible materials and meeting the minimum requirements set in terms of the energy efficiency of the buildings

24. Verano Brianza (Monza and Brianza): project for area AT22
(under way since 2013)

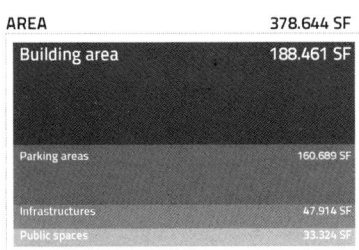

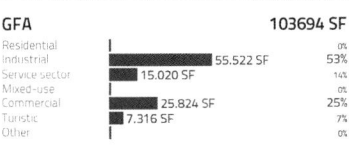

The project for area AT22 regards the definition of the rules for a complicated zone included in the Territorial Management Plan of Verano Brianza.

This is an area of production included in the plan for the purpose of redeveloping a part of the territory occupied over the years by small businesses and buildings through a process typical of the region, thus causing severe fragmentation of the settlement system. The division into countless small plots of land and the density of the production system have had major repercussions on circulation, which is crippled by the presence of many access points and a confused, non-hierarchical and disorganized road system.

The presence of some vacant lots of building land prompted the Territorial Management Plan to redefine the area as a whole and attempt an approach that has always proved complex in Italian urban planning, namely the transfer of building rights from one area to another so as to concentrate construction in some places and free others. This transfer procedure makes it possible to define the places where buildings must be erected, thus concentrating the areas for the parking spaces and facilities required by an industrial area and those for the concentration of green spaces at the points best served by the road system. Above all, it makes it possible to draw up a single set of rules for transformation and guide the individual operations within a single project in step with the progress of construction. The difficulty of the area and the particular nature of an instrument of this kind involved concrete experimentation with the use of an urban-planning design to develop the functioning of the rules in depth.

Design simulations were used to examine the modes of implementation for the area, monitoring the behaviour of the individual parties concerned and envisioning the results of the design as a whole on the basis of their greater or lesser capacity to operate in terms of building concentrations. The design thus governs implementation, monitoring the schedules and also deciding which works and which burdens for the municipality are to be guaranteed as well as their quantity and the plans and procedures to be adopted.

Implementation is thus related to the ability to the parties concerned to grasp the importance to acting in accordance with a coordinated design of public character but strongly linked to the real and effective possibilities of private concerns to put its content into effect, overcoming the traditional separation of provisions and actual implementation by anticipating at the time of formulating provisions all the typical problems and difficulties as regards their implementation.

The overall design born out of this has no particular compositional merits. The nature of the area, the complexity of the site and the very ordinary character of the context permit nothing more than an orderly design susceptible of correct implementation and above all capable of guiding the parties involved over time and persuading them to comply with urban-planning and morphological rules that are new for the context.

Planivolumetric plan. The volumes generated by the individual lots into which the project area is divided are organized and rationalized by means of a single master plan designed to coordinate the activities of the different parties involved and to minimize the consumption of land. The project envisages the concentration of volumes in buildings aligned with one another and with the existing and planned frontage on the street and a high environmental standard through the planning of large green areas serving also to attenuate the visual impact of the new buildings. Running alongside the planted areas are new cycle tracks and pedestrian paths designed to extend the existing system of slow mobility but also to link up with the circuit of cycle tracks envisaged at the supra-municipal level. At the same time, the presence of passageways for motor vehicles ensures an adequate level of infrastructure, which is necessary in order to connect the new activities with their context of reference. Unlike the circuit of slow mobility, the system of road transport penetrates the built-up fabric, thus avoiding the positioning of parking places on the perimetric road system

URBAN PLANNING

The project is seeking to create a field of production and trade, without compromising the quality and efficiency of public spaces often ignored in the design of similar areas. The two large car parks, the south one at service of the shopping complex, the second one, central, that serves all of the production buildings, avoid the design of on-street parking, so as not to hinder traffic, and leave space for the mitigation and green spaces pedestrian, often ignored

Functions and operations. The building volumes inside the area of transformation are predominantly connected with production (in purple), located on the northern perimeter of project area and served by the planned link road. A shopping and hotel segment is envisaged on the Via Comasina in a more attractive location as regards visibility and accessibility. The production plants are to be served by three public parking spaces screened by trees and located inside the built-up fabric, never directly on the road

Opposite
Planning indications. The focus in terms of architectural composition is on the integration of built-up and unbuilt areas through the planning of volumes obeying a precise compositional order as regards the alignment of façades and the imposition of a general criterion of design. This should serve to ensure recognizability as a unified operation rather than a sum of different parts in accordance with the drive for general coordination that accompanied its conception. Priority is given in particular to a morphological approach that harnesses layouts and positions deduced from the anthropic context of reference as generating lines for the structural arrangement planned

Architectural conception. The construction of homogeneous volumes governed by precise compositional criteria is envisaged also from the architectural standpoint. Even though the expressive possibilities are limited by the functional vocation envisaged, an attempt is made to regulate the vocabulary through a simple but rigorous formal repertoire. The composition of façades is organized in horizontal sections with a base differentiated by colour and material from the main part of the building, where the primary openings are made for access and the loading and unloading of goods, and the upper section, where the window frames will be as uniform as possible in materials and colour. With a view to meeting the requirement set in the dossier on the planned area, the buildings will also need to meet the standards for the upper level of energy class B, a prerequisite for development of the planned SLP

Road system and compositional rules. The road system and compositional aspects are conceived so as to reduce the impact of the new segment on the surroundings while at the same time fostering connection of the built-up fabric with its territorial and anthropic context of reference.
For this reason it is planned to build a link road inside the site to serve all of the production plants internally. The street sections are developed so as to ensure alignment of the façades also along the new main road, as emphasized by the line of the canopies of the buildings located along it. The hierarchy of the elements planned is regulated by criteria of scale and requirements imposed on the parties responsible for execution so as to ensure compliance with the criteria of homogeneity and uniformity in force throughout the area

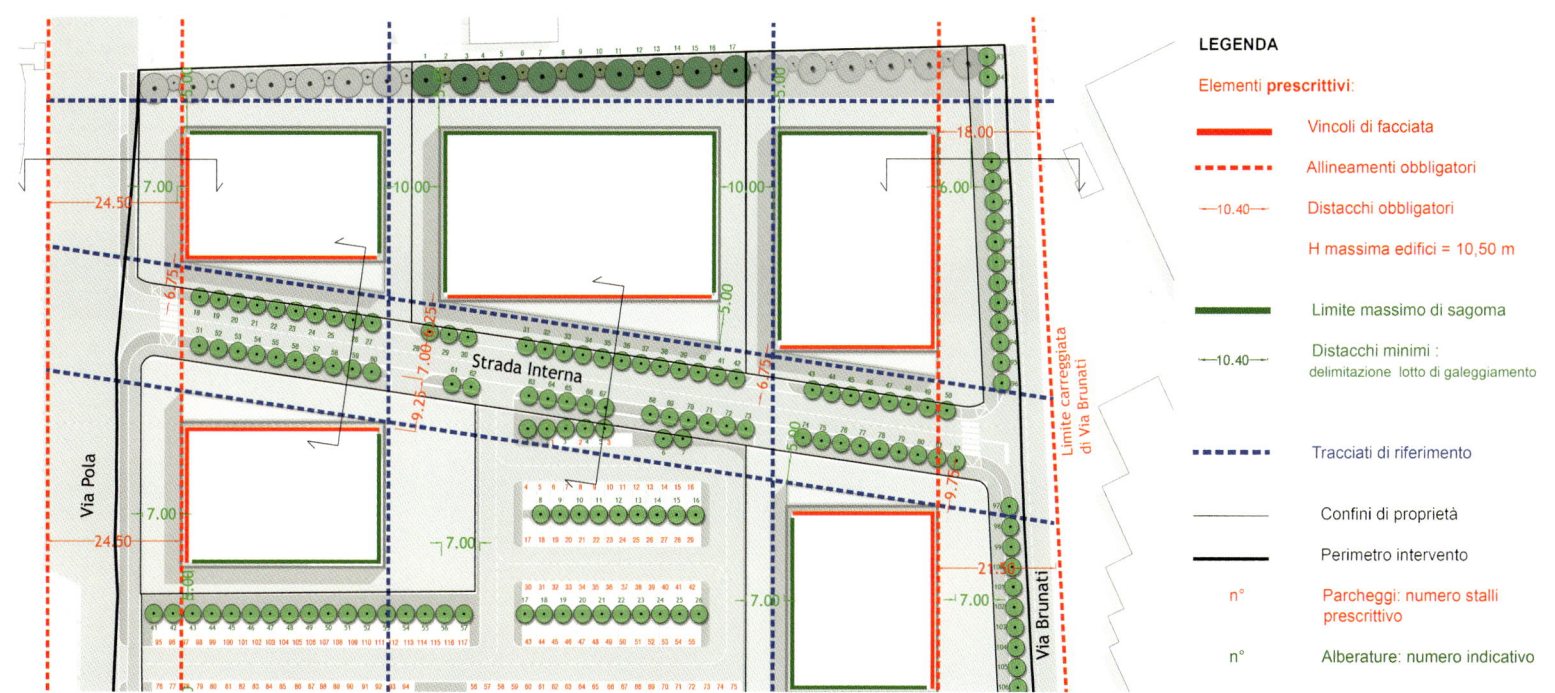

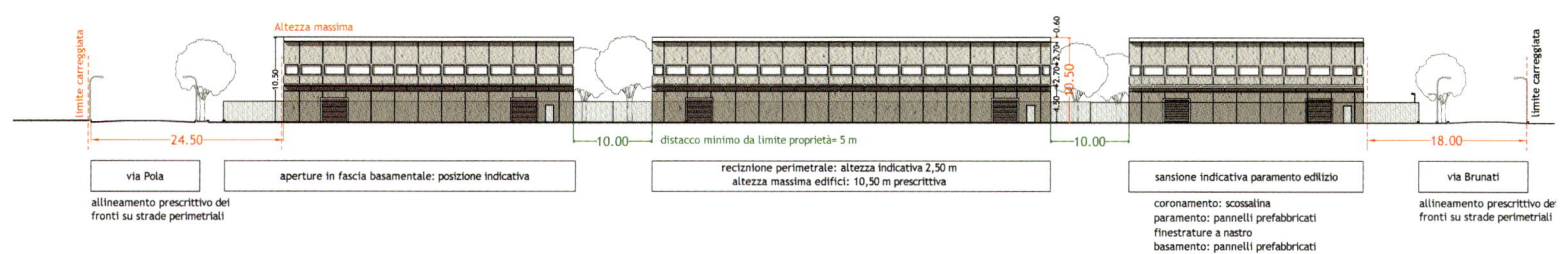

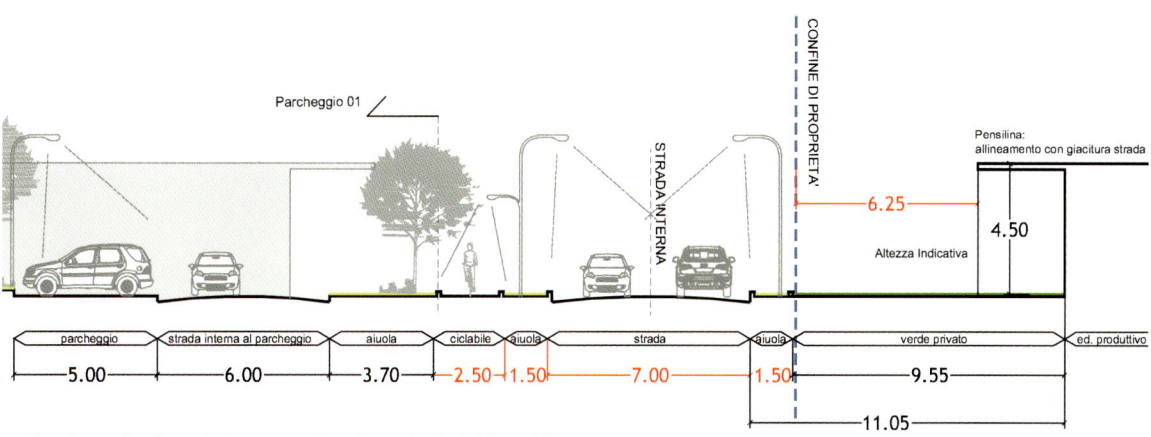

Sezione 3 - Strada Interna, Parcheggio Pubblico 01

2. ARCHITECTURE

1. Carrara: pedestrian access to the beach (2005–06)
2. Cornaredo: shopping mall (2007)
3. Trezzo sull'Adda (Milan): Bureau of Productive Activities procedure (SUAP) and Integrated Action Plan (PII) for the Tollgate and Furnace areas (2007–10)
4. Lainate (Milan): Integrated Action Plan (PII) for a new centre on the A8 (2008)
5. Rozzano (Milan): Integrated Action Plan (PII) for the multifunctional area of Via Manzoni (under way since 2008)
6. Roncello (Monza and Brianza): Integrated Action Plan (PII) for the new town centre (2009–12)
7. Verano Brianza (Monza and Brianza): Integrated Action Plans (PII) for the Core, Montegrappa and Borgonovo areas (2010)
8. Pozzo d'Adda (Milan): enlargement and restructuring of an industrial building (2010)
9. Inzago (Milan): public plan for cooperative residential buildings (2010–11)
10. Rozzano (Milan): building for commerce and services (under way since 2010)
11. Cassano d'Adda (Milan): projects and plans for redevelopment of the area of the disused Linificio Canapificio Nazionale factory (under way since 2010)
12. Peschiera Borromeo (Milan): plan for redevelopment of the Cascina Deserta (under way since 2010)
13. Arcene (Bergamo): master plan for environmental restoration and residential development of a quarry (2011)
14. Cassina de' Pecchi (Milan): feasibility study for redevelopment of the Cascina Bindellera (2011)
15. Cassina de' Pecchi (Milan): feasibility study for a new sports centre (2011)
16. Missaglia (Lecco): residential Integrated Action Plan (under way since 2011)
17. Missaglia (Lecco): residential buildings on the area of the Integrated Action Plan (under way since 2011)
18. Essaouira (Morocco): preliminary project for villas on sea (2012)
19. Kiev (Ukraine), metropolitan area: feasibility study for public housing projects (2012)
20. Minsk (Byelorussia), metropolitan area: preliminary project for a shopping mall (2012)

ARCHITECTURE

1. Carrara: pedestrian access to the beach (2005–06)

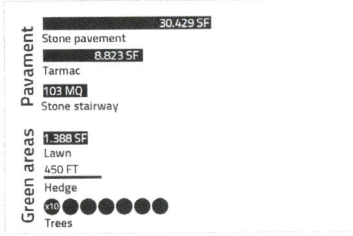

The project for access to the beach at Carrara pursued two aims, not only a new design for the pedestrian route together with the necessary urban furnishings but also and above all the creation of a tool capable of resolving the chaos generated over the years by the combined presence of the harbour, inner harbour activities and commercial structures connected with the beach. A situation typical of the condition of many Italian shorelines, proving beyond the capacity of planning and everyday management to ensure the orderly organization of public areas, access through the eastern harbour gateway had become indispensable to the safety of a pedestrian walkway in open conflict with the harbour and inner harbour activities. The project was therefore conceived as a strategic master plan in order both to develop the overall design and above all to create a tool for dialogue with the many parties involved, from the Harbour Authority to the owners of the commercial enterprises along the pathway, as they all had to be asked to sacrifice a small portion of their respective space and redefine their frontage or modify its appearance aesthetically. This was by no means easy for such a consolidated context pervaded by a very low sense of quality. The master plan strategically stimulated participation in the project of various parties, working on the design and the proposals for urban furnishing. In particular, it displayed the ability to employ a project apparently restricted to urban furnishing in more territorial terms, albeit on the local scale, creating new connections also with nearby pathways, designing new squares and offering new viewpoints on the seafront. In addition, the master plan was used to handle relations between the various bodies involved – the Harbour Authority, as primary owner of the areas crossed by the walkway; the Italian Navy, as owner of some structures there; and town council of Carrara – in a particular condition midway between municipal instruments of urban planning, special instruments like the harbour plan, and local instruments of implementation regarding transformations then under way.

The end result is evidently marked by the different purposes for which it was conceived. It was thus decided to forgo the use of materials or urban furnishings of any particular quality and rely on the overall urban quality control of the operation in the knowledge that this opening made it possible not only to ensure the safety of a dangerous crossing for the many users of the beach but also to develop, through use of the master plan, cooperation between different bodies and tools of planning.

Setting. The project area is located in a non-homogeneous context characterized by the presence of the harbour and associated service activities as well as the coastal landscape

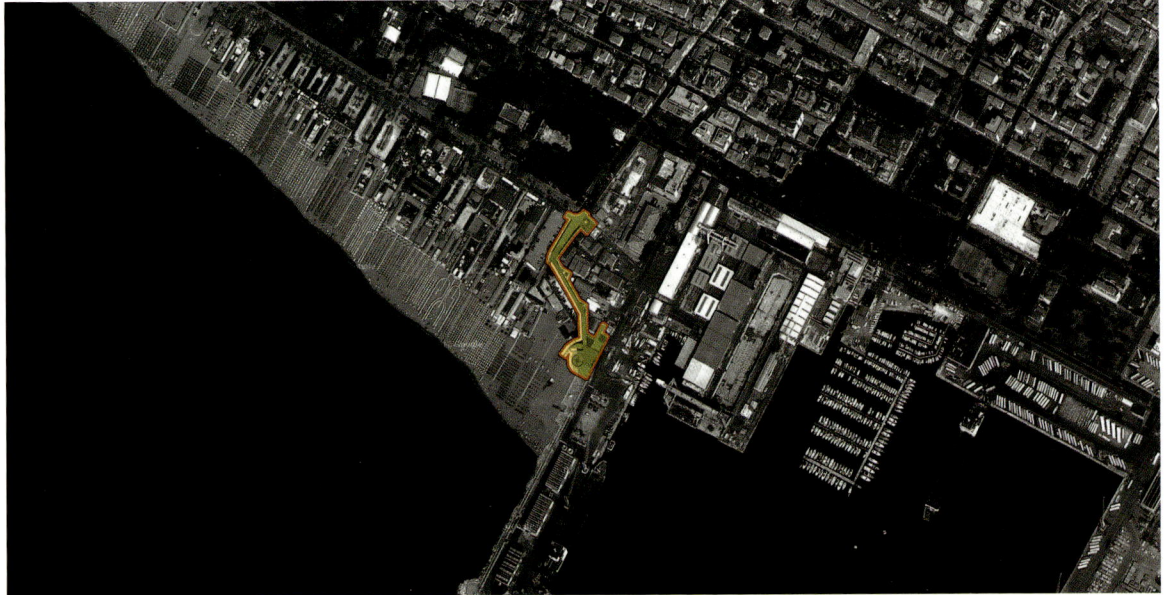

Project plan. The pedestrian pathway develops around three linear layouts on an irregular design. There is a stopping area at the end of each linear stretch

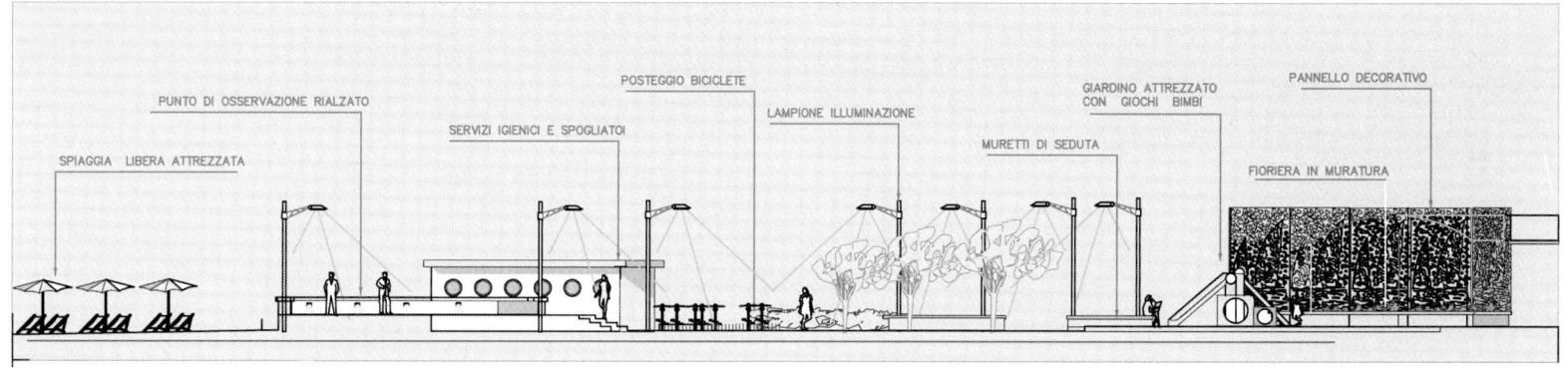

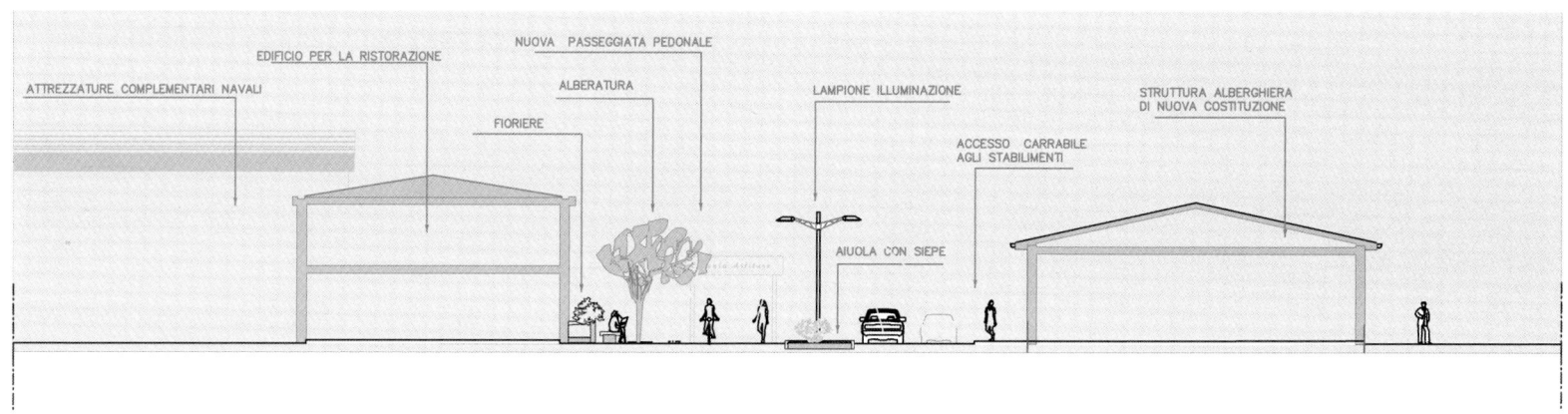

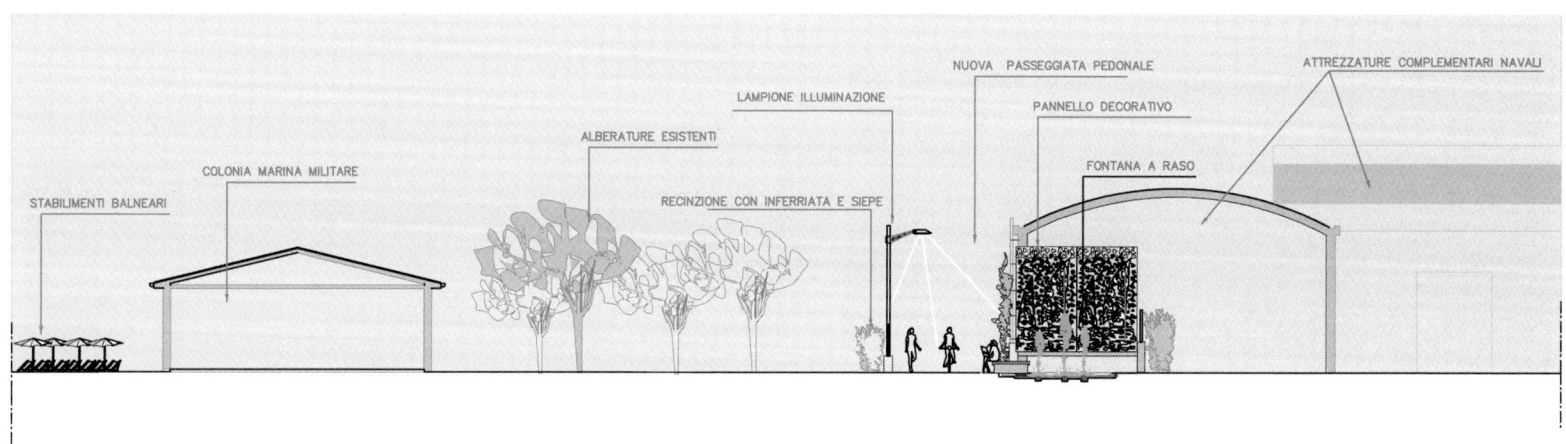

Views. The absence of high-quality materials does not impair the urban quality of the space planned

ARCHITECTURE

2. Cornaredo (Milan): shopping mall (2007)

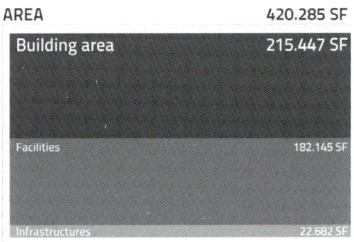

PUBLIC REVENUES 1.662.276 €

Due to the location of the new shopping mall of Cornaredo directly on a provincial highway, the plan for the area was used to coordinate provisions at both municipal and provincial level. The instrument leading to construction designed the greens areas, the new road system and the supplementary works, such as the new nursery school envisaged as a qualitative standard.
The shopping mall is a compact rectangular block of 400 x 262 ft with façades 32 ft in height. It was decided to locate it at the back of the site, allowing for the creation of a green buffer strip of about 64 ft along Via Milano (SS 11) and a tree-lined free space for parking paved with Erbablock.
A deep ring of planted green space all the way around the perimeter of the site creates a natural environmental barrier that connects with the adjacent sites and existing buildings as well as those planned for construction.

The ground floor presents a gallery with overhead lighting, with a hypermarket and twelve shops opening off it, for a total length of 290 ft. Great importance was attached to natural lighting, with skylights installed in the gallery and the stores, as conducive to human well-being and significant savings on energy.
The architectural vocabulary adopted for the interior and exterior of the building is characterized by innovation and tradition: innovation with the use of modern materials and technologies such as ventilated façades, insulated windows, the point-fixed glass system and aluminium cladding; tradition with the use of facing slabs of marble, a natural material with historical connotations used in two colours, yellow ochre and red earth, which combine with the expanses of glass and metal to create an innovative chromatic equilibrium. Vertical panels with a finish of crushed

marble similar in colour to the stone facing are used for the less significant parts at the back of the building.
The gallery is paved inside with marble and decorated with geometric patterns using the Botticino, Verona Red and Alpine Green types of marble.
The high glass wall of the gallery, facing south onto the road, is protected by a portico that regulates the incidence of sunlight during the day. In the evening during winter it is perceived as a glowing transparent window and acts, together with the entrance towers, as a visible sign on the threshold of the town of Cornaredo.

Setting. The project looks directly onto the provincial highway that separates the residential areas to the north from the industrial zone to the south

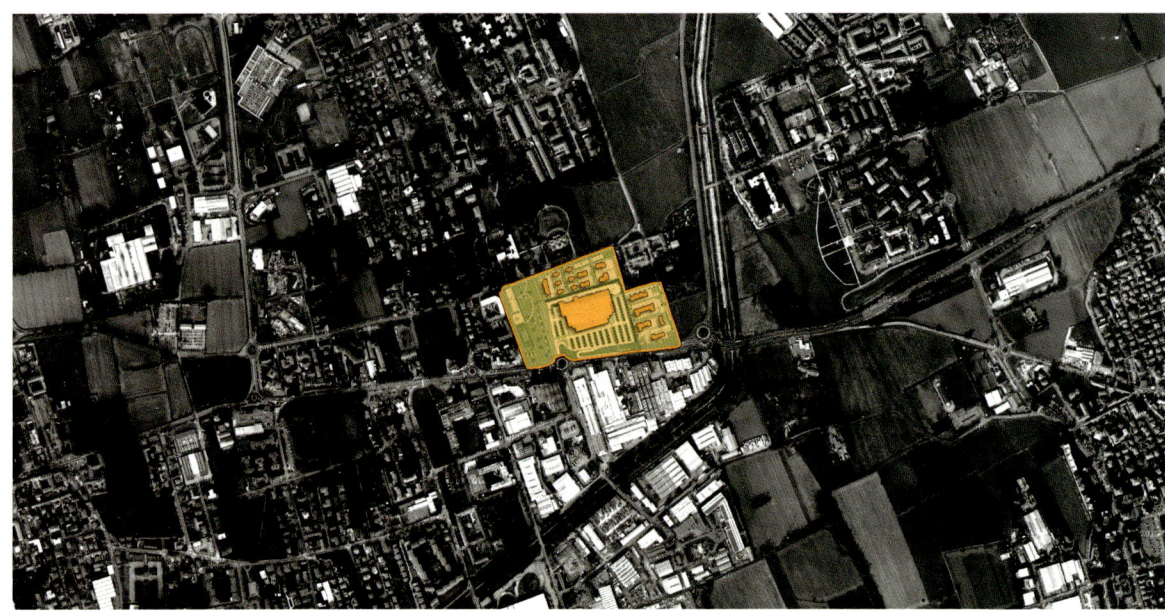

External spaces and shopping mall. The quality of a project also depends on the careful planning of external spaces. In this case, the need for a large parking area for the shopping mall is combined with an effort to minimize impact and inject urban quality. The choice of materials for the outer shell endows a building of considerable size with elegance and reduces the risk of anonymity

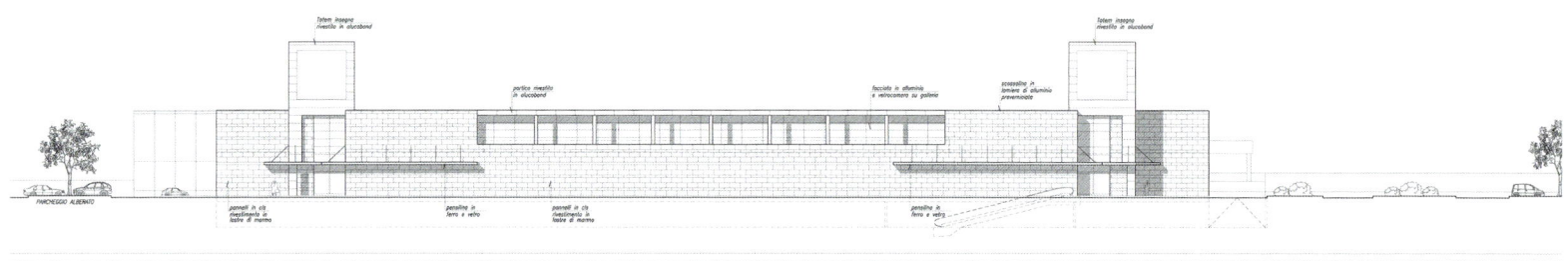

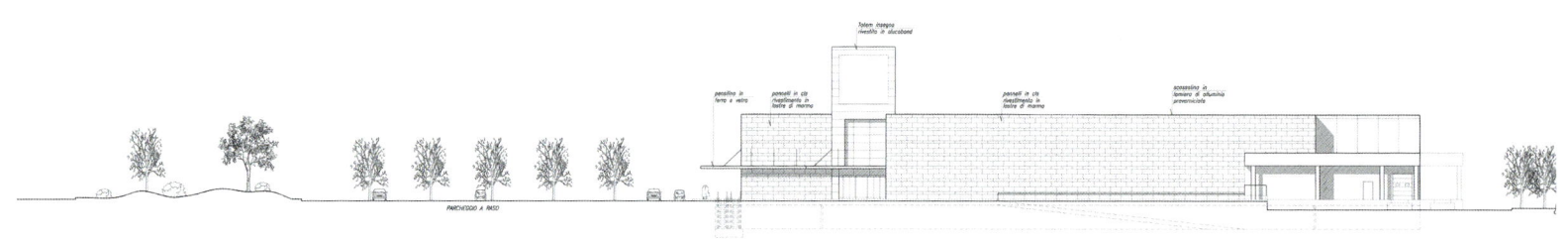

Elevation on the road. Developed as a long wall parallel to the road with a tower at either end. The gallery faces south and receives natural light through large windows in the centre of the main section

Exterior of glazed area

Opposite
Interior. Commercial gallery

ARCHITECTURE

3. Trezzo sull'Adda (Milan): Bureau of Productive Activities procedure (SUAP) and Integrated Action Plan (PII) for the Tollgate and Furnace areas (2007–10)

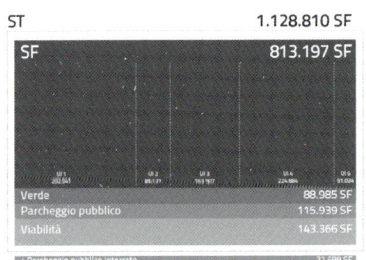

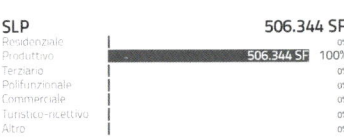

The aim of the project for Trezzo sull'Adda was to provide a centre and space for numerous companies interested in establishing themselves on the municipal territory so as to take advantage of its particular location, not least in the wake of the enlargement and improvement of the motorway. Recourse to the tool of a bureau of productive activities was required in order to coordinate the numerous parties involved and define the presence on a broader territory of a major opportunity for economic development and employment in a particular context where a considerable environmental heritage has survived the pressure of past and recent urbanization. Recourse to a strategic instrument capable of establishing direct relations with all the actors involved was also indispensable in order to make the transformation compatible with the Territorial Management Plan then being drawn up. By means of a mechanism of visualization and anticipation through the use of master plans, the two projects were thus constructed and combined – both in their conception and in the compensatory systems they set in motion – with the management policies of the municipality and the bodies involved. For the area around the new motorway Tollgate, the project sought a rational distribution of the constructions envisaged in a small space with many constraints with a view to safeguarding the envisaged agricultural park of supra-local interest and the archaeological site discovered in a neighbouring area. The master plan envisaged a broad environmental buffer strip and a distributional layout so as to attenuate the visual impact of the new buildings on the agricultural surroundings. The system of constructions envisaged revolves around different types of functions and uses other than those offered by the context. In point of fact, the project constitutes an important opportunity for redevelopment also in functional terms of the then primarily residential area of Via Cavour, defining its sphere as an episode of mostly urban character in which some productive functions are concentrated, including a high-quality production centre and a service centre for haulage firms parallel to the acquisition of areas for the park. As in the area of the furnace, commercial and logistic activities were excluded.

Attention to environmental issues develops in two directions: on the one hand, through the definition of a high standard of green areas (a buffer zone of 18,000 yd² and 30,000 yd² of agricultural land, serving as an initial nucleus for the creation of the

PII Tollgate, location. The project area is located in the vicinity of the motorway tollgate on the municipal outskirts and far away from the town

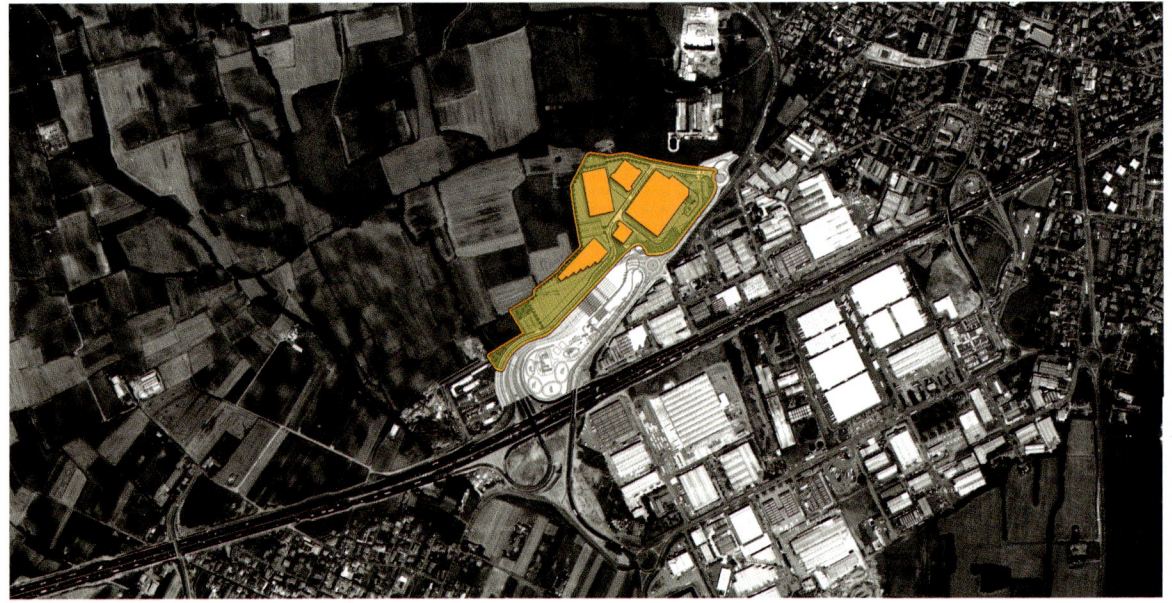

ARCHITECTURE

PII Tollgate, master plan. The rational distribution of volumes is the result of careful appraisal of the constraints and limits in the area as well as the paramount need for road construction to connect the tollgate and for adequate spaces to develop the activities envisaged

ARCHITECTURE

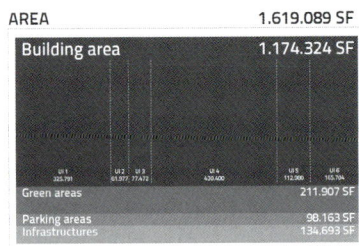

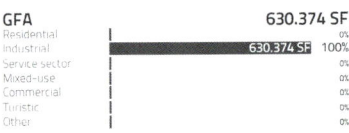

agricultural park); on the other, through reduction of the parking lots so as to create a broad strip of greenery encircling the area.

The complex of buildings is given a markedly urban character precisely in order to highlight the potential of the area, located near the tollgate, in relation to the territory as a whole. As a new centrality, it has a strong presence of public areas and areas of public use, both constructed and open, and the composition of an innovative functional mix combines functions of a more markedly urban nature with functions of a territorial kind, thus experimenting precisely with one of the territorially distributed urban nodes provided for by the project.

The area of the Furnace presents different environmental requirements.

The permission for structures additional to those already built in the historical sphere of the Adda furnace was prompted by the need to request in return for landscaping of the quarry to the rear, ecological restoration of the area, and the transfer of a large restored agricultural area to enhance the compactness and size of the green heart of Trezzo sull'Adda. The master plan thus experimented with mechanisms of compensatory transfer, obliging concerns to transfer substantial areas of land in return for building along the provincial highway. Wide green strips and large buffer zones avoid the typical "shop-window" effects of construction along the roads in the past. Here too, efforts are made above all to identify a functional mix capable of enhancing the area's vocation in both local and territorial terms.

Furnace location. The project regards an isolated area halfway between the towns of Trezzo sull'Adda to the east and Busnago to the west

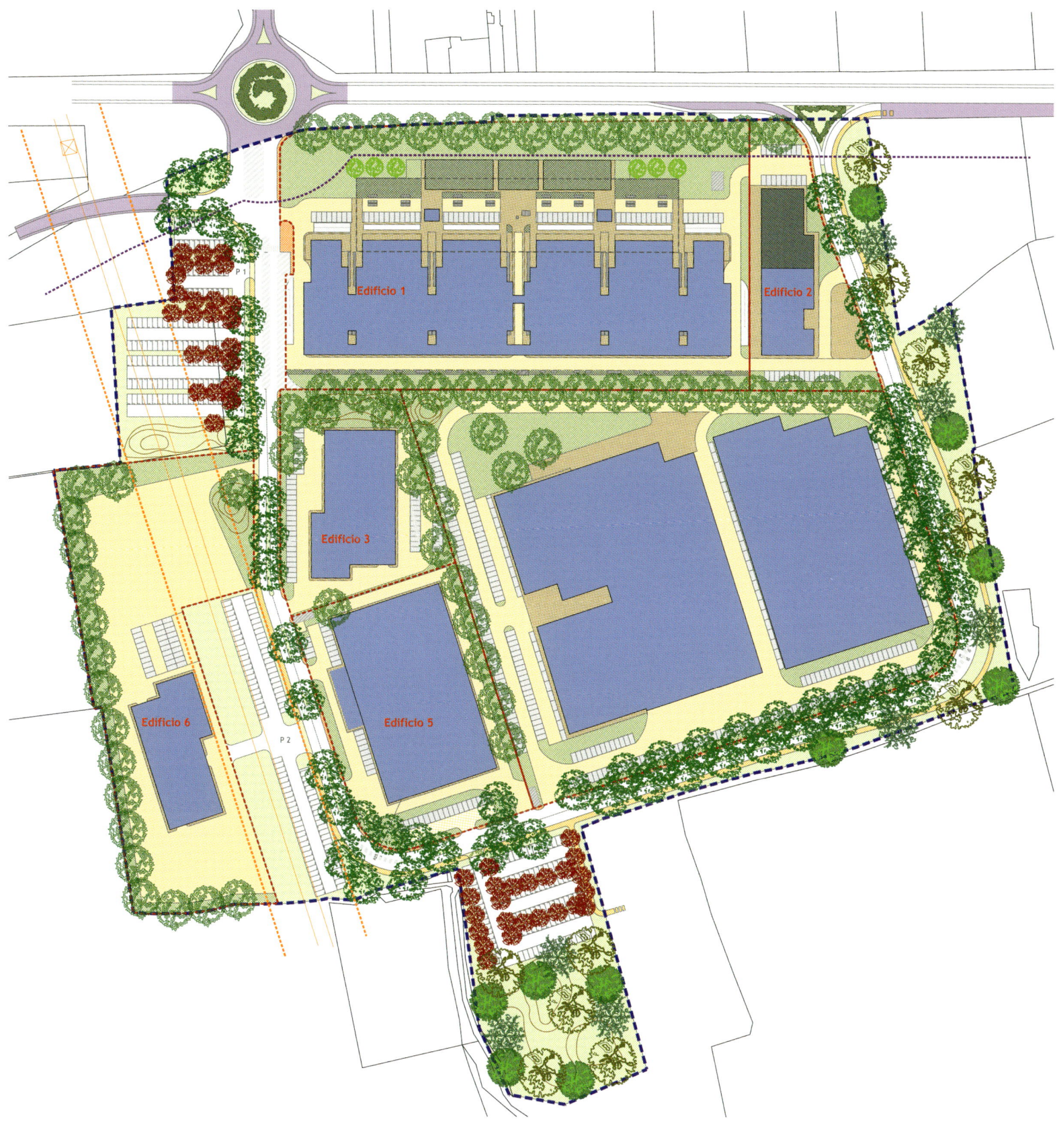

Furnace, master plan. The master plan focuses on the search for planning solutions oriented towards attenuating the transformation through a precise choice of types of tree for the various requirements of impact minimization, setting and environmental restoration

Furnace, sections

Furnace, master plan. The transformation of the territory is defined by a process the plan of which undergoes change and evolution while always maintaining a recognizable structure

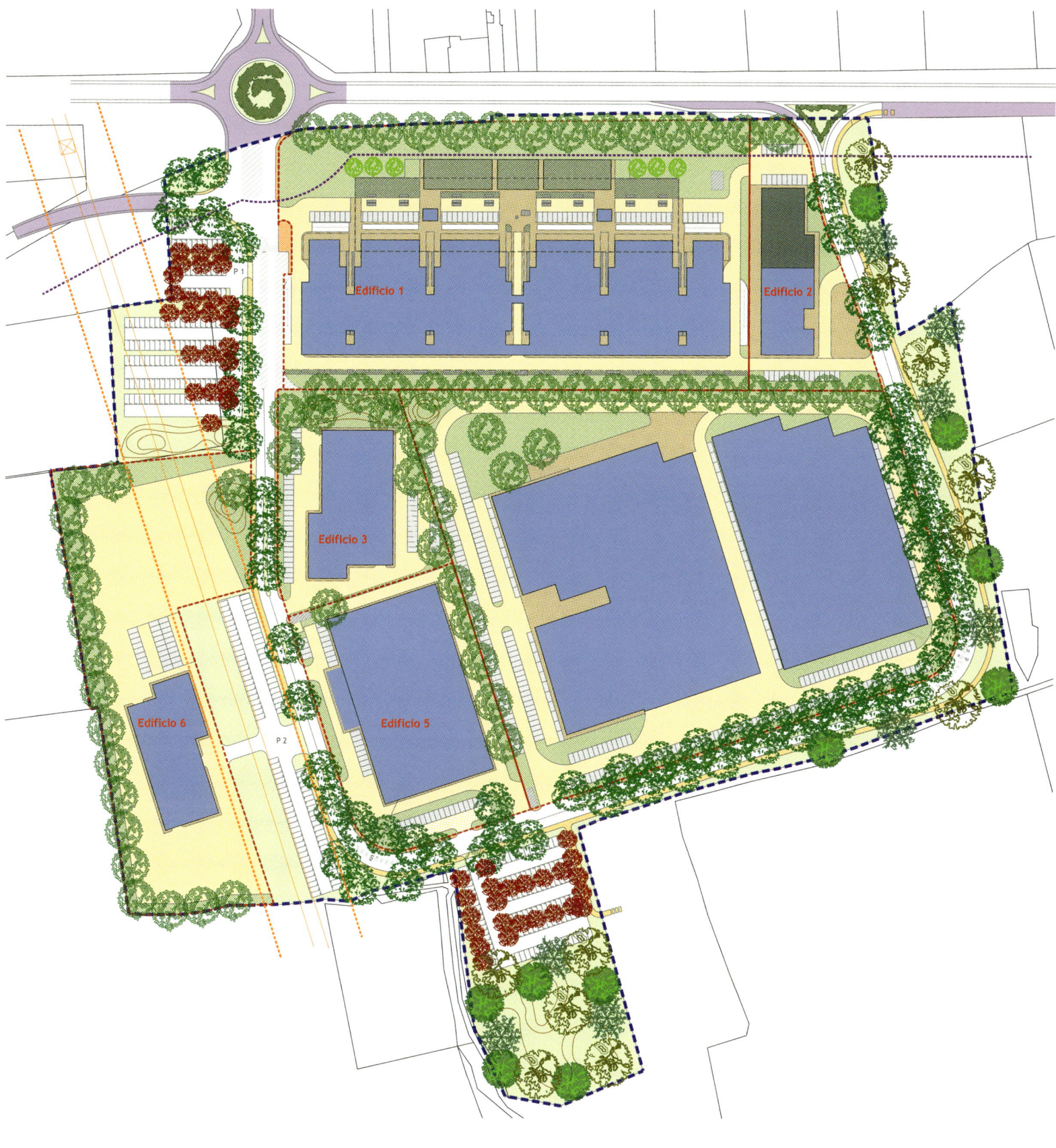

Furnace, master plan. The master plan focuses on the search for planning solutions oriented towards attenuating the transformation through a precise choice of types of tree for the various requirements of impact minimization, setting and environmental restoration

Furnace, sections

Furnace, master plan. The transformation of the territory is defined by a process the plan of which undergoes change and evolution while always maintaining a recognizable structure

PII Furnace, elevations

Furnace, view

ARCHITECTURE

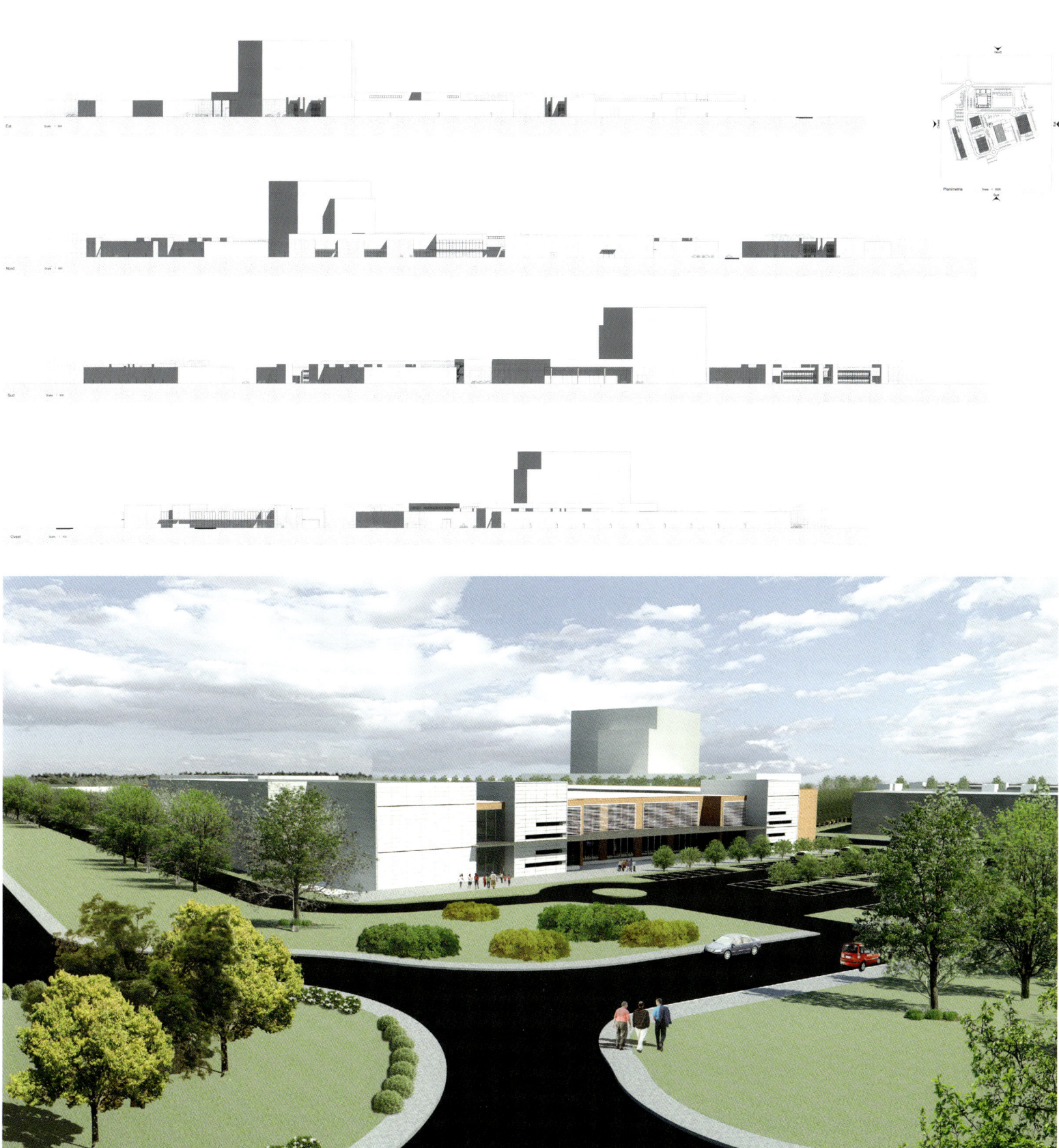

ARCHITECTURE

4. Lainate (Milan): Integrated Action Plan (PII) for a new centre on the A8 (2008)

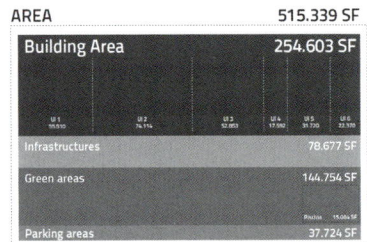

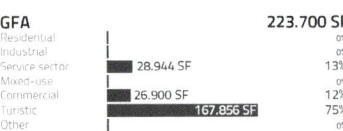

The Integrated Action Plan (PII) transforms an unused area on the A8, from Milan to Varese and Malpensa, not far from the 2015 Expo area and close to the Lainate motorway tollgate. Apparently one of the many spaces of little use and no environmental or settlement quality, the area actually possesses great potential. Located between the Malpensa airport and the Expo, close to the city and near the two nuclei of Lainate, between the main settlement and the area of Grancia and Barbaiana, it can play a major role as a gateway to the town, as a central urban node of the Lainate settlement system and, above the local scale, as part of a larger and more complex territorial system stretching from the airport to the city. The risk was of repeating one of the many operations exploiting the shop-window effect offered by the motorway, above all because of the great attraction to be expected as a result of the construction of the 2015 Expo complex and the associated provisions for fast transit between Malpensa and Milan. It was decided to install some functions of territorial scale, drawn both by the Expo and by the large-scale nature of the context in general, establishing dialogue at the local level and constructing a small, new urban centrality for the territory of Lainate. Thus avoiding the construction of containers devoted exclusively to major functions, the project draws a map in the form of area of strong urban character with a wide, tree-lined central boulevard and large public spaces. Buildings of the envisaged types stand on either side: hotels, commercial areas, personal services, a conference centre and functions on a smaller scale. The aim is to create an urban area of linkage between Lainate, the motorway and the separate parts of the town in which the buildings contribute to the construction of a markedly central and urban context. Provision is made for large greens areas and pedestrian zones, and connections with the pedestrian and cycle systems to and from the town are ensured by restructuring the viaduct over the A8.

The project therefore addresses the role of areas like this along the motorway in a context that is only locally and apparently decentralized. It avoids the risk of being drawn excessively by the motorway and the associated territorial values, and follows the more prudent path of contributing to the creation of a new centrality in a territory of sprawl devoid of quality as a centre capable of gathering together the scattered elements and of hosting territorial functions in a fabric able to establish dialogue with the local scale and offer it opportunities for new centralities. Only thus is it possible to maintain the inherent large-scale role of the infrastructural corridor of the motorway while respecting the nature of the contexts and offering them an increase in settlement quality.

Planivolumetric plan. The area, upon which the motorway has a marked effect, is organized in terms of an orthogonal design that the arrangement of the plans of the buildings makes readily recognizable

Setting. The operation concerned a small, marginal area delimited all along its perimeter by the road infrastructures of the Lainate motorway tollgate

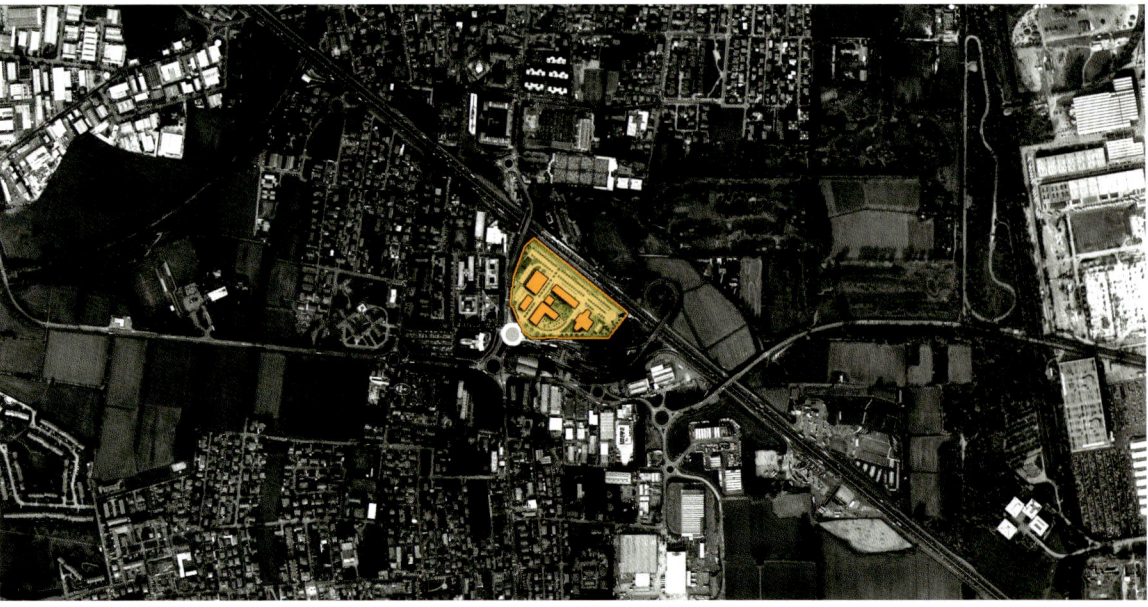

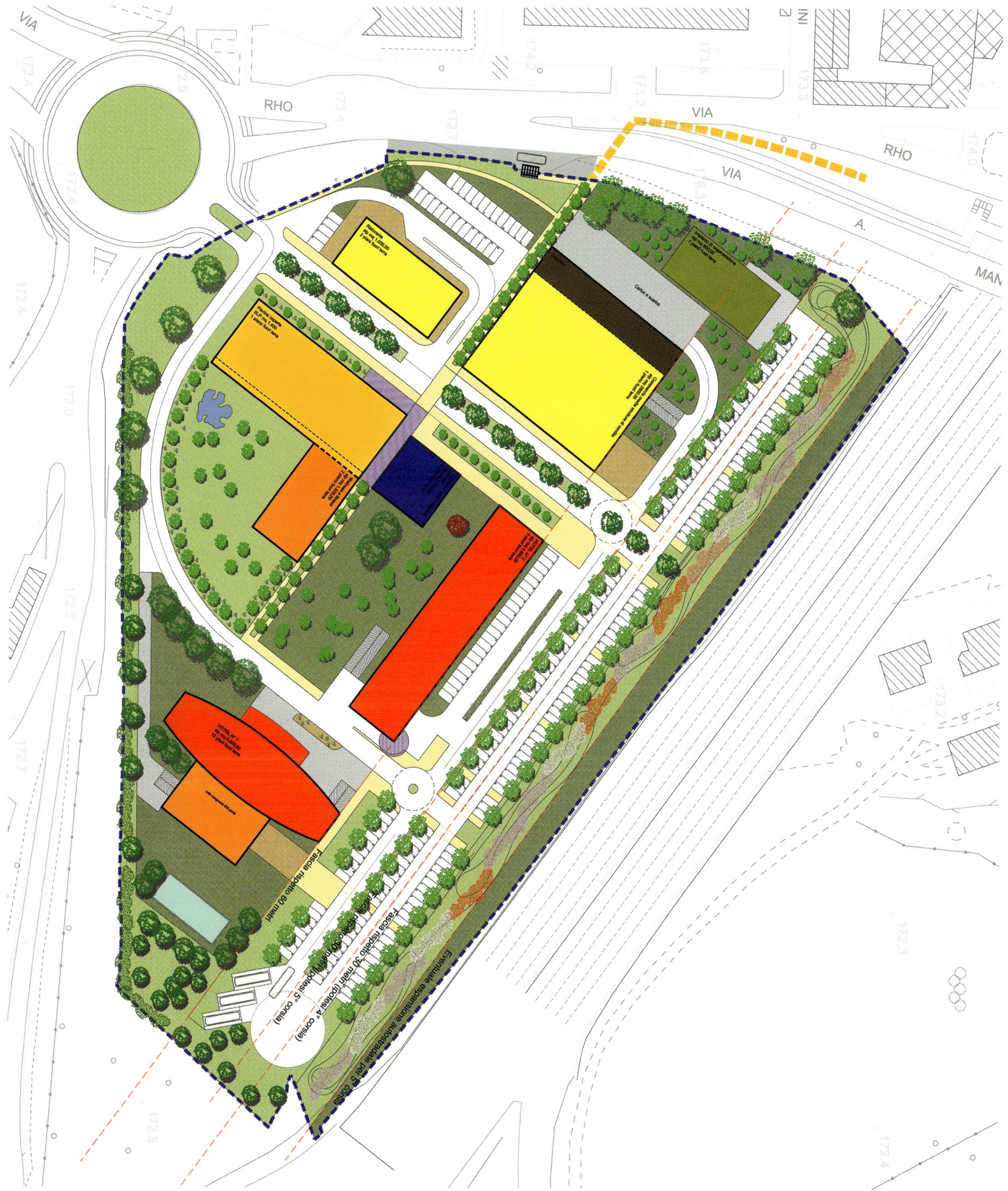

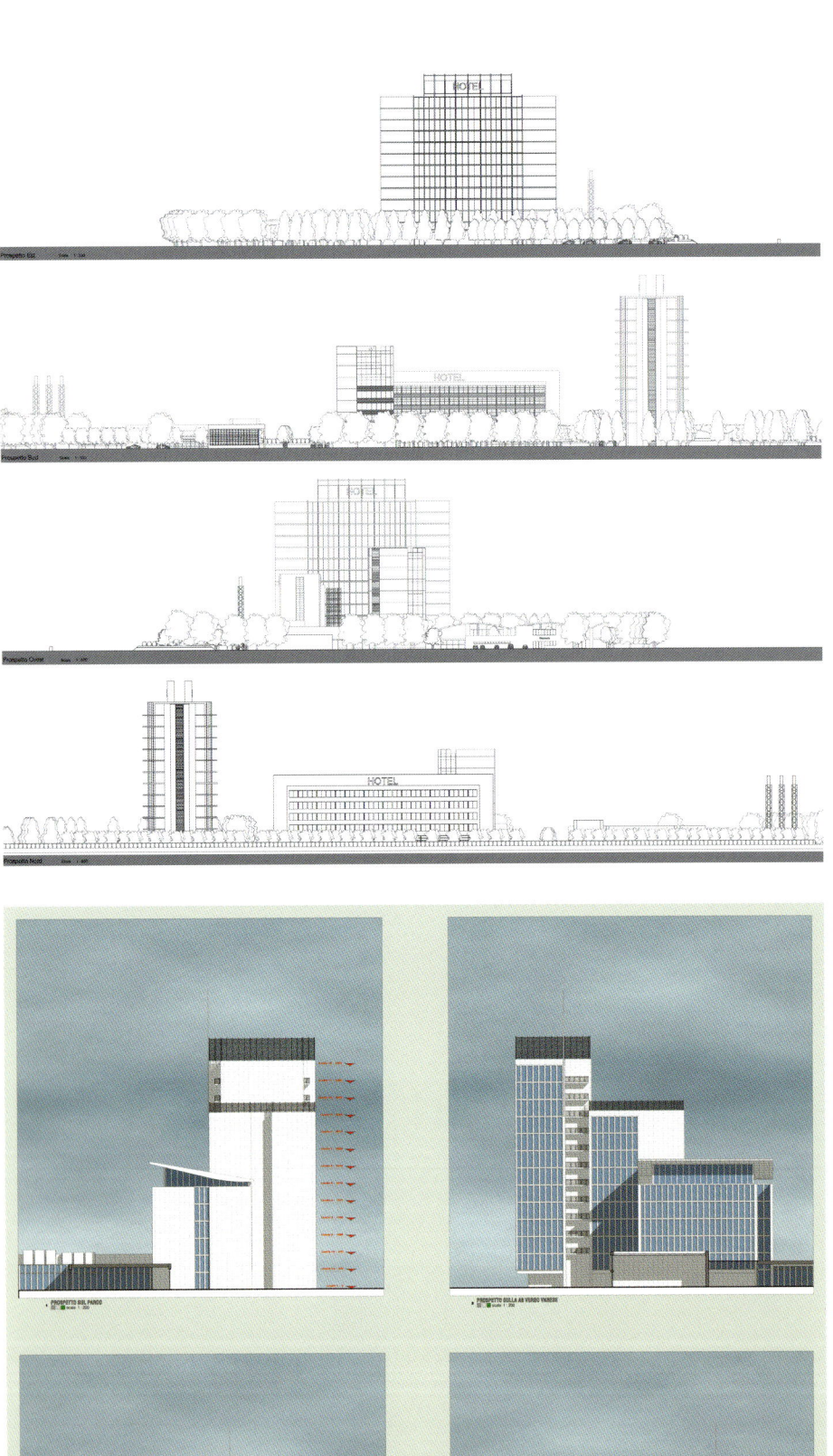

Elevations. The buildings are arranged in the space so as to give visual predominance to the hotel structure south of the area

Elevations. Initial version

Initial master plan. Despite the volumetric differences, it is easy to identify the structure of the area's design. The tree-lined avenue, parking areas parallel to the motorway, orthogonal arrangement of buildings and large public spaces constitute the compositional elements that give the operation its structure

View

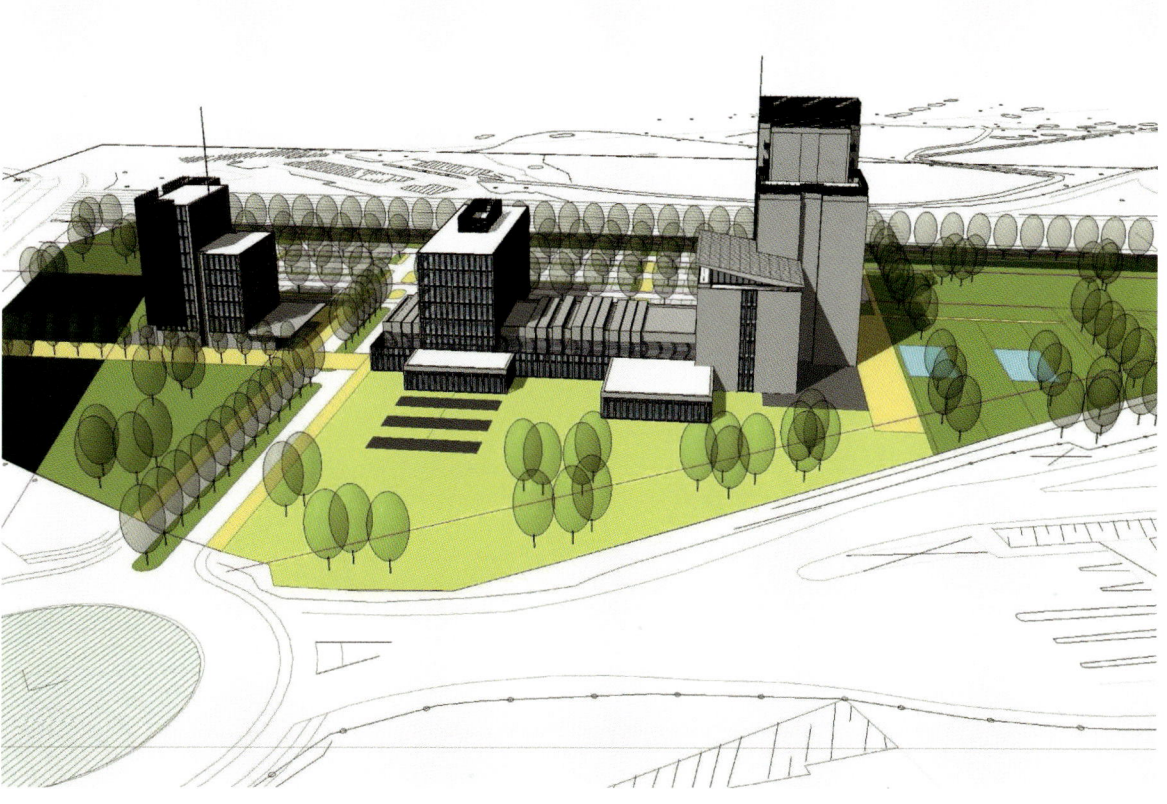

ARCHITECTURE

5. Rozzano (Milan): Integrated Action Plan (PII) for the multifunctional area of Via Manzoni (under way since 2008)

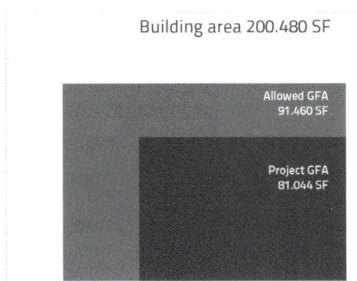

PUBLIC REVENUES
Not observed

The Integrated Action Plan (PII) for Rozzano is designed to participate in the redevelopment of unused, underused and low-quality areas along the axis of Via Manzoni, which has taken on ever-greater territorial importance, especially in the last few years. Connecting Milan, Rozzano and Basiglio, it constitutes a continuous prolongation not only of the road connections between the city and the hinterland but also of the built-up area. The developments along it include some key episodes in Milanese urban planning with public housing projects located too far from the city, private building sadly typical of an era, and shopping malls capable of upstaging many central areas, like Rozzano, impoverished and devoid of any particular meaning. The section along Via Manzoni is a succession of industrial, commercial and disused areas, including the one addressed by the Integrated Action Plan. On the corner with Via Brodolini, the area was occupied by a dense wood made up of trees and bushes planted in the 1950s but never pruned and left to grow wild. Already earmarked for construction by the existing urban-planning scheme, the area is reconsidered with a view to greater dialogue not with the existing city, which is weak in the expression of quality, but with the city one would like to expect along the road. Unbalanced by the presence of the shopping mall in the north and the Humanitas hospital complex in the south, Via Manzoni has the potentiality to become a road of quality services, both public and private, so as to enrich an economic and urban fabric that is very weak but crossed by more than considerable flows and forming part of the major territorial axis between Milan and Basiglio through Rozzano.

Given the need to eliminate the wood, the PII adopts a compensatory approach and reduces by nearly half the volume of construction provided for by the city planning scheme, which envisaged far more extensive building in the area, including very large industrial and commercial structures. Reducing this by nearly half, the PII engages in dialogue with the municipal and provincial authorities to identify areas of reforestation within the municipal territory amounting to approximately twice the area of woodland lost. It modifies the area's functions and coverage ratios, recognizing on the front the possibility of constructing an initial sphere of private services, commercial and otherwise, and a second sphere of support for the Humanitas hospital complex in the shape of a residence and guest-quarters. To the rear, on the two remaining units, the project confirms the existing residential uses with provisions for moderate expansion in relation to the housing already constructed. The PII thus participates in redevelopment of the territorial axis of Via Manzoni, making a substantial contribution in terms of public works with the restructuring of three crossroads, especially the main one towards the centre of Rozzano, the environmental restoration of the Pizzabrasa stream, which runs along the north side of the settlement, and redevelopment of an old industrial parking lot south of the area. The project is therefore conceived as an instrument for revaluation of an area capable of intense dialogue with the territorial role of the axis, transforming small-scale local uses into others of a more appropriate character so as to generate quality and intensity of interest along the road while adapting infrastructures and services at the same time and providing abundant compensation for the losses that construction in any case inflicts upon the existing environmental system.

Location of the project area. The transformations envisaged by the Integrated Action Plan (PII) are located along Via Manzoni, a primary axis connecting Milan, Rozzano and Basiglio as well as a corridor where many important service and commercial functions have been concentrated in recent years

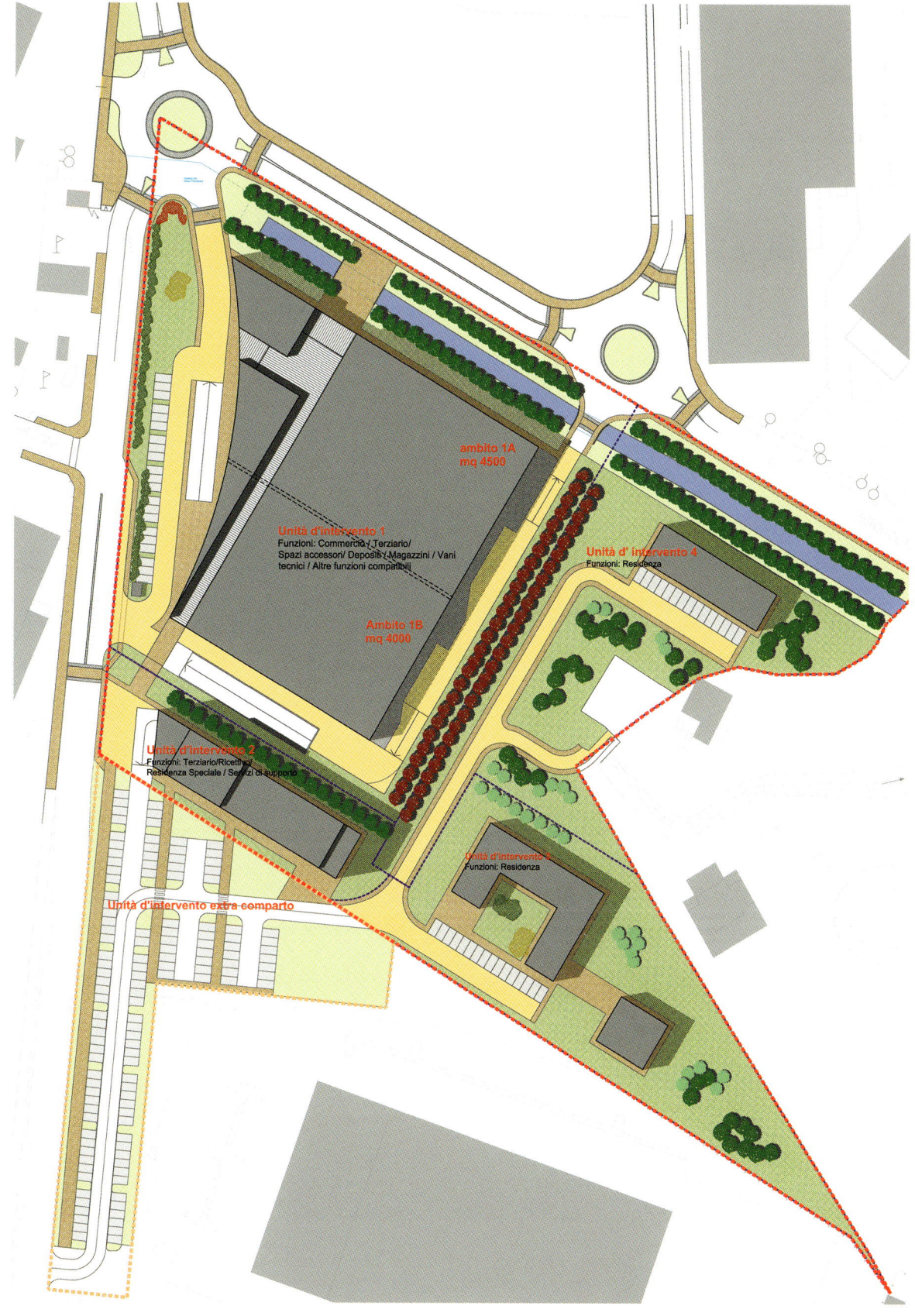

General plan. The alignment of the north side along the watercourse and the curve of the main façade on Via Manzoni

ARCHITECTURE

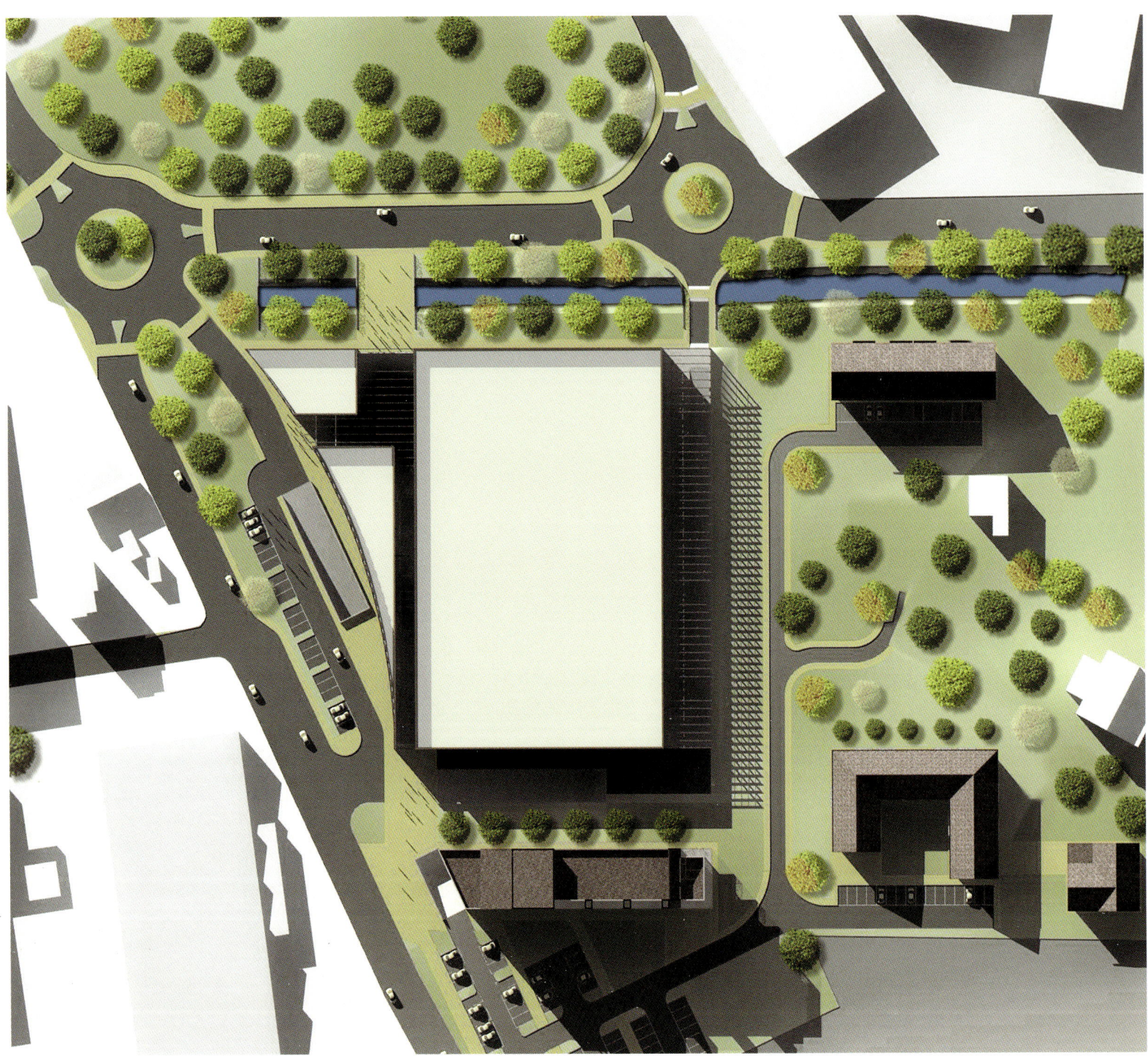

Overall planimetric and volumetric plan

View from the south

View from the west along the north side. Upgrading of the Roggia Pizzabrasa watercourse

ARCHITECTURE

View from the north

Opposite
West elevation

North elevation

East elevation

South elevation

View from the south

View from the west along the north side. Upgrading of the Roggia Pizzabrasa watercourse

ARCHITECTURE

View from the north

Opposite
West elevation

North elevation

East elevation

South elevation

Prospetto Ovest

Prospetto Nord

Prospetto Est

Prospetto Sud

ARCHITECTURE

6. Roncello (Monza and Brianza): Integrated Action Plan (PII) for the new town centre (2009–12)

AREA 330.687 SF

GFA 94.214 SF
AT 01	16.925	transferred	16.925 SF
AT 02 a	22.596	transferred	22.596 SF
AT 02 b	10.975		10.975 SF
AT 03			Undefined
AT 04	11.997	16.699	14.999	43.707 SF

PUBLIC REVENUES 574.117 €

Roncello is a small town in the northern sector of the Martesana Adda area in the east of the province of Milan. Formerly devoted entirely to agriculture, Roncello has undergone the same fate as many other towns in this part of the territory, with strong residential expansion around a small historical centre of clearly rural appearance. This growth has not allowed the territory to develop adequate structures and the breadth of the expansion has not proved able in itself to shape the public structure of the municipality. The small square on which the church stands is certainly unable to bear the weight of the new part of the town, and the building of the new town hall on a site away from the old centre has increased the sense of impoverishment in terms of public space and places of public interest and importance.

Designed to offer a continuous series of spaces, places for relations, structures for public use and green areas, the project involves a number of central areas near the church square, the farmhouse that closes the south side (already the object of a redevelopment project) and the space behind it as well as various more peripheral areas. Its purpose is to increase the availability of free, public areas equipped for social relations and thus increase public interaction between the inhabitants.

To this end, it alters the zoning of the areas involved, transferring building rights from the central areas to the outskirts so as to free land and design a new series of publics spaces. The focal point is the construction of the new town hall and refurbishment of the small library. The project reflects on the nature of the construction of a public area and a new public building in a stylistically chaotic context. For this reason, it works on the essential characteristics of the town as built up over the years, taking up key elements like the main square, the belfry and the portico as well as characteristic architectural features like the fretted brick façade, the shallow pitched roofs and the arcade. The result is a major complex of restrained monumentality. The public structures, first and foremost the town hall and belfry, express the centrality of the area and the importance of the functions they accommodate. The open areas connect all the corners involved in the project with those of the existing territory, which takes on new meaning only in this way.

The buildings not erected on the project areas are shifted to more recent residential contexts, which also see an increase in green space and connections with the system of cycle paths. The project thus engages in dialogue with the territory and offers it the possibility of a small new centrality of monumental character with forms capable of giving new significance it its surroundings, again by harnessing the potential of the territorial and urban approach to the architectural project.

Setting. The PII (Integrated Action Plan) provides for various projects regarding both central and peripheral areas of municipal territory. In a town devoid of communal spaces, the possibility of reinventing a central area offers a key opportunity to endow the system of public gathering spaces with continuity and an organic character

ARCHITECTURE

Elevations. The profile of the new buildings is harmonious and fits into the context of the town. The tower of the town hall is juxtaposed to the church bell tower as a new landmark of the municipal territory

Town hall, elevations and sections. The building is made up of two distinct sections, one horizontal and the other vertical. The project proposes a mixture of elements typical of a historical town centre, such as the arched portico, and more modern elements like the façades of the tower

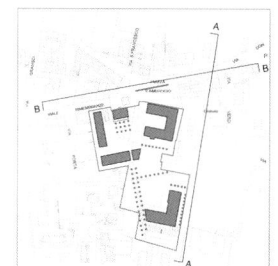
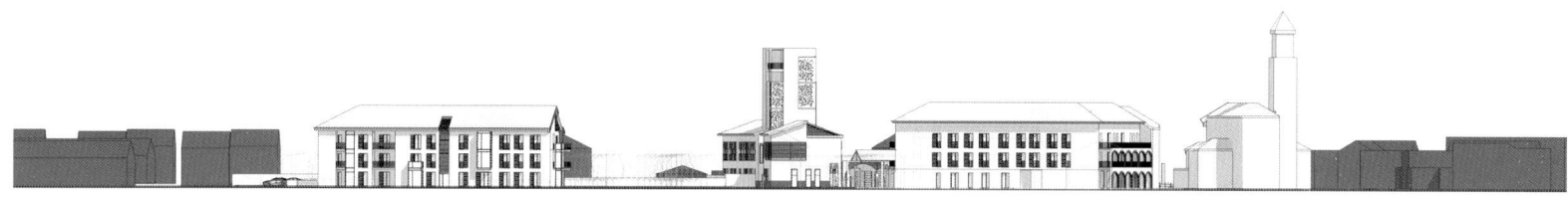

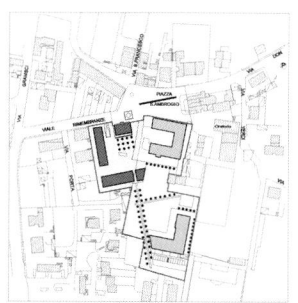

183

ARCHITECTURE

Master plan. The project envisages renovation of the existing courtyard and the building in front of it. Two new L-shaped buildings are also inserted to the west to accommodate the new public functions and a residential building to the southeast. The public space is designed as a void with respect to the solids of the buildings planned. The centrepiece of the entire project is the tower of the town hall, the meeting point of the linear axes of the public spaces, buildings, tree-lined avenues and vistas

Materials for the tower. The use is envisaged of traditional materials, like brick, copper and wood

ARCHITECTURE

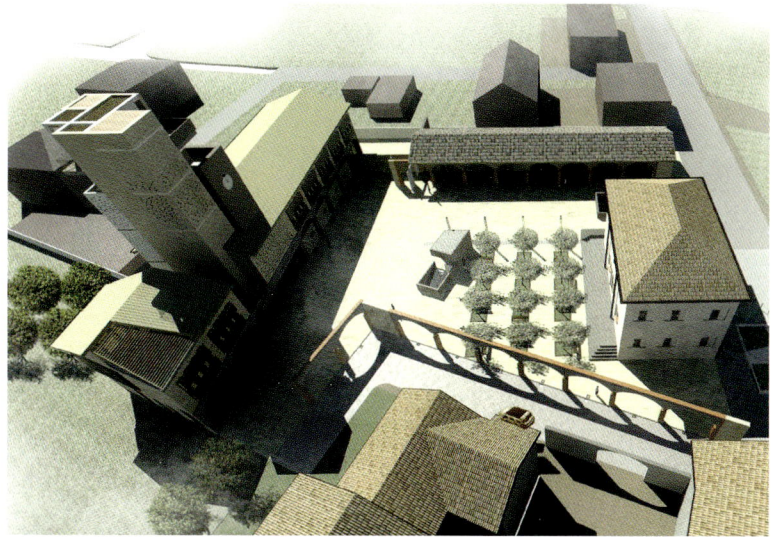

Bird's eye view of the public space in front of the town hall

View of the piazza

View of the park

View of the public space with a closing element in the foreground

ARCHITECTURE

Residential building. Simple, linear volumes are endowed with variety by their materials and the handling of the various external elements such as terraces, windows, staircases and roofs

Residential building, elevations

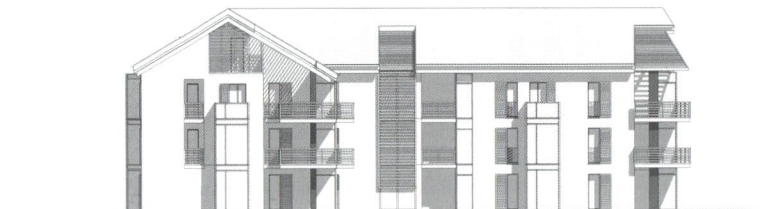

Nord

Ovest

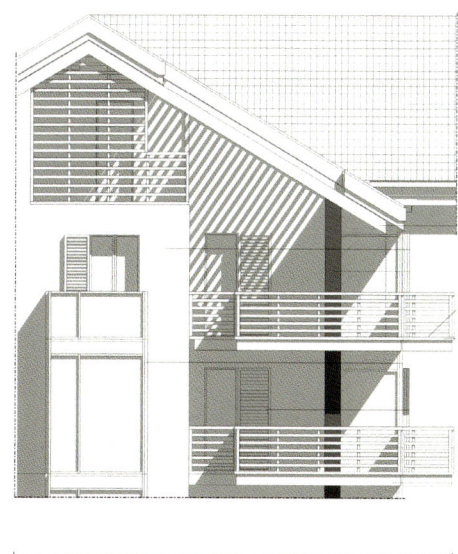

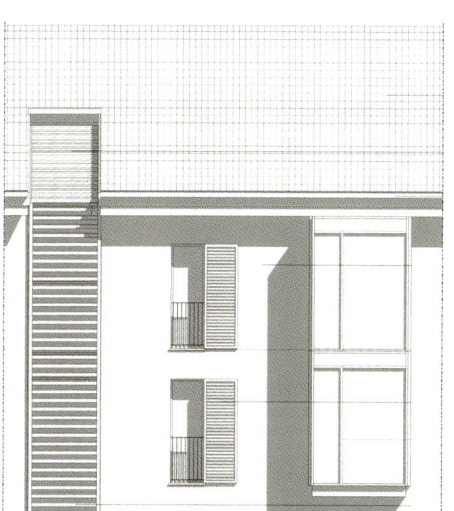

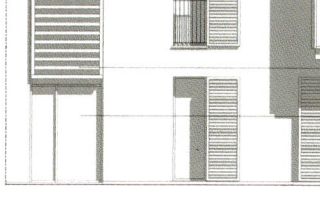

Materials. Wood, plaster, brick

Residential buildings. Within the peripheral area to the east, the PII (Integrated Action Plan) envisages the construction of six residential buildings with three storeys above ground. The choice of materials and compositional elements unifies the different parts of the project

ARCHITECTURE

7. Verano Brianza (Monza and Brianza): Integrated Action Plans (PII) for the Core, Montegrappa and Borgonovo areas (2010)

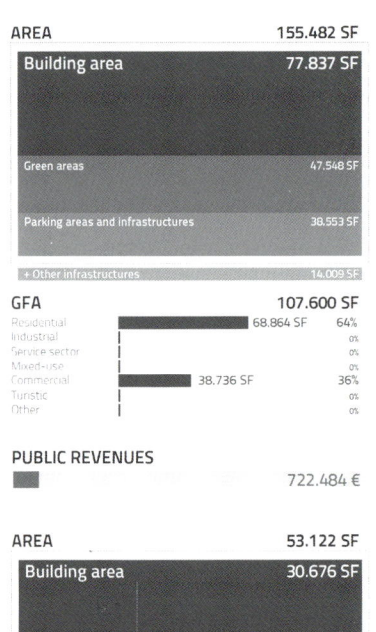

AREA	155.482 SF
Building area	77.837 SF
Green areas	47.548 SF
Parking areas and infrastructures	38.553 SF
+ Other infrastructures	14.009 SF

GFA		107.600 SF
Residential	68.864 SF	64%
Industrial		0%
Service sector		0%
Mixed-use		0%
Commercial	38.736 SF	36%
Turistic		0%
Other		0%

PUBLIC REVENUES

722.484 €

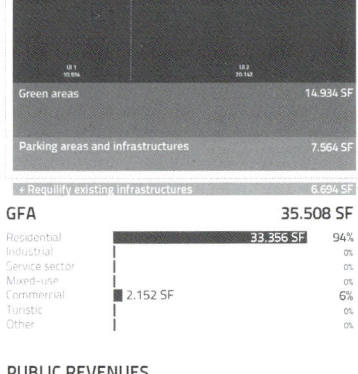

AREA	53.122 SF
Building area	30.676 SF
Green areas	14.934 SF
Parking areas and infrastructures	7.564 SF
+ Requalify existing infrastructures	6.694 SF

GFA		35.508 SF
Residential	33.356 SF	94%
Industrial		0%
Service sector		0%
Mixed-use		0%
Commercial	2.152 SF	6%
Turistic		0%
Other		0%

PUBLIC REVENUES

195.007 €

Location of the areas involved in the PII (Integrated Action Plan). The Core and Montegrappa areas are situated close to the town's residential fabric south of the Via Valassina. The Borgonovo area is on the outskirts in the southwest

The desire of the municipal administration to anticipate some choices of the Territorial Management Plan and immediately test its capacity for response to transformation stimuli took concrete shape in three Integrated Action Plans (PII) drawn up parallel to the Territorial Management Plan. Great importance attaches to the attempt to anticipate choices already present in an urban-planning scheme. The experiment made it possible to test the system of rules, regulations and design set up by the said scheme and ascertain the capacity both of the context to respond to the project and of the bodies involved to put it into effect. Finally, it also made it possible for the plan to monitor the effects of the projects and their implementation or otherwise so as to absorb any negative and maximize any positive aspect. The use of a master plan for the three projects also made it possible to anticipate the formal implementation of the projects. Precisely due to the essence of the master plan as an instrument capable of visualizing the transformations and morphological effects of the rules defined by the project itself, the three projects were designed on the basis of more general morphological, typological, infrastructural and urban-planning rules. Engaging in dialogue with the needs expressed by the territory, they base their choices on the content of the Territorial Management Plan, which therefore includes the impact of the rules, regulations and precise urban-planning decisions (such as indices and construction volumes). In addition, the use of a master plan made it possible to present and build up consensus on a simulation whose construction was in turn made possible precisely by compliance with the precise rules and insertion into the general urban-planning context.

The three master plans regarded the transformation of three different areas. The Borgonovo quarry, a wholly typical case of exploiting underground resources, is situated in the western sector of the

Master plan of the Core PII (Integrated Action Plan). A functional mixture characterized by three units. The first, situated in the northwest segment of the area as a whole close to the new roundabout, is distinguished by the presence of a one-storey commercial structure with a maximum height of six metres. The other two, residential in character, are separated by a public space that permits correct dialogue between the project and the consolidated urban fabric already in existence

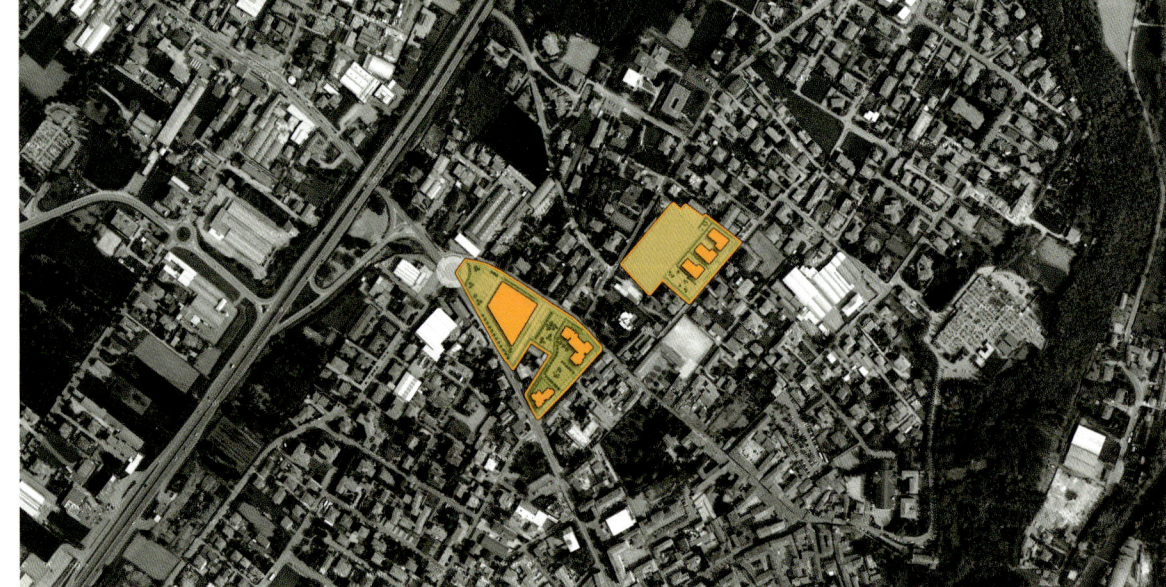

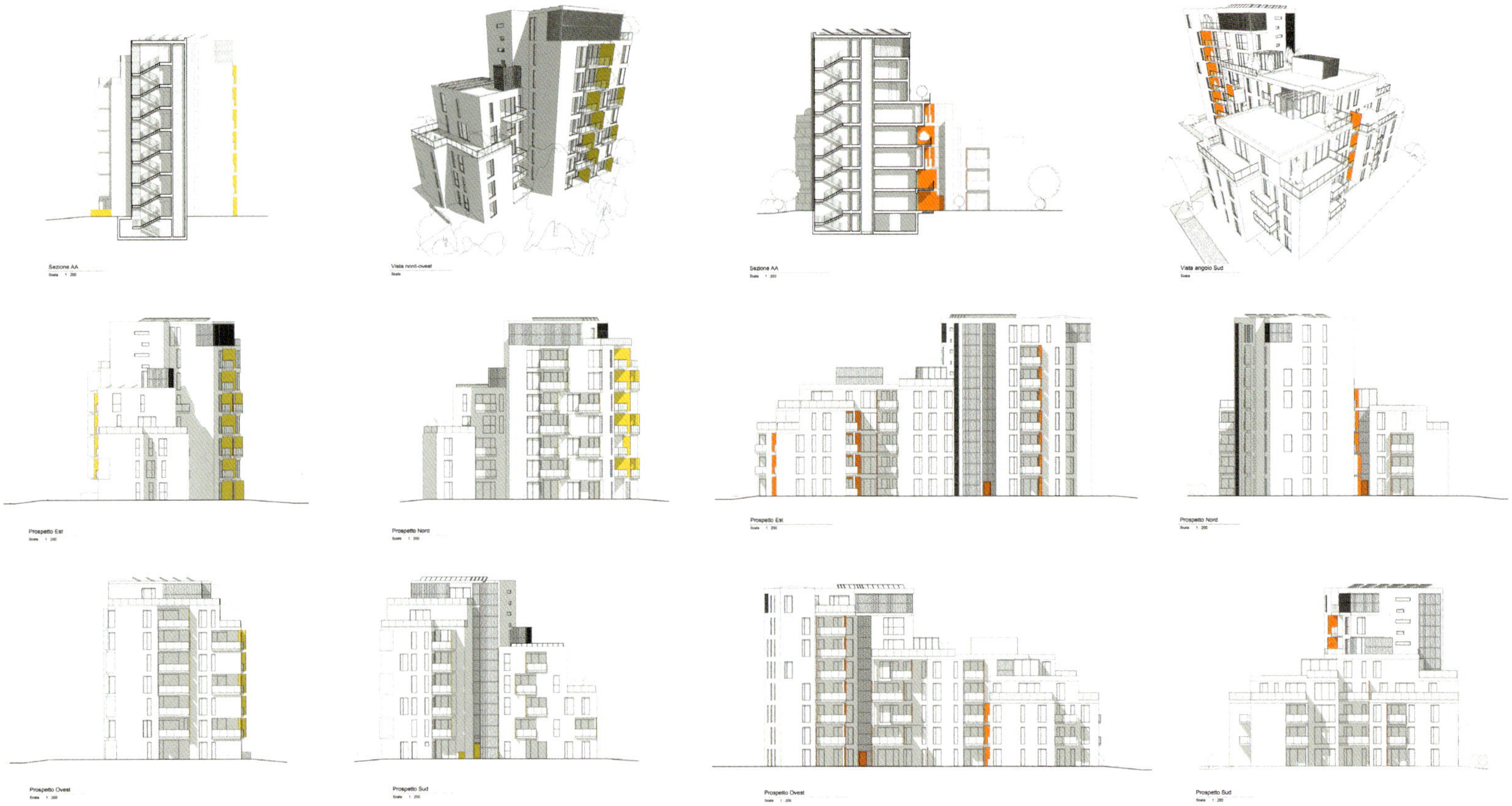

Sections and elevations showing the "stratified" composition of the two residential buildings. The different heights of the buildings make it possible to create large terraces and a sort of architectural "breakdown" that enlivens both of them

Elevations. The elevations show the volumetric variation of the residential buildings sloping down towards the public space of the project, thus ensuring the harmonious insertion of the structures into the context and embracing the open spaces

Prospetto 1
Scala 1 : 500

Prospetto 2
Scala 1 : 500

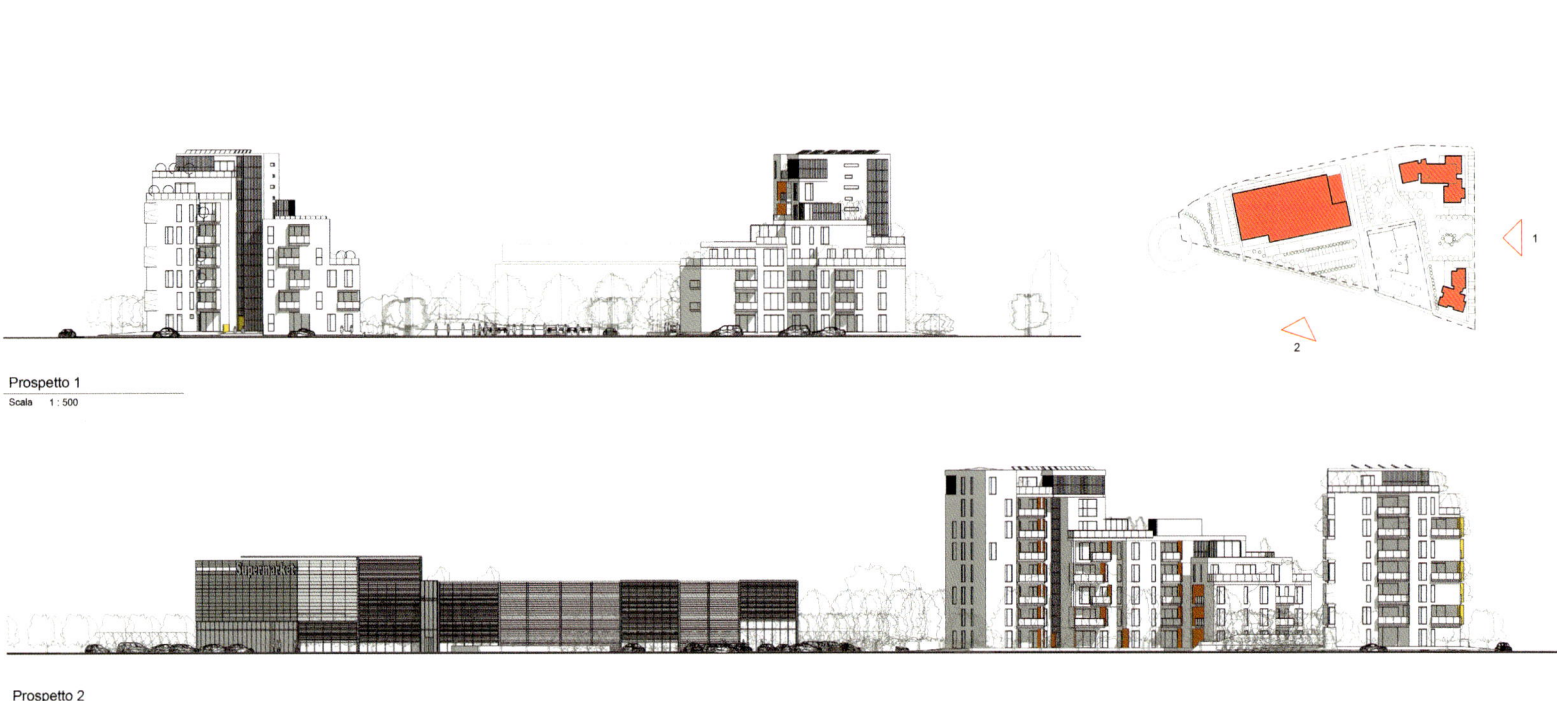

Compositional materials and elements

Perspective view from Via IV Novembre. Regular, sharply defined lines and forms characterize the façade of the building. Terraces and loggias endow a minimalistic solid form with lightness. The use of wood and the presence of roof and terrace gardens contribute to the creation of a structure with high aesthetic and architectural standards

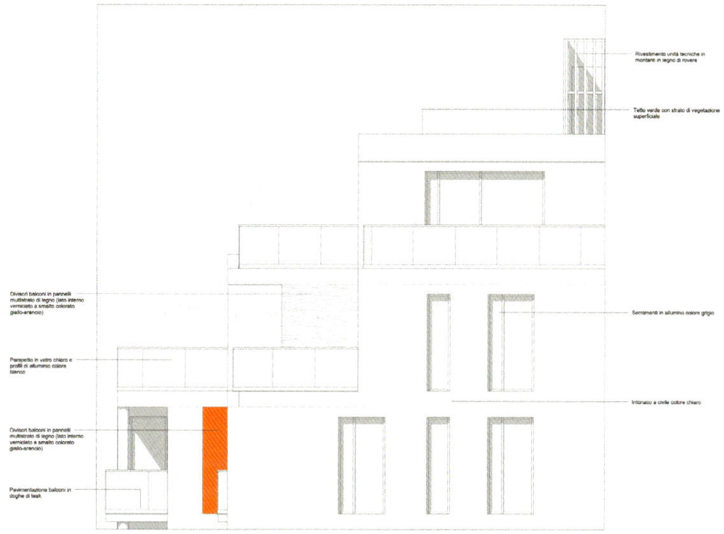

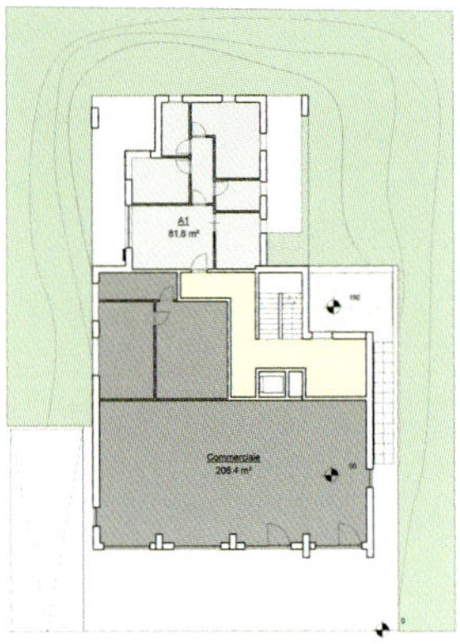

Prospetto 1

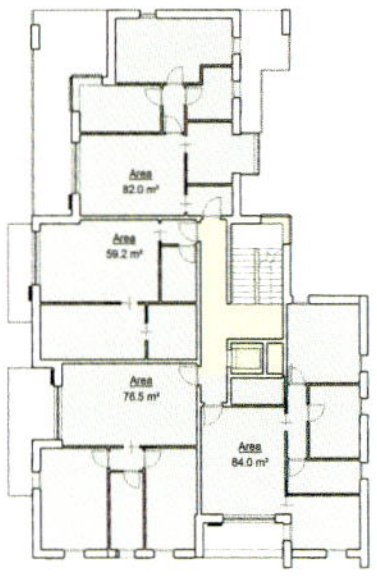

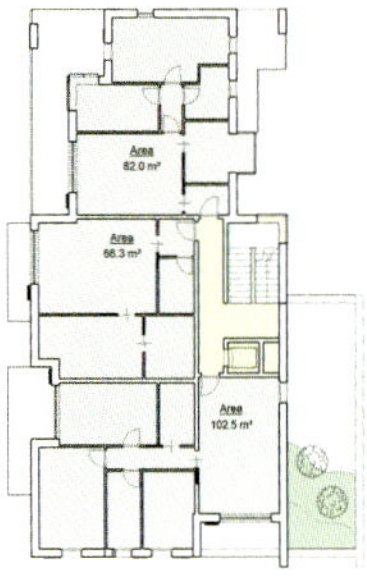

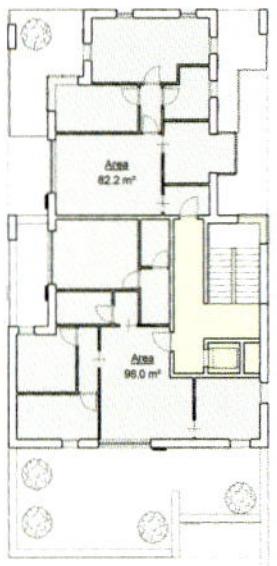

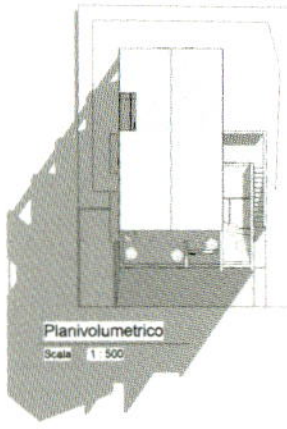

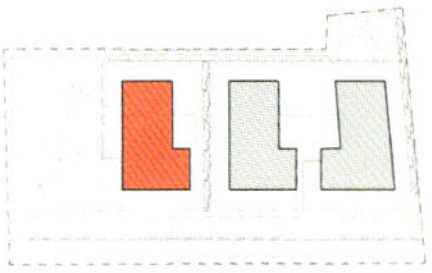

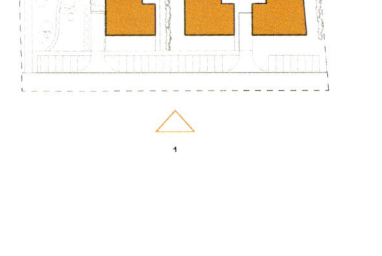

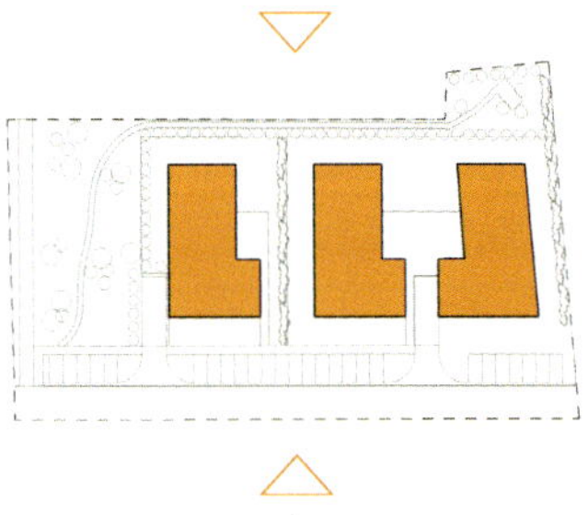

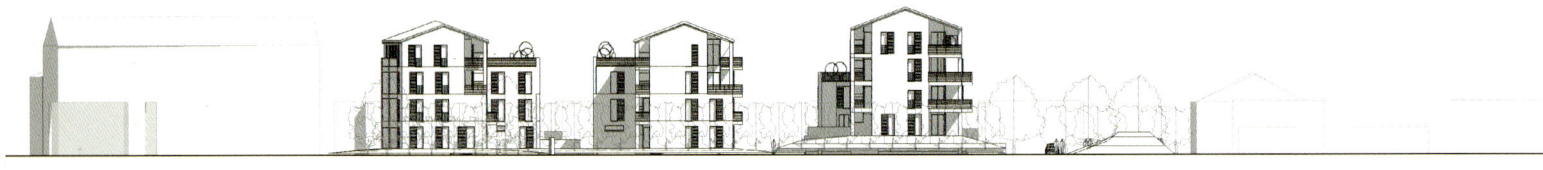

Prospetto 2

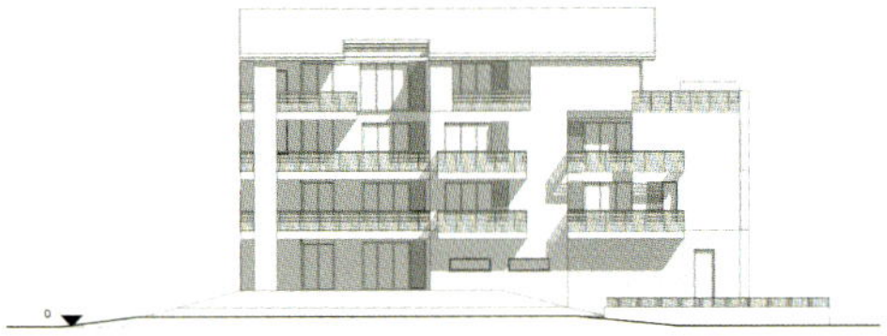

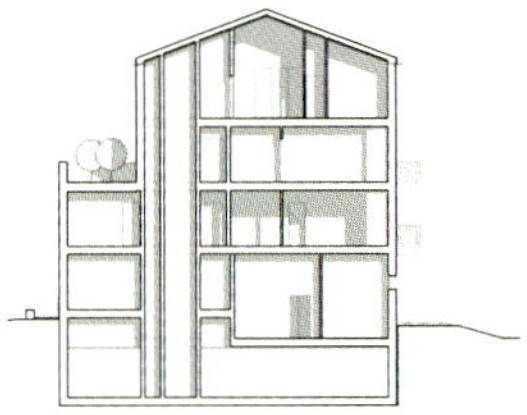

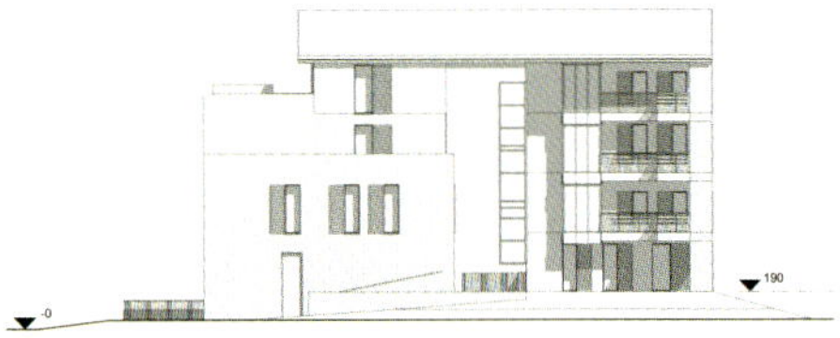

Opposite
Model unit. Plans, elevations, section and view. The commercial space on the ground floor on the main road and the residential part on the upper floors

Overall views of the project

Detail of the materials used for the façade. Use is made of traditional materials such as plaster, copper, brick and stone

Overall view. Insertion of the proposal into the existing built-up fabric

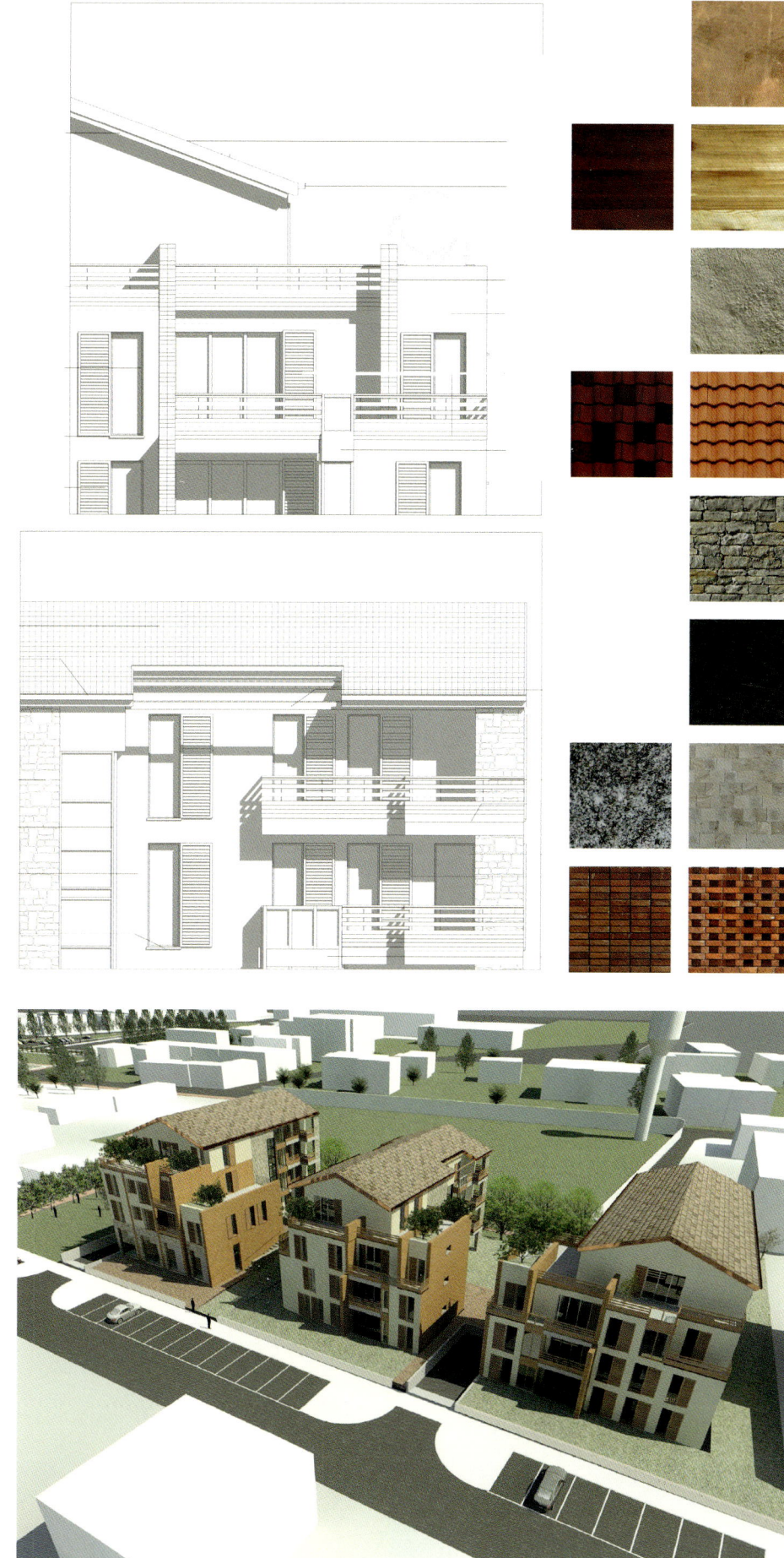

ARCHITECTURE

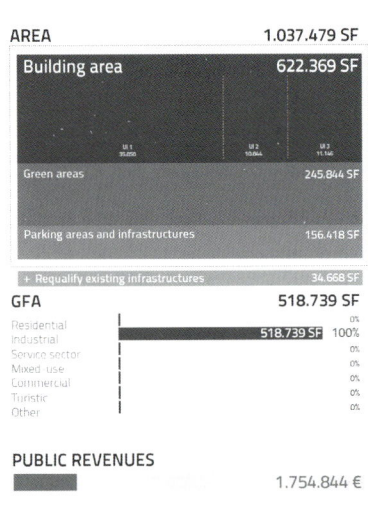

municipality, close to industrial areas and the border with neighbouring municipalities but above all to the axis of the Comasina highway, handling a major flow of traffic and capable of attracting substantial commercial developments. Core is an abandoned industrial district of great potential situated in the north on the town's main road (Via Nazario Sauro) close to the north exit the Valassina provincial highway. Finally, the much smaller area of Via Montegrappa is embedded in a small-scale settlement system generated in recent years by the urban sprawl of the eastern sector of the town, devoid of quality, public structures and green spaces. All three projects provided for large quantities of works, spaces and public structures, and each focused on a specific theme.
The project for the Borgonovo quarry addressed the new industrial system envisaged with a substantial cycle lane and a less rigid relationship with the Comasina highway. The project for Core took full advantage of its position, concentrating the volume of construction in a tall building and a commercial complex so as to leave space for the major infrastructural work required to restructure the connection with the Valassina highway. The project for Montegrappa necessarily envisaged ordinary architecture, albeit of good quality, in order to give new meaning to its position in the ordinary residential fabric of the town's eastern sector.
The Territorial Management Plan approved the projects' provisions and incorporated them in its own planning, taking advantage of the experimentation made possible by the rules in order to structure the system for the management and implementation of other similar projects, which together defines the areas of greatest transformation and redevelopment of the territory.

Location of areas involved in the PII. The area of the Borgonovo quarry at Verano Brianza

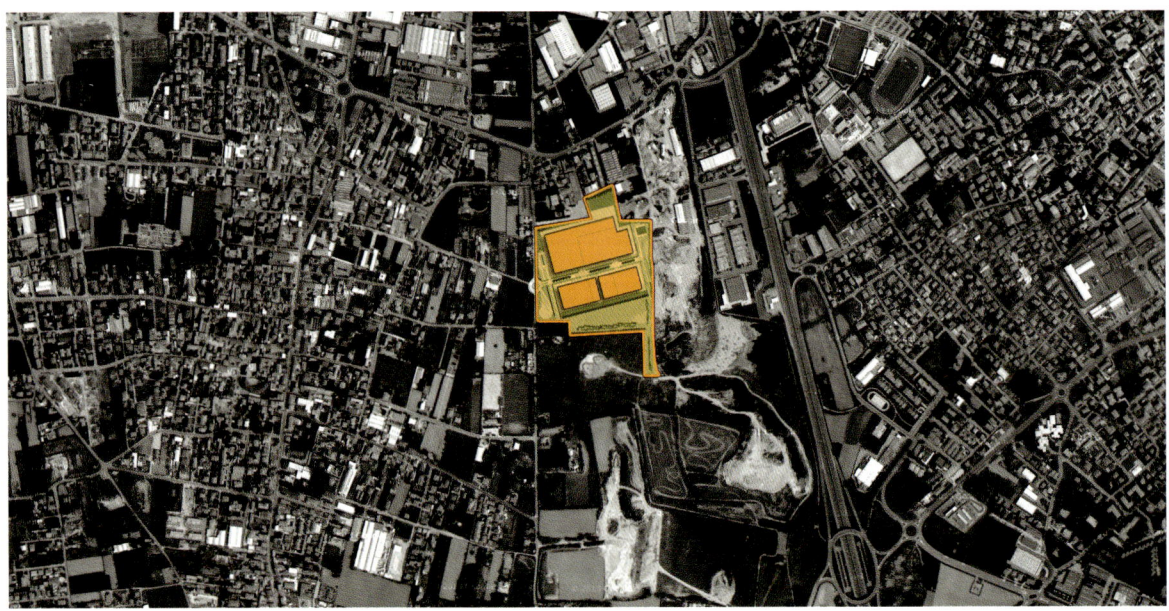

Overall planimetric and volumetric plan

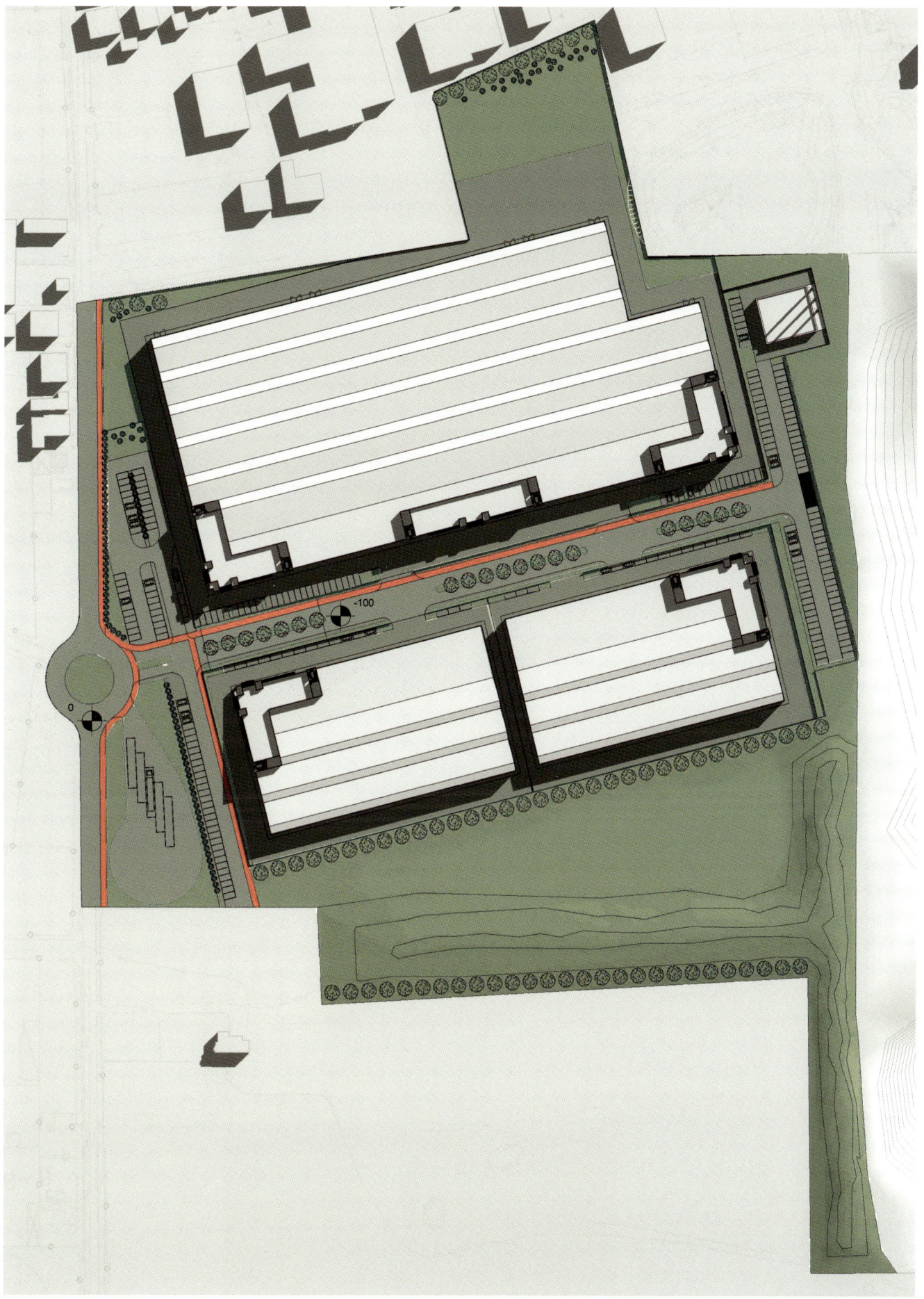

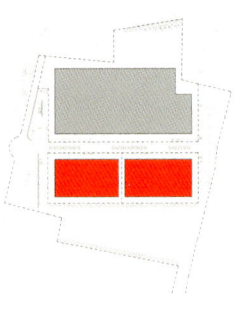

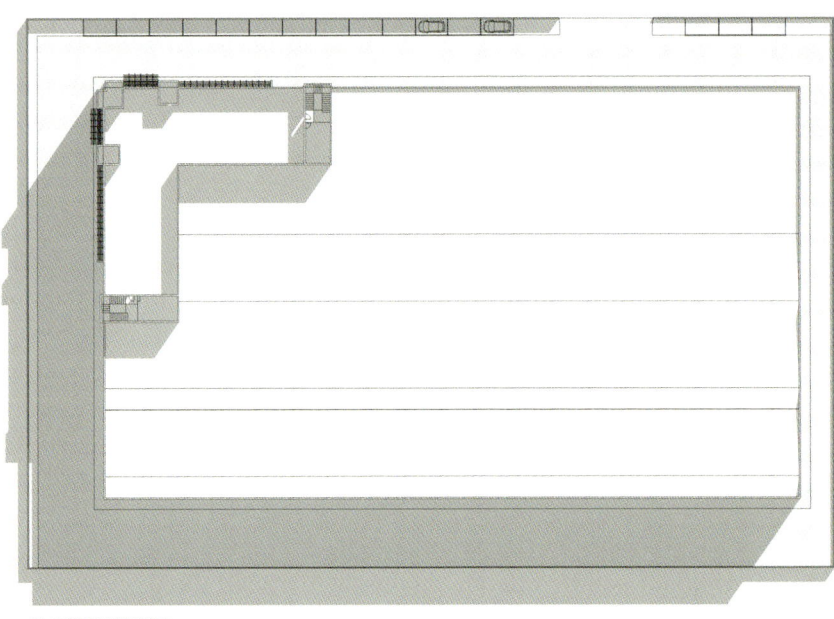

Planimetric and volumetric plan and elevations of the southern section

Overall views of project in the southern section

PLANIVOLUMETRICO
Scala 1 : 500

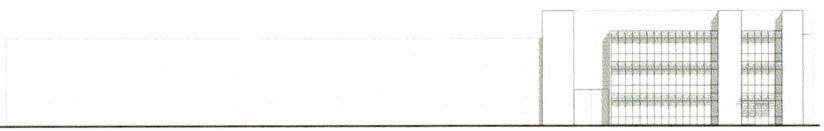

PROSPETTO NORD
Scala 1 : 500

PROSPETTO SUD
Scala 1 : 500

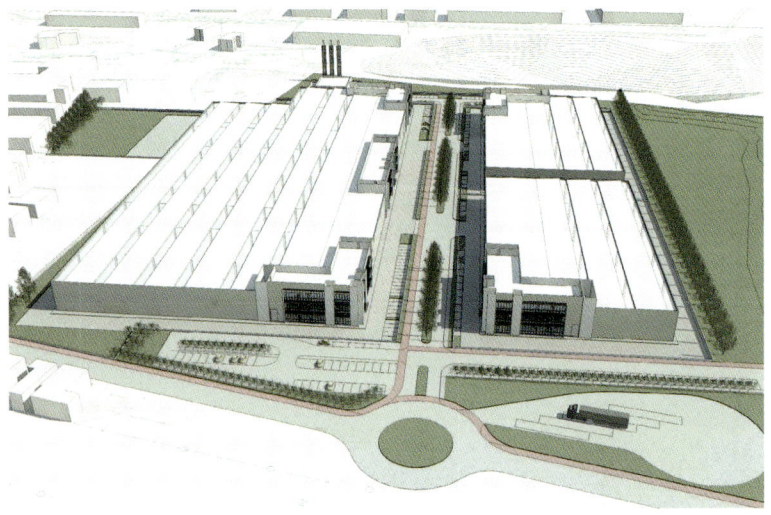

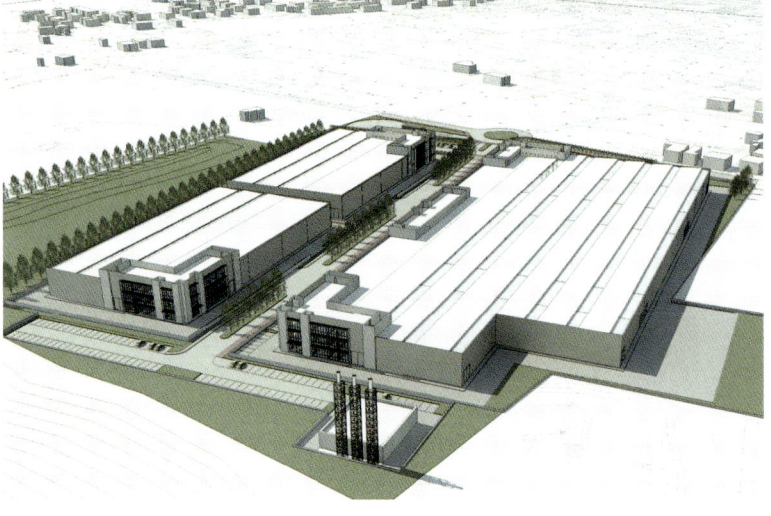

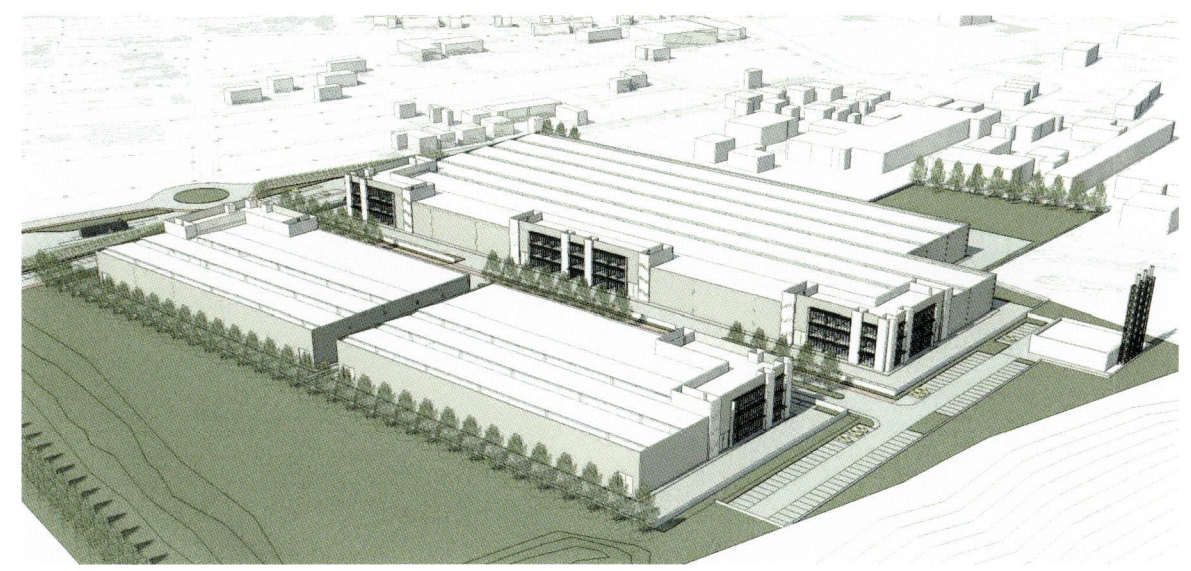

Overall view of project in the northern section

Planimetric and volumetric plan and elevations of northern section

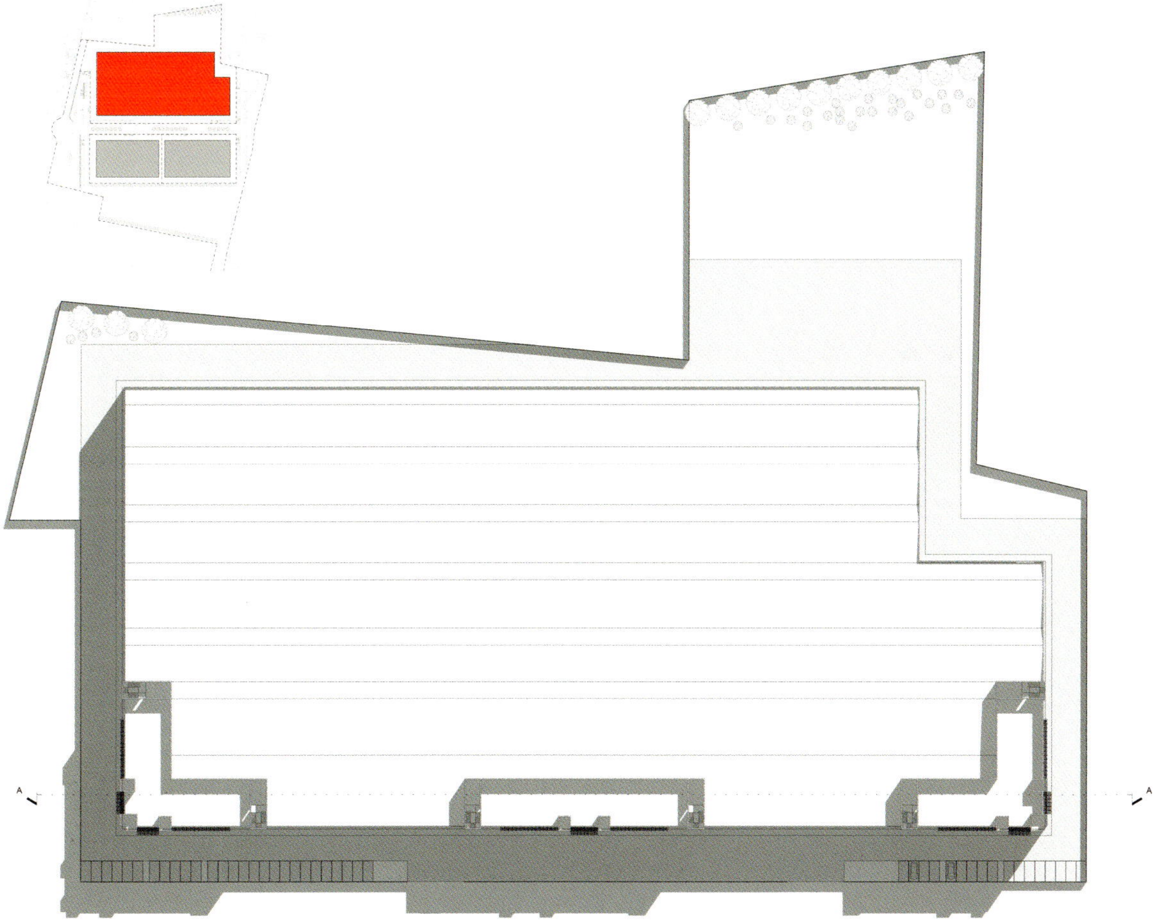

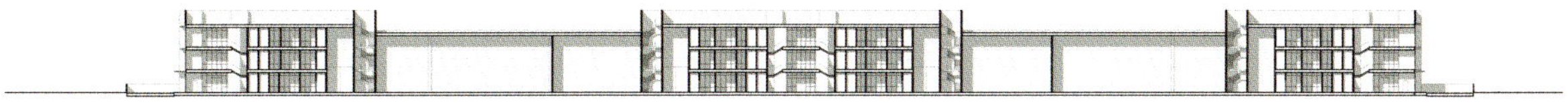

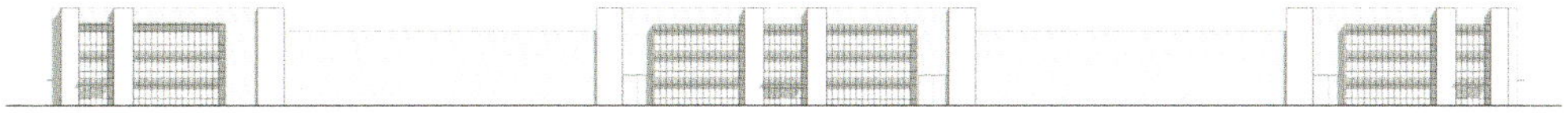

197

8. Pozzo d'Adda (Milan): enlargement and restructuring of an industrial building (2010)

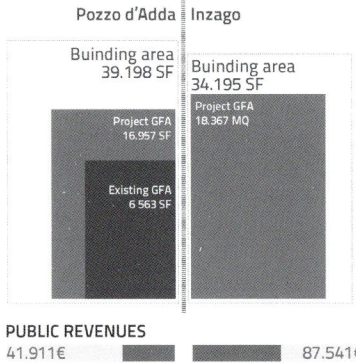

The complex at Pozzo d'Adda, located in an industrial context on the 525 provincial highway from Milan to the Vaprio bridge and wholly lacking in quality, was made up of three connected and staggered buildings following the slope of the road, albeit in a context of buildings aligned instead with provincial highway 180. Requirements of production and expansion of the activities carried out inside it as well as reorganization of the company's premises made it advisable to take advantage of the building land made available by the Territorial Management Plan of Inzago just over the boundary of the area. The enlargement of the built-up area thus offered an opportunity to rethink the complex as a whole, not least in relation to the possible restructuring of highway 525 with the opening of a new front and access.

The project envisaged two different systems: a construction to the south capable of housing the production and processing units of a company manufacturing installations for trade fairs and exhibitions, and enlargement of the system of offices on the west side towards the road. The new volume is enveloped in a single uninterrupted skin capable to lending homogeneity to the whole, both the existing part and the new, and of using the space between the new building and the old to conceal facilities such as the space for waste disposal. This skin thus thickens the outer shell to the point of endowing it with volumetric substance and giving the complex a new image. The existing part and the new are connected by a new staircase unit that handles the flow between the expanded spaces and provides the new point of access.

Structured as a tool capable of managing construction on an area straddling the territory of two different municipalities, namely Inzago and Pozzo d'Adda, the project developed a particular pathway with a view to direct implementation and obtaining rapid agreement among different bodies called upon for a contribution towards the enlargement and restructuring of an existing parking lot in the industrial area in return for the indirect public benefit of the operation. The architectural project thus once again broadens its horizons and presents itself as a tool for the implementation of provisions regarding not only construction but also urban planning.

Territorial location. The project area is situated on the outskirts of Pozzi d'Adda in the existing industrial district along the 525 highway. The strategic position of the buildings concerned suggested a planning strategy aimed at enhancing their symbolic value and visibility through the expansion and reconfiguration of the façades

ARCHITECTURE

Planivolumetric plan. The project regards the building of a new structure containing storage spaces and offices to serve the existing industrial buildings, to which a new outer shell of organic profile is added to serve as a unifying element for the complex. The new building is aligned with provincial highway 180, thus differing in compositional logic from the surrounding settlement and vigorously emphasizing the new construction. The open space is reorganized and made more functional, including a ramp for access to the basement floor, some street-level parking places and a large green area

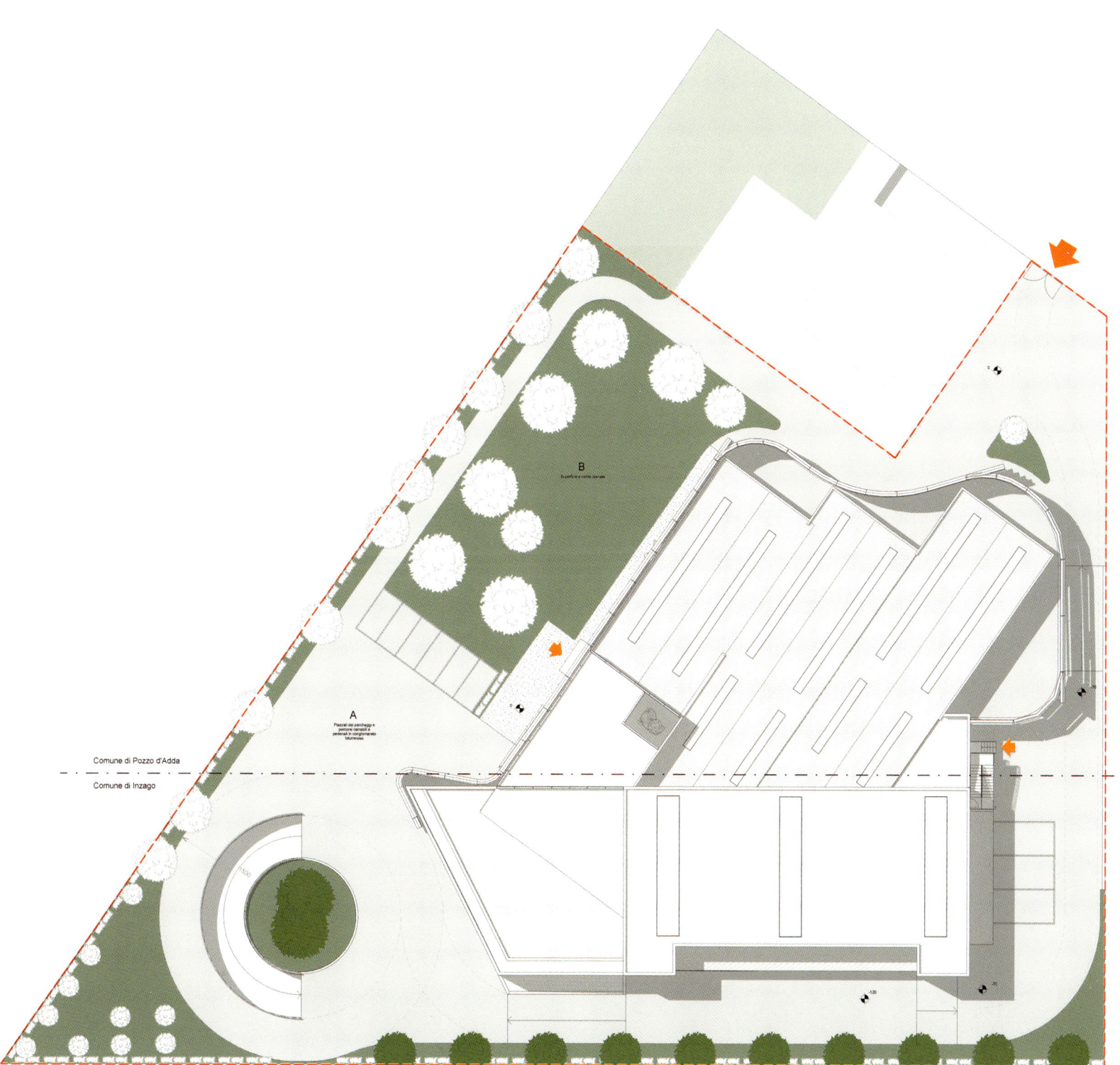

ARCHITECTURE

Elevations. The fragmented front of the existing buildings is unified by means of a fluidly moulded shell of painted sheet-metal panels capable of linking the industrial buildings in one architectural sweep. The new building, characterized by a simple formal vocabulary, is taller than the existing ones but adds no elements of physical and expressive complexity

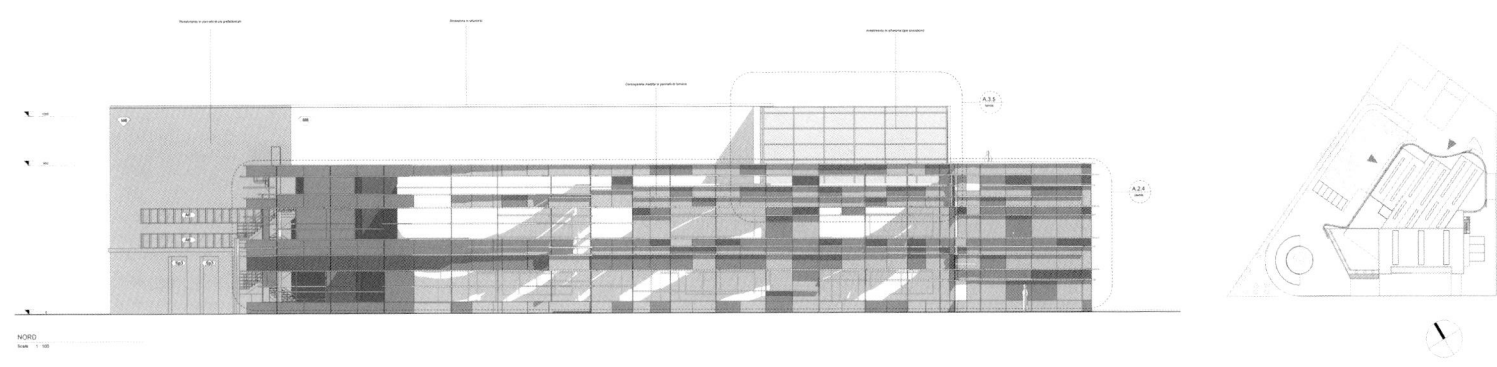

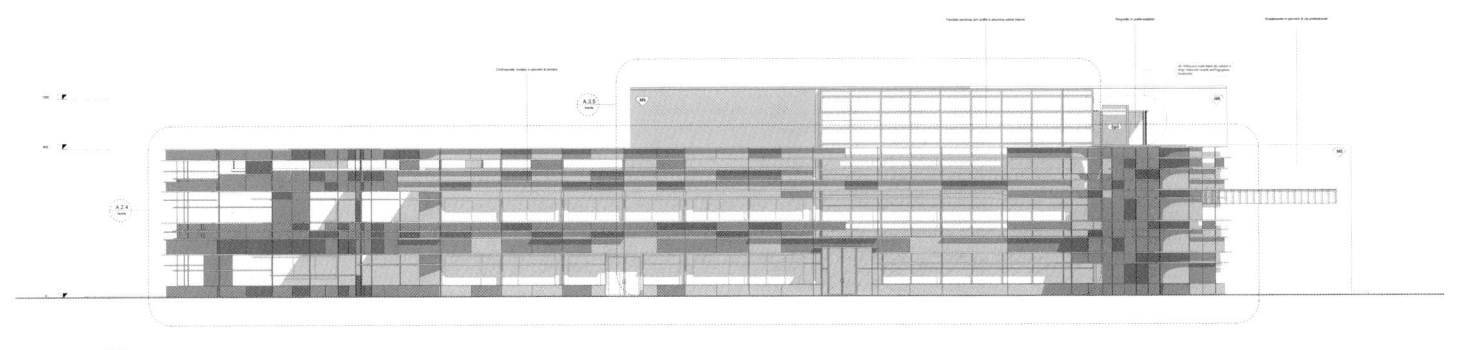

Plan of ground floor and first floor. The new building, situated alongside the tertiary workshops, has two floors that serve the existing factories as a storage depot. The upper floor is expanded to include a section for offices and reception facilities, which use part of the roof of the new building as a terrace with plants

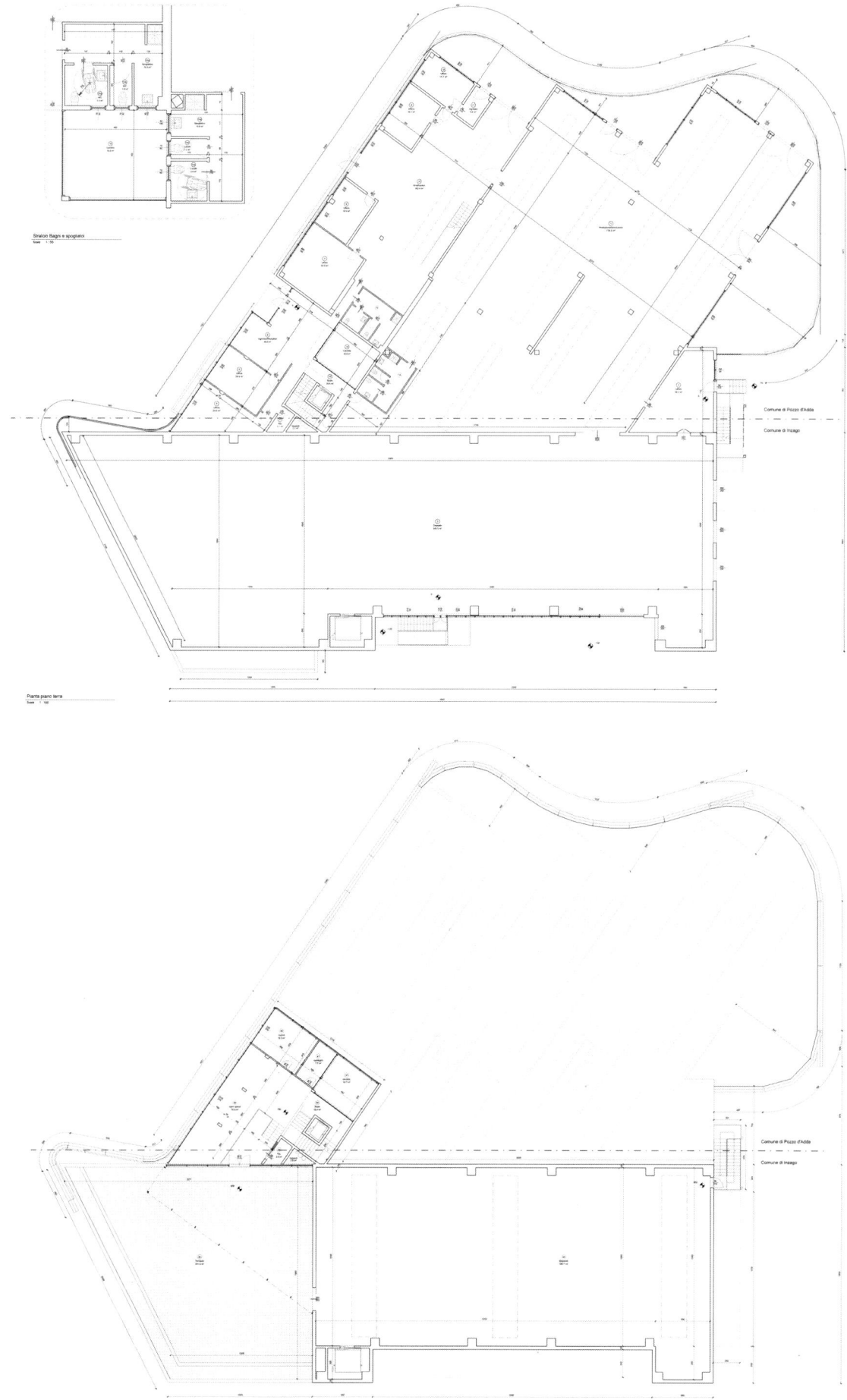

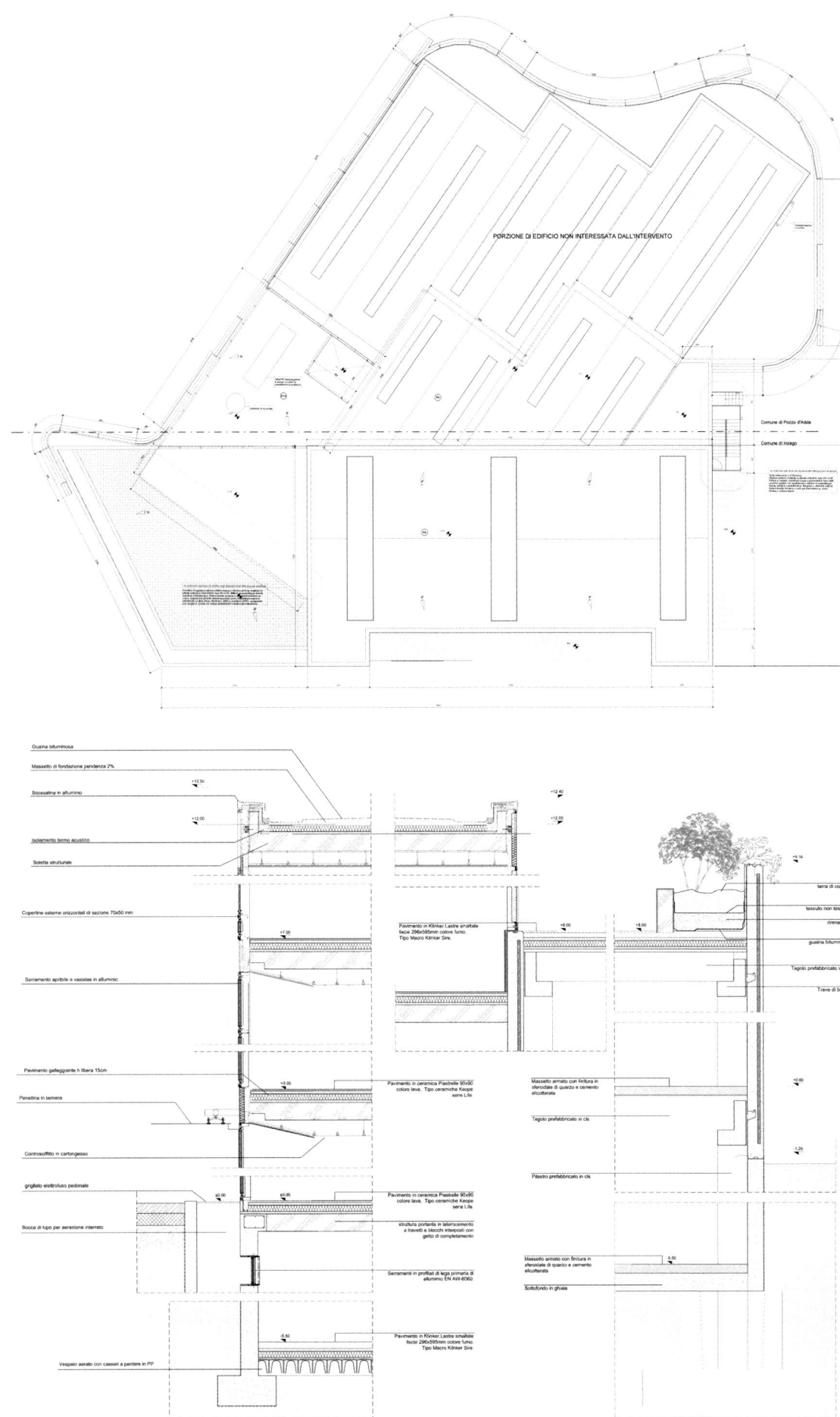

Construction section of the new building and overall views. The new building is made entirely of prefabricated elements with a flat roof. The new shell of painted sheet metal functions as unifying element for the various structures inside the project perimeter by virtue of its highly distinctive shape of marked visual impact. The choice in terms of form and material marks a deliberate departure from the vocabulary of the existing structures and adds an element of complexity to simple and otherwise inexpressive edifices

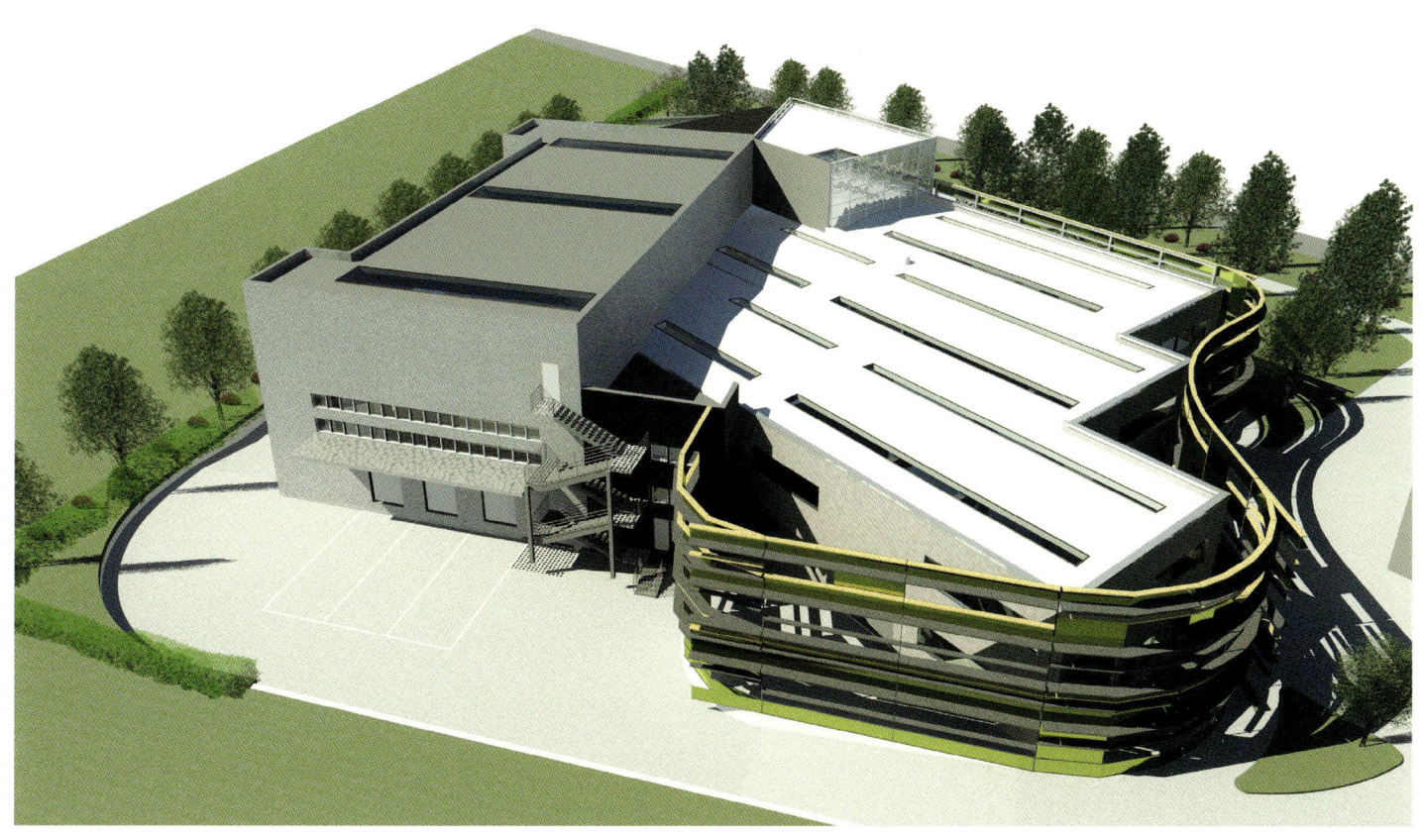

ARCHITECTURE

9. Inzago (Milan): public plan for cooperative residential buildings (2010–11)

AREA	152.340 SF
Building area	67.142 SF
Green areas	43.696 SF
Parking areas	11.416 SF
Infrastructures	14.213 SF
Public spaces	15.871 SF

GFA		68.551 SF
Residential	68.551 SF	100%
Industrial		0%
Service sector		0%
Mixed-use		0%
Commercial		0%
Turistic		0%
Other		0%

PUBLIC REVENUES

535.164 €

The Territorial Management Plan of Inzago earmarked the area on the northeast side of the centre for the construction of public housing to be carried out by the cooperatives that have historically operated on the territory and made up for the lack of exclusively public policies. The town council and the plan envisaged a project for the area capable of boosting the quality of the peripheral and marginal northeast sector, slightly rundown above all due to the presence of a less recent public housing complex of shabby appearance facing onto the project site. The area is characterized by the rich environmental system typical of these contexts with the presence of streams and canals. The proximity of agricultural land gives greater breadth and focuses attention on the need to respect these characteristics.

The project thus took into consideration these aspects and some strong constraints. Attention to the requirements of the cooperatives prompted discussion on their habitual practices as regards construction and customary conception of building projects in very dogmatic and traditional terms that unquestionably work only because they always have worked and only because the results could ensure a certain level of performance and appeal for members. The town council and the plan sought to focus attention on the nature of the operation and its possible role at the territorial level, above all due to the fact that the cooperatives presented a project wholly closed to the territory and the surrounding settlement fabric, where the green spaces were all fenced-in and private, and the buildings turned their back on the agricultural territory and the settlement system to create a small and entirely defensive enclave. The plan developed completely reversed this perspective, seeking to place the architectural project within broader urban-planning horizons, to establish dialogue with the territory, and above all to address the town's constitutive characteristics. The square, the park and the built-up area must work towards the construction of a small new centrality capable of enhancing the settlement quality of the eastern sector and opening up the new development to the territory. Above all, the new settlement must fully belong to the important tradition of public housing complexes and cannot be allowed to sink into the anonymity of urban sprawl.

A central square attracts buildings to look onto it and share their inhabited and illuminated façades, reducing the area occupied by construction and increasing the urban sense of the development. The park occupies the southern part of the area, where ecological restoration is envisaged for the streams and canals. A main road provides vehicle access without running through the area. A cycle track and a pedestrian path run through the buildings and are alone allowed access to the main square, to which they give shape through modification of design. With water, trees and urban furniture for seating, the square comes to life and equips itself to become the central hub of the settlement. The cycle track organizes the parts and the pattern of the paving is altered to mark its passage. The shapes of the residential buildings are calculated to enhance a more dynamic volumetric composition, highlighting the major angles and heights looking onto the square and sloping away towards the exterior.

Developed in the form of a guiding master plan, the project includes some prescriptive norms for aspects such as the alignment of façades and the position of the square and the green space so as to avoid any distortion of the architectural approach and its urban-planning nature during implementation.

Location of areas involved in the project. Project site in the eastern section of the municipality of Inzago

204

Planivolumetric plan. Drawing inspiration from the northwest alignment of the building, the project disrupts and alters the structure of the context by creating a new line of transversal alignment. The distances between the buildings thus avoid areas of shadow and increase the exposure to natural light

ARCHITECTURE

Elevations. The façades on all sides show the extent to which the project pursues movement and the overlapping of visual planes. Solids and void are juxtaposed and the higher parts of the buildings are balanced by the lower

Overall view. The photovoltaic systems installed are indicative of the focus on sustainability and environmental aspects that informs the project as a whole

ARCHITECTURE

Prospetto est

Prospetto nord

Prospetto ovest

Prospetto sud

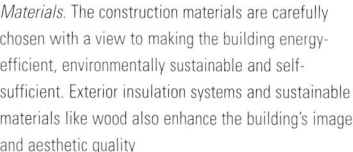

Elevations. The façades accentuate the variety of modules devised, displaying a harmonious blend of higher and lower sections and the use of light and opaque surfaces

Materials. The construction materials are carefully chosen with a view to making the building energy-efficient, environmentally sustainable and self-sufficient. Exterior insulation systems and sustainable materials like wood also enhance the building's image and aesthetic quality

207

3D views. The image gives a complete idea of the project for private and public spaces. Paving and green areas interweave to create a wholly usable space

Infrastructural detail. The central roundabout ensures correct distribution of the flows of access to the buildings

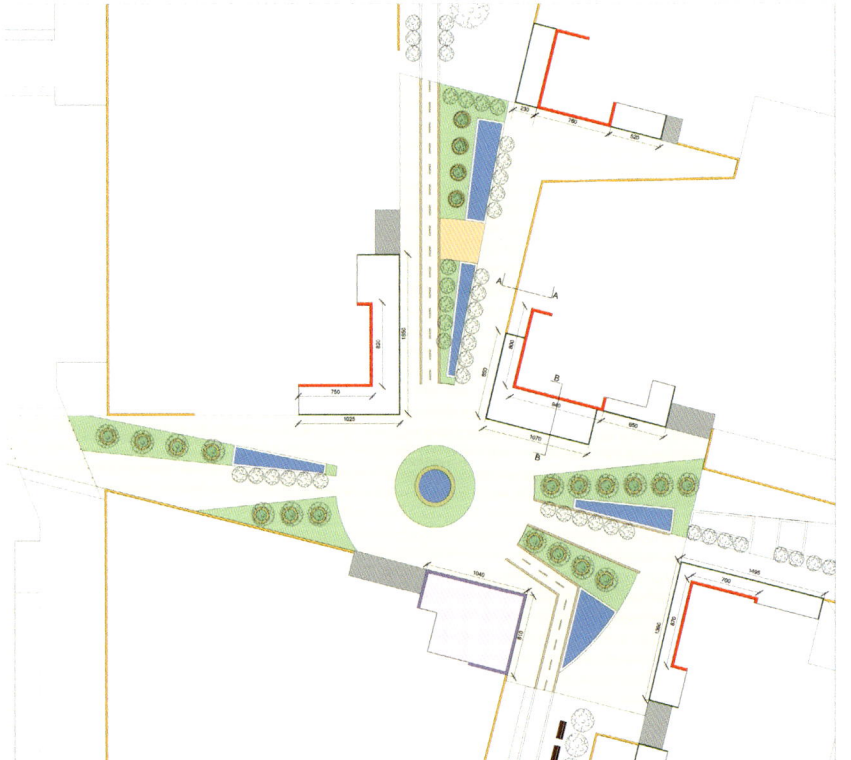

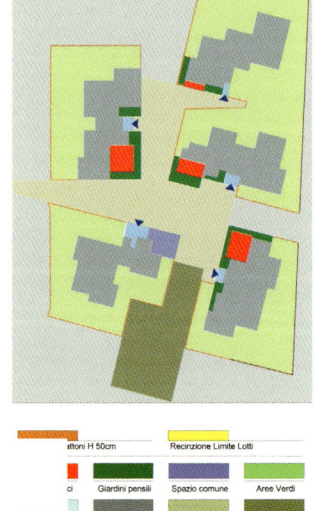

ARCHITECTURE

Green areas. The sustainability concept includes correct planning of green space. Public and private green areas interweave and complement one another to become an integral part of the compositional design of the district as a whole

3D view of the central buildings. Perspective view of the central green backbone and the central buildings characterized by façades that vary in terms of compositional modules and colour

3D view of public space. The base of the buildings in direct contact with the public space to create an environment of high residential quality

ARCHITECTURE

10. Rozzano (Milan): building for commerce and services
(under way since 2010)

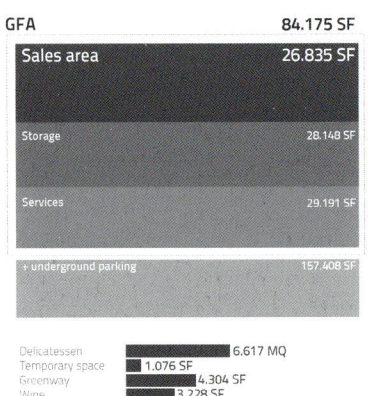

GFA	84.175 SF
Sales area	26.835 SF
Storage	28.148 SF
Services	29.191 SF
+ underground parking	157.408 SF

Delikatessen	6.617 MQ
Temporary space	1.076 SF
Greenway	4.304 SF
Wine	3.228 SF
Desing market	10.006 SF

The largest unit of the redevelopment project for the area along Via Manzoni regards the building with the largest surface area of the section as whole. Taking advantage of the particular location between Via Manzoni and Via Brodolini, the project envisages a building with two particular elements: a sharp and prominent point visible from a distance, serving as a landmark for the crossroads and establishing dialogue with the territory brought into communication by the road; and a broad, gentle curved side on Via Manzoni capable of evoking the more winding course it once followed, marked by the presence of a small and ancient bridge over the Pizzabrasa stream. These two features make up a particular façade of great impact and visual significance. Though constituting a territorial landmark of importance, with respect to the functions housed by the building, predominantly commercial together with large surfaces devoted to supporting services, the façade presented the defect of facing southwest and thus being fully exposed to the sun in the afternoon, thus posing a major problem for the public activities carried out inside. The west side, in addition to bending in accordance with the former course of the road, is thus hollowed out and given a double skin. With a double arch originating in the southwest corner of the building, the façade opens up to increase its volume and thickness to such an extent that the windows are inserted into this thickness, not directly flush with the façade, and face north rather than west. The same windows design a continuous vertical cadence to accompany the eye in transit along Via Manzoni, its thickness being marked also by the continuation of the glazed surfaces at the top with the construction of skylights. The thick façade opens up to accommodate the points of access to the commercial surfaces, the importance of the entrance being indicated by its height, and folds to end in the point near the stream. The other façades are more subdued in character, again with the repetition of the rhythm of thicknesses along the north side to accompany the building's second public façade looking onto the environmentally restored and redeveloped areas by the stream. While the east and south façades are smooth and homogeneous, the east includes some service structures such as loading and unloading areas. Environmental minimization along this side, close to the surviving areas of woodland, includes the construction of a green dune with a canopy for growing plant species.

It was decided to conceal the parking spaces. Precisely in order to increase the territorial revaluation of the area, these are housed in two underground storeys, whose construction presented no few challenges with respect to the overall building system of the area. Here the watery terrain of the lower Po Valley presents layers of sand and mud with clay only at the bottom.
A complex system of bulkheads, 82 ft in depth, made it possible to create a cavity of about 14,400 yd^2 to house the two-storey car park with a foundation slab about 3,28 ft in thickness to counter the considerable thrust of the water table.
The building is constructed in accordance with the class A energy standards through the use of particular devices to insulate the façades and the installation of photovoltaic solar panels on the roof, concealed by the taller top of the façade, as well as systems to harness geothermal energy with the construction of heat pumps and shafts.
This complex edifice performs the various roles derived from its location and genesis, and expresses them through the dynamic handling of volume and the composition of the façades.

Location of areas involved in the project. Operational area 1 along Via Manzoni and Via Brodolini in the municipality of Rozzano

Design of Blossom Market interior. The aisles and display units constitute thematic islands with the goods on show rather than traditional rows of shelves. The use of different display systems, such as raised platforms and containers, creates a new approach to the sales space and fosters greater interaction with the goods and their qualities

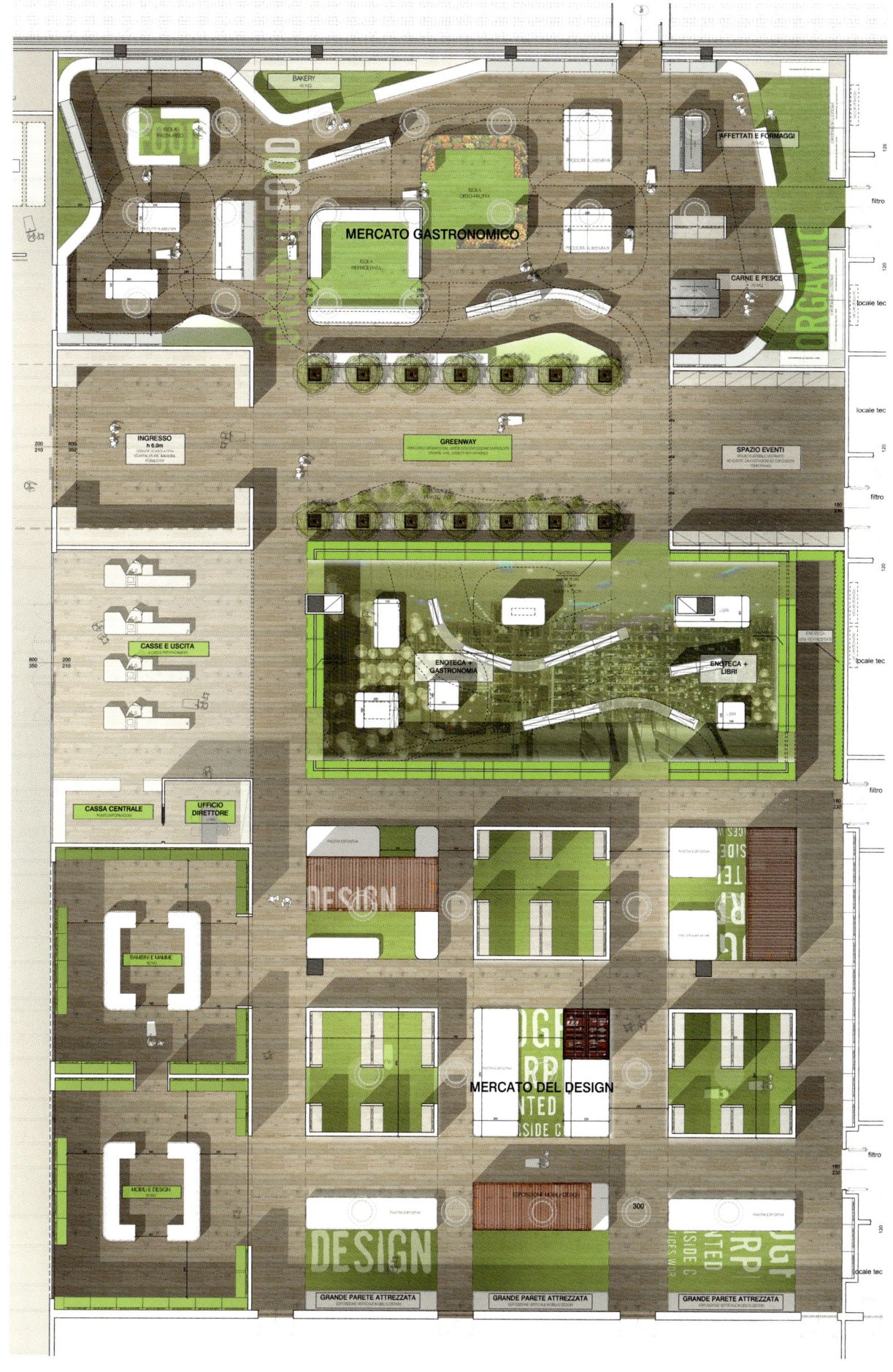

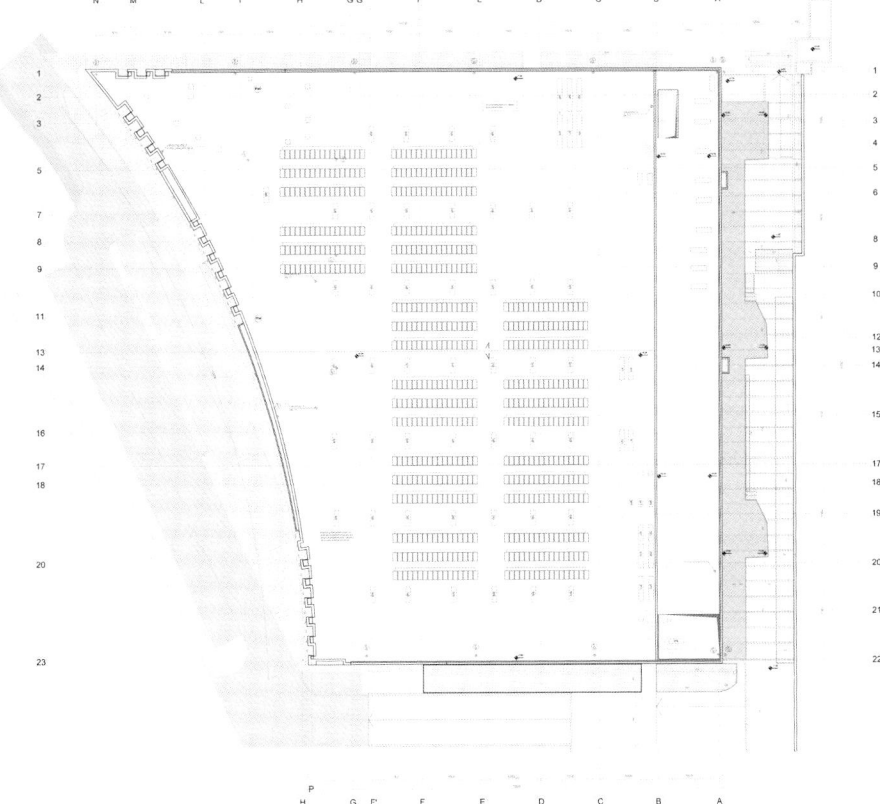

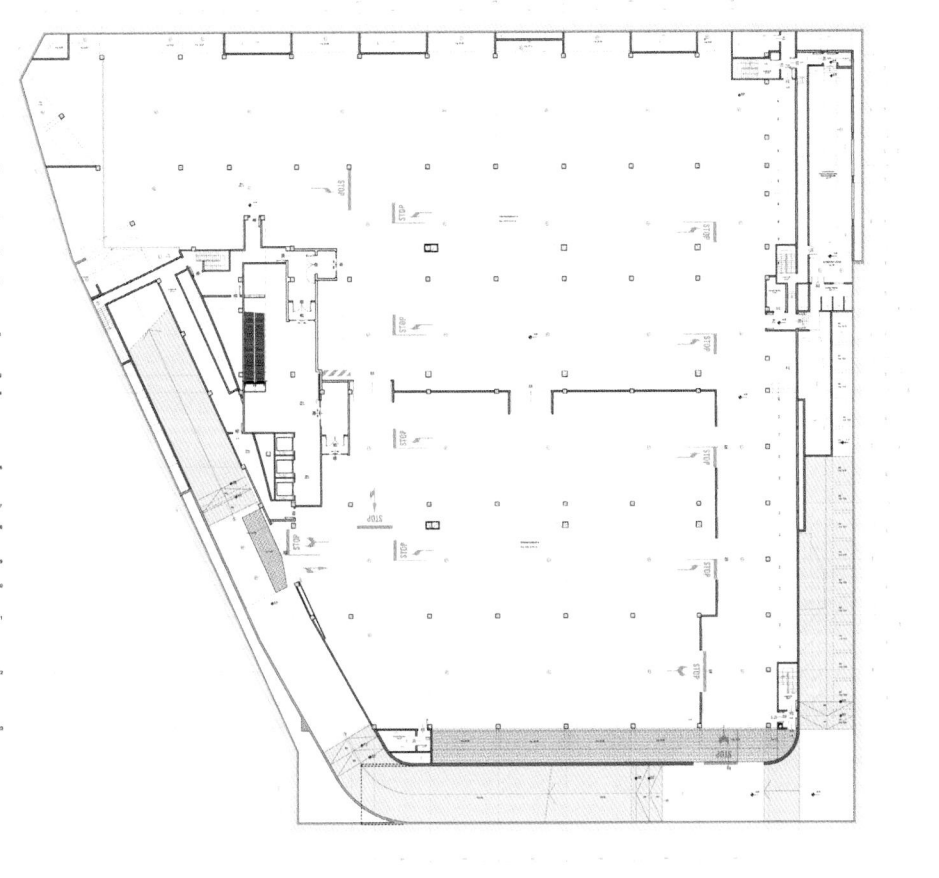

Plan of basement -1. Garage, stairway and mechanical rooms

Roof plan. It is possible to distinguish the three sections of the main body, the roof of the mezzanine and the canopy of the short-term storage area for dispatch. Garage, stairway and mechanical rooms

Plan of basement -2. Garage, stairway and mechanical rooms

Plan of ground floor. The gallery with the entrances from the south and west, the sales area and the areas used for storage and services

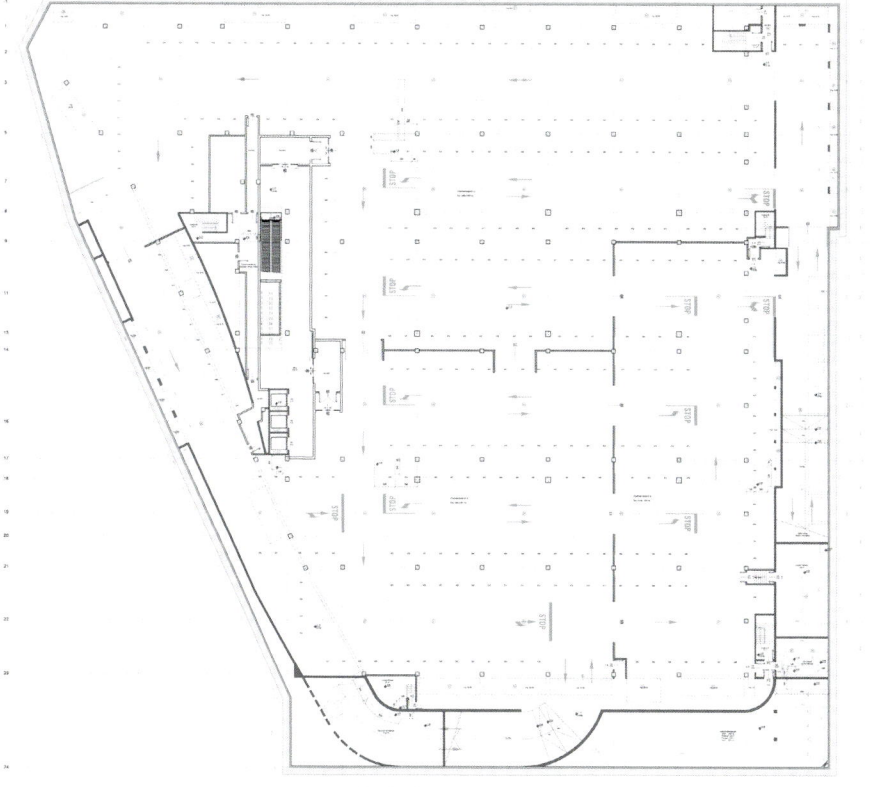

ARCHITECTURE

Elevations. The main façade presents a rhythmic arrangement of vertical modular elements interrupted by the closer rhythm of the entrance and the hiatus of the long sign. The side façades mask the service exits with a contrasting interplay of light-coloured walls and larger expanses of dark colour

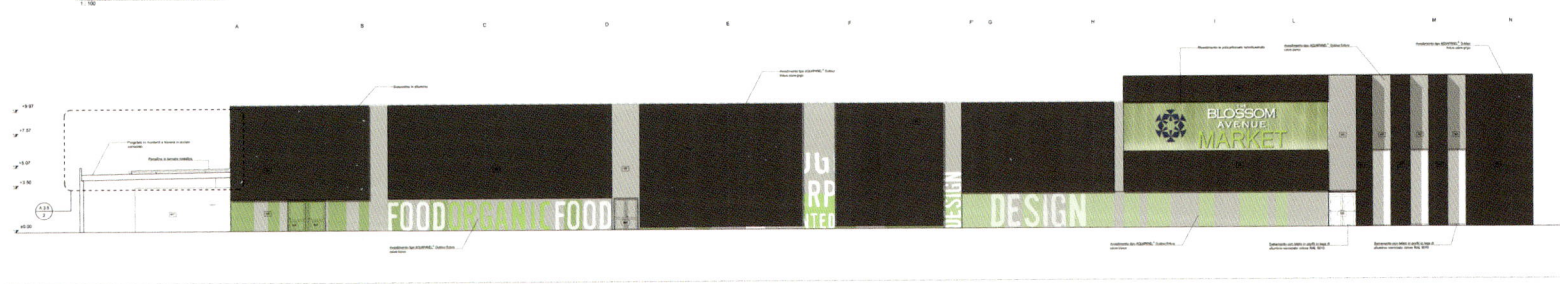

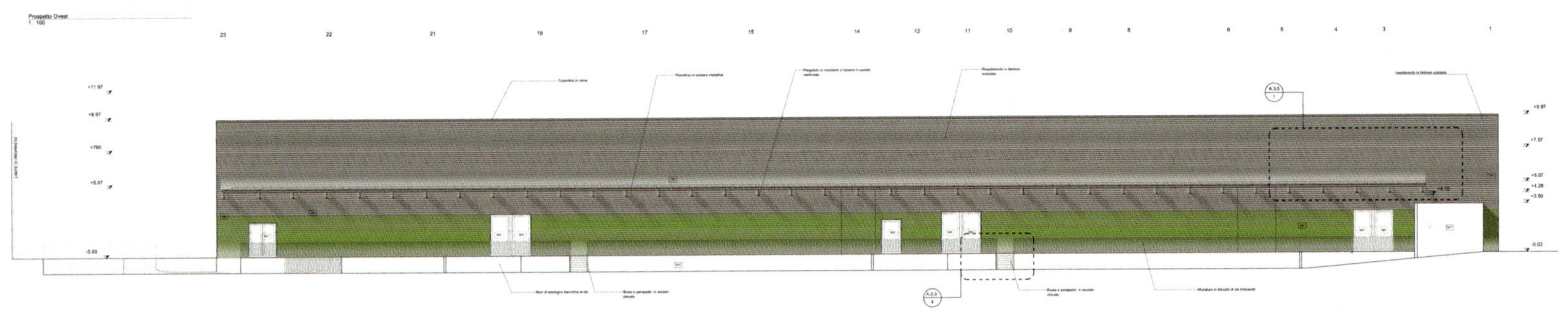

Building sections. The lighting systems are clearly seen through the interplay of open and closed sections of the façade

ARCHITECTURE

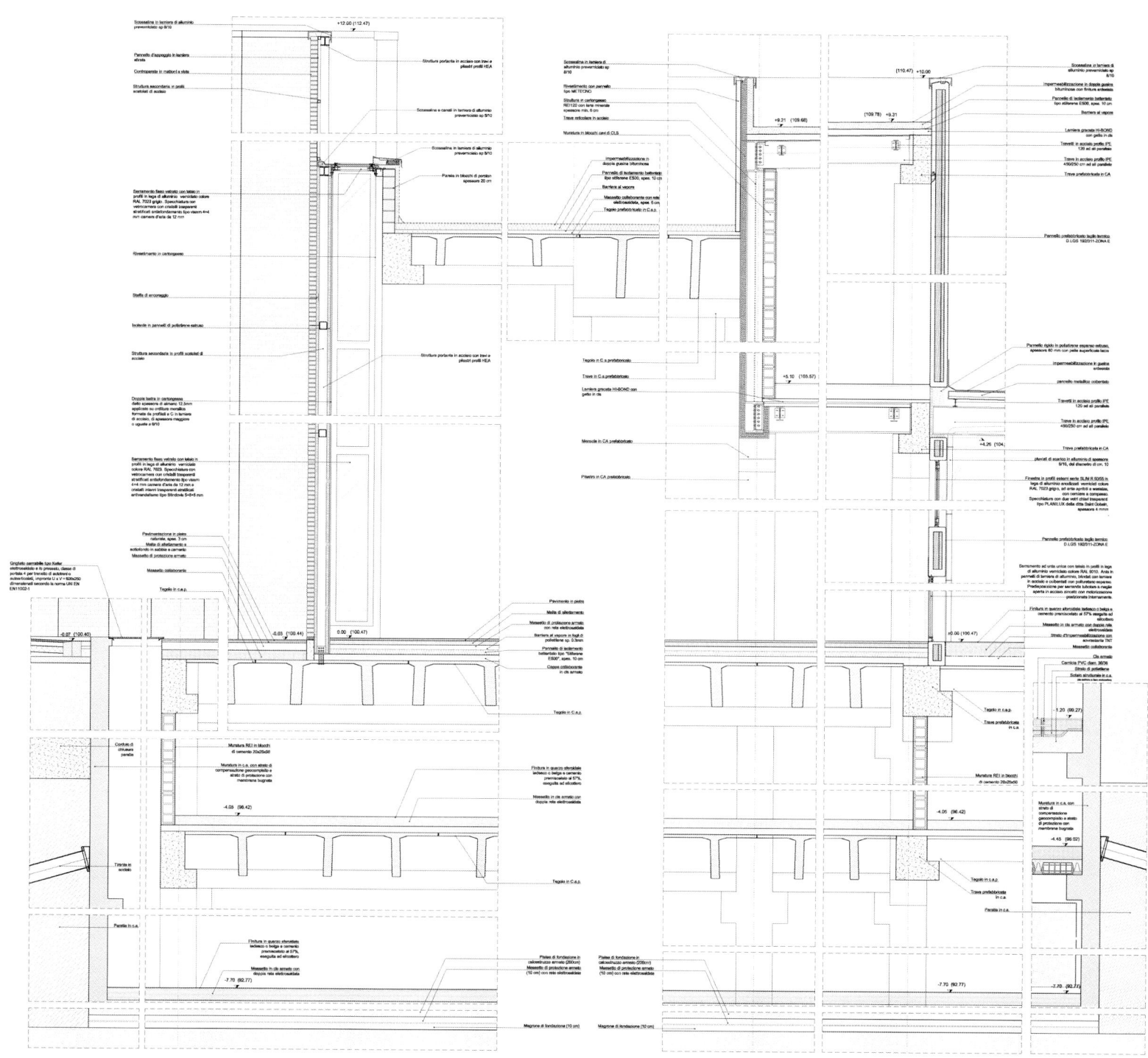

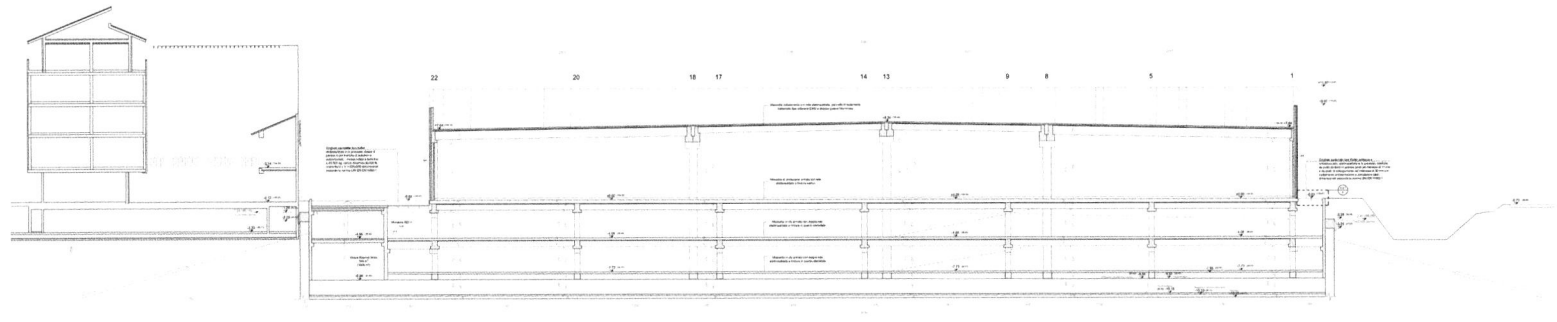

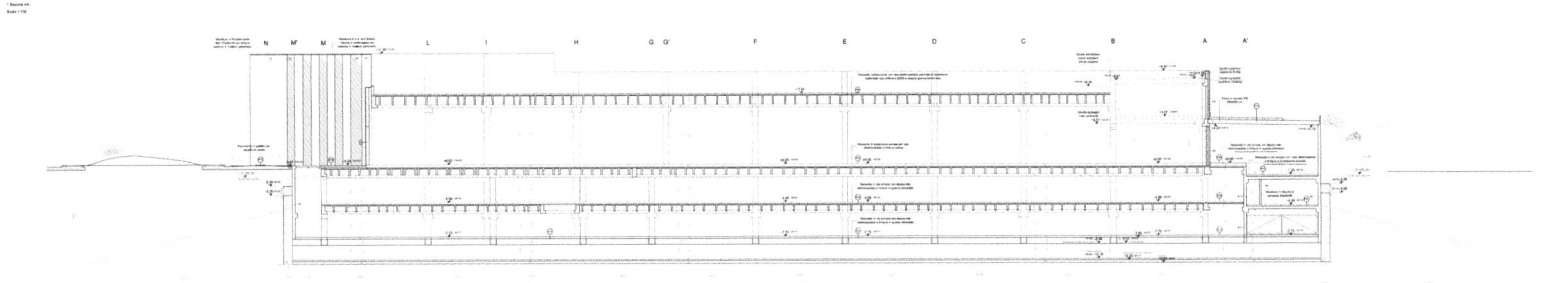

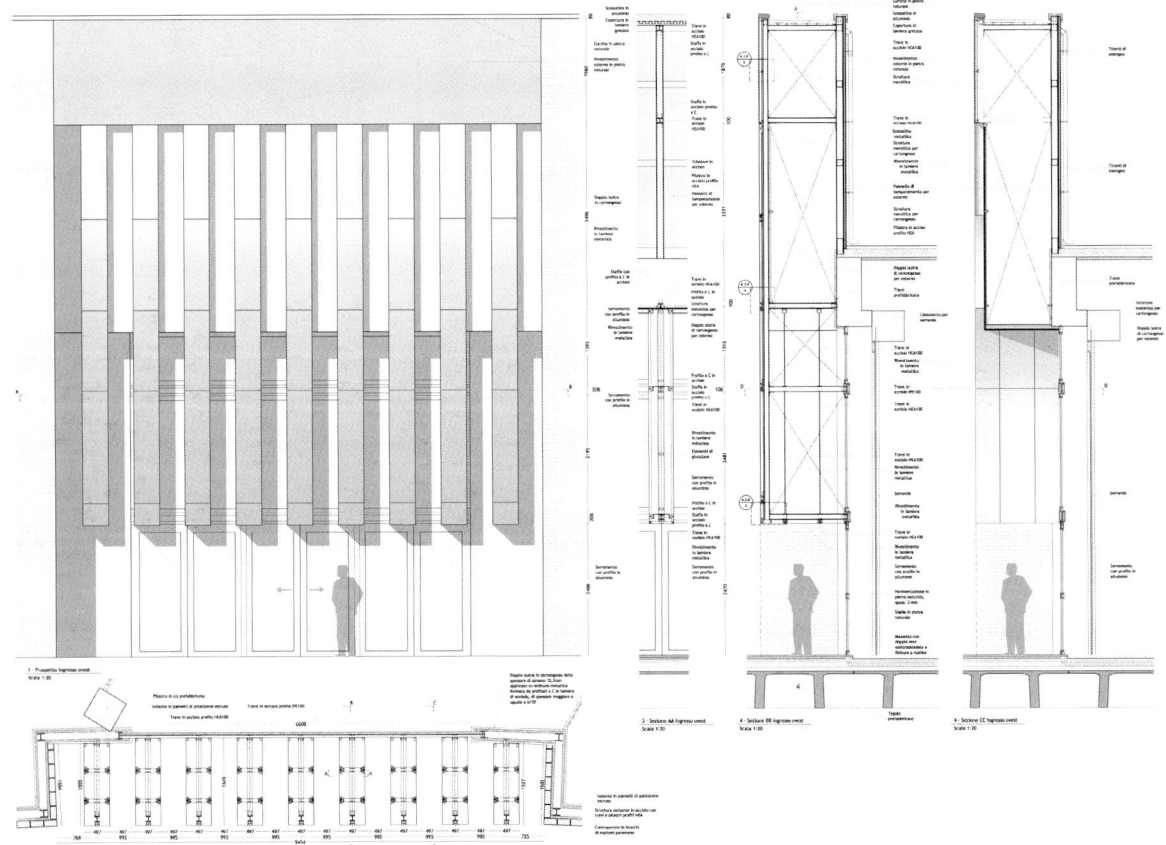

Longitudinal cross section. The large foundation slab and the prefabricated structure of the underground garages and the roof

Main entrance, detail. The large window is fitted with vertical aluminium sun baffles that recall the modular rhythm of the façade on a smaller scale

ARCHITECTURE

View of the south entrance by night. The use of lighting emphasizes the primary compositional elements

Construction. Assembly of the prefabricated structure

ARCHITECTURE

11. Cassano d'Adda (Milan): projects and plans for redevelopment of the area of the disused Linificio Canapificio Nazionale factory (under way since 2010)

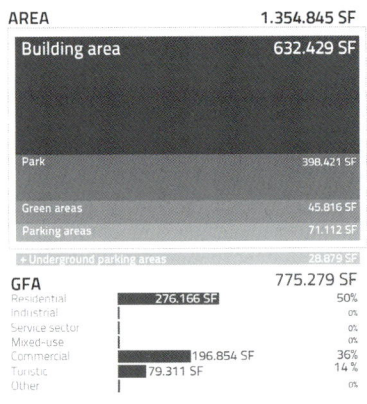

The Linificio Canapificio Nazionale complex at Cassano d'Adda is a very particular area embedded in the context of the anthropization and industrialization of the course of the river Adda, between industrial areas founded about a century ago, hydraulic works to channel the waters of the river, dams and power stations.
A particular landscape rich in history and remains of hydraulic and industrial engineering and endowed at the same time with particular environmental value, increased by the abandonment of industrial activities under way for some time, which has allowed nature to gain the upper hand over the buildings. In the case of Cassano, the former industrial area is constructed on a platform nearly at the level of the canal of the linen factory, which draws its waters from the Adda, passes through the power station and the lock, and joins up again with the Adda downstream, thus drawing the boundaries of the Borromeo island.
The platform is lower than the settlement of Cassano, spread out over the terrace on the plain overlooking the valley of the Adda, but close to the historical centre, higher up but nearby, and to the heritage presented by the centre on the edge of the terrace, starting with the castle. We thus have an area of great local interest and territorial value belonging to a long series of similar towns and disused industrial systems along the river. A heritage that merits the utmost attention and the highest possible level of planning with a view not only to salvaging the buildings and associated areas but also to harnessing the environmental aspects, the relations with historical centres and in general with the settlement system of the Adda. This is, however, run by the North Adda Park, a body that has failed over the years to address redevelopment with the degree of courage required to prevent the destruction of the heritage through waste and the ravages of time with no overall breath and vision. Though endowed with this courage, the project developed has repeatedly been at risk over the years of drowning in the muddy waters of public administration and being deviated from its true purpose of redeveloping a major heritage and doing justice to its twofold role at the local and territorial levels. It took off again with inclusion in the Territorial Management Plan of Cassano d'Adda and attained its definitive form and structure ready for implementation.
Proximity to the historical centre and the presence of the canal are the two elements on which the project focuses in order to express its character and potential with respect to the local context, by maximizing the image of the extension of the historical centre with new constructions, and to the territorial system, by taking advantage of the canal to define all the linear elements, including the green system, cycle tracks and pedestrian connections. The project thus takes shape, expressing the area's vocation to accommodate a settlement in the form of a prolongation and extension of the historical centre of Cassano capable of constituting a centrality of markedly urban character and strong territorial attraction in the knowledge that urban life involves a mixture of functions and compact aggregation of volumes. Three pathways constitute the project's backbone and the basic structure of the settlement. First, a pathway along the canal, with the reconstruction of the longer disused Corderie building to give new volume to a symbolic place for Cassano and the entire context of the Adda, capable of accommodating a cycle lane and a pedestrian pathway of sufficient weight to attract public spaces and central places beneath the rebuilt factory roof. Second, a central pedestrian pathway of many uses

Location of the site for redevelopment of the Linificio factory at Cassano d'Adda (Milan)

Overall plan of the final solution, designed to explore the area's potential, for implementation of the rules of the PGT (Territorial Management Plan) and verification of the volumes located there. The design develops a complex system of relations between open spaces, spaces for relations and constructed spaces both at the local microscale and at the macro level of relations with the rest of the municipal territory

ARCHITECTURE

Plans, from basement to roof, of the renovation of the central structure of the Linificio

and functions in the form of an urban promenade, like a riverside or waterfront, with shops, leisure facilities, cafés, restaurants, residential buildings and private service functions clustered along the main living street, the true backbone of the settlement. Third, a greenway that gives shape to the project with the design of a major backbone along the canal, which overlaps with the Corderie pathway, shapes the park, and branches out through the built-up area to expand the environmental value of green areas in the midst of constructed space.

Key importance attaches to salvaging the buildings that have survived neglect and decay. The historical nucleus of the Linificio Canapificio Nazionale, a splendid two-storey building with a steel frame and outer shell of masonry once occupied by major machinery, and some small buildings of lesser importance with the markedly industrial character of the period make up the heritage of the linen factory earmarked for conversion and together accommodate the most important public functions.

New accommodation facilities for Cassano are hosted in the most historical complex, through which a central pathway is constructed to connect with the territorial pathways leading to the linen factory and the adjacent steel-frame building. Gymnasiums and wellness centres increase the public leisure facilities in the area, opening up to the green areas and the park and taking advantage of the water as an element characterizing all these functions. A public square linking this section and the park is located in the most symbolic and central place of the entire area so as to gather its inhabitants and users precisely in the point of most importance.

The architecture seeks out a particular vocabulary. Establishing dialogue at a distance with approaches focusing on the urban character of new settlements, such as New Urbanism in the USA, it modulates the volumes carefully in relation to the urban-planning scheme in the conviction that urbanity is attained through a blend of structures, public networks, spaces for relations, open spaces, constructed spaces, uses and functions. It also designs surfaces with materials connected with the local tradition, the industrial past of the area and the contemporary requirements of energy saving and environmental performance. Larger and smaller buildings engage in dialogue with the public pathways, squares and green space, almost as though to acknowledge the greater importance of the public space and systems in a context abased for too many years by the ravages of time and a misconceived approach to management of the territory. The Linificio will take shape as a major area of transformation capable with its urban character of renewing the role of the town and increasing its overall quality.

Volumetric simulation of the central area with refurbishment of the historical structures of the Linificio factory, the addition of new buildings and the design of open space. The central backbone makes it possible to design a single pathway capable of connecting both the new spaces and the renovation of the historical central structure of the area

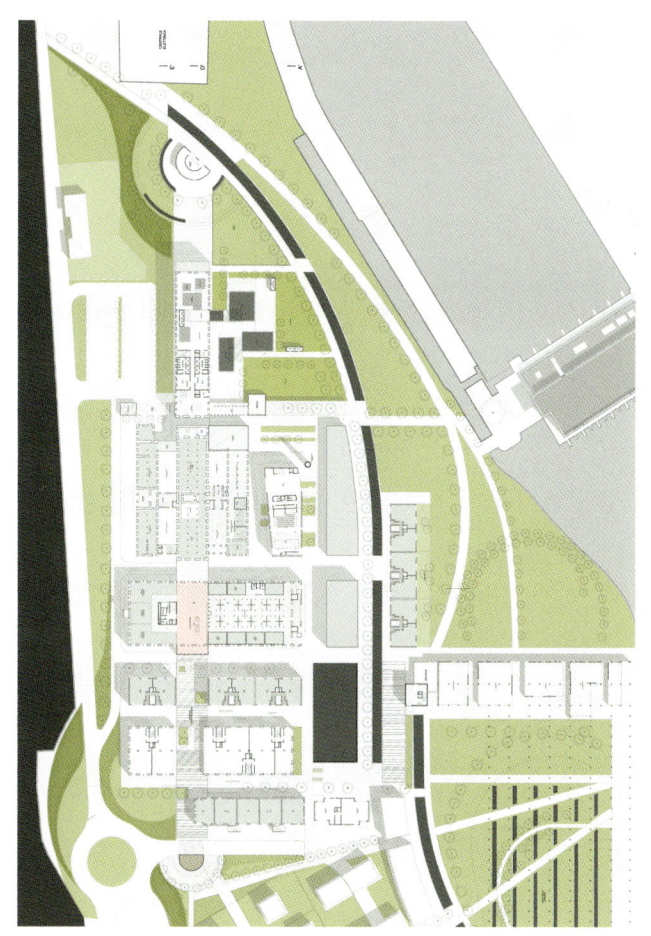
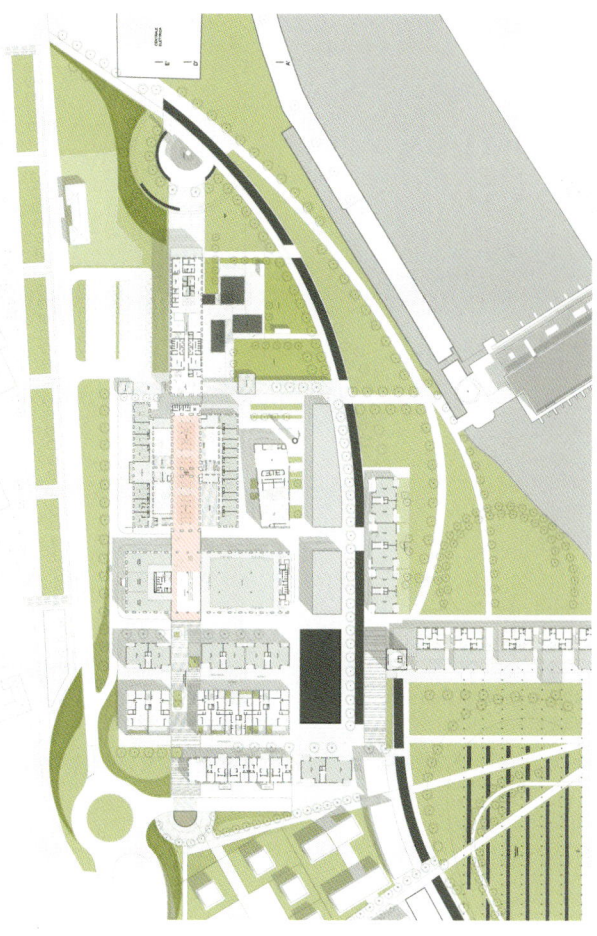
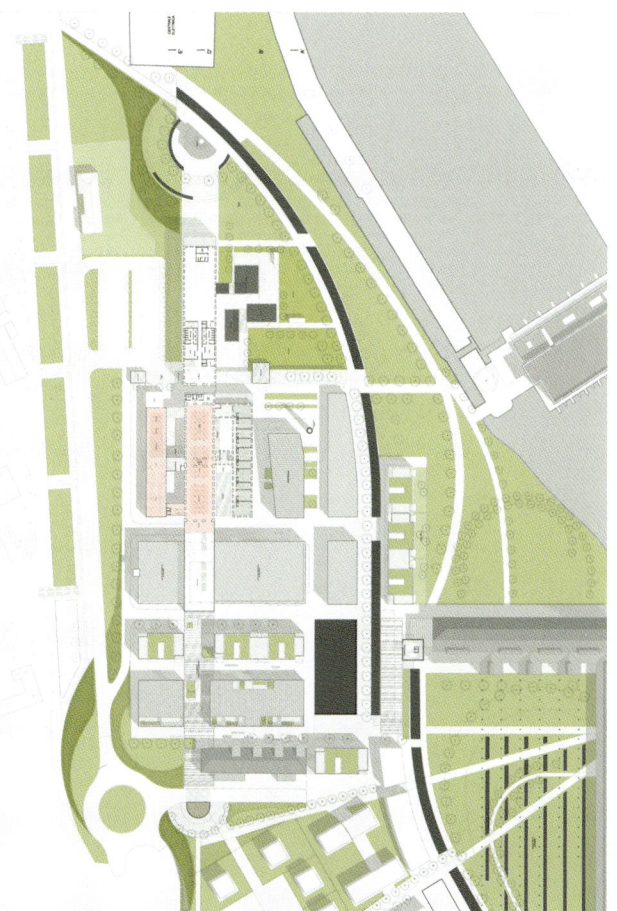
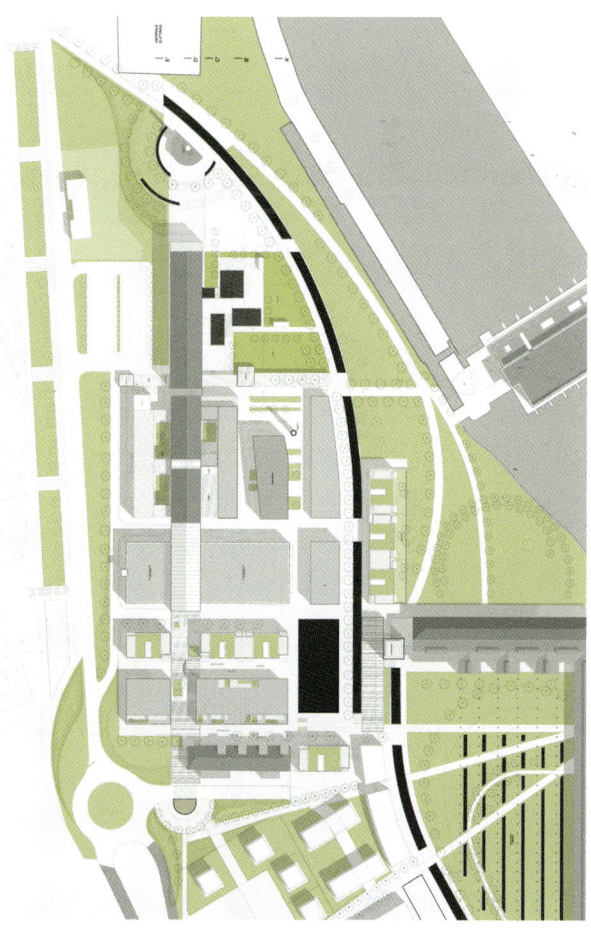

ARCHITECTURE

Cross-sections of the renovation of the central structure of the Linificio and the context

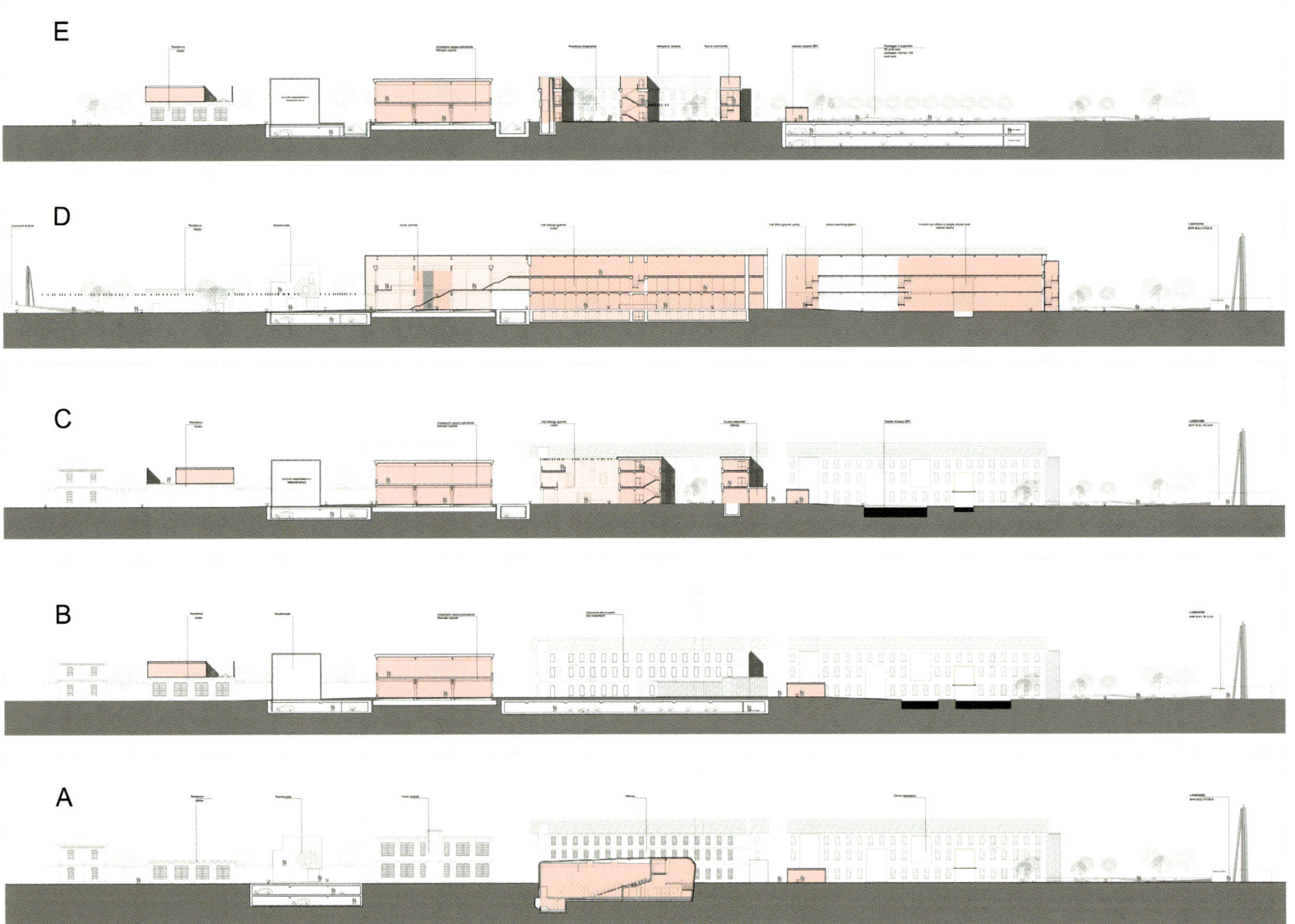

222

Sections and elevations of the renovation of minor structures in the central area of the Linificio

ARCHITECTURE

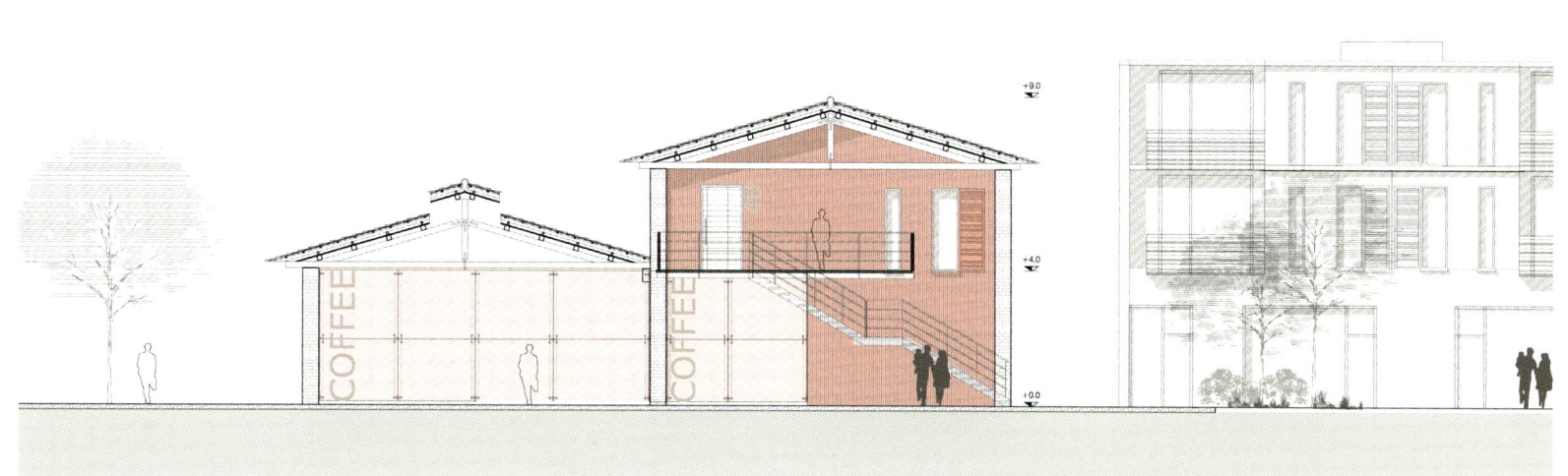

223

ARCHITECTURE

Elevations and plan of the renovation both of the minor structures to house apartments, offices and studios, and of the water tower

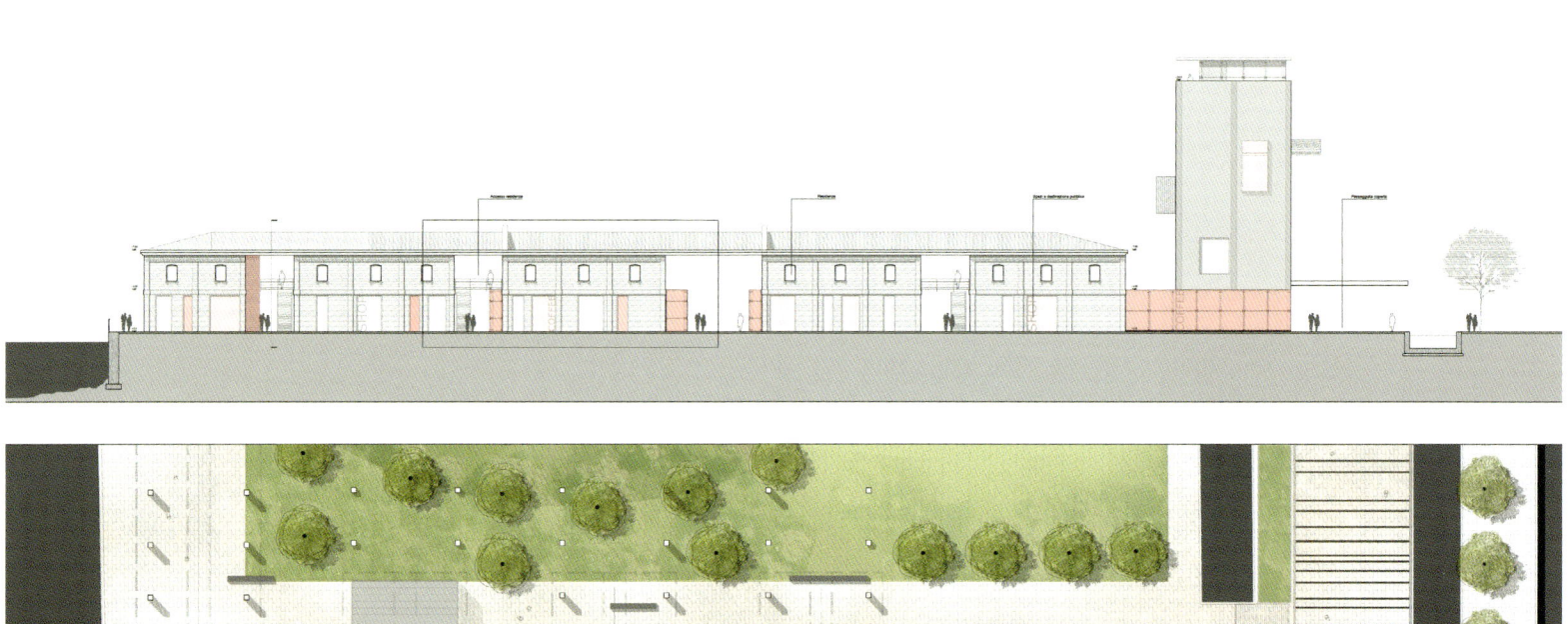

General plan of areas of volumetric concentration, services, public use and roads

General plan of the systems of open space: green avenues, parks, gardens, paved pedestrian areas and green spaces belonging to the residential units

ARCHITECTURE

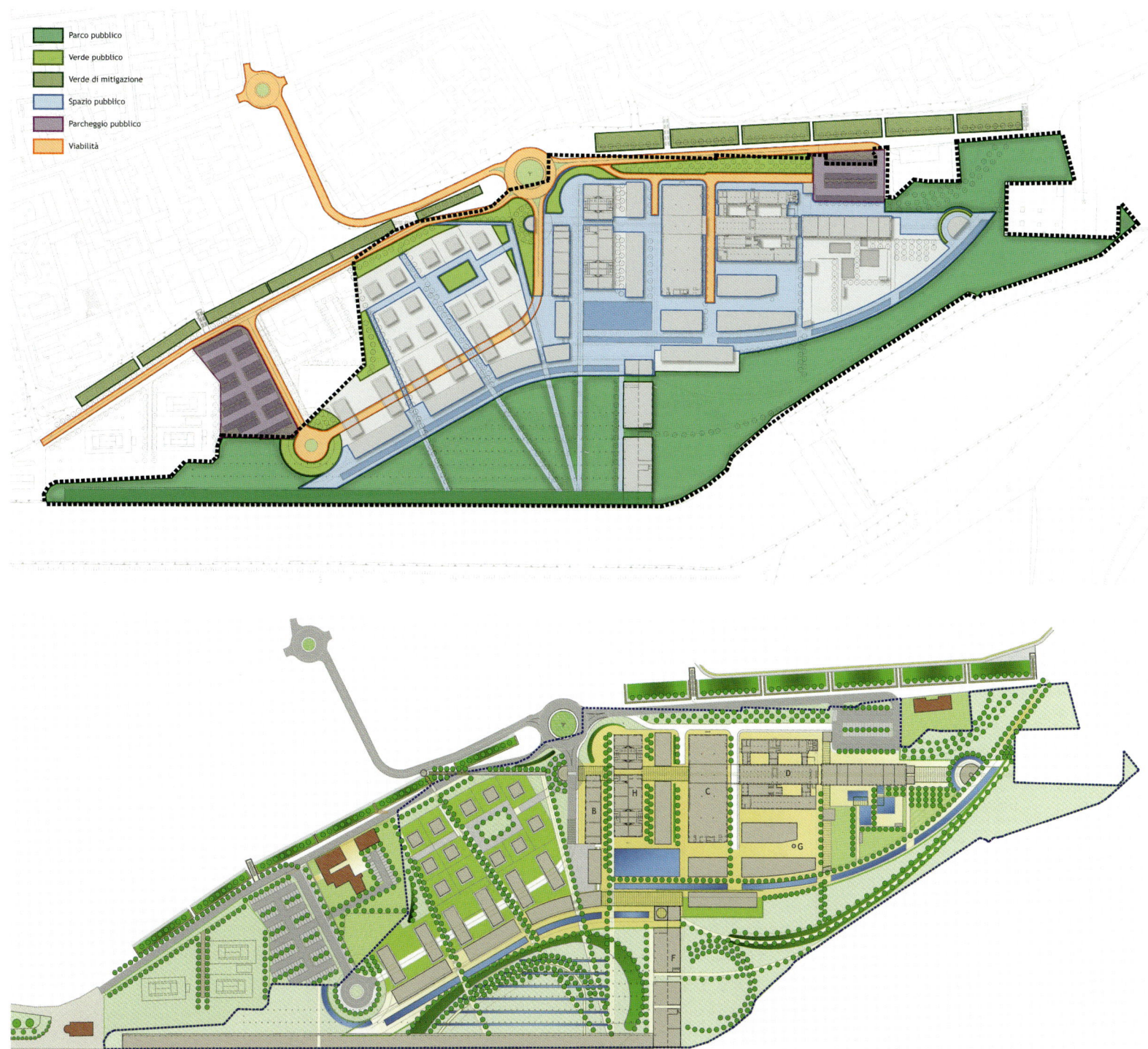

ARCHITECTURE

12. Peschiera Borromeo (Milan): plan for redevelopment of the Cascina Deserta (under way since 2010)

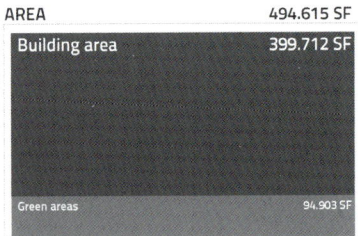

AREA — 494.615 SF
Building area — 399.712 SF
Green areas — 94.903 SF

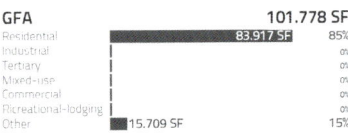

GFA — 101.778 SF
Residential — 83.917 SF — 85%
Industrial — 0%
Tertiary — 0%
Mixed-use — 0%
Commercial — 0%
Recreational-lodging — 0%
Other — 15.709 SF — 15%

PUBLIC REVENUES — 1.459.804 €

The Cascina Deserta at Peschiera Borromeo is located on agricultural land protected by the South Milan Agricultural Park between the rear of the Idroscalo (an artificial lake constructed as a seaplane airport) and the town. The broad expanse of space and the richness of the environmental system endow the area with great potential. The Cascina Deserta has the typical forms and structure of the Lombard agricultural context, opening out around a central courtyard and designed in full accordance with the geometry and layout of the agricultural system. Work carried out over the years with no authorization and certainly no respect for the complex and the natural environment under the pressure of the earlier building frenzy has altered its character and added new sections. Fortunately, the presence of the Agricultural Park has protected the surrounding areas from major transformation, even though some service-sector operations to the north of the farmhouse have reoriented the territorial system towards the Rivoltana highway and the Linate area. Midway between the agricultural system of the southern part of the plain and the tertiary development of the Rivoltana, crushed towards the south of the territory precisely by the increased weight of the highway and its ongoing expansion within the broader framework of the strengthening of Milanese infrastructures, the farmhouse is given a new role by a plan for redevelopment of its structures for settlement purposes.
Careful historical reconstruction has made it possible to give new architectural dignity and form to many buildings maimed over the years by unauthorized operations that have altered their nature and volumetric composition, in addition to reconstructing the image and composition of other historical buildings in a state of collapse or abandonment. The old ice house, built like a chamber with an apse in the northern part, and the main building, attributed to Piermarini, give dignity to the whole and give some idea of the importance it once had.
The project rids the farmhouse of the unauthorized additions and buildings, bringing the complex back to its truest historical nature and scale with the utmost respect. The courtyard structure still visible between the ice house to the north, the long building to the west, the central storage facility, the main house on the corner and the unauthorized buildings to the south is consolidated and repeated to the south so as to have two adjacent but separate courtyards connected by the central section of the buildings. The highest degree of environmental quality is pursued. The courtyards and surrounding area are treated as green areas of public or private use in full continuity with the agricultural system. The stream and spring regain their full environmental dignity. The parking area and roadway are placed underground out of sight. The architecture reinterprets the typological characteristics of Milanese agricultural buildings. Brick walls, arches and porticos, shallow pitched roofs, openings and open parts make up simple, unadorned volumes capable of expressing the settlement character already inherent in the Lombard farmhouse, where working and living areas are accommodated together in a sequence of open and constructed spaces with relations concentrated in the open central section. The project minimizes the degree of urbanization so as to preserve the agricultural character of the farmhouse in the midst of greenery and avoid the risk of betraying its very nature under increasingly strong pressure from the north and the Rivoltana system.

Territorial setting. The project is located inside the South Milan Agricultural Park alongside provincial highway 160 in the vicinity of the Gambarone watercourse. The area includes a building complex of rural character, which will be salvaged entirely through a project of conservative restoration. The considerable environmental value of the site and its proximity at the same time to the Rivoltana highway and the city of Milan constitute elements of great strategic interest

General plan of areas of volumetric concentration, services, public use and roads

General plan of the systems of open space: green avenues, parks, gardens, paved pedestrian areas and green spaces belonging to the residential units

ARCHITECTURE

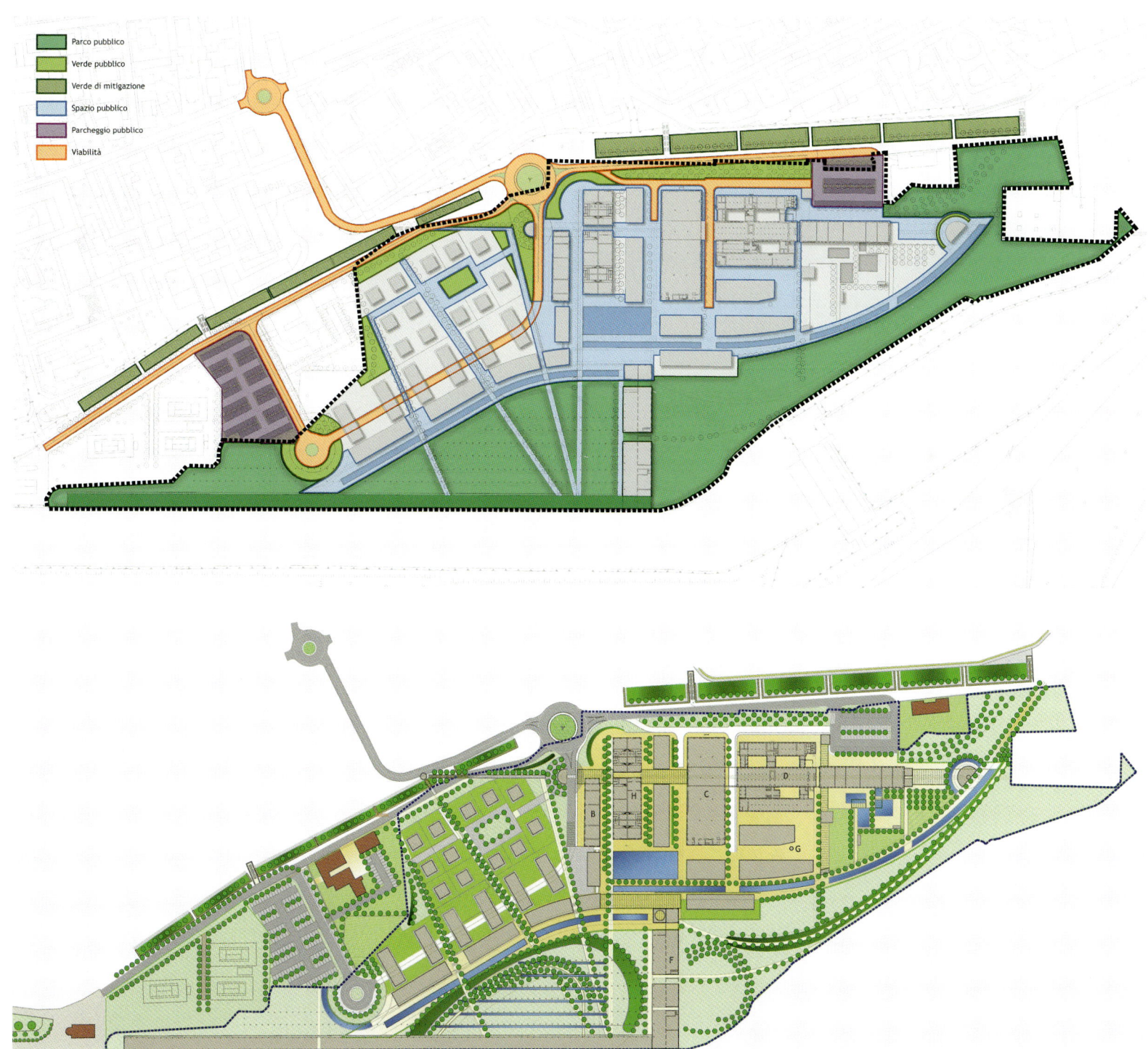

12. Peschiera Borromeo (Milan): plan for redevelopment of the Cascina Deserta (under way since 2010)

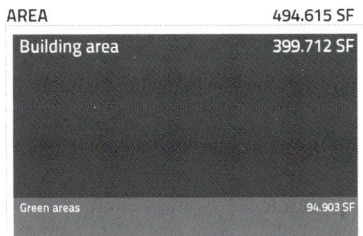

AREA — 494.615 SF
Building area — 399.712 SF
Green areas — 94.903 SF

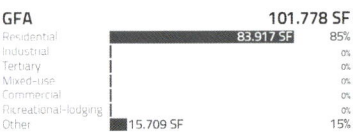

GFA — 101.778 SF
Residential — 83.917 SF — 85%
Industrial — 0%
Tertiary — 0%
Mixed-use — 0%
Commercial — 0%
Recreational-lodging — 0%
Other — 15.709 SF — 15%

PUBLIC REVENUES — 1.459.804 €

The Cascina Deserta at Peschiera Borromeo is located on agricultural land protected by the South Milan Agricultural Park between the rear of the Idroscalo (an artificial lake constructed as a seaplane airport) and the town. The broad expanse of space and the richness of the environmental system endow the area with great potential. The Cascina Deserta has the typical forms and structure of the Lombard agricultural context, opening out around a central courtyard and designed in full accordance with the geometry and layout of the agricultural system. Work carried out over the years with no authorization and certainly no respect for the complex and the natural environment under the pressure of the earlier building frenzy has altered its character and added new sections. Fortunately, the presence of the Agricultural Park has protected the surrounding areas from major transformation, even though some service-sector operations to the north of the farmhouse have reoriented the territorial system towards the Rivoltana highway and the Linate area. Midway between the agricultural system of the southern part of the plain and the tertiary development of the Rivoltana, crushed towards the south of the territory precisely by the increased weight of the highway and its ongoing expansion within the broader framework of the strengthening of Milanese infrastructures, the farmhouse is given a new role by a plan for redevelopment of its structures for settlement purposes. Careful historical reconstruction has made it possible to give new architectural dignity and form to many buildings maimed over the years by unauthorized operations that have altered their nature and volumetric composition, in addition to reconstructing the image and composition of other historical buildings in a state of collapse or abandonment. The old ice house, built like a chamber with an apse in the northern part, and the main building, attributed to Piermarini, give dignity to the whole and give some idea of the importance it once had.

The project rids the farmhouse of the unauthorized additions and buildings, bringing the complex back to its truest historical nature and scale with the utmost respect. The courtyard structure still visible between the ice house to the north, the long building to the west, the central storage facility, the main house on the corner and the unauthorized buildings to the south is consolidated and repeated to the south so as to have two adjacent but separate courtyards connected by the central section of the buildings. The highest degree of environmental quality is pursued. The courtyards and surrounding area are treated as green areas of public or private use in full continuity with the agricultural system. The stream and spring regain their full environmental dignity. The parking area and roadway are placed underground out of sight. The architecture reinterprets the typological characteristics of Milanese agricultural buildings. Brick walls, arches and porticos, shallow pitched roofs, openings and open parts make up simple, unadorned volumes capable of expressing the settlement character already inherent in the Lombard farmhouse, where working and living areas are accommodated together in a sequence of open and constructed spaces with relations concentrated in the open central section. The project minimizes the degree of urbanization so as to preserve the agricultural character of the farmhouse in the midst of greenery and avoid the risk of betraying its very nature under increasingly strong pressure from the north and the Rivoltana system.

Territorial setting. The project is located inside the South Milan Agricultural Park alongside provincial highway 160 in the vicinity of the Gambarone watercourse. The area includes a building complex of rural character, which will be salvaged entirely through a project of conservative restoration. The considerable environmental value of the site and its proximity at the same time to the Rivoltana highway and the city of Milan constitute elements of great strategic interest

Master plan. The plan for the Cascina Deserta farmhouse is designed to preserve the typological characteristics of the old rural settlement through restoration of the courtyard buildings, which will retain their original residential function, and the functional conversion of the icehouse in the north into offices.

The open spaces are designed so as to establish clear links between the different structures involved, emphasizing the generating position of the built-up fabric with a tree-lined pedestrian pathway.

The major axis along which the residential buildings are laid out culminates in the apsidal edifice, which will thus become the fulcrum of the new settlement and house a tertiary-sector complex.

The east boundary of the area is reinforced with a row of closely-planted trees to screen the residential section from the provincial highway, while the southern part of the project area is developed as a park with large expanses of greenery

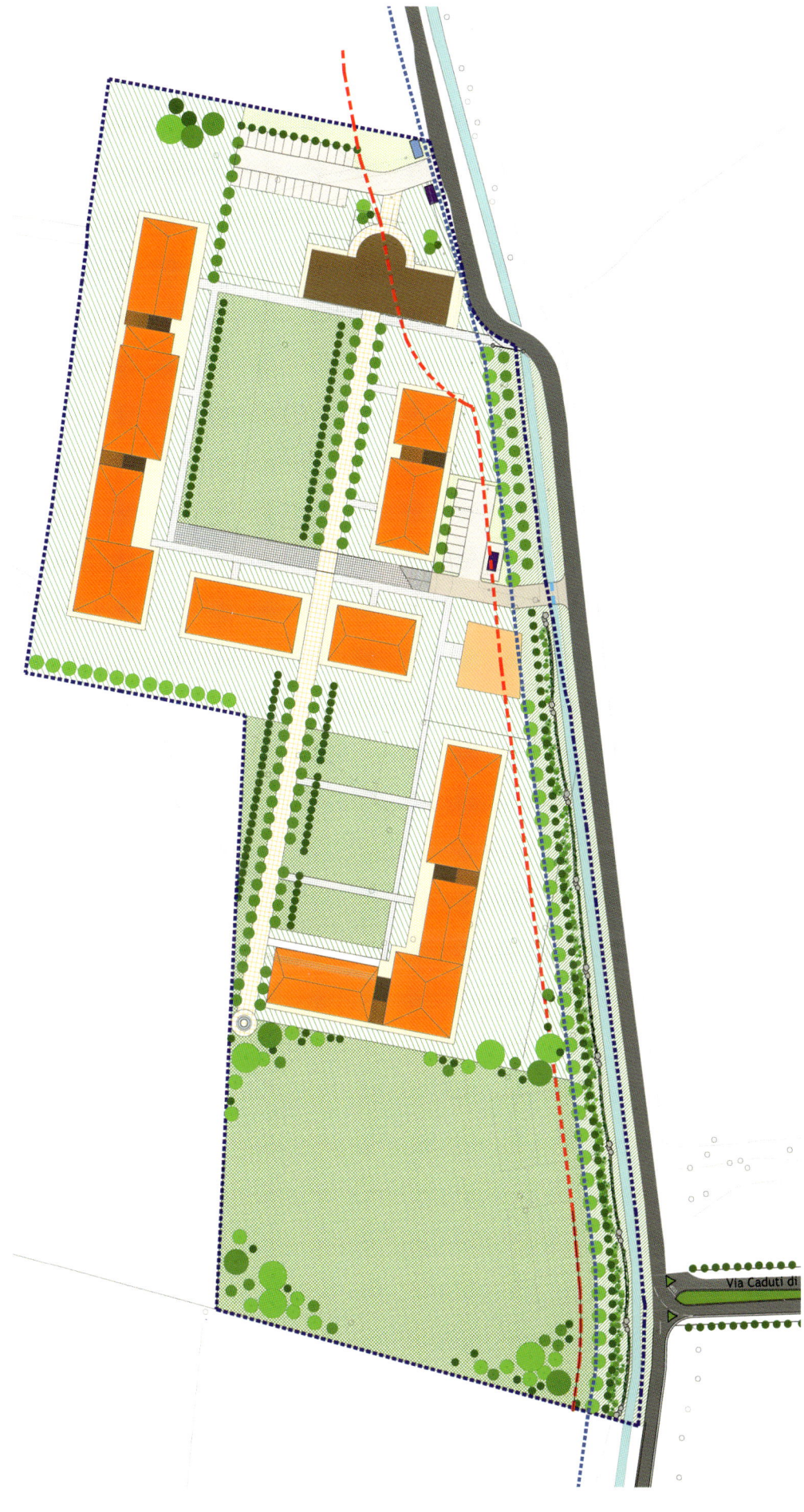

General plan. The courtyard building typology and the internal layouts of the individual buildings are maintained in accordance with a respectful approach to the historical matrix of the complex. At the same time, the project is distinguished by an effort to restore the original characteristics of the settlement developed through intense archival research that made it possible to distinguish and refurbish the original architectural elements and eliminate later additions to the complex

ARCHITECTURE

Longitudinal profiles. The project adopted a conservative approach to the original architectural characteristics in both typological and physical terms, restoring the original vocabulary of the exteriors of the buildings. The residences thus present the distinctive characters of rural buildings, with façades marked by regular windows and doorways, light-coloured plastered walls and tiled, pitched roofs

Perspective view of the operation. The plan restores the original characteristics of the settlement, underscored by its planimetric layout and distribution. It aim is both renovation of the buildings and the planning of a space for public use of marked environmental value through the reorganization of internal pedestrian pathways underscored and reinforced by the green element

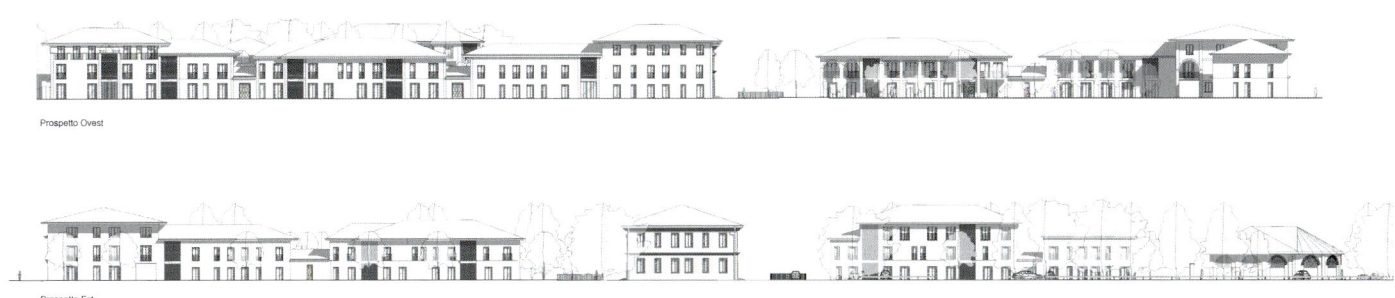

ARCHITECTURE

13. Arcene (Bergamo): master plan for environmental restoration and development of the quarry (2011)

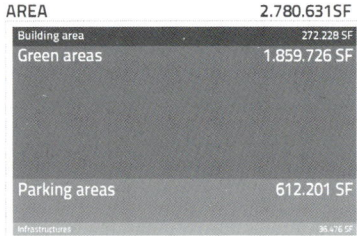

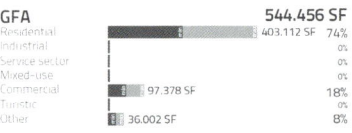

PUBLIC REVENUES
Not observed

The environmental restoration of the Arcene quarry involves a very large area between the Treviglio-Bergamo railway line and provincial highway 144 to the south, partly used as a quarry and partly unused. The site's strength is the presence of the railway, being made accessible by the regional rail service and quick connections with Bergamo.

The environmental restoration of a quarry is a subject of particular interest in the plain between Milan, Bergamo and Brescia. Exhausted older quarries and newer ones opened also in relation to the works under way to improve the region's road and rail infrastructures are present in the plain and impair its agricultural continuity and regular surface level. Their restoration is no easy task, above all in financial terms.

The reclamation of areas of extraction, infill to restore the ground level and work to ensure the safety of the sides are complicated and expensive operations. For this reason, the project maintains its economic feasibility in proposing the creation of a settlement, part on the quarry area and part on the adjoining land used for services, and taking advantage of its particular position and link with the infrastructures. The location endows the project with both local and territorial breadth, its major measurements being drawn from the territorial axes and its minor measurements from the ancient boundaries of centuriation. Developing a functional mix that includes housing, shops, services and an ample amount of green areas and sports facilities, the complex is equipped with a system of low-impact streets, mostly through furrows in the ground, and a system of green trails and cycle tracks capable of establishing relations between the layout of the area and the lines and structure of centuriation. Like the small plots once created during the phases of colonization or land reclamation, these macro and micro networks divide the areas earmarked for housing, with longitudinal sites capable of structuring the constructed part with the minimum consumption of land. Like a project for a new town, the plan permits the construction of a new settlement, a small "colony" near the railway line, through reclamation of the quarry area for the countryside and the settlement system.

Territorial context. The high level of accessibility offered by the context, relations with railway lines of regional importance and supra-municipal road connections endow the disused extraction site with major potential for transformation

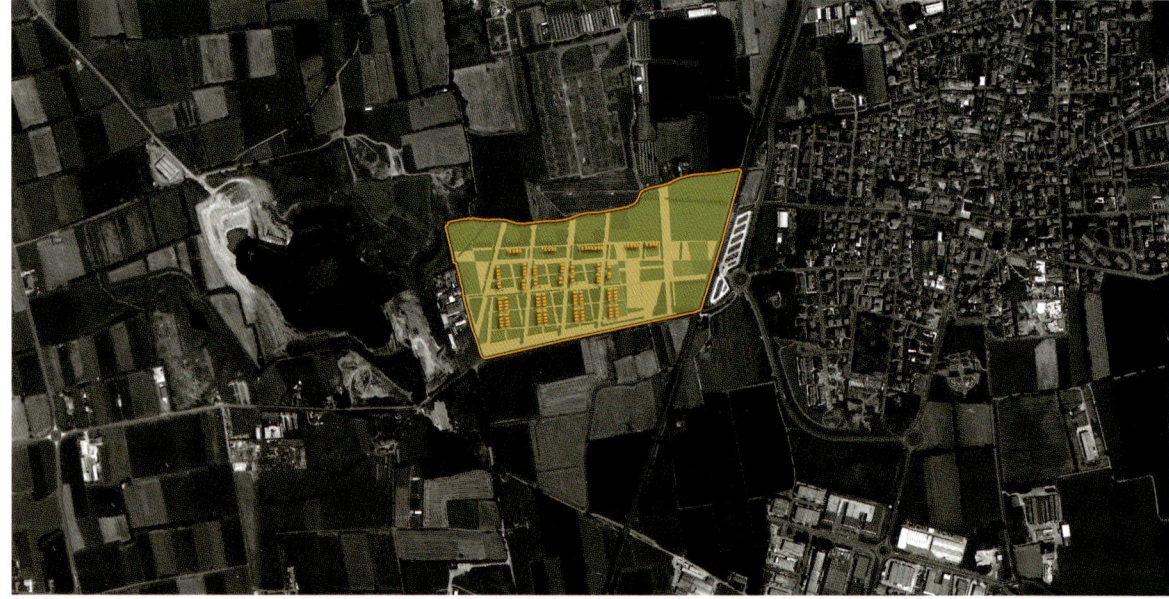

230

ARCHITECTURE

Master plan. The compositional rules are developed around a low-impact system of greenways and cycle tracks that follow and interrelate the lines of the ancient centuriation of the countryside and the future design of area development. The predominance of green areas plays a fundamental connective role for the settlement and endows the project as a whole with environmental and landscape quality

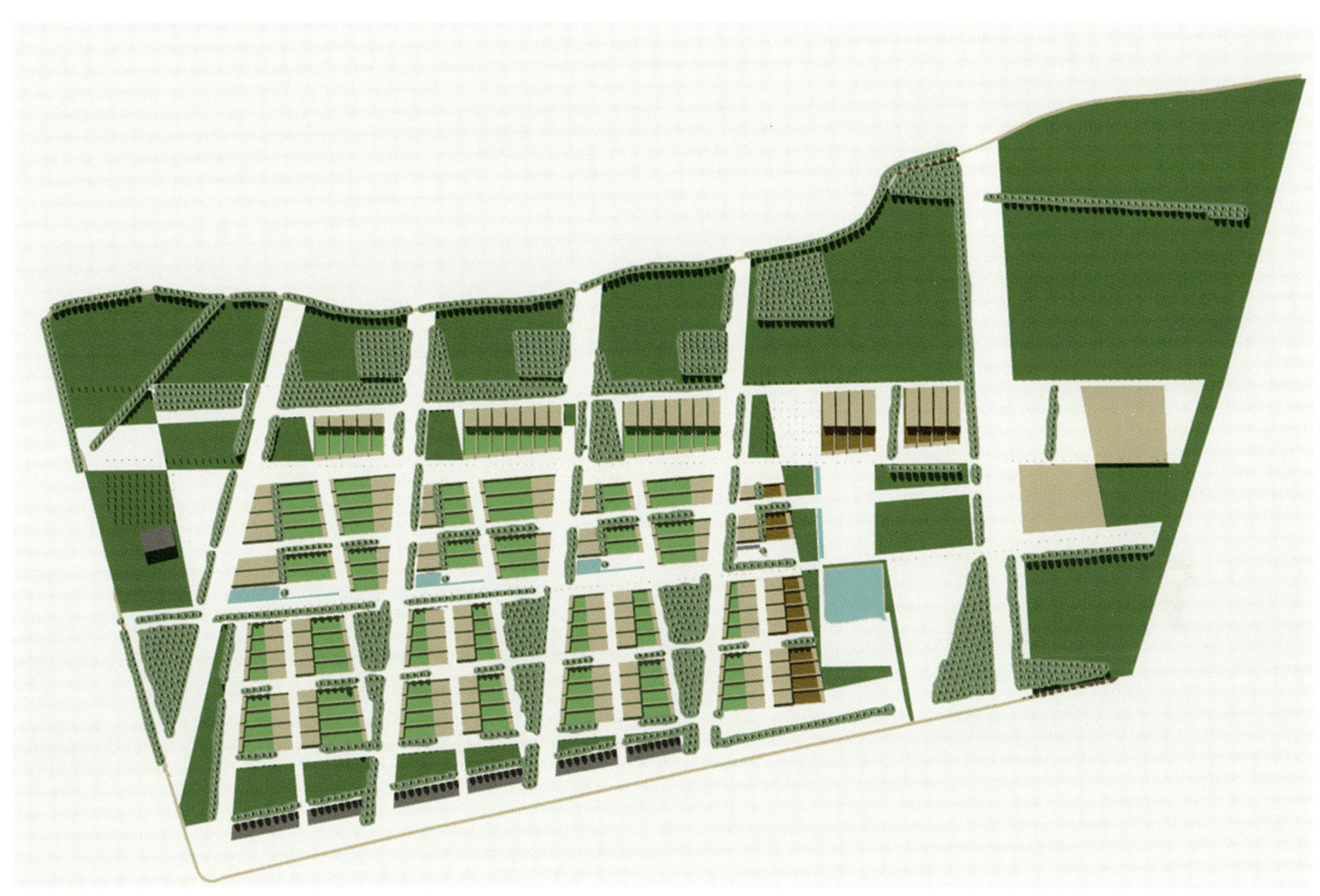

ARCHITECTURE

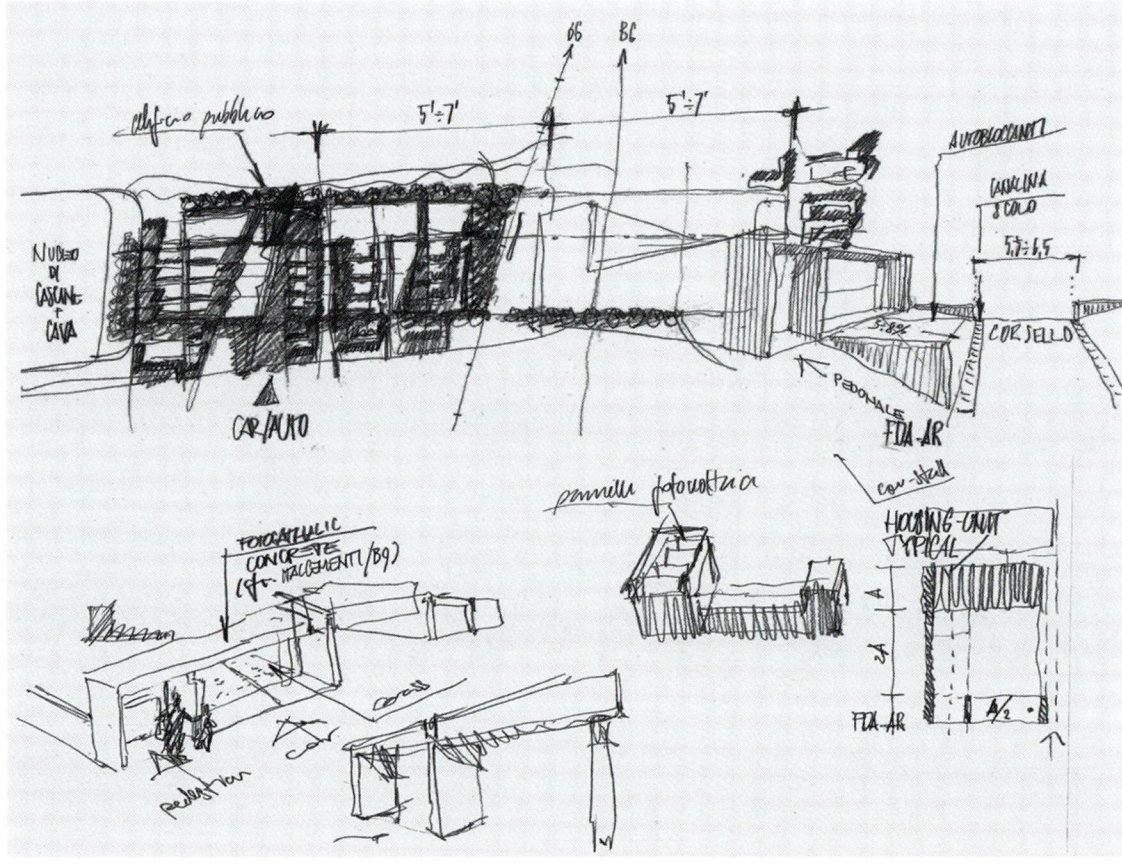

Configuration, planimetric and volumetric layouts. Concept of complex and residential unit

Road system and underground utilities. The infrastructural system is planned on the basis of a precise hierarchical and functional structure: axes and accesses of the cycle tracks and pedestrian pathways and first-level nodes, axes and accesses of passageways for vehicles and intersections between the slow mobility and vehicle systems where attention is focused in particular on the safety of the more vulnerable user

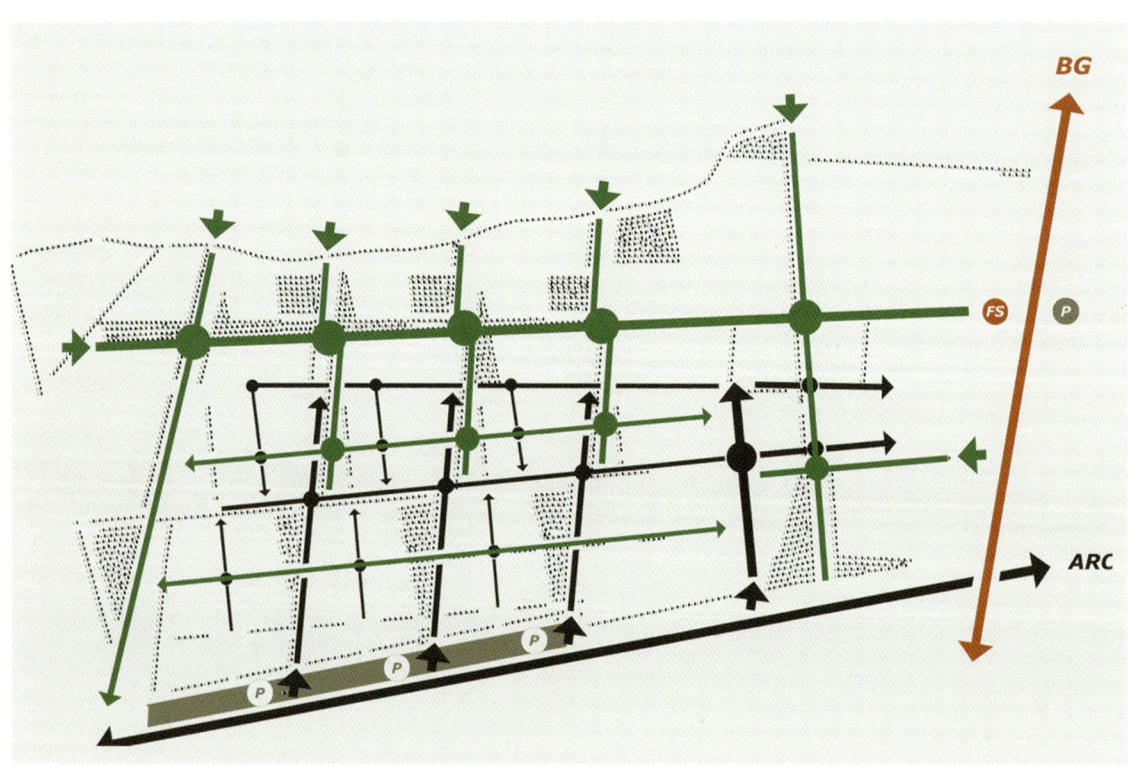

Configuration. Study of the geometry and travel times of the historical centre

Three-dimensional modelling. Bird's eye view with opening towards the railway station

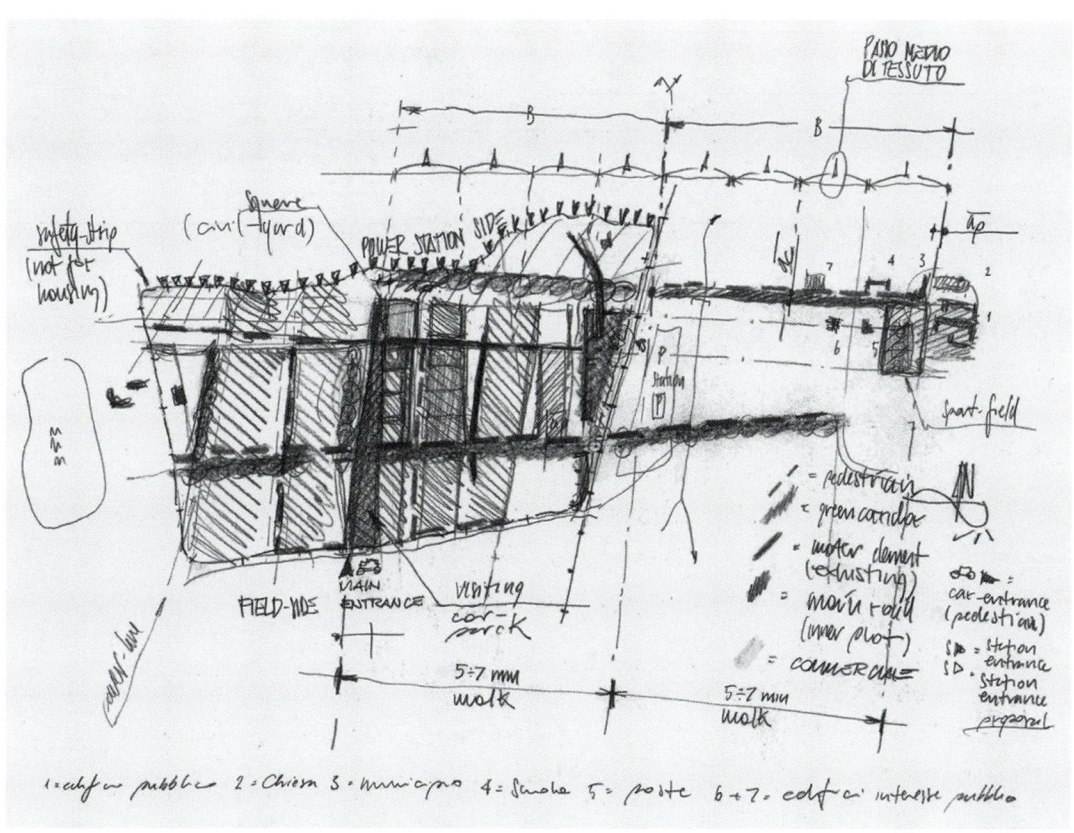

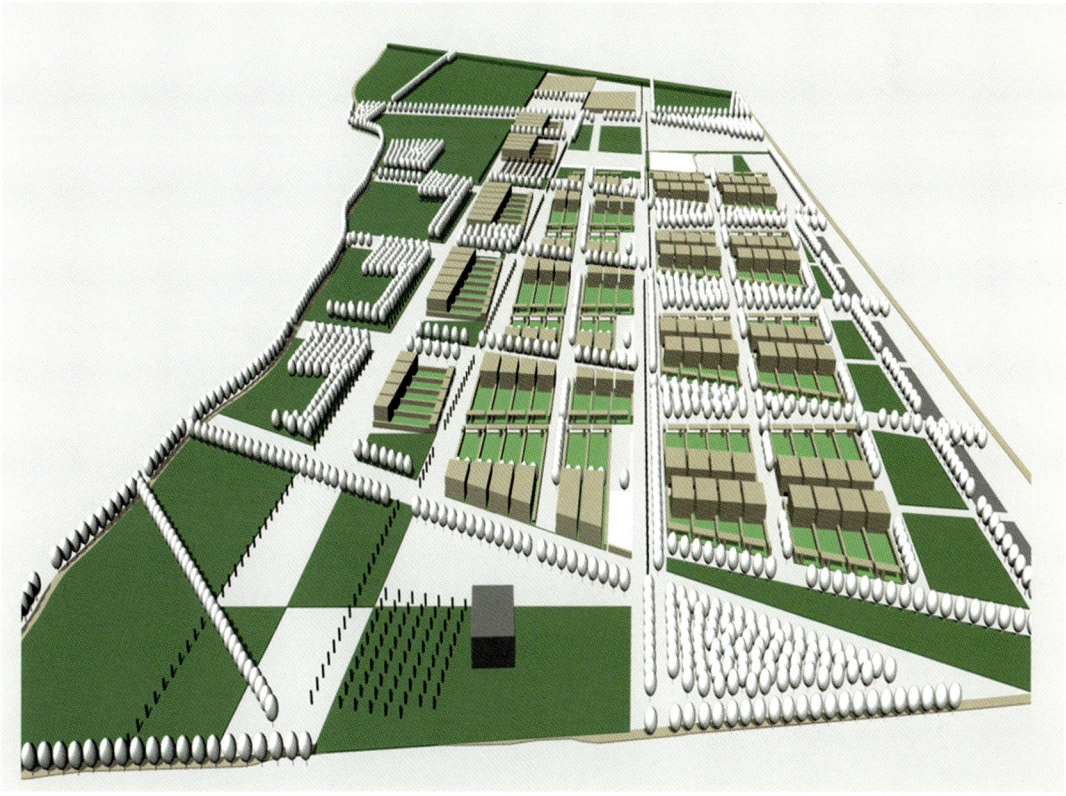

ARCHITECTURE

14. Cassina de' Pecchi (Milan): feasibility study for redevelopment of the Cascina Bindellera (2011)

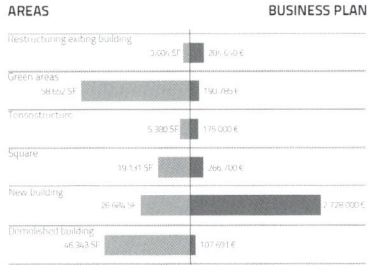

The project for redevelopment of the Cascina Bindellera takes on a territorial role of great importance in the parallel path followed by the town's Territorial Management Plan. The farmhouse is located in the protected area of the South Milan Agricultural Park, barycentric between the hamlet of Sant'Agata and the main territory of Cassina. It thus occupies a position of particular importance if the void of the agricultural system is regarded as the true centre of the municipal territory. In the absence of a real, consolidated historical centre, with only a few areas around the town hall and the station regarded as central, and with the particular division between Cassina and the Sant'Agata, the farmhouse can become the new green centre of the town. The project thus reinterprets the remnants, takes advantage of their form, and provides for restoration of the structures and open spaces with some additions capable of reconstructing the compactness of the overall volume and the integrity of the area's shape. The farmhouse is earmarked to accommodate functions of public interest and events for the local inhabitants. The restoration project adopts the vocabulary of the traditional farmhouse while adding crisp, solid, neutral volumes so as to maintain a clear distinction between existing and new structures. The external space is designed to accommodate many functions of a public character and above all in connection with plans for a greenway to connect the town and the hamlet.

Study of the architectural characteristics of farmhouses makes it possible to develop a project adopting the correct designs and materials in full compliance with the regulations of the Agricultural Park.
The tool used is the master plan, which anticipates the provisions the Territorial Management Plan, tests the strength of the desire for transformation, and visualizes its effects through a concrete project. The master plan thus contributes to definition of the town's areas of transformation, works together with the Territorial Management Plan in order to understand its strategies and visualize the results, and stimulates the qualitative redevelopment of the town's places of primary interest.

Master plan. The image presents the compositional idea for development of the area designated to house usable public spaces for the town. The planning of green space becomes a key element for correct dialogue with the agricultural areas of the context

Setting. The Cascina Bindellera farmhouse is situated in a key position within the agricultural system and has the potential to become the fulcrum of the public city of Cassina de' Pecchi

ARCHITECTURE

Planimetria piano terra
Scala 1 : 350

ARCHITECTURE

ARCHITECTURE

Opposite
Elevations and profiles. The profiles indicate the slight increase in volume proposed with a view to redefining the overall layout of the area. The renovation of the farmhouse draws inspiration from the morphology of the context

3D views. The compositional design concentrates the envisaged volumes so as to create a large courtyard embedded in a park designed and organized in terms of themes and activities. Long rows of trees join and connect the various points of the area. The use is proposed of traditional building materials with a view to restoration in not only physical but also visual terms and reinforcing the identity of one of the town's few historical elements

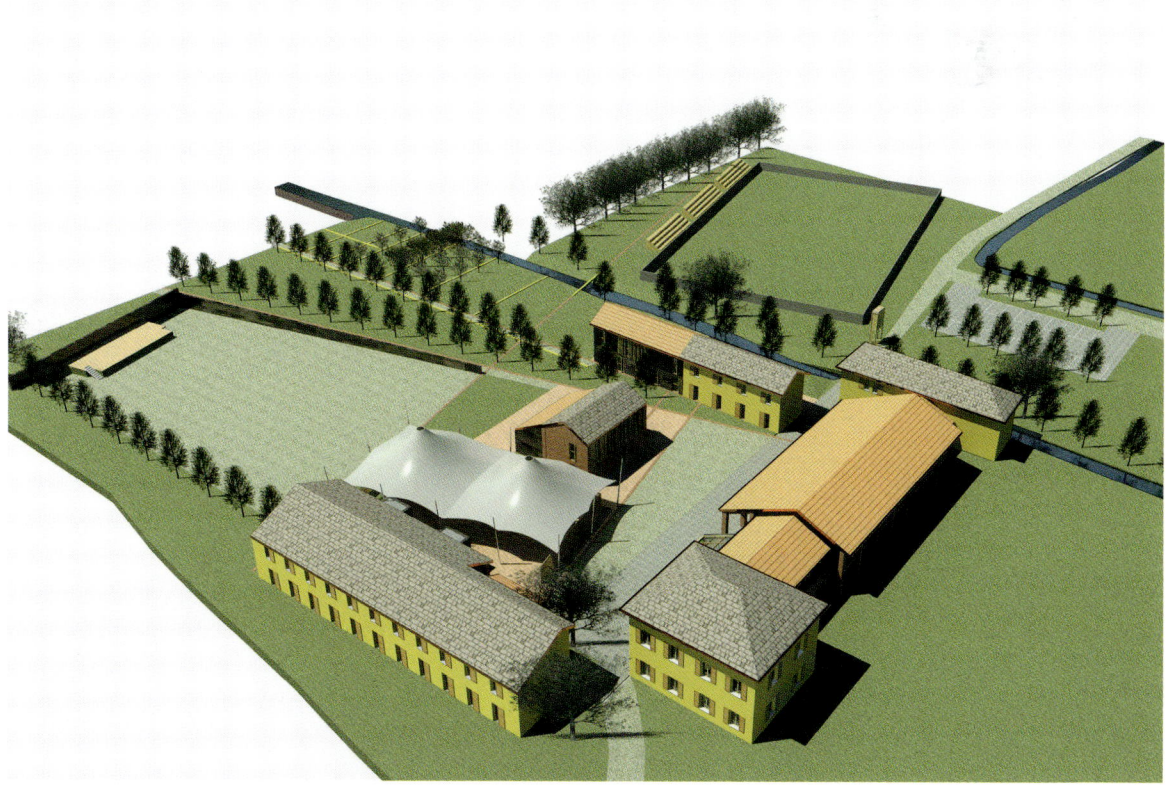

237

ARCHITECTURE

15. Cassina de' Pecchi (Milan): feasibility study for a new sports centre (2011)

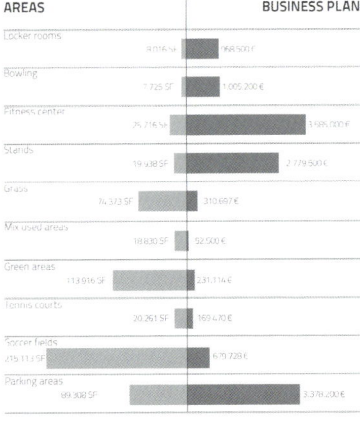

Like the project for redevelopment of the Bindellera farmhouse, the feasibility study for the new sports centre establishes close dialogue with the provisions of the Territorial Management Plan. One of the latter's strategies is to upgrade the system of services, investing in particular on those already existing, increasing the supply and constructing them in the form of new centralities capable of serving the town and neighbouring areas. Situated on outskirts of the municipal territory of Cassina close to the South Milan Agricultural Park, the sports centre is designed to perform two functions in the project: providing the town and its inhabitants with new sports facilities and constituting a small urban gateway to the most dense and central part of Cassina. To this end, different spaces of different weight are designed to house different functions. The west side is constructed with greater severity only in plan view, as a green dune is actually created to house the parking spaces and mask the construction of the stands of the sports fields while engaging in dialogue with the nearby boundary of the South Milan Agricultural Park. The north side along the Padana highway is redesigned as a gateway to the town, increasing the amount of public space and creating a landmark for the territory and the change in character. The resulting structure is aligned on the hard edge of the west side and open to the countryside to the south and east. Here too, the project is conceived and illustrated through the use of a master plan, a tool for developing a project, anticipating its formal choices and volumetric provisions, and assessing the results expected from the implementation of planning provisions. The master plan illustrates and expresses the choices of the Territorial Management Plan, makes its solutions visible, and makes it possible to build up the necessary consensus around real visions. In precisely this sense it has played a key role in assessing the feasibility of the solutions proposed, not only stimulating discussion on itself but also presenting a concrete picture of what is required in terms of funding, commitments and the use of public areas.

Setting. The area of study is adjacent to the town of Cassina de' Pecchi south of the provincial highway

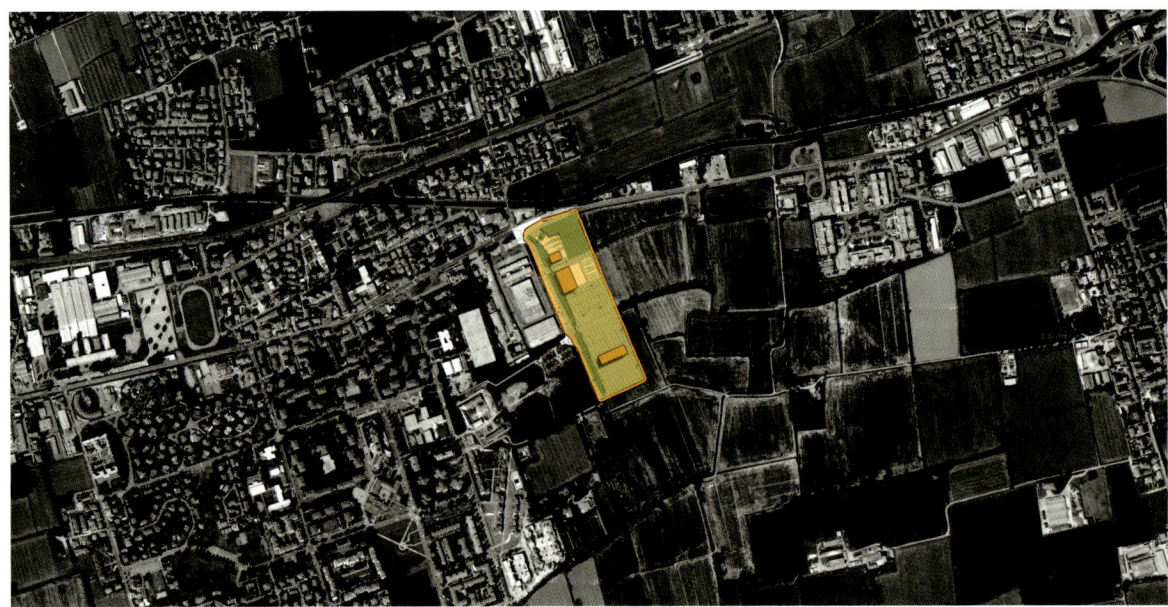

Master plan. The project envisages the creation of fields for various sporting activities. An access road will be constructed on the side adjoining the town to connect with the north through the insertion of a roundabout. A tree-lined dune along the road serves both the attenuate the impact and as a site for structures of the sports centre such as stands and changing rooms

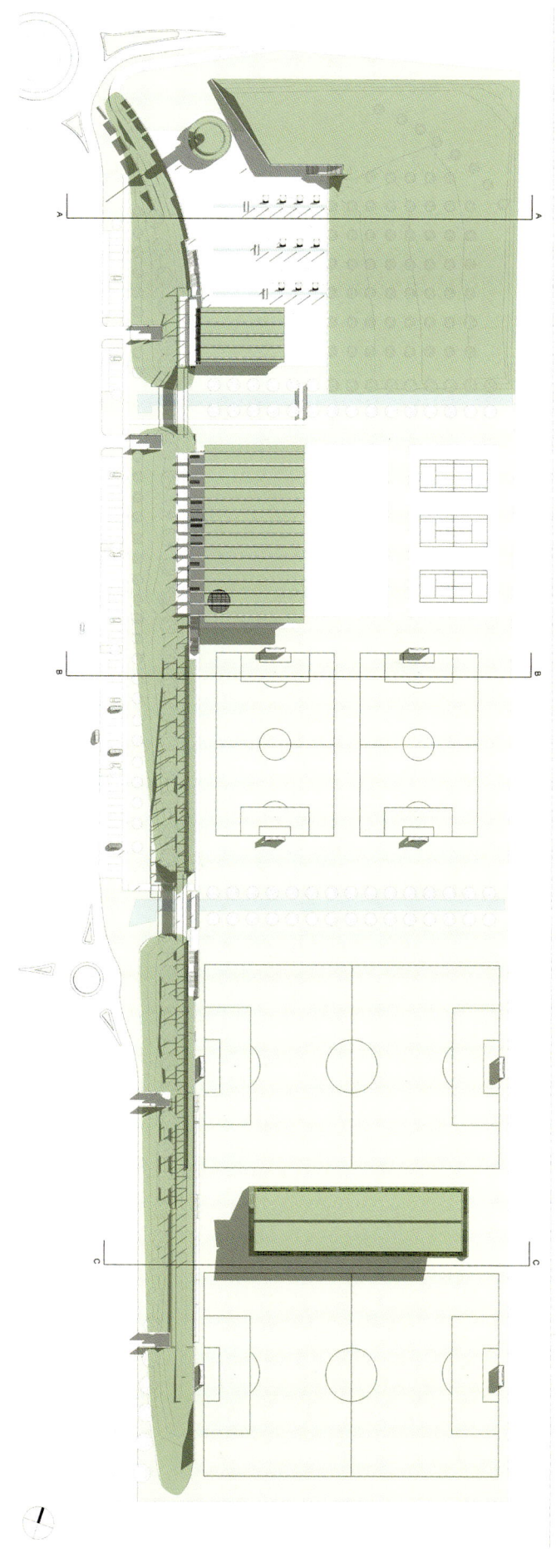

ARCHITECTURE *Elevations*

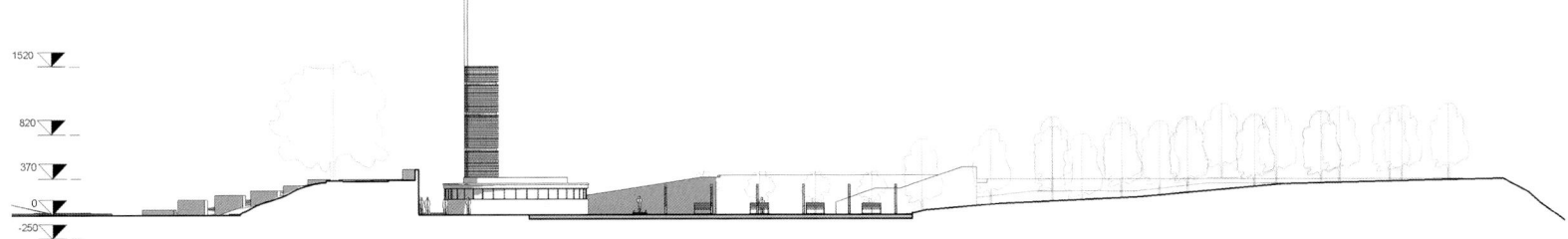

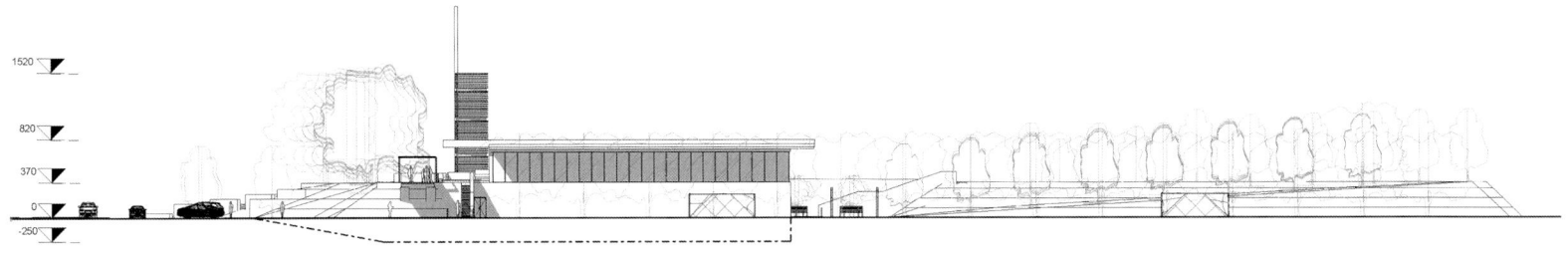

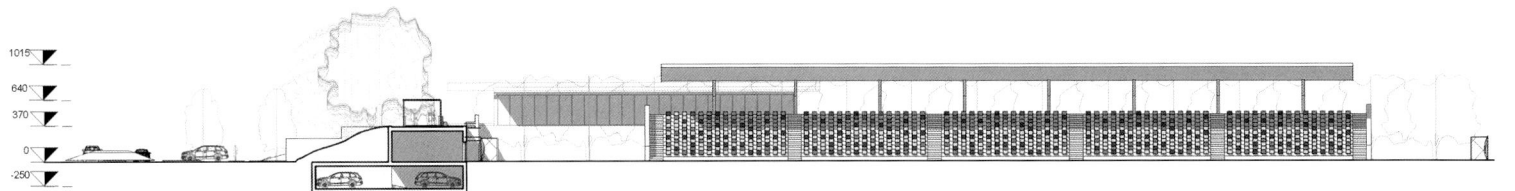

View of the tree-lined dune

ARCHITECTURE

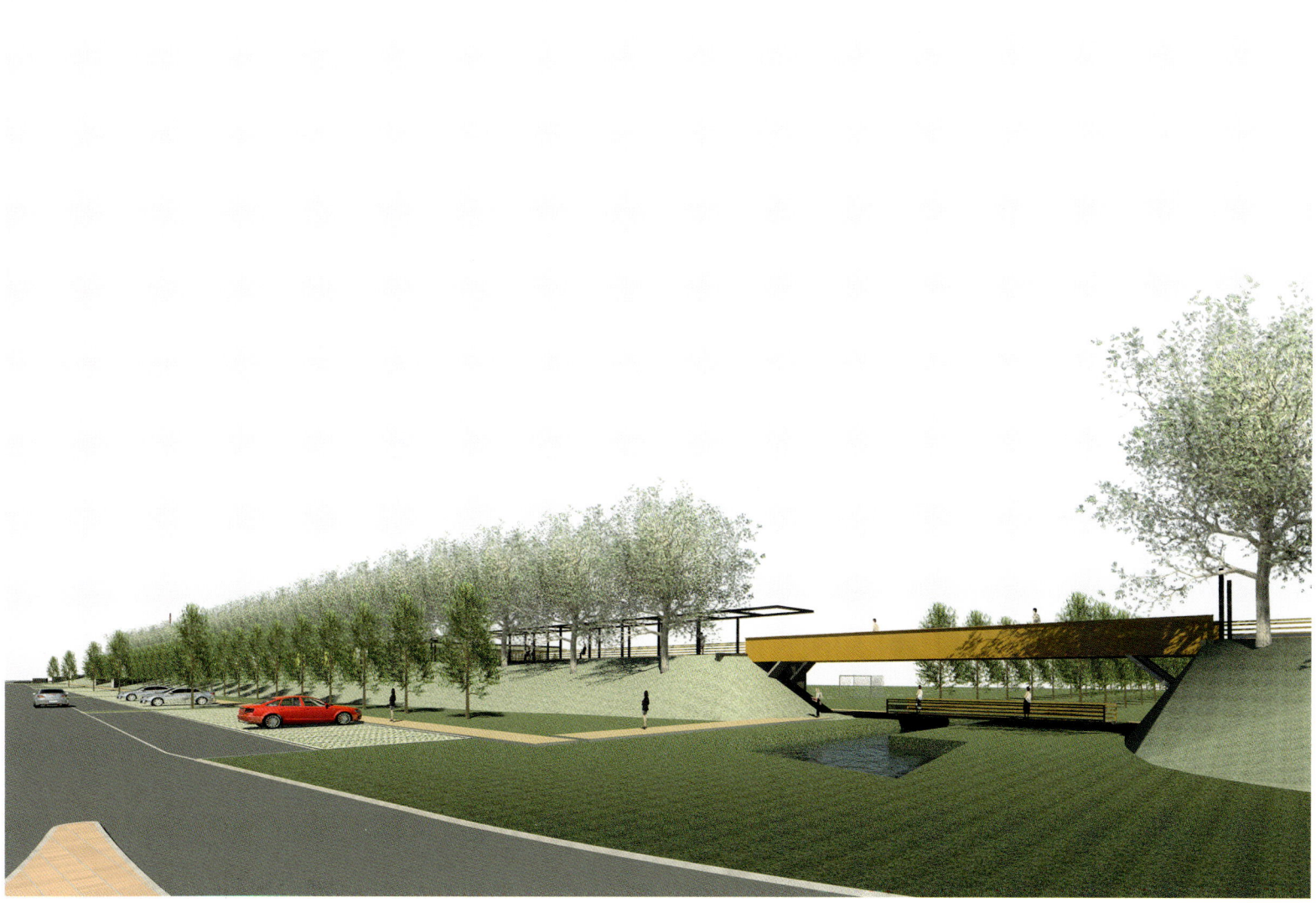

241

ARCHITECTURE

16. Missaglia (Lecco): residential Integrated Action Plan
(under way since 2011)

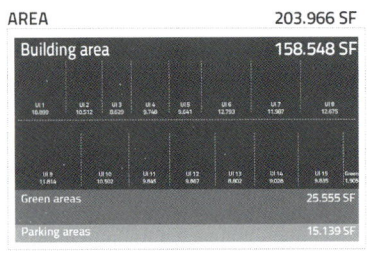

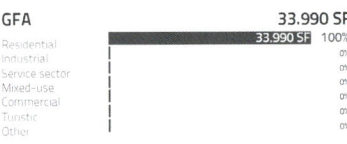

The project area is located in Contra, a hamlet of the town of Missaglia, on a hill between Via Battisti and Via Agazzino sloping down towards the west. It is part of a much larger holding that includes late 19th-century villas and agricultural estates with vineyards. The urbanization under way in Brianza over the last seventy years has almost spared this corner, where the small size of the hamlet and the wealth of residences maintain a character of great overall quality. The project was drawn up in opposition to one already submitted by the owner of the area to the local authorities, which found little favour, probably because of its recourse to forms of planning traditionally employed for areas of no particular settlement quality or environmental merit.

The project included within the Integrated Action Plan took a completely different approach, taking advantage of the slight unevenness of the terrain to define an innovative system and attempt to open up the view to the west for all the residences.

The design is based on a private sunken road system, partly covered, partly open and partly lined with vegetation, providing access to the private residences, which have their own garages and parking places along its length. The houses fall into the category of the extra-urban villa and closely follow its characteristics as established over time. While just a few works of the 1970s and 1980s experimented with a vocabulary borrowed from traditional and agricultural buildings, the construction of extra-urban villas in these contexts was generally developed with the broadest freedom of expression but not always with results of high quality. The houses envisaged thus return to the centrality of the living space opening onto a garden, organized around the fireplace and protected by a wide roof. Given the slope of the hill, the living room, kitchen, study and utilities room are placed at the level of the garden with the bedrooms, bathrooms and wardrobes on the upper half-floor and the laundry room, cellars and garage downstairs. Particular attention is focused on the design of the pathways, examining the solutions best suited to the middle-class residence, about which so much has been said in the recent past. The materials express the sense of the place with the use of brick, wood and stone but also large windows opening up to the outside, which is again regarded as an integral part of the residence, equipped with a swimming pool and in dialogue with the planned gymnasiums. The settlement is innovative also as regards energy, as the buildings are registered as class A, and particular devices for the recycling of water. The interiors are designed in accordance with the Acanto philosophy in pursuit of the correct Italian style in line with the stylistic choices of the exterior.

A long cycle track is created to the south of the project area as a continuation of the Contra cycle track.

Territorial setting. The new settlement is located along the south boundary of the town of Missaglia in the locality of Contra in a territorial context of great environmental importance. The project is integrated with the natural surroundings through a linear design and particular attention to of the existing trees

View of the tree-lined dune

ARCHITECTURE

241

ARCHITECTURE

16. Missaglia (Lecco): residential Integrated Action Plan
(under way since 2011)

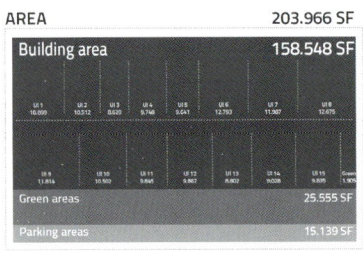

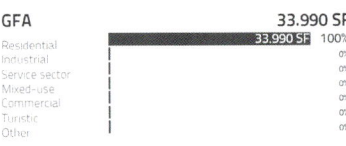

The project area is located in Contra, a hamlet of the town of Missaglia, on a hill between Via Battisti and Via Agazzino sloping down towards the west. It is part of a much larger holding that includes late 19th-century villas and agricultural estates with vineyards. The urbanization under way in Brianza over the last seventy years has almost spared this corner, where the small size of the hamlet and the wealth of residences maintain a character of great overall quality. The project was drawn up in opposition to one already submitted by the owner of the area to the local authorities, which found little favour, probably because of its recourse to forms of planning traditionally employed for areas of no particular settlement quality or environmental merit.

The project included within the Integrated Action Plan took a completely different approach, taking advantage of the slight unevenness of the terrain to define an innovative system and attempt to open up the view to the west for all the residences.

The design is based on a private sunken road system, partly covered, partly open and partly lined with vegetation, providing access to the private residences, which have their own garages and parking places along its length. The houses fall into the category of the extra-urban villa and closely follow its characteristics as established over time. While just a few works of the 1970s and 1980s experimented with a vocabulary borrowed from traditional and agricultural buildings, the construction of extra-urban villas in these contexts was generally developed with the broadest freedom of expression but not always with results of high quality. The houses envisaged thus return to the centrality of the living space opening onto a garden, organized around the fireplace and protected by a wide roof. Given the slope of the hill, the living room, kitchen, study and utilities room are placed at the level of the garden with the bedrooms, bathrooms and wardrobes on the upper half-floor and the laundry room, cellars and garage downstairs. Particular attention is focused on the design of the pathways, examining the solutions best suited to the middle-class residence, about which so much has been said in the recent past. The materials express the sense of the place with the use of brick, wood and stone but also large windows opening up to the outside, which is again regarded as an integral part of the residence, equipped with a swimming pool and in dialogue with the planned gymnasiums. The settlement is innovative also as regards energy, as the buildings are registered as class A, and particular devices for the recycling of water. The interiors are designed in accordance with the Acanto philosophy in pursuit of the correct Italian style in line with the stylistic choices of the exterior.

A long cycle track is created to the south of the project area as a continuation of the Contra cycle track.

Territorial setting. The new settlement is located along the south boundary of the town of Missaglia in the locality of Contra in a territorial context of great environmental importance. The project is integrated with the natural surroundings through a linear design and particular attention to of the existing trees

ARCHITECTURE

General plan. The project comprises fifteen residential units inside a large private park. The buildings are laid out in accordance with the natural slope of the land so as to offer each villa a particular view over the green spaces inside the project perimeter and the thickly wooded strip along the perimeter road system west of the area. The course of the newly-built cycle track and pedestrian pathway of steel and wood stretching through the forest of plane trees is designed so as to preserve all of the existing trees and enhance the landscape of the site

Plan of the lower ground basement level. The project focuses particular attention on safeguarding the landscape through numerous measures aimed at preservation of the natural element and the harmonious insertion of the buildings into their environmental context. For this reason it was decided to construct a sunken internal road system and leave the ground level for the private gardens and communal green areas. Large opening are made along the sunken passageway so as to ensure the natural lighting of communal spaces

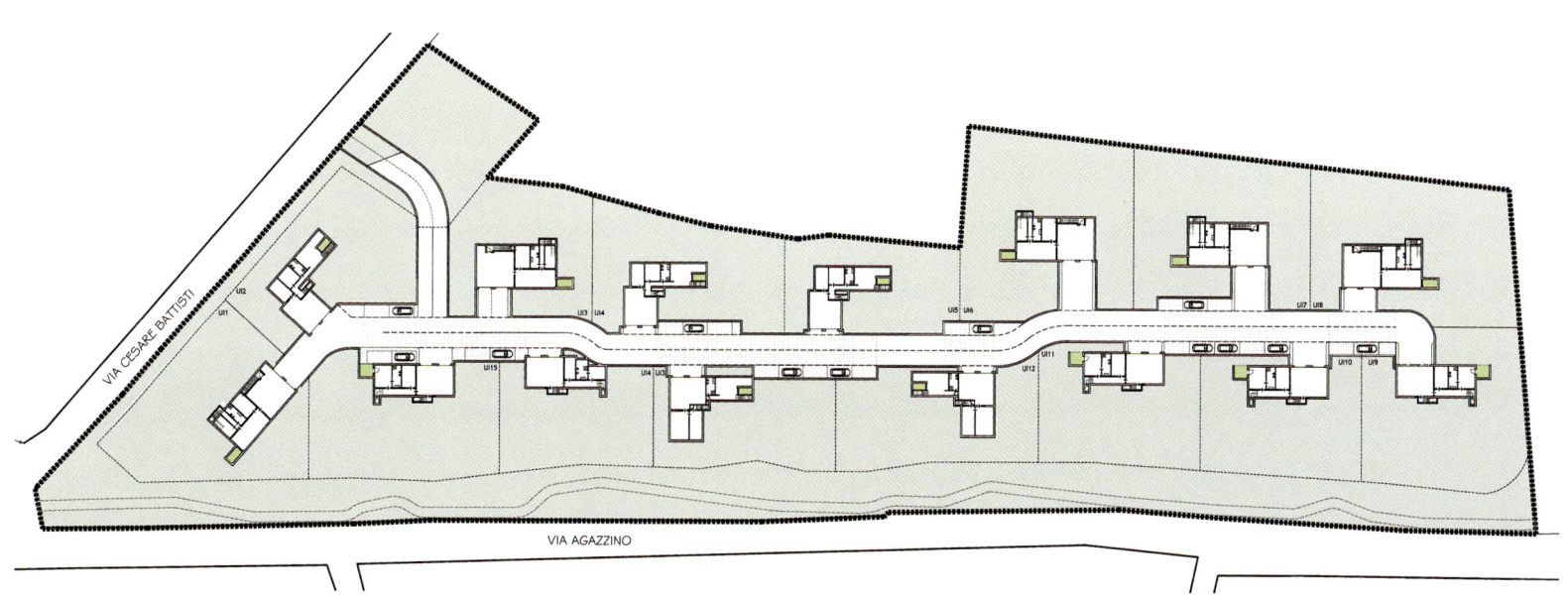

ARCHITECTURE

Longitudinal profile. The morphology of the project site made it possible to take advantage of the lie of the land and design the villas so as to ensure that each has an unimpeded view of the surroundings. Moreover, the residential units are reciprocally staggered so that the living rooms look out onto the wood of plane-trees, thus adding a further element of merit to the architectural project

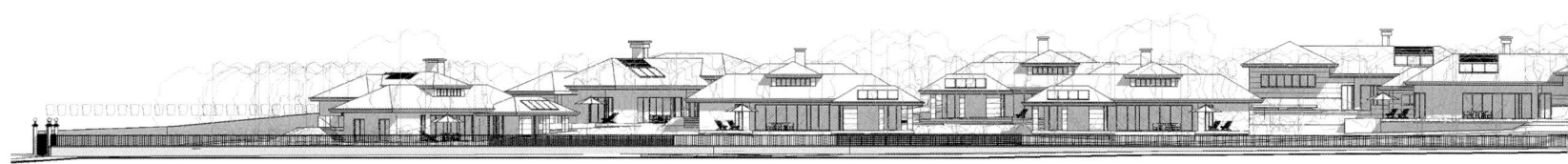

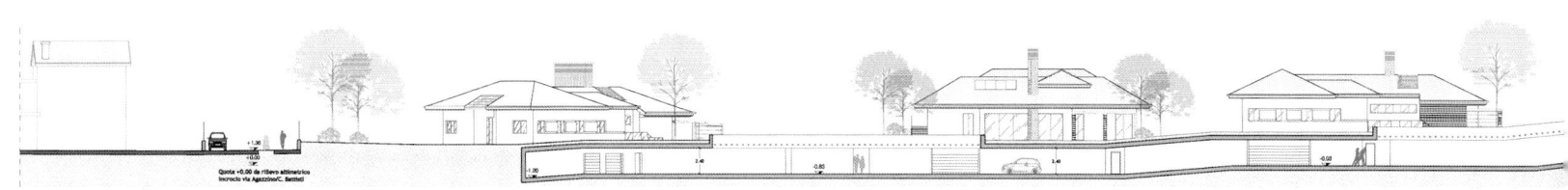

Sezione HH
Scala 1:200

General cross section along the sunken roadway.
The design of the façades adopts a simple, minimalist vocabulary capable of integrating traditional elements like exposed brick and stone paving with the context and reducing the impact of the planned new buildings on the natural character of the site. At the same time, the architecture reveals close attention to composition and details of construction

ARCHITECTURE

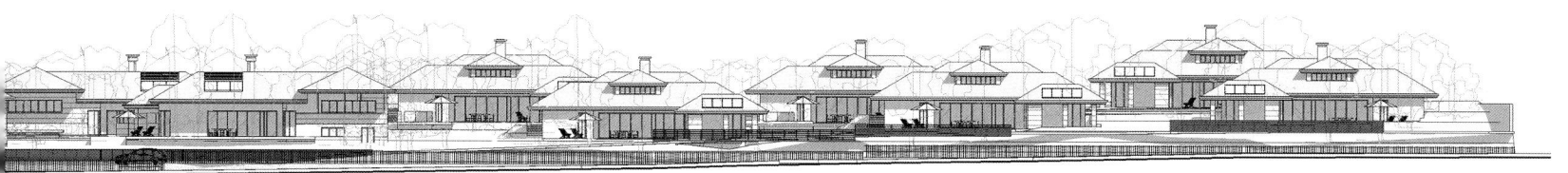

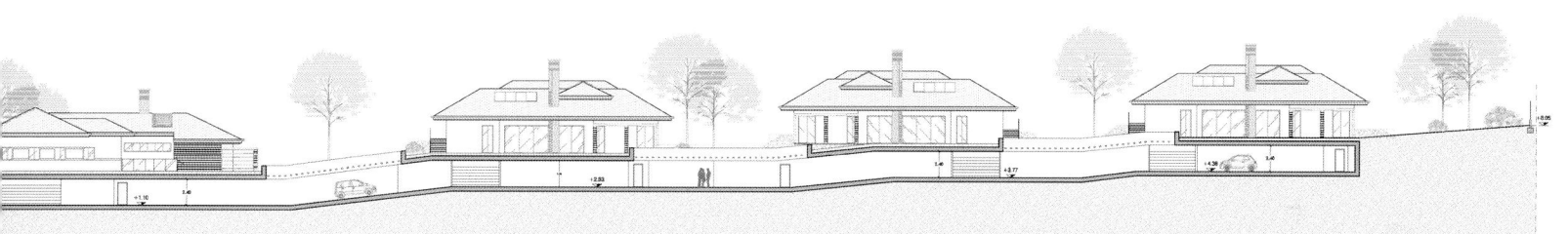

ARCHITECTURE

17. Missaglia (Lecco): residential buildings on the area of the Integrated Action Plan (under way since 2011)

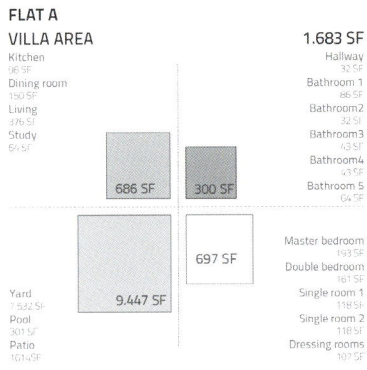

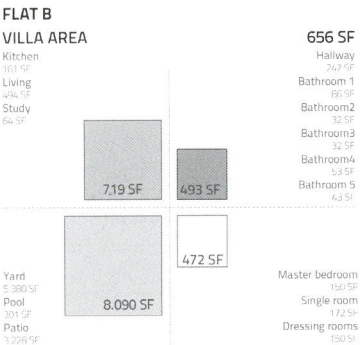

The residences planned return to the tradition of the large extra-urban villas with a great deal of space outside that were built all over Brianza from the 1960s to the end of the 1980s, offering an alternative to urban life. Given the whole variety of styles used for their construction, the project for Missaglia takes up the attempts made in the 1960s by various great masters to create a recognizable style, studying various typological characteristics and materials while at the same time analyzing the organization of the internal pathways and the layout of spaces in the middle-class residences of the period. The villas are thus large, laid out on two levels plus a third, and engage in constant dialogue with the exterior through large windows, outside facilities such as swimming pools, ponds and large covered paved surfaces. They are organized around a large fireplace, the compositional fulcrum and key element of the plan. The basement level houses the garage, parking spaces for visitors, facilities and cellar as well as a small patio adjoining the laundry room. The house opens up to the outside at the garden level and develops around the fireplace, including the living room, dining room, kitchen, bathrooms, study, open gymnasium connected with the outside and the pool, and utilities room. The upper half floor to the rear houses the master bedrooms and guest rooms with bathrooms and wardrobe. The house is thus divided up in relation to functions and times of the day with no separation of space but rather fluid movement around some key points such as the fireplace.

While the project provides for class A buildings of the maximum energy efficiency, the use of facing materials such as wood, stone and brick permits direct dialogue with tradition and respect for the setting. In the choice of materials, facings and furnishings, the interior design developed by Acanto returns to the tradition of the Milanese middle-class home on which the masters worked so much, reviving a handling of space and a taste that are not easy to find in other contemporary works, far removed from architectural fashion and more in line with the history of style.

Territorial setting. The residential project area lies inside the perimeter of the PII close to the wood of plane trees from which it takes its name (I Platani). The aim is to attain a high degree of integration between anthropic and natural environment, built-up and unbuilt space. The villas stand in a green area where the natural component retains its dominant role

General plan of the lower floor

*General plan of the ground floor and the development
of green space and gardens*

ARCHITECTURE

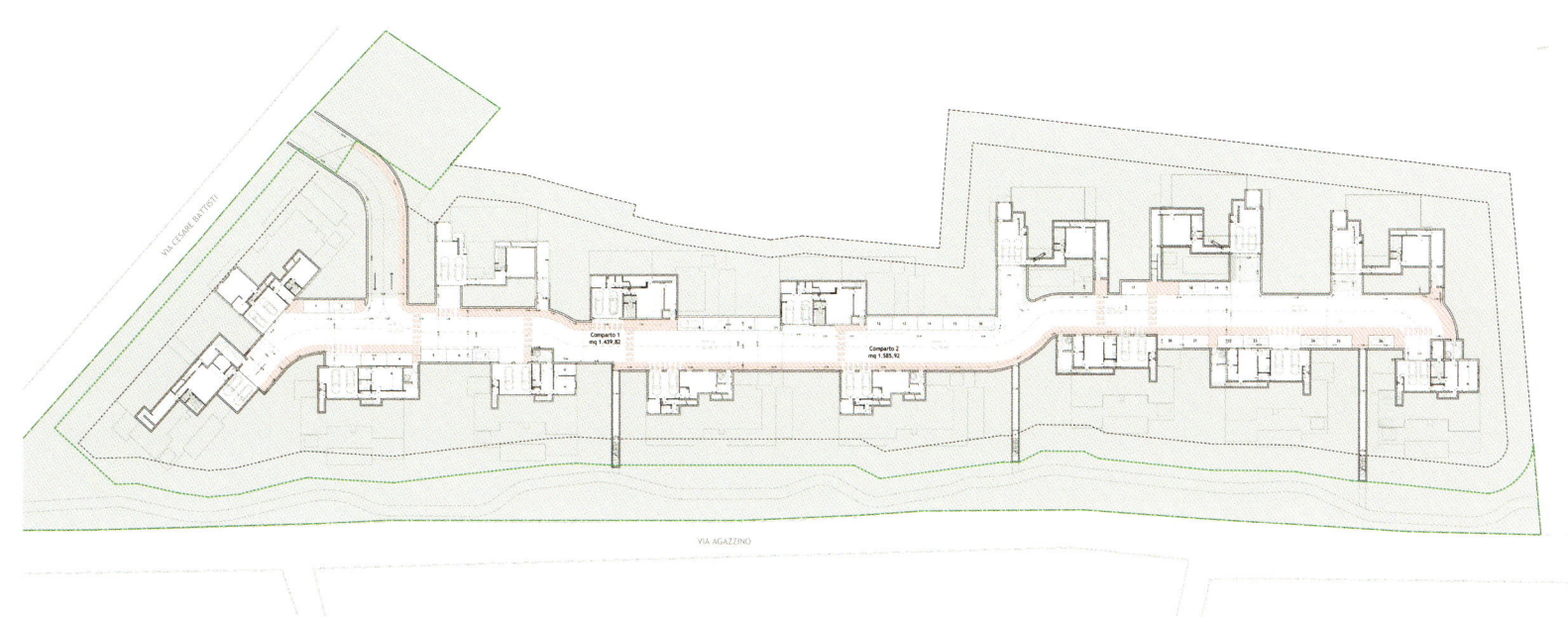

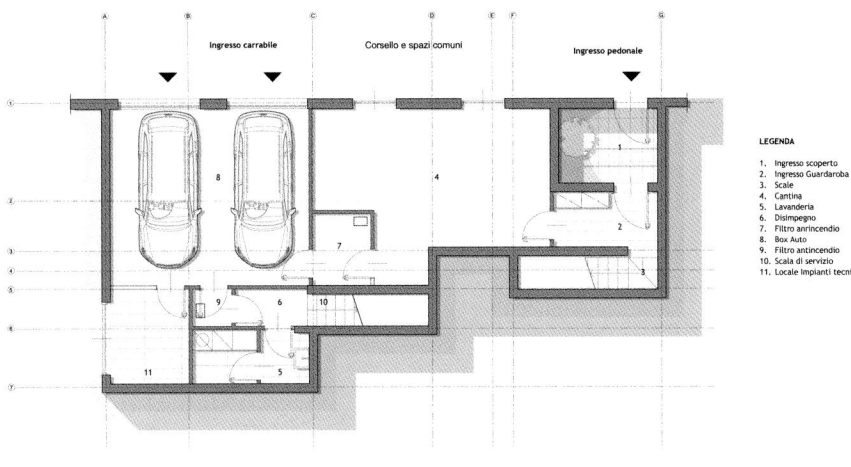

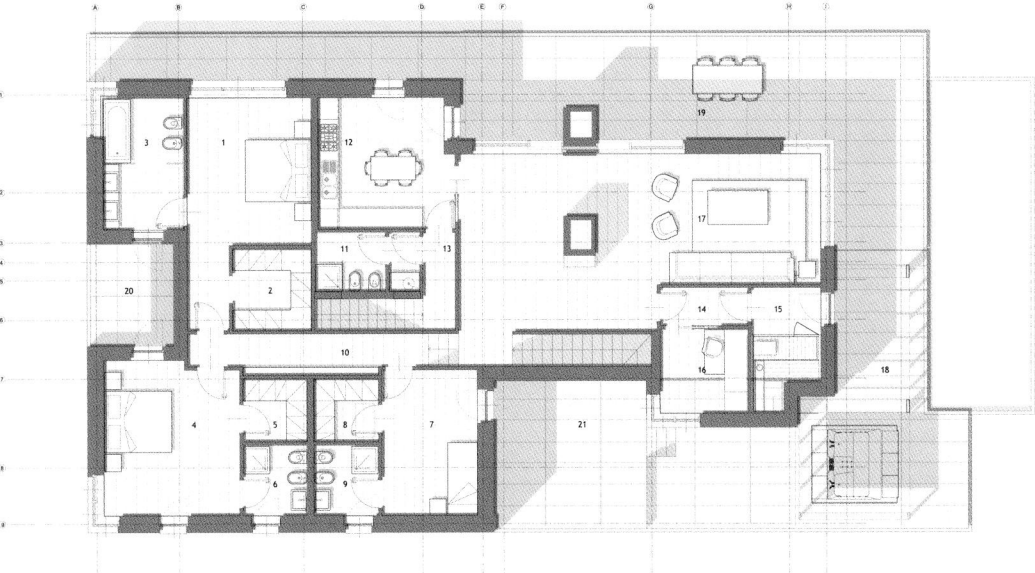

Types of building. The villas are designed in two different types that are equivalent as regards facilities and surface area and share the same formal vocabulary. The internal layout opts for large spaces with views of the surroundings that receive light from large, full-height windows and skylights positioned to serve the corridors and the rooms in the centre of the house. The design of the interiors opts for high standards of quality and envisages numerous accessory spaces such as built-in wardrobes and en suite bathrooms for all the bedrooms characterized by top-quality materials and finishes

Environmental section. The presence of floors at different levels and the natural slope of the site make it possible to avoid visual obstructions between the buildings. In addition to raising the qualitative standard of the villas with pleasant views of the natural surroundings through large windows in the living room, this also ensures that all the residential units on the site have a high degree of exposure to sunlight in accordance with the overall energy strategy

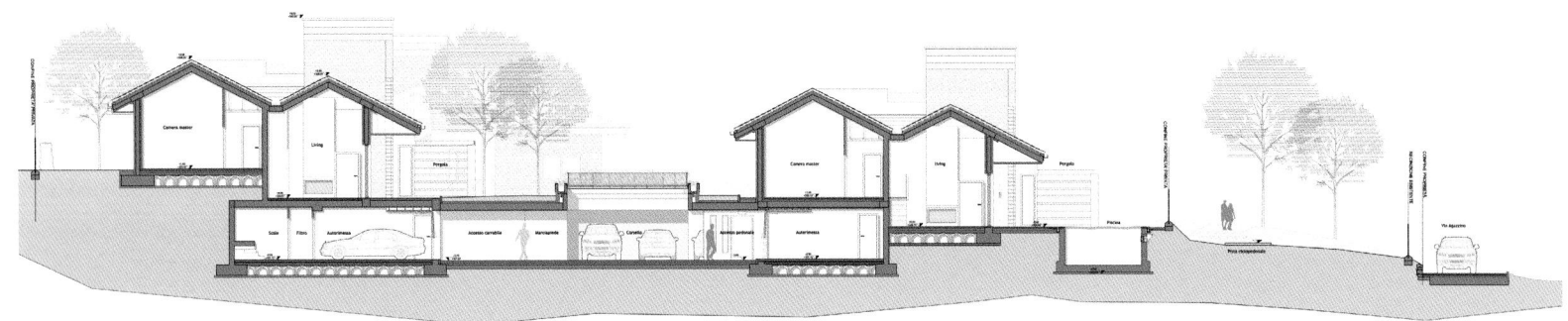

General plan of the lower floor

*General plan of the ground floor and the development
of green space and gardens*

ARCHITECTURE

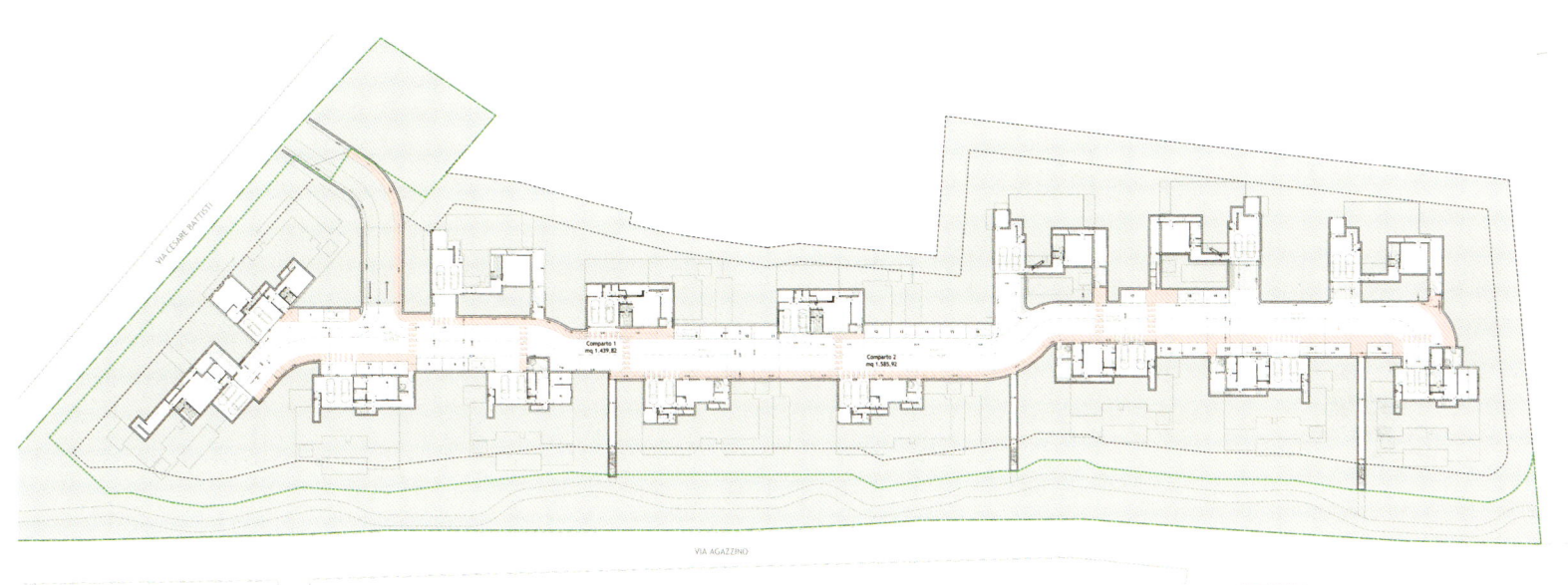

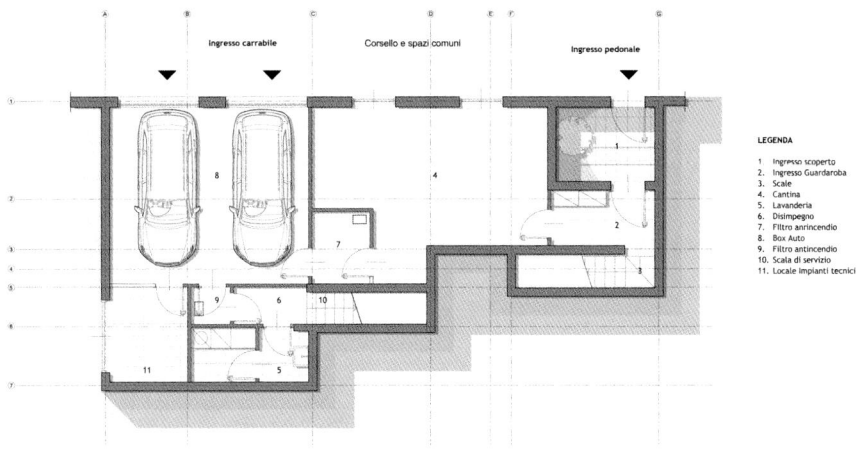

LEGENDA
1. Ingresso scoperto
2. Ingresso Guardaroba
3. Scale
4. Cantina
5. Lavanderia
6. Disimpegno
7. Filtro antincendio
8. Box Auto
9. Filtro antincendio
10. Scala di servizio
11. Locale impianti tecnici

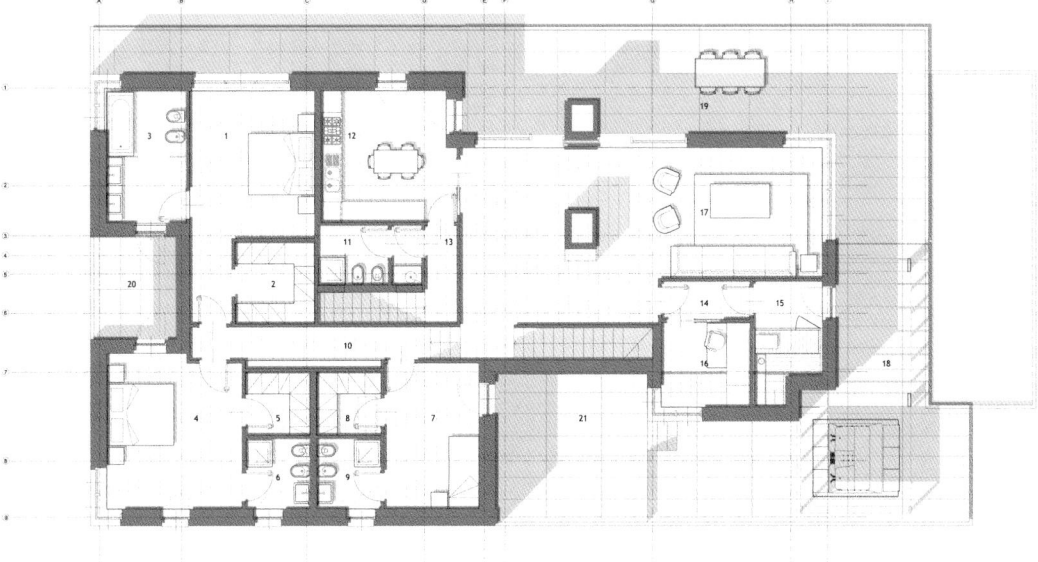

LEGENDA
1. Master Bedroom
2. Cabina Armadi Master
3. Bagno Master
4. Camera doppia
5. Bagno doppia
6. Cabina Armadi doppia
7. Camera singola
8. Cabina armadi doppia
9. Bagno doppia
10. Disimpegno camere
11. Bagno di servizio
12. Cucina/pranzo
13. Disimpegno locali di servizio
14. Disimpegno
15. Home SPA
16. Studio
17. Living
18. Pergola con piscina e vasca idromassaggio
19. Dehor con caminetto esterno
20. Terrazzo Camere
21. Terrazzo Singola

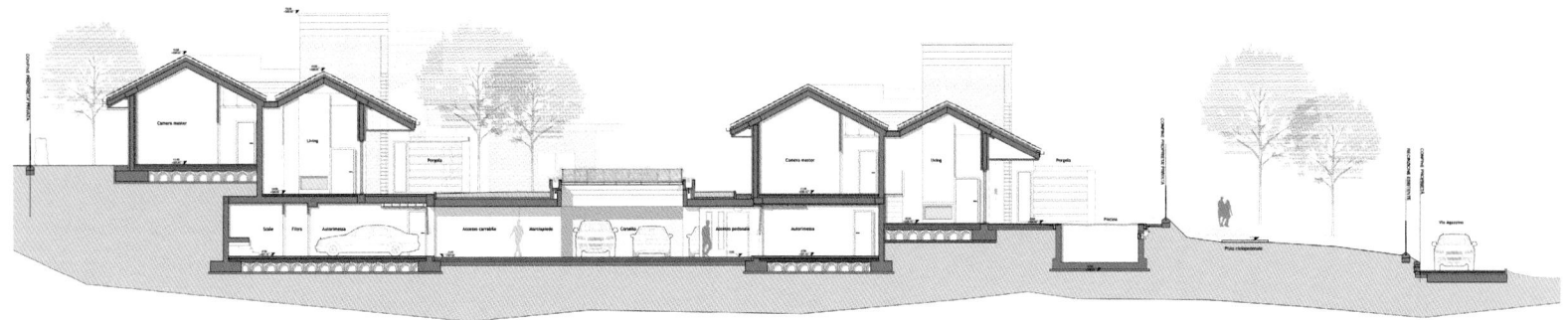

Types of building. The villas are designed in two different types that are equivalent as regards facilities and surface area and share the same formal vocabulary. The internal layout opts for large spaces with views of the surroundings that receive light from large, full-height windows and skylights positioned to serve the corridors and the rooms in the centre of the house. The design of the interiors opts for high standards of quality and envisages numerous accessory spaces such as built-in wardrobes and en suite bathrooms for all the bedrooms characterized by top-quality materials and finishes

Environmental section. The presence of floors at different levels and the natural slope of the site make it possible to avoid visual obstructions between the buildings. In addition to raising the qualitative standard of the villas with pleasant views of the natural surroundings through large windows in the living room, this also ensures that all the residential units on the site have a high degree of exposure to sunlight in accordance with the overall energy strategy

ARCHITECTURE

Types of building. The villas are designed in two different types that are equivalent as regards facilities and surface area and share the same formal vocabulary. The internal layout opts for large spaces with views of the surroundings that receive light from large, full-height windows and skylights positioned to serve the corridors and the rooms in the centre of the house. The design of the interiors opts for high standards of quality and envisages numerous accessory spaces such as built-in wardrobes and en suite bathrooms for all the bedrooms characterized by top-quality materials and finishes

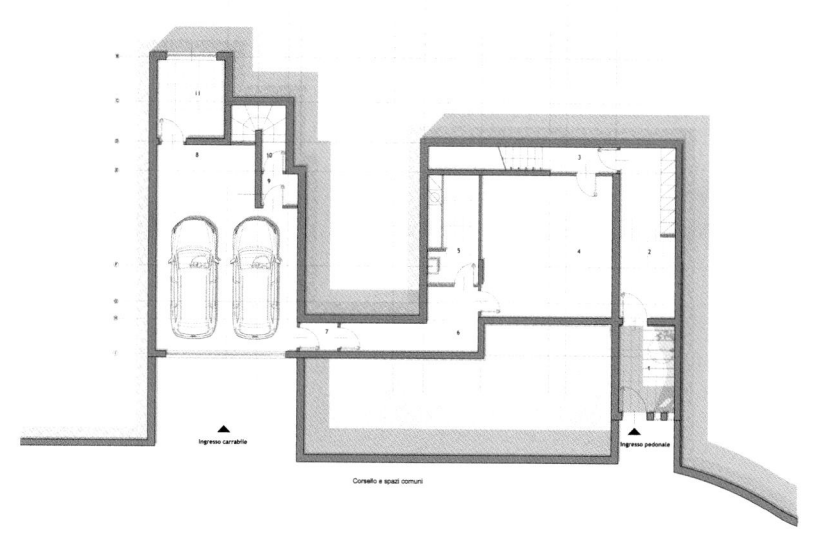

LEGENDA

1. Ingresso scoperto
2. Ingresso Guardaroba
3. Disimpegno/scale
4. Cantina
5. Lavanderia
6. Disimpegno
7. Filtro antincendio
8. Box Auto
9. Filtro antincendio
10. Scala di servizio
11. Locale impianti tecnici

LEGENDA

1. Master Bedroom
2. Cabina Armadi Master
3. Bagno Master
4. Camera singola
5. Bagno singola
6. Camera doppia
7. Bagno doppia
8. Cabina armadi doppia
9. Disimpegno camere
10. Cucina
11. Sala da pranzo
12. Bagno di servizio
13. Living
14. Disimpegno
15. Studio
16. Home SPA
17. Vasca idromassaggio esterna
18. Dehor con piscina
19. Pergola
20. Terrazzo Master
21. Terrazzo doppia

249

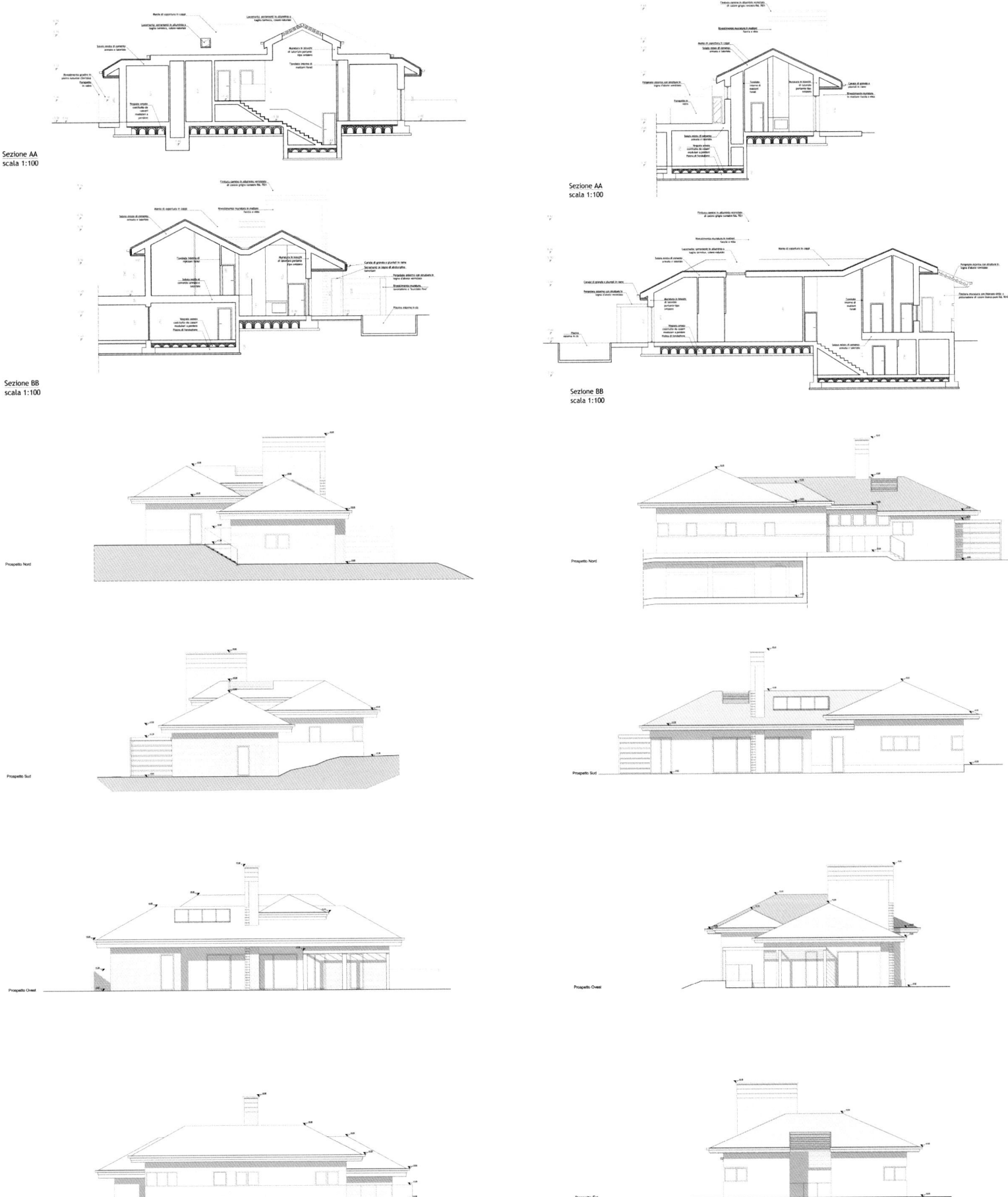

Opposite

Sections and elevations. The residential units have a lower ground level connected with the sunken road, a ground floor and a mezzanine. The spaces are designed so as to ensure separation of private sections like the bedrooms from the living area through the staggered mezzanine. At the same time, the various parts of the house are integrated in a unified and harmonious functional layout around the focal point the two-sided fireplace in the living room

Construction section. The design of the villas focuses particular attention on environmental sustainability, which is pursued through the choice of construction technologies capable of reducing the building's ecological footprint. In particular, the wall stratigraphy is characterized by a high degree of thermal inertia obtained through the introduction of solid elements such as a facing of full bricks. The shell is also thermally insulated by means of panels installed on the outer walls and the roof. The strategy as regards utilities focuses on systems with a high degree of energy efficiency powered by photovoltaic panels for air conditioning, while tanks are installed to collect rainwater and permit substantial savings on water consumption. The residential units are certified as belonging to energy class A through the application of these planning measures and some criteria of sustainable architecture

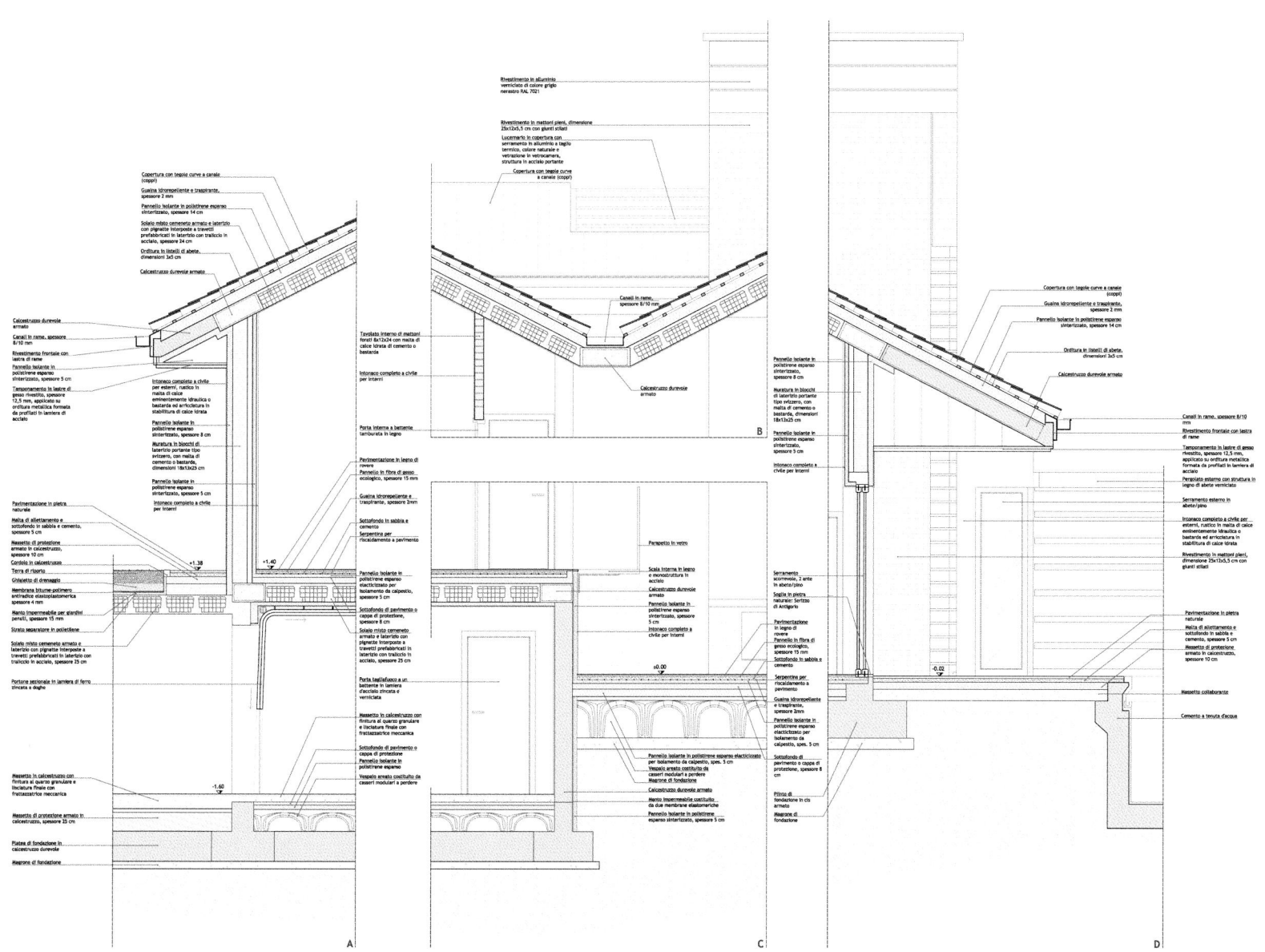

View of a type A villa

View of a type B villa

252

ARCHITECTURE

18. Essaouira (Morocco): preliminary project for villas on sea (2012)

FLAT AREA   1.937 SF

Located on the Moroccan coast near the town of Essaouira, the houses are set in a private area of great importance and reinterpret the concept of the private enclave, inside which the elements of the house are arranged, albeit with strong connections with the outside.
The complex of villas nestles on the coast looking out over the ocean. The model studied is enclosed by a low wall in accordance with tradition. Inside, two paths that cross make it possible to divide the main body into various units separated by open corridors and covered by pergolas. The circulation of air divides the house into various separate rooms that are private but open onto the communal central space, which is again covered by a pergola.
Like the Roman *domus* and many other Mediterranean houses, the villa is concentrated around a central patio crossed by two paths. The first leads from the entrance to the interior, serves the external parking space, skirts and supports the swimming pool looking out towards the sea, and separates the living area from the rest of the house. The second runs through the house from north to south, defines the other side of the patio, crosses the living area and leads to a balcony with a view of the sea. The two paths ensure the centrality of the patio and allow the rooms to have points of references, albeit separate. The garden, the exterior and the patio enter the volumes and divide their form so as to make the divisions between inside and outside disappear in the continuous interplay of open, closed and covered parts, thus discovering how architecture can be enriched with new possibilities thanks to climate.
The interiors are designed in accordance with the Acanto philosophy, so that the choice of materials, coverings, furnishings and particular solutions takes up the local tradition but retains the characteristic Acanto style. The external volumes are rational in their compositional simplicity and so are the interiors, which allow the bright sunlight to flood in and endow the space with form and colour. Wood, glass and plaster are the basis and the canvas on which carpets, upholstery, coverings and woodworks as well as the objects and furniture bring their varied hues into play in pursuit of an elegant balance between architecture and decoration. Displaying great respect for the light and the landscape to be seen all around, the villas constitute an initial experimental project for the Moroccan coast and attempt a more sophisticated model of settlement than the simple occupation of land along the coasts found in so many places.

Territorial setting. The site is located in a landscape of quality from which the project draws inspiration, adopting the light and colours of the surrounding territory in order to endow the architectural forms with new meaning

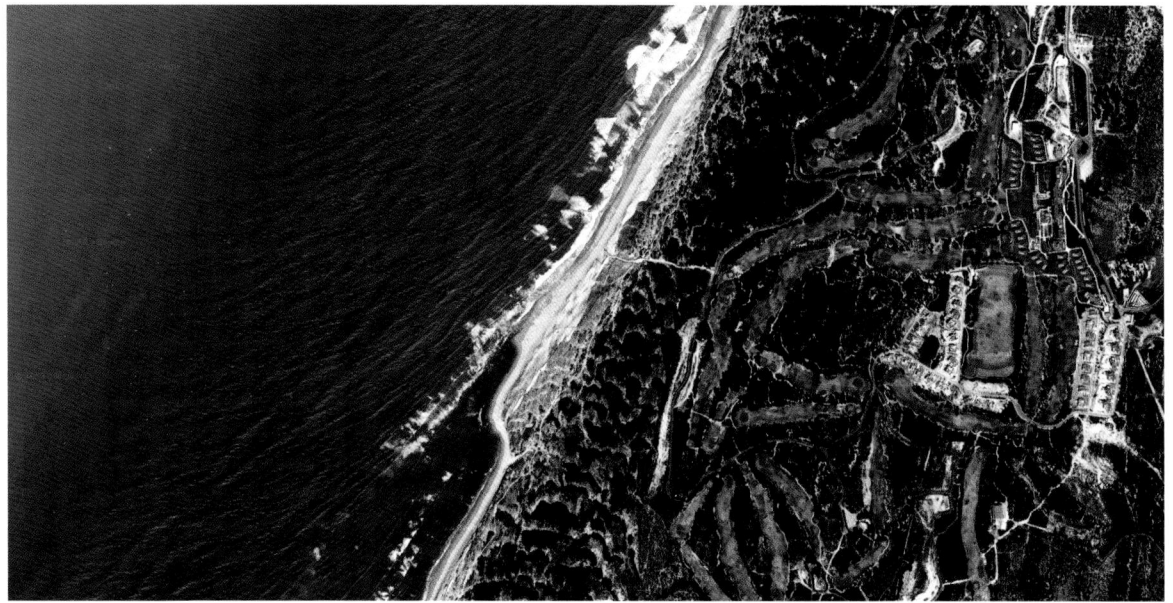

Type A/B. Layout of the ground floor. The project identifies two different residential models sharing the same compositional elements: a central patio around which the various rooms are laid out, a swimming pool, a living area and a sleeping area in a constant interplay of light and shadow opening up to the coastal landscape

ARCHITECTURE

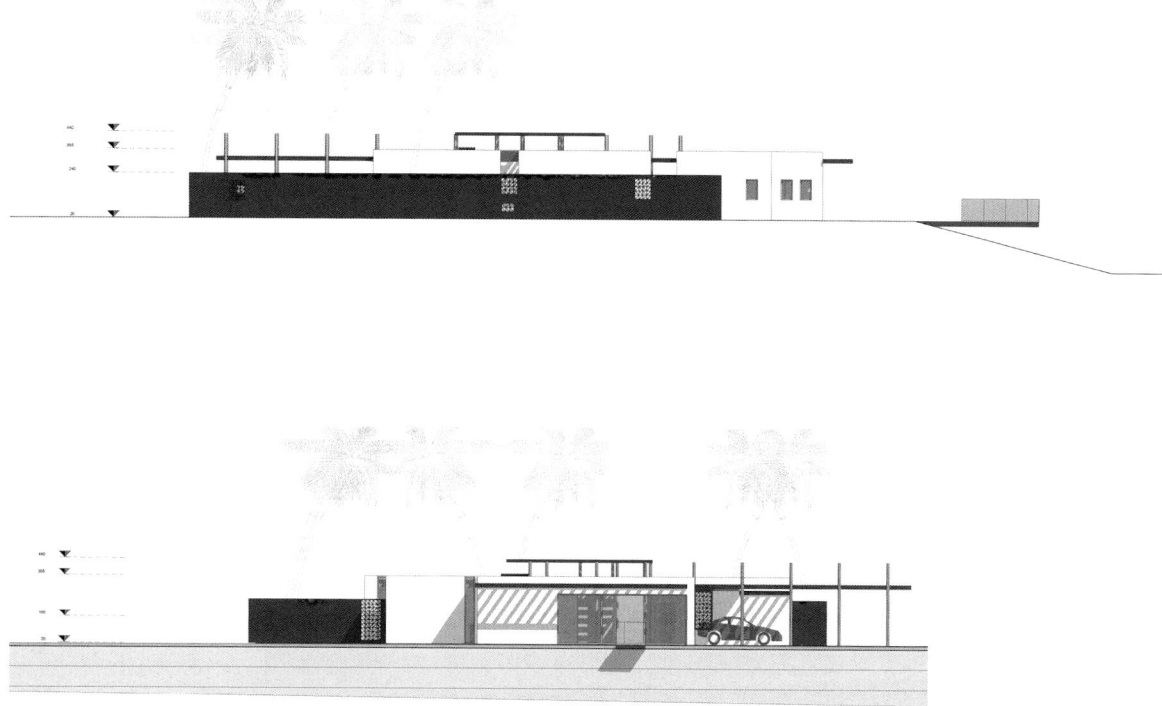

Elevations. Arrangement of the buildings and rooms

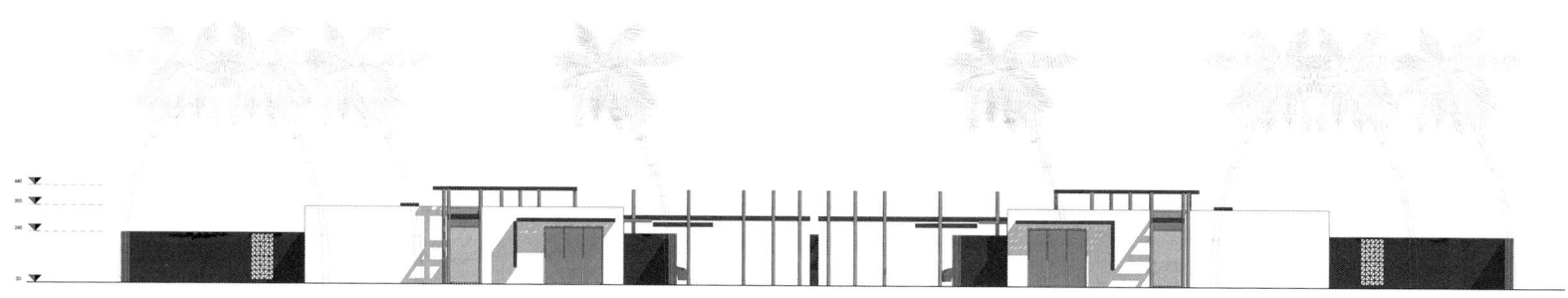

Central patio. The focal point of the project and fulcrum round which the spaces and rooms are laid out, drawing inspiration from the characteristic residential models of the historical Mediterranean landscape

3D views

ARCHITECTURE

257

ARCHITECTURE

19. Kiev (Ukraine), metropolitan area: feasibility study for public housing projects (2012)

FLAT A
FLAT AREA   645 SF

Kitchen and dining room
129 SF
Living
194 SF

Living 323 SF
Service 151 SF
Yards 129 SF
Bedrooms 172 SF

Balcony
129 SF

Entrance
43 SF
Bathroom 1
25 SF
Bathroom 2
12 SF

Bedroom
172 SF

FLAT B
FLAT AREA   656 SF

Kitchen and dining room
118 SF
Soggiorno
237 SF

Living 355 SF
Service 54 SF
Yards 43 SF
Bedrooms 247 SF

Balcony
43 SF

Bathroom 1
32 SF
Bathroom 2
22 SF

Bedroom 1
108 SF
Bedroom 2
140 SF

Plans for the metropolitan area of Kiev envisage new public housing projects using innovative techniques of prefabrication. It is therefore necessary to ensure compatibility between the demands of building production and an architectural image that does not necessarily express the way in which the houses are constructed. It is indeed precisely architectural design that gives value to the building, which is otherwise addressed with less thought and consideration. Two models were designed and put forward, one with nine storeys and one with six, reinterpreting the tower and the apartment block, two tried and tested forms typical of public housing. The first is planimetrically organized around the central core of the stairs and elevator, with the apartments arranged so as to take the best advantage of the views on every side. The presence of terraces and openings is maximized in both plan view and elevation. The second repeats the standard block of so many public housing projects but with greater richness as regards the composition of the façades and the expressive qualities of the roof.

Here too, particular emphasis is given to the column of terraces and balconies, which is repeated on the two sides. The aim is to pinpoint a particular element of the building, both the tower and the block, and make it a recognizable and repeatable hallmark to be picked up in all the buildings and distinguish the complex as a whole. Prefabrication is bent to comply with more complex compositional rules in the interplay of the plan and the development of the elevations, thus making the settlement more varied in general and the layouts of the buildings more structured so as to avoid the bleakness and monotony of traditional prefabricated constructions. The savings obtained on construction costs are used for greater detail of the façades and better employment of materials like plaster and brick. The project is set in the framework of collaboration with some companies of prefabrication and the country's plans for development in the housing sector.

Territorial setting. Completely embedded in the metropolitan area of Kiev, the project seeks to stand out with respect to the context by adopting different architectural materials and solutions to put forward new residential models for the country's urban development programme

ARCHITECTURE

Type A. Internal layout. The six-storey residential model displays intense planimetric development around a central nucleus consisting of the primary utilities so that the apartments can look out onto the outside as much as possible

Type A. Interiors. The model apartment opens onto a large living area receiving abundant light from outside and offering a view

Type A. Six-storey model. The project is enhanced by an ample array of balconies and terraces that interrupt the compositional monotony of the prefabricated structures, thus offering new rules conducive to the creation of a varied and pleasant settlement

Type A. Six-storey model. The project is enhanced by an ample array of balconies and terraces that interrupt the compositional monotony of the prefabricated structures, thus offering new rules conducive to the creation of a varied and pleasant settlement

Type B. Interiors. The model apartment develops around the dining room, which becomes the heart of the apartment separating the living and sleeping areas

721 (85%) - жилая
127 (15%)- общего пользования

848 - всего

727 (86%) - жилая
121 (14%)- общего пользования

848 - всего

Opposite
Type B. Nine-storey model. The second type is characterized by original composition of the façade and expressive richness of the roof, with particular emphasis placed on the exteriors so as to ensure the recognizability of the settlement as a whole

View of the south elevation of the type B building

ARCHITECTURE

20. Minsk (Byelorussia), metropolitan area: preliminary project for a shopping mall (2012)

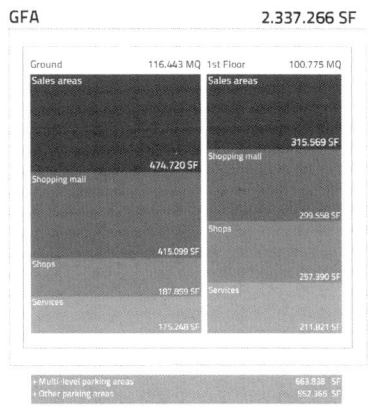

The construction of a new shopping mall in the metropolitan area of Minsk provided an opportunity for reflection on the type of building and its meaning. A now familiar type of construction, a new shopping mall generally triggers further development in free areas, causing the known phenomena of urban sprawl to which much of our thinking is opposed by the conviction that a compact city functions far better. Nevertheless, in a growing country with an expanding metropolitan area characterized by rapid and chaotic phenomena, the building of a structure like a shopping mall can provide an opportunity for reflection on the role of a container of private functions for public use a context devoid of any other services. For this reason, the project also expanded to include a large winter garden, not only bringing inside something otherwise unobtainable for many months of the year in such a cold region but also taking up the tradition of the structures for wintertime leisure so deeply rooted in the history of these countries. The provision for a winter garden inside the covered structure makes it possible to alter the plan and layout of the mall, two traditionally monotonous elements. An entrance gallery mediates immediately between the space of the garden and the space of the mall. It is as though the garden forced its way between the structures traditionally devoted to shopping, thus becoming central in the layout and leaving the sides and outer areas of the construction to the shops and larger commercial surfaces. The project is in any case always for a sort of huge block surrounded by emptiness and thus with no possibility of establishing territorial dialogue or relations with the outside. For this very reason, the definition of a strong, central and important structure inside the building offers not only an focal point for its layout but also a constraint for future constructions in the area which, if correctly interpreted, can give orderly shape to the complex and to the territory of the future.

Territorial setting. The project is located in the metropolitan area of Minks in Byelorussia, a quickly growing city undergoing marked urban expansion

Elevations

ARCHITECTURE

Winter garden. The project breaks the typical compositional rules for shopping malls by placing a large winter garden inside the structure and thereby altering its ground floor layout and plan

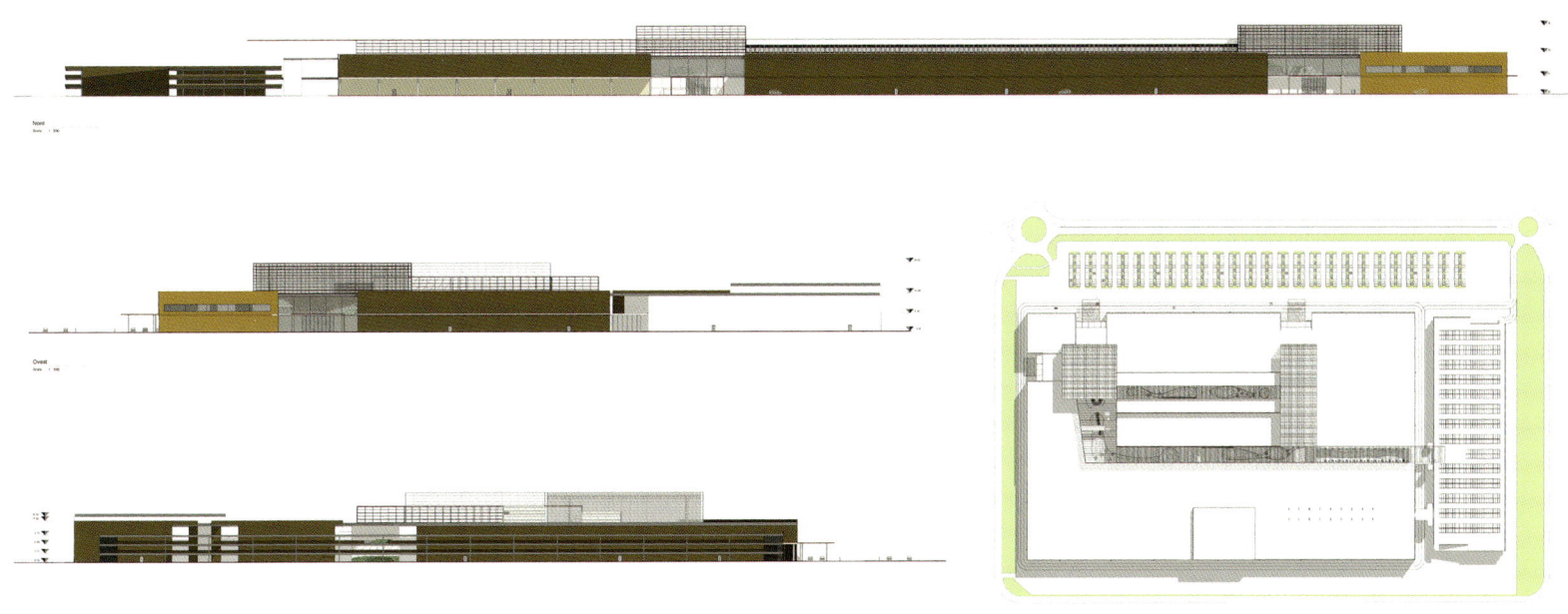

Winter garden. Rendering. The entrance gallery mediates between the commercial space and the large winter garden, thus becoming an element of dialogue between outside and inside

Opposite
Relationship with context. The use of materials and composition of the façade become model elements for the area as a whole, providing guidance and inspiration for the future development of the context

3. INTERIOR DESIGN

3. INTERIOR DESIGN

3. INTERIOR DESIGN

1. Milan: apartment,
   Via Giulio Romano 25 (2009)
2. Milan: La Gavetta, restaurant,
   Via Donizetti 3 (2010)
3. Verano Brianza (Monza
   and Brianza): wine shop (2010)
4. Siena: apartment,
   Viale Vittorio Emanuele 56
   (2012–13)
5. Milan: apartment,
   Corso Italia 15 (2012–13)

INTERIOR DESIGN

1. Milan: apartment, Via Giulio Romano 25 (2009)

FLAT AREA   936 SF

Kitchen   70 SF
Living Room   344 SF
Dining Room   129 SF

Entrance   75 SF
Dressing room   21 SF
Bathroom 1   75 SF
Bathroom 2   43 SF

Balcony   75 SF

Bedroom   172 SF

The project regarded a classic apartment in a condominium built in 1955 on Via Giulio Romano during the city's years of growth. Built on the site of a factory forming part of the Beruto Plan, the condominium exemplifies the typical characteristics of the normal building of the period, as did the design of the apartment before refurbishment. Regularly divided by a central corridor, the living area looked onto the street and the bedrooms, kitchen and bathroom onto the interior.

Taking advantage of the space of the corridor and altering the size of all the other rooms, the project worked on the idea of a fluid space capable of accommodating a number of flows and pathways while avoiding the sharp closure of doors and walls. The space thus flows, cut only by the volumes designed by the rooms and eliminating the shape of doors and jambs: between the kitchen and the dining room, the entrance hall and the living room, the living room and the bedrooms. In its spatial fluidity, the apartment presents three distinct areas: the central living room and focal point of flow, facing west and enjoying the light and warmth of sunset; the kitchen, dining room, bathroom and utilities; and the sleeping area with the master bedroom, bathroom and two fitted wardrobes. The design focuses on layout, and it is in terms of layout that the flows and functions are developed. This rational approach is then reflected in the materials and colours, which are characterized by sobriety and simplicity of style. The project thus experiments with the possibility of reversing the traditional organization of apartments and making every room and the function it accommodates also an element of connection and linkage so that movement can give shape to the apartment as a whole.

Location. Via Giulio Romano, Milan, within the historical nucleus of the Beruto Plan. The building replaced an artisanal area in the 1950s

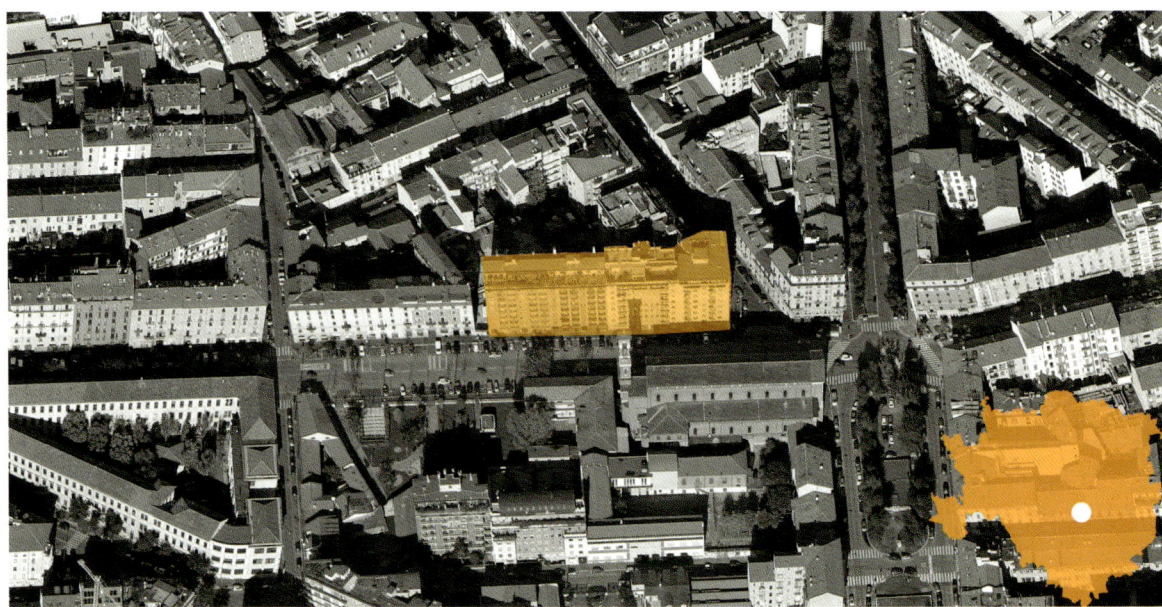

270

Plan as built. The plan as built shows the ordinary architectural character of the apartment and the building

INTERIOR DESIGN

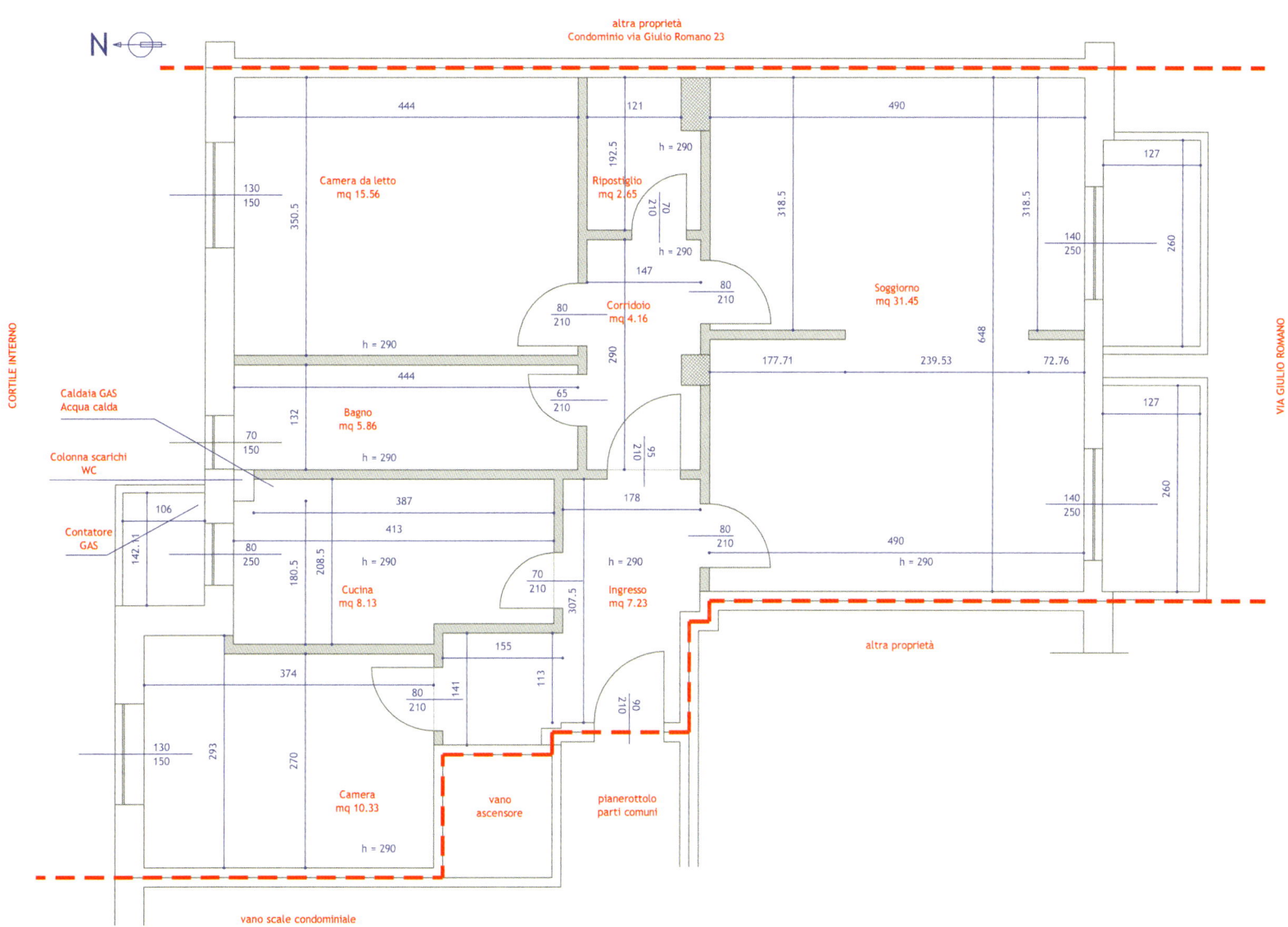

271

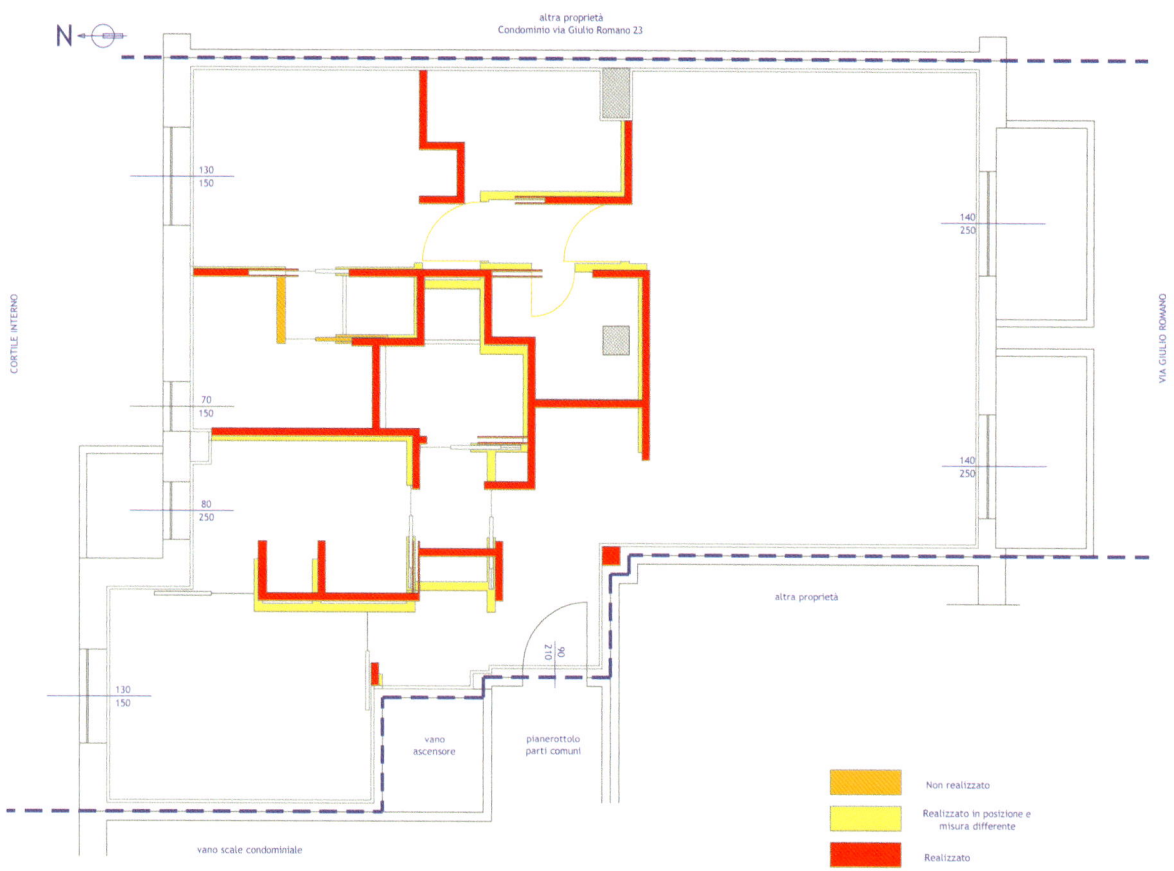

Plan of demolition and construction work. The demolition and construction plan shows the intended structure and layout of the apartment

Project plan. The project plan highlights the new characteristics of the apartment, identifying three distinct areas: the central lounge, which enjoys the best (western) exposure to sunlight; the sleeping area, including the suite, two built-in wardrobes and bathroom; and the central areas of utilities

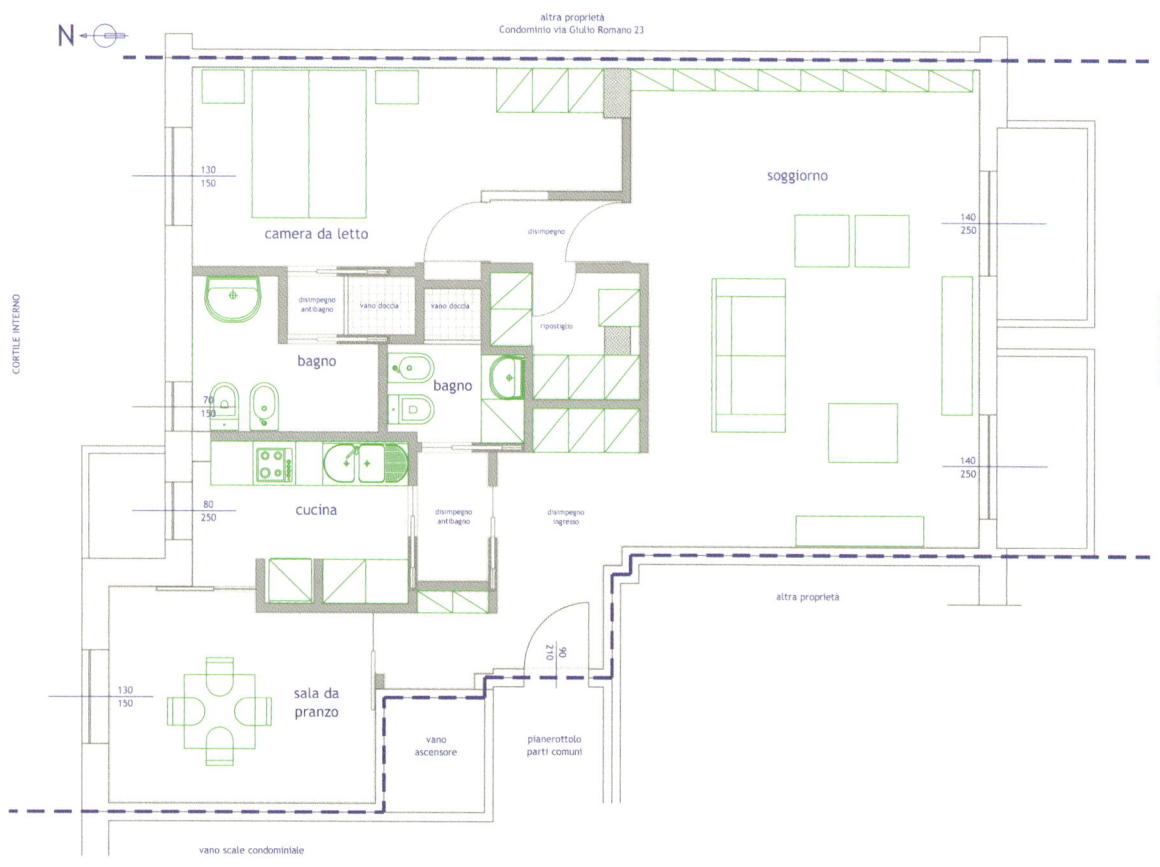

Materials and interior design. The rational planning choices find agreement also in the choice of materials and sober, delicate colours to create an pleasant environment

INTERIOR DESIGN

273

INTERIOR DESIGN

2. Milan: La Gavetta, restaurant, Via Donizetti 3 (2010)

AREA   914 SF

The design of the space for La Gavetta, a new restaurant, gave shape to premises for a new catering chain devised around a new project with a traditional Italian object, namely the *gavetta* or mess tin, as its hallmark. The idea is for the customer to fill a *gavetta* with hot and/or cold food from the restaurant's counter. Given the portable nature of the container, he or she can then decide whether to eat on the premises or elsewhere. The design involved the construction of a central counter running diagonal to the regular layout of the restaurant, preceded by a circular element for the *gavette*, which are immediately visible to customers, and surmounted by a domed fireplace. The centre of the restaurant is thus occupied by the central feature of the catering project and its trademark. The counter projects into the middle of the premises its most important part, namely the food and the way in which it can be consumed: the sophistication of gastronomic quality and the culture surrounding the object.

The many simple materials used include wood, plaster, steel and panels of woven straw. The vocabulary is kept deliberately simple, recalling the simplicity and the cornerstones on which the gastronomic project rests. A service area is placed to the rear of the counter to leave room for the toilets and other minimal items of equipment required by refurbished premises. Tables are arranged around the central counter for those choosing to dine in the restaurant. The aim is to ensure that the design of the physical space reflects the entrepreneurial project. Everything in the restaurant echoes its gastronomic project. Every element of the design and the architecture speaks of the central role of the *gavetta* and communicates the innovative underlying idea, thus transforming the refurbishment project into an opportunity to present a business strategy and a new brand.

Location. Via Donizetti, Milan

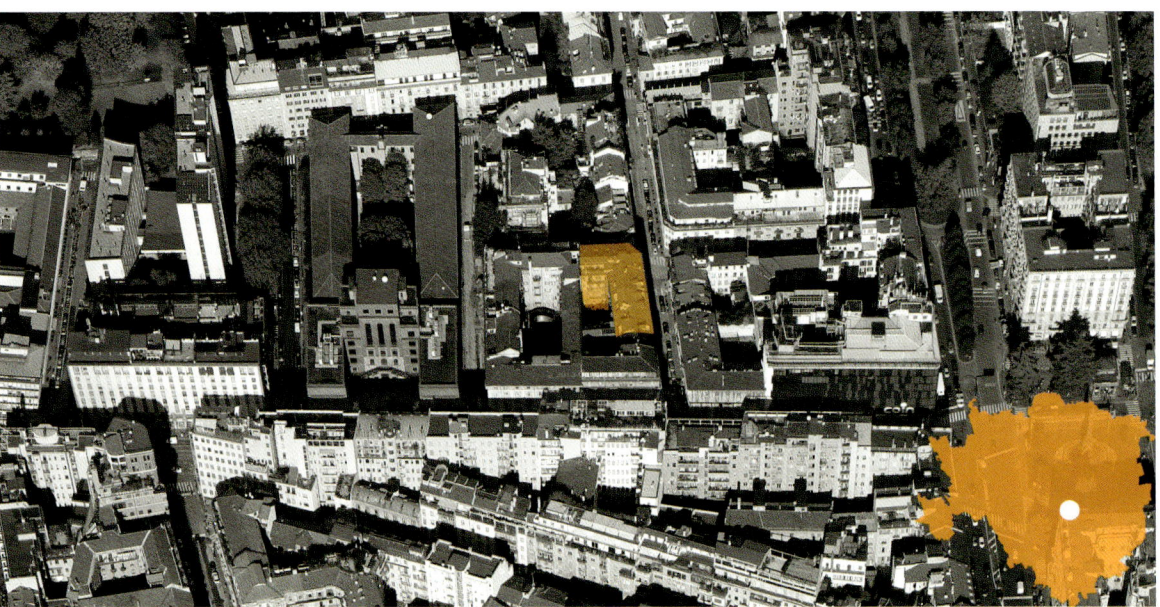

Plan as built

Project plan. The plan highlights the role central of the projecting counter, which becomes the physical and visual fulcrum of room as a whole

INTERIOR DESIGN

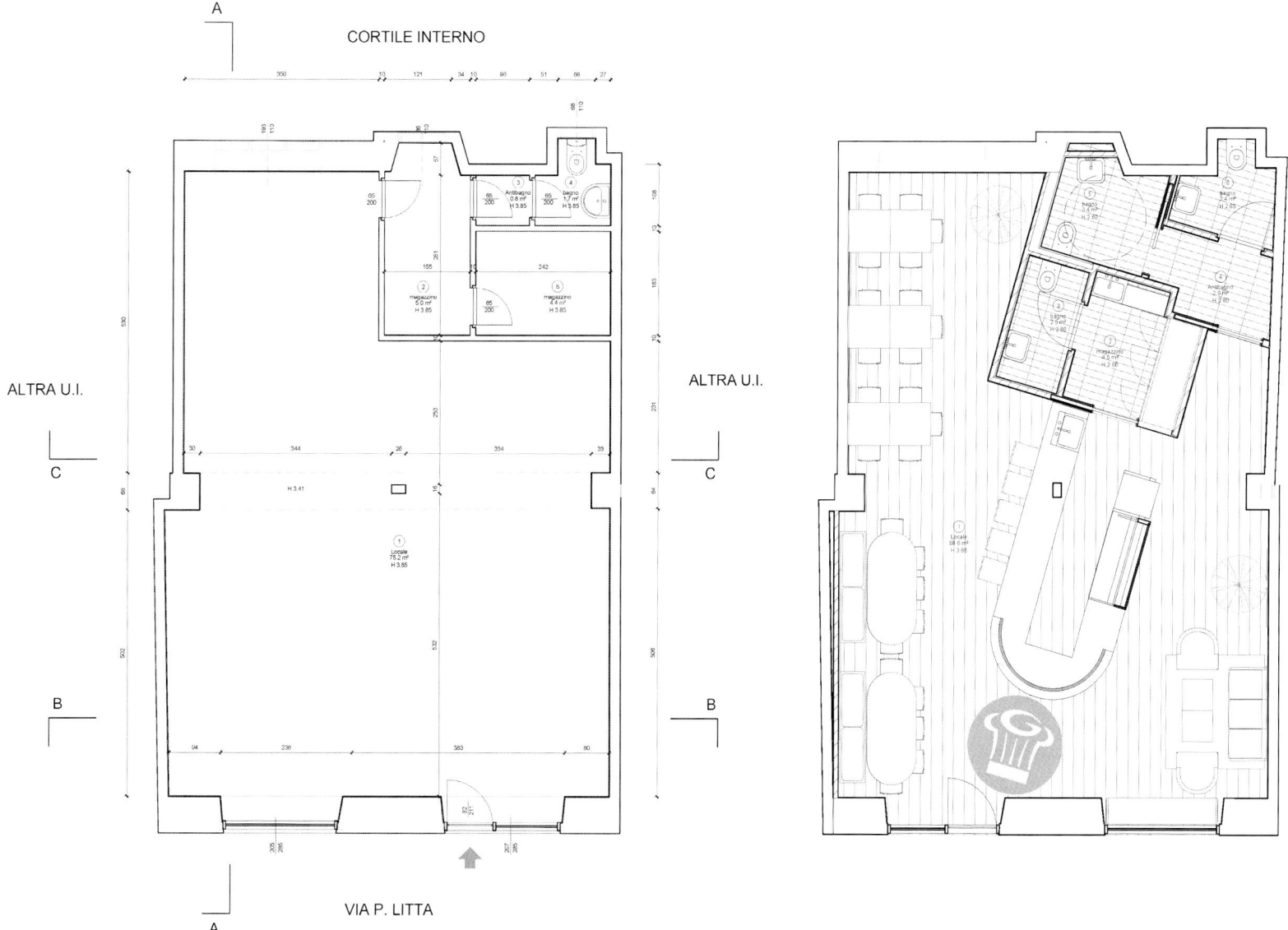

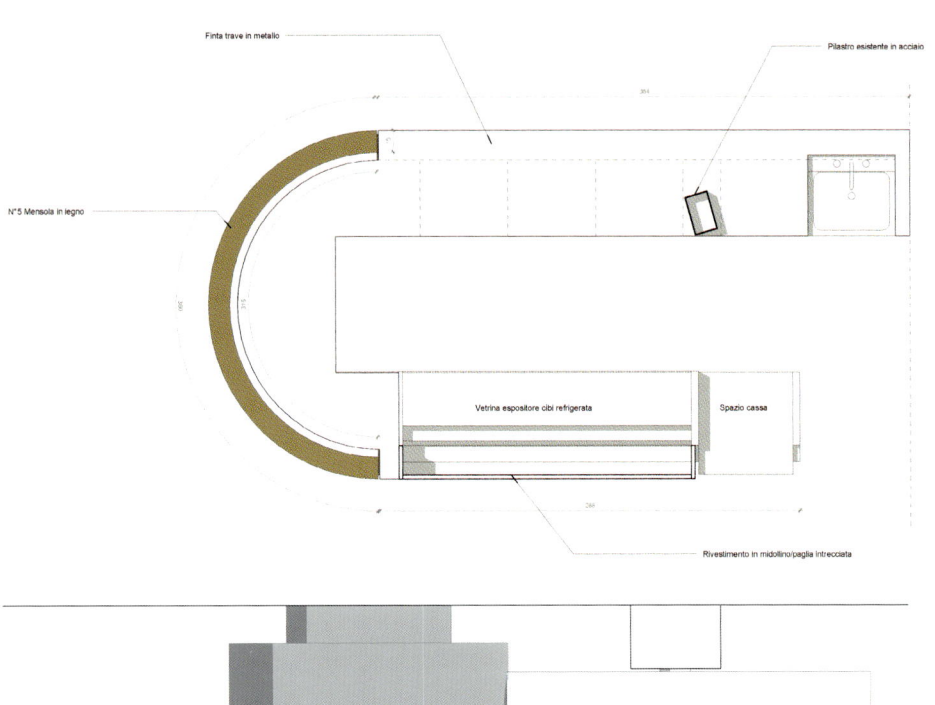

Plan of the central counter. The focal point of the space is the counter, the form and materials of which recall a *gavetta* or mess tin, the object from which the restaurant takes its name

Elevations of the counter. The elevations highlight the variety of spaces and views offered from different points in the premises. Key importance attaches to the juxtaposition of opaque and shiny spaces and the balance of solids and voids

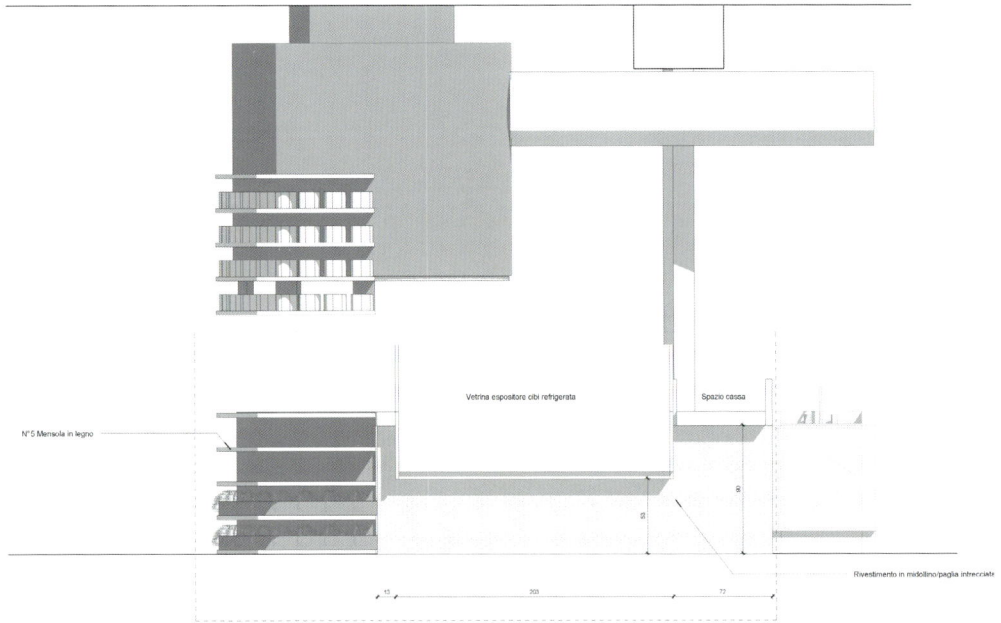

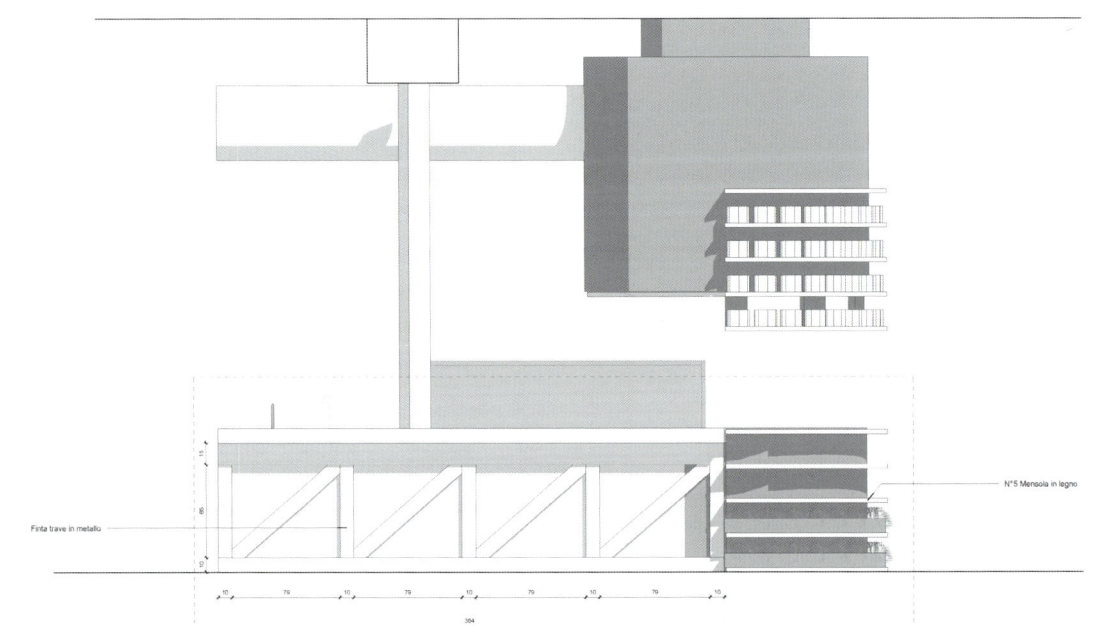

3D view. The imposing character of the counter, as reflected also in the choice of materials, contrasts with the lightness of the surrounding furniture, the simple chairs and the overall sharp definition of forms. The wooden floorboards are light-coloured and laid longitudinally. The natural lighting is backed up by lamps with crisp lines in the same materials as the counter

INTERIOR DESIGN

INTERIOR DESIGN

3. Verano Brianza (Monza and Brianza): wine shop (2010)

AREA 1032 SF

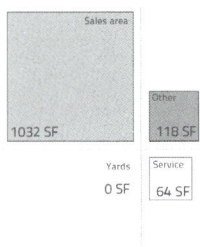

The project for the wine shop envisaged from the outset a space organized around a strongly identifying central element capable not only of ordering the distribution of all the other parts but also and above all of characterizing the functions to be performed inside and outside in relation to time of day and context.

By occupying the centre not with the mere function of the display and sales area but with the flow of human activities, the project designs a central island in which to represent the figure of the person called upon to manage the space. In this it seeks the strong and authentic connotation of a time when the person running a business of public use or access in a small town like Verano became an integral part of it, a representative and depositary of a small area of knowledge and a small world serving as a point of reference for customers. Focusing not on function and primary purpose but on the nature of human figures, of their professions and social connotation in the context of belonging, this design approach studies their behaviour patterns and organizes the space accordingly. All the pathways spread out from the central island in the free arrangement of shelves for the display of bottles, with the space of greatest public use for the events to be held on the premises placed in front.

Research on materials made it possible to identify types of wood for the display units and floor as well as a colour scheme for the walls and lighting system capable of presenting a traditional image of the space so as to accentuate the centrality of the human figure and the knowledge of which the shopkeeper is the depositary. It is on the central space that the lights, the design and all the pathways of display and use converge.

The daring of the project lies precisely in its decision to highlight and focus on the professional figure of person running the business in the conviction that the starting point for the design of the space should be the human connotation of whoever is called upon to inhabit it on a daily basis. This was the first design to be developed in this way, and the experience was to give birth for THE BLOSSOM AVENUE of a peculiar philosophy characterized by the organization and design of space around the human figure and the social function performed by the same in that particular context. Every element of the design is thus related to the public function of the architectural setting.

Location. Via Cadorna, Verano Brianza

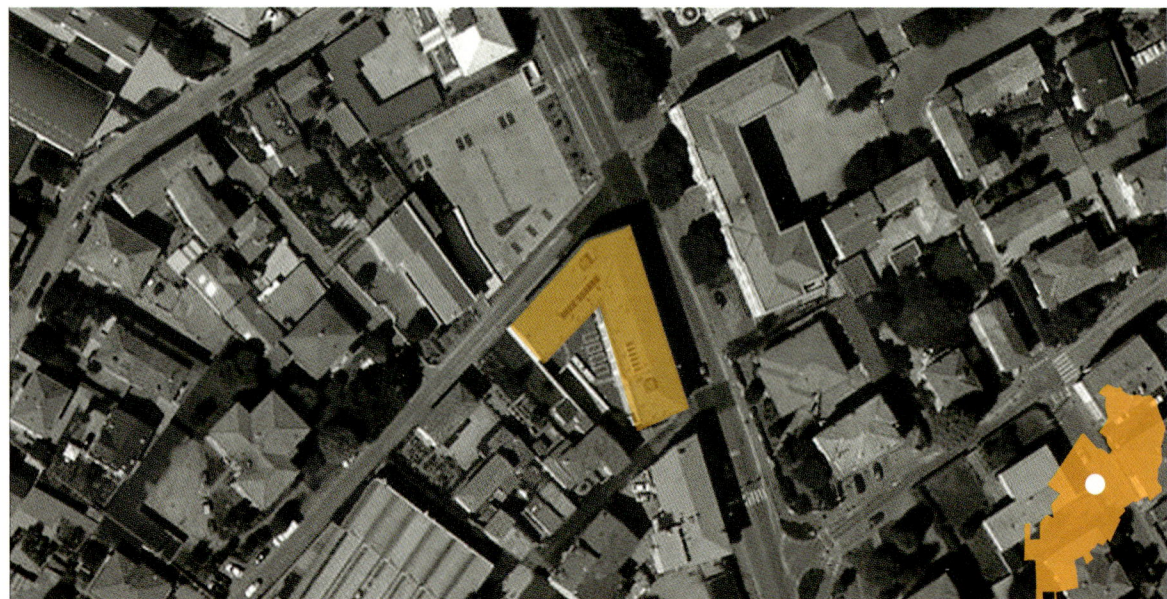

Plan of the wine shop. The central counter organizes the space so as to ensure that the pathways are fluid and highlight the role of the shopkeeper

INTERIOR DESIGN

4. Siena: apartment, Viale Vittorio Emanuele 56 (2012–13)

FLAT AREA 968 SF

Kitchen 96 SF
Living Room 333 SF
Dining Room 140 SF

Entrance 32 SF
Bathroom 1 63 SF
Bathroom 2 49 SF

53 MQ
11 MQ

Yards
0 MQ

Bedrooms
25 MQ

Bedroom 1 161 SF
Bedroom 2 118 SF

The refurbishment of an apartment on Viale Vittorio Emanuele in Siena addressed the question of intervention in an historical context at the gates of the walled city in an area affected here and there by the transformations to which Siena was subjected prior to the Astengo town planning scheme of 1956. The apartment is on the first floor of a building classified as one of the offshoots of the historical centre, i.e. the first to be built also outside the walls after 1860. Historical in character but located outside the city walls, the building is characterized by having just two storeys on Viale Vittorio Emanuele, with a brick facing that ennobles its appearance, but a number of storeys on the other side towards the valley as a result of the slope of the terrain outward from the city gate (Porta Camollia). Its particular construction thus reflects various aspects of the city's territorial, geographic and historical development.

The project offered an opportunity to go much further than envisaged in redesigning the layout. The extension of ownership also to the floor above made it possible to raise the ceiling and transform the traditional apartment into one with a height of about five meters up to the central beam. Consolidation of the roof, also in relation to the elimination of many points of support and many internal walls upon which the whole rested, made it possible to design trusses, repeated in four sections, that become the most important visual element of the apartment. The arrangement of the rooms creates a fluid, open space with just one clean break between the living and sleeping areas. The focal point around which the space of the living area as a whole rotates is the main pillar supporting the building's central truss, against which the chimney of the fireplace descends from the roof. The presence of this single dividing element, slender and contained though it is, makes it possible without other walls to ensure the recognizability and compactness of three rooms – two living rooms and the kitchen – without separating or dividing them.

Once again, the open plan and the contiguity of rooms make the apartment freely habitable. The interior design developed by ACANTO focuses both on sobriety and on variety in terms of the chromatic range, deciding on the appropriate colour scheme room by room in relation to the light while maintaining uniformity with the soft hue of the parquet floors and the tiles of the bathrooms. The final effect is of great and above all unexpected impact on climbing the stairs and seeing the large sheet of opaque glass that channels the light from the skylight above the stairwell into the apartment and gives an immediate glimpse of the innovative interplay of volume and height.

Setting. The building is located on the boundary of the historical fabric of the walled city in a context where alterations and additions have been limited

Plan as built. Situated in a two-storey building that stands out in a context of higher buildings, the apartment has a regular plan that makes it possible to imagine new spaces and perspectives, also taking advantage of the height of the rooms

Project plan. The layout is regular and fluid with a large living area developed around the fulcrum of a central pillar. The size of the rooms and openings is redefined to create a central corridor for the sleeping area and utilities

INTERIOR DESIGN

Plan as built. Situated in a two-storey building that stands out in a context of higher buildings, the apartment has a regular plan that makes it possible to imagine new spaces and perspectives, also taking advantage of the height of the rooms

Project plan. The layout is regular and fluid with a large living area developed around the fulcrum of a central pillar. The size of the rooms and openings is redefined to create a central corridor for the sleeping area and utilities

INTERIOR DESIGN

Opposite
Rendering. The central pillar of the living area, into which the fireplace is inserted, and the use of the roof trusses to create a skylight define a space characterized by variety of viewpoints and clear-cut lines

Construction work. The heights reach a maximum of five metres. The consolidation of the roof and the elimination of some points of support make it possible to redefine the rooms and spaces

INTERIOR DESIGN

5. Milan: apartment, Corso Italia 15 (2012–13)

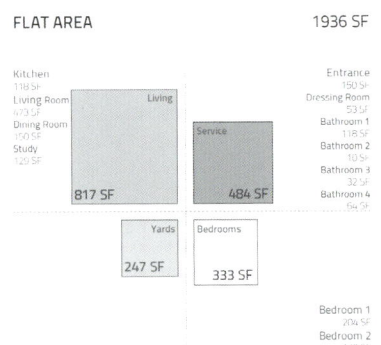

FLAT AREA — 1936 SF

The renovation of an apartment at Corso Italia 15 was an opportunity to address one of best-known modern buildings in the centre of Milan, built by Luigi Moretti between Corso Italia and Via Sant'Eufemia. The major complex has one building on Corso Italia, which respects the height of the existing urban frontage, and a taller building in the centre of the site, with floors 7 to 13 occupied by apartments and those below by offices. In addition to enjoying a complete view of the centre and the city, the apartment on the 11th floor is close to the axis of pedestrian and vehicle access running from the edge of the site on Corso Italia through the middle of the block and to Via San Senatore, thus appearing to hover in midair over the passageway.
The renovation project changes the layout completely, working once again on the concept of fluid, open space and also reinterpreting some important points of residential architecture of the 1950s and '60s. The apartment initially presented a traditional central corridor with rooms opening off it on either side. This was widened, reoriented by 90 degrees, and opened up to the home as a whole. Taking advantage of the particular depth of the building, the project concentrates all the spaces not requiring windows in the middle, creating two blocks on either side of the two walls of the corridor, one for the laundry room and a small powder room, and the other for closets, part of the master bathroom and a fitted wardrobe. The rest of the house develops around these two walls of the corridor, expanded to contain the utilities: from the through kitchen between the living room and dining room to the fluid spaces of the master bedroom, bathroom and dressing room. Small corridors lead off the wide, central corridor but are incorporated into the rooms in order to reduce their presence and impact and endow them with the spatial fluidity of the apartment as a whole. Now running perpendicular rather than parallel to the façade, the corridor connects the two sides, the side looking east onto Milan Duomo and the warmer side looking west onto the city, Monte Rosa and the sunset.
The corridor central frames the passageway like a telescope, arranges the space and organizes the apartment as a whole with no division or closure. Two walls of transparent glass close the two ends of the corridor, occupied by the study and the dining room, leaving all the rest free and allowing the space to flow and change with no impediment in its everyday perception. The interior design project developed by ACANTO included particular research on the original furnishing and decoration. Marble, stone, wood are used to define and shape the rooms so as to ensure their physical solidity and compactness.

Setting. The apartment is situated on the eleventh floor of one of the most particular and interesting buildings of the Milanese modern period

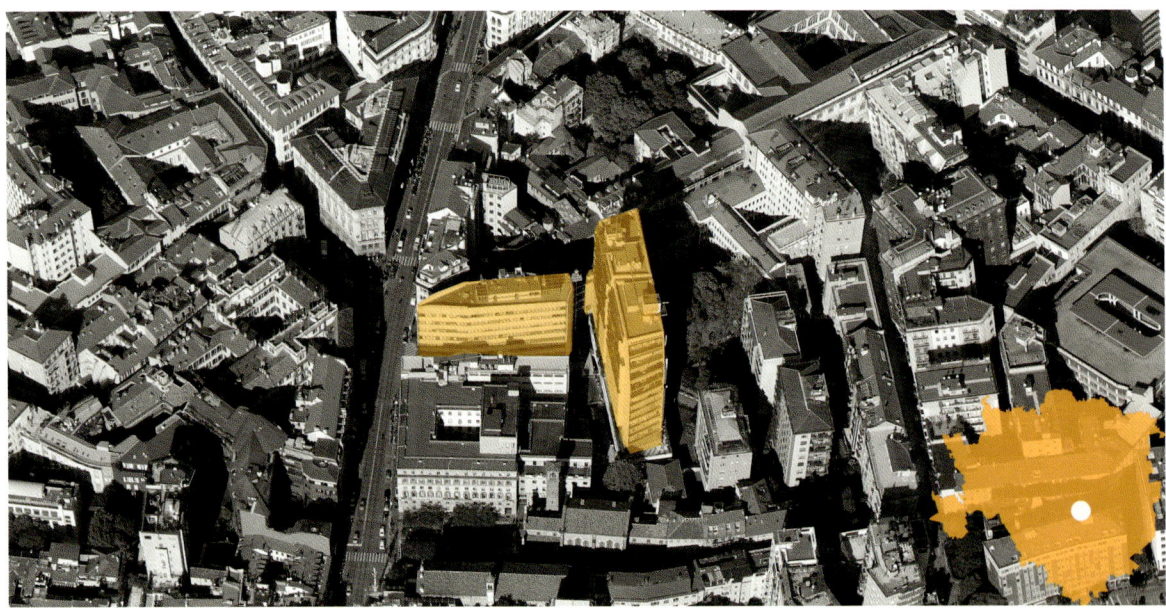

Project plan. The project transforms the layout of the apartment. Taking advantage of its large size and the central corridor, it positions all the areas that have no need of windows in the centre and the others around them, connected by means of short corridors that are incorporated into the rooms so as to diminish their impact and enhance the fluidity of the spaces

INTERIOR DESIGN

INTERIOR DESIGN

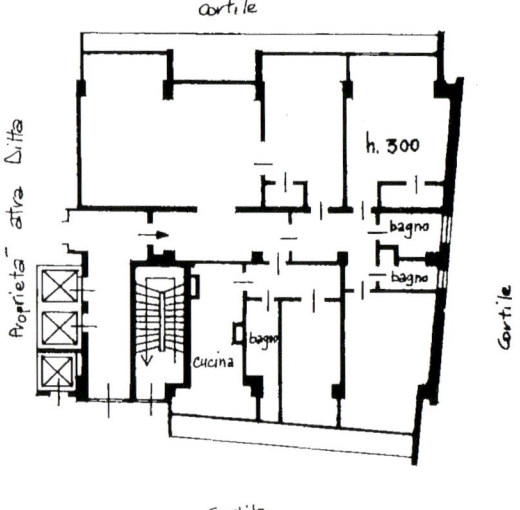

Internal courtyard of the building

Plan as built. The long central corridor initially represents the element dividing and serving the different parts of the apartment

INTERIOR DESIGN

View from the living area. East-side view towards the Velasca Tower and Milan Duomo

View of the study facing west

INTERIOR DESIGN

View of the master bedroom and bathroom

View of the bathroom of the guest room

Central corridor. Transformed with respect to its original position, the central corridor serves the windowless inner spaces of the apartment such as the utilities room and a small powder room. The clear, light colours of the floor and the doors and walls make the space light and airy

Dining area. The clarity and lightness of the chromatic choices for furnishings also continue in the dining area, where white predominates in contrast with the vivacity of the view of Milan offered by the large windows

Living area. Through the use of elements of design and furnishings with sharply defined lines and light hues as well as the careful selection of upholstery, the living area creates a pleasant and relaxing environment where the large bookcase and renowned *Barcelona* chairs designed by Mies van der Rohe stand out by virtue of their aesthetic presence

Living area. Panorama and views from the living area

Biography

Marco Facchinetti and Marco Dellavalle began to work together on joint projects in 2003 and founded FDA INTERNATIONAL in 2005. Marco Facchinetti is an architect and graduated from the Milan Polytechnic in 1996. The last student to graduate under the supervision of Giuseppe Campos Venuti, together with Federico Oliva and Valeria Erba, he took the path of urban studies and planning, first in the post-graduate school of Patrizia Gabellini at the Polytechnic and then with a research doctorate in urban, environmental and territorial planning at Florence University. He completed his studies in New York, however, at the Robert F. Wagner Graduate School of New York University with a dissertation on the sense of urban transformations around the strengthening of infrastructural nodes. The consolidation of relations with the United States saw a period as visiting professor at the department of geography and planning of the State University of New York at Albany. Responsibility for the workshop in urban planning and the course of international urban planning from 2003 to 2005 was an important experience providing insight into how the traditions of the practice and technique of urban planning vary in the western world to define and create different urban environments. In the meantime, he consolidated his teaching at the Milan Polytechnic, where he became a first-level professor in 2007. It was on the drawing boards of the Polytechnic that he met Marco Dellavalle, his brightest student.

Marco Dellavalle graduated with a survey thesis on recent transformations in the Milanese area, examined and interpreted through the lens of settlement quality and the sense of habitation in those territories. Concepts like settlement quality and the relations between lifestyles and territorial forms were thus highlighted for the first time together with a reading the phenomenon of urban sprawl under way in that very period. The research project and the question to be addressed, as formulated by Marco Dellavalle and Marco Facchinetti, were thus grounded on the same assumptions, prompting them to work together in 2003 and join forces definitively in 2005 to found FDA INTERNATIONAL. The firm's mission has been very clear from the outset: to work for private and public bodies, developers and investors in the conviction that urban contexts, both small and large, and the city in general offer the best opportunities to generate development. It is indeed sustainable, balanced, respectful and innovative development that lies at the heart of the work on which FDA concentrates. In drawing up plans, projects, regulations, master plans and designs, the firm grasps the problematic dynamics of the evolution of the discipline of urban planning and the uncompleted transition of urban contexts, torn between pressures for internal transformation and the persistence of strong dynamics of external growth. The firm began work straight away with municipalities and private bodies in Italy and the United States, investing on the one hand in the reform of urban planning under way in Lombardy, Piedmont, Tuscany and other places, and on the other in developing a different concept of quality.

The growth of the firm led to the need for a new structure, born out of reflection on what had been accomplished in ten years of activity, eight of which very intense. The major strength is the capacity to invent processes for the virtuous production of quality spaces. Within their plans, in designing planning solutions and managing processes and dynamics of transformation, the two partners demonstrate the ability to take advantage of every opportunity to increase the capacity of a project to produce quality and embed itself in the context in such a way as to become a point of reference also for development on a broader scale. The production of territory is the activity that the firm has shown its ability to perform best, at both the large and the small scale, and it is on this basis that reorganization was carried out in 2012 and 2013 with the absorption of FDA INTERNATIONAL and F&D PROJECTS, the New York office, into THE BLOSSOM AVENUE. It is the blooming and blossoming of initiatives, ideas and projects over these years that has distinguished the firm, which has demonstrated its supreme quality in seizing opportunities and bringing them to fruition in initiatives for new development in the conviction that the city and its components are the best container and the road the primary organizing element of human activity. THE BLOSSOM AVENUE thus leads FDA INTERNATIONAL and F&D PROJECTS together towards the projects of the future while also developing new initiatives like ACANTO. Founded by Marco Facchinetti and Marco Dellavalle in 2013, ACANTO works to broaden the concept of interior design, understood as a set of techniques for designing interiors, towards a more organic idea capable of involving the possibility of designing space in such a way as to express the identity, of those who will inhabit it, their vision and philosophy, for example, in the case of spaces for firms and companies. The ultimate goal is for the space thus designed to express the personal brand of whoever commissioned it. ACANTO works on this idea, drawing upon the Italian culture of design and demonstrating that it can be used in all its variety and depth far better than any other tradition to construct the personal identity of every space.

4. LIST OF PROJECTS

LIST OF PROJECTS

URBAN PLANNING

  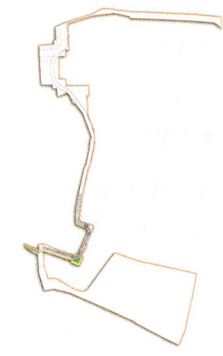

2005

Renovation of the MM2 Station central area (2005)
Cassina de' Pecchi

Province of Milan
Client: Town Council of Cassina de' Pecchi

Projects for the Cascina Pellizzara commercial area (2005)
Trecate

Province of Novara
Client: Impresa Tacchino

Feasibility study for the functional renovation and restoration of the Visconti Walls (2005)
Oleggio

Province of Novara
Client: Town Council of Oleggio

  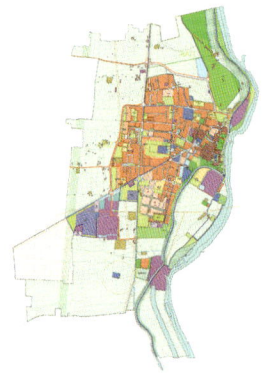

2006

Strategic plan and design for reorganization of areas PL 4 and 8 (2006)
Grezzago

Province of Milan
Client: Town Council of Grezzago

Preliminary plan for development of the PEEP area (2006)
Grezzago

Province of Milan
Client: Town Council of Grezzago

Municipal Territorial Management Plan (PGT) (2006–07)
Vaprio d'Adda

Province of Milan
Client: Town Council of Vaprio d'Adda

LIST OF PROJECTS

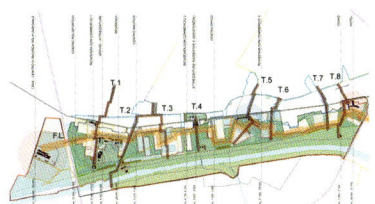

Preparing the framework of strategic actions for the Municipal Territorial Management Plan (PGT) (2005)
Pozzuolo Martesana

Province of Milan
Client: Town Council of Pozzuolo Martesana

Consultation of urban planning and infrastructures and territorial context – Urban Transformation Study (STU) (2005–07)
Le Piagge, Florence

Client: Ernst & Young

Municipal Territorial Management Plan (PGT) (2006–07)
Pozzuolo Martesana

Province of Milan
Client: Town Council of Pozzuolo Martesana

Municipal Territorial Management Plan (PGT) (2006–08)
Grezzago

Province of Milan
Client: Town Council of Grezzago

Plan of Services (2006–09)
Melzo

Province of Milan
Client: Architect Roberto Pozzoli

LIST OF PROJECTS

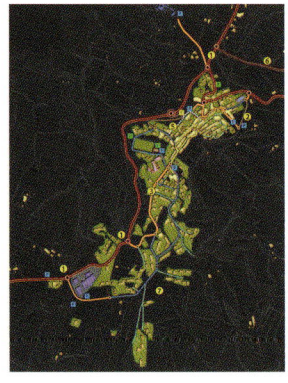
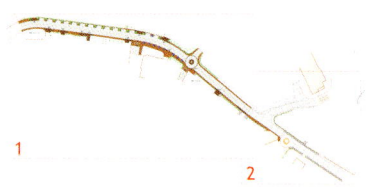

2007

Urban Traffic Plan (2007)
Cambiago

Province of Milan
Client: Town Council of Cambiago

Urban Traffic Plan (2007)
Gambassi Terme

Province of Firenze
Client: Town Council of Gambassi Terme

Project for renovation of the Via Gramsci urban road system (2007)
Gambassi Terme

Province of Florence
Client: Town Council of Gambassi Terme

Variance to the General Town-Planning Scheme (PRG) – L.r. 23/1997 (2007)
Melzo

Province of Milan
Client: Town Council of Melzo

Framework of Aims and Objectives (*Documento di Inquadramento*) (2007)
Pognano

Province of Bergamo
Client: Town Council of Pognano

Municipal Territorial Management Plan (PGT) (2007–08)
Cologno al Serio

Province of Bergamo
Client: Town Council of Cologno al Serio

Municipal Territorial Management Plan (PGT) (2007–09)
Cambiago

Province of Milan
Client: Town Council of Cambiago

LIST OF PROJECTS

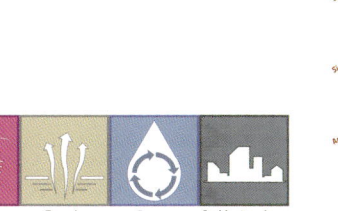  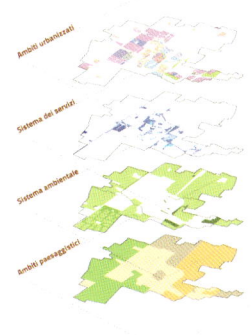 

Strategic Environmental Assessment (VAS) Planning Document (2007)
Vignate

Province of Milan
Client: Town Council of Vignate

Territorial Information System – Municipal Territorial Management Plan (PGT) (2007)
Cambiago

Province of Milan
Client: Town Council of Cambiago

Territorial Information System – Municipal Territorial Management Plan (PGT) (2007)
Vignate

Province of Milan
Client: Town Council of Vignate

Strategic plan – Technical consultation (2007)
Selargius

Province of Cagliari
Client: Criteria S.r.l.

Municipal Territorial Management Plan (PGT) (2007–09)
Vignate

Province of Milan
Client: Town Council of Vignate

297

LIST OF PROJECTS

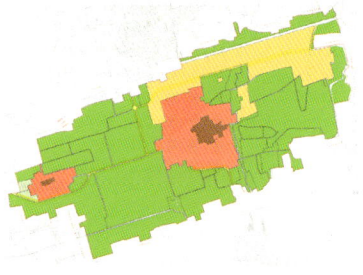  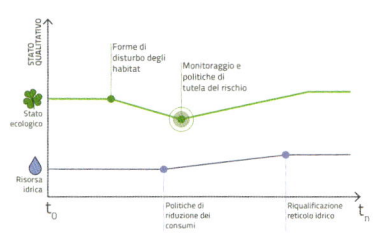

2008

Municipal regulations for installation of advertising structures (2008)
Cambiago

Province of Milan
Client: Town Council of Cambiago

Strategic Environmental Assessment (VAS) Planning Document (2008)
Cologno al Serio

Province of Bergamo
Client: Town Council of Cologno al Serio

Strategic Environmental Assessment (VAS) Planning Document (2008)
Inzago

Province of Milan
Client: Town Council of Inzago

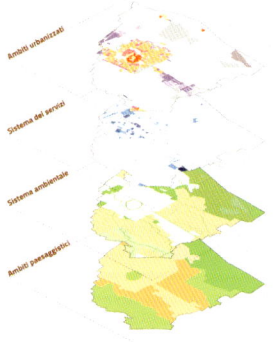 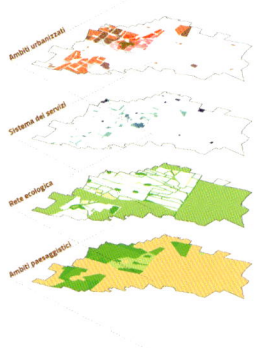 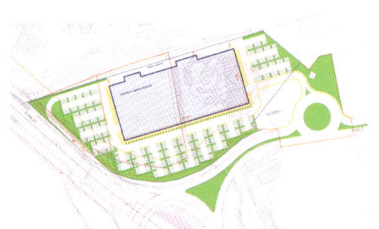 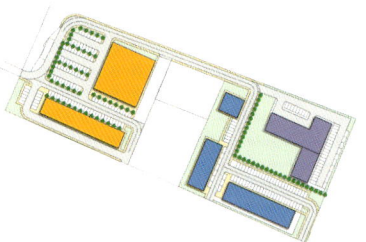

Territorial Information System – Municipal Territorial Management Plan (PGT) (2008)
Cologno al Serio

Province of Bergamo
Client: Town Council of Cologno al Serio

Territorial Information System – Municipal Territorial Management Plan (PGT) (2008)
Liscate

Province of Milan
Client: Town Council of Liscate

Integrated Action Plan (PII) for a shopping mall (2008)
Lodi

Province of Lodi
Client: V. Sironi

Preliminary project for the CDX area (2008)
Grezzago

Province of Milan
Client: Severgnini – Mattavelli

LIST OF PROJECTS

Strategic Environmental Assessment (VAS) Planning Document (2008)
Cassina de' Pecchi

Province of Milan
Client: Town Council of Cassina de' Pecchi

Ascertainment of applicability of Strategic Environmental Assessment (VAS) Planning Document (2008)
Pozzuolo Martesana

Province of Milan
Client: Town Council of Pozzuolo Martesana

Territorial Information System – Municipal Territorial Management Plan (PGT) (2008)
Inzago

Province of Milan
Client: Town Council of Inzago

Territorial Information System Variance to Municipal Territorial Management Plan (PGT) (2008)
Pozzuolo Martesana

Province of Milan
Client: Town Council of Pozzuolo Martesana

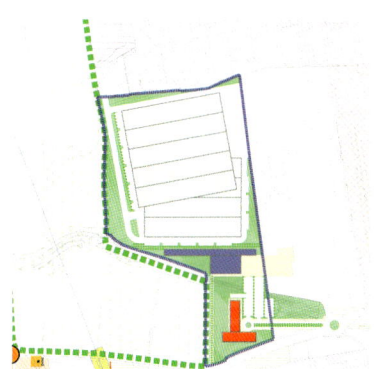   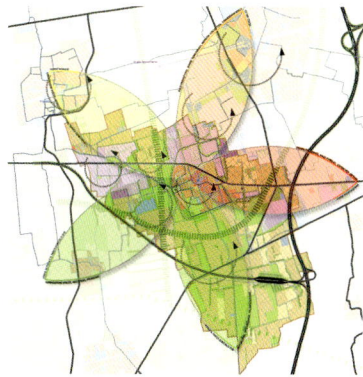

Feasibility study for the AS1 area (2008)
Vignate

Province of Milan
Client: Town Council of Vignate

Variance to Municipal Territorial Management Plan (PGT) (2008–09)
Pozzuolo Martesana

Province of Milan
Client: Town Council of Pozzuolo Martesana

Municipal Territorial Management Plan (PGT) (2008–10)
Inzago

Province of Milan
Client: Town Council of Inzago

Municipal Territorial Management Plan (PGT) (2008–12)
Liscate

Province of Milan
Client: Town Council of Liscate

LIST OF PROJECTS

Municipal Territorial Management Plan (PGT) (2008–12)
Novedrate

Province of Como
Client: Town Council of Novedrate

Municipal Territorial Management Plan (PGT) (2008–13)
Canzo

Province of Como
Client: Town Council of Canzo

Municipal Territorial Management Plan (PGT) (2008–13)
Cassina de' Pecchi

Province of Milan
Client: Town Council of Cassina de' Pecchi

2009

Rectification of Municipal Territorial Management Plan (PGT) (2009)
Vaprio d'Adda

Province of Milan
Client: Town Council of Vaprio d'Adda

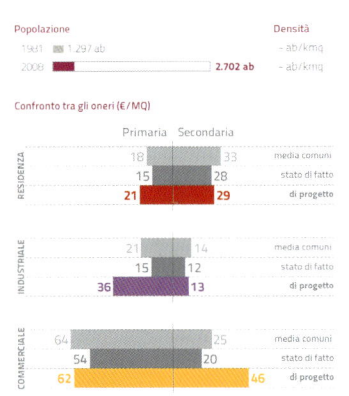

Updating of urbanization costs (2009)
Grezzago

Province of Milan
Client: Town Council of Grezzago

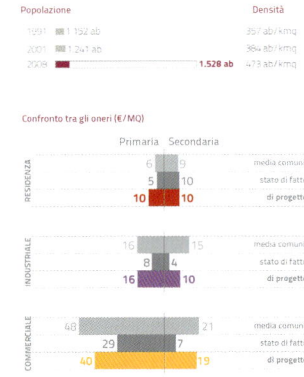

Updating of urbanization costs (2009)
Inzago

Province of Milan
Client: Town Council of Inzago

LIST OF PROJECTS

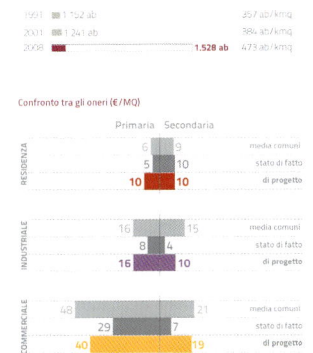 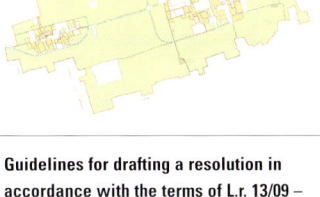  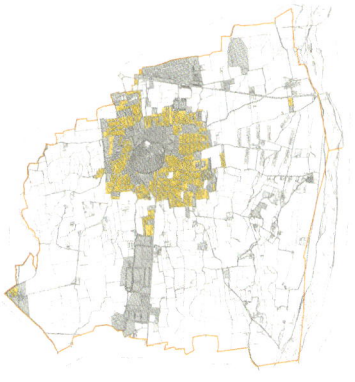

Updating of urbanization costs (2009)
Pognano

Province of Bergamo
Client: Town Council of Pognano

Guidelines for drafting a resolution in accordance with the terms of L.r. 13/09 – Housing Plan (2009)
Cambiago

Province of Milan
Client: Town Council of Cambiago

Guidelines for drafting a resolution in accordance with the terms of L.r. 13/09 – Housing Plan (2009)
Cassina de' Pecchi

Province of Milan
Client: Town Council of Cassina de' Pecchi

Guidelines for drafting a resolution in accordance with the terms of L.r. 13/09 – Housing Plan (2009)
Cologno al Serio

Province of Bergamo
Client: Town Council of Cologno al Serio

LIST OF PROJECTS

 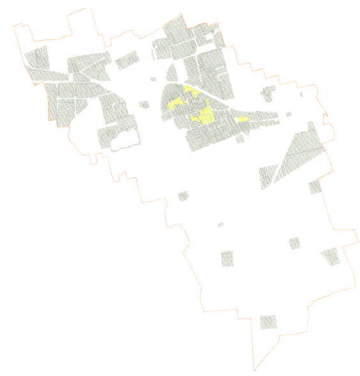  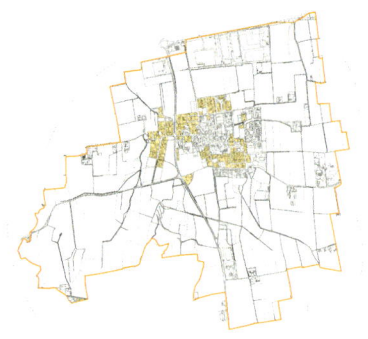

Guidelines for drafting a resolution in accordance with the terms of L.r. 13/09 – Housing Plan (2009)
Inzago

Province of Milan
Client: Town Council of Inzago

Guidelines for drafting a resolution in accordance with the terms of L.r. 13/09 – Housing Plan (2009)
Liscate

Province of Milan
Client: Town Council of Liscate

Guidelines for drafting a resolution in accordance with the terms of L.r. 13/09 – Housing Plan (2009)
Novedrate

Province of Como
Client: Town Council of Novedrate

Guidelines for drafting a resolution in accordance with the terms of L.r. 13/09 – Housing Plan (2009)
Pognano

Province of Bergamo
Client: Town Council of Pognano

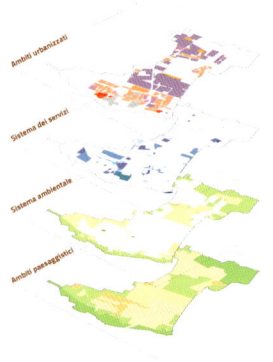 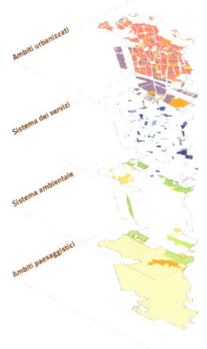 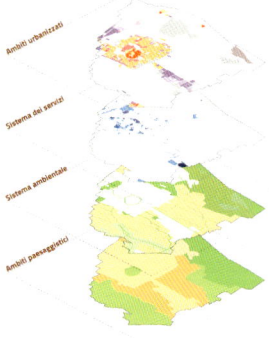 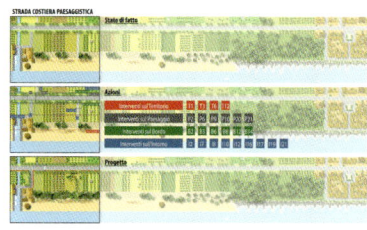

Territorial Information System – Municipal Territorial Management Plan (PGT) (2009)
Novedrate

Province of Como
Client: Town Council of Novedrate

Territorial Information System – Municipal Territorial Management Plan (PGT) (2009)
Verano Brianza

Province of Monza and Brianza
Client: Town Council of Verano Brianza

Territorial Information System Variance to Municipal Territorial Management Plan (PGT) (2009)
Cologno al Serio

Province of Bergamo
Client: Town Council of Cologno al Serio

Guidelines for environmental renovation of infrastructures (2009–10)
Regional Territorial Landscape Plan

Puglia Region
Client: Puglia Region

LIST OF PROJECTS

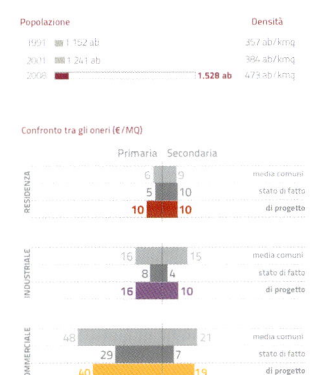 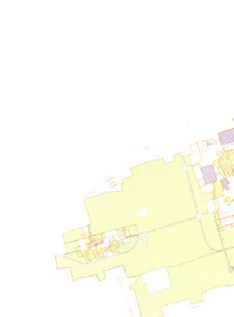  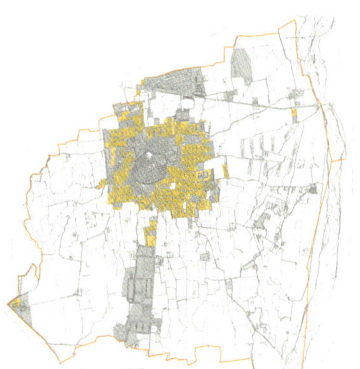

Updating of urbanization costs (2009)
Pognano

Province of Bergamo
Client: Town Council of Pognano

Guidelines for drafting a resolution in accordance with the terms of L.r. 13/09 – Housing Plan (2009)
Cambiago

Province of Milan
Client: Town Council of Cambiago

Guidelines for drafting a resolution in accordance with the terms of L.r. 13/09 – Housing Plan (2009)
Cassina de' Pecchi

Province of Milan
Client: Town Council of Cassina de' Pecchi

Guidelines for drafting a resolution in accordance with the terms of L.r. 13/09 – Housing Plan (2009)
Cologno al Serio

Province of Bergamo
Client: Town Council of Cologno al Serio

LIST OF PROJECTS

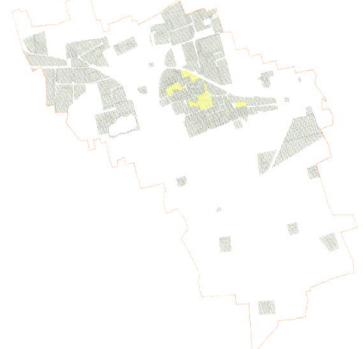
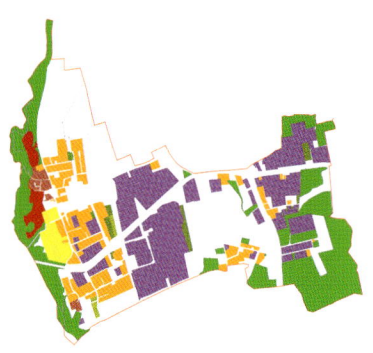

Guidelines for drafting a resolution in accordance with the terms of L.r. 13/09 – Housing Plan (2009)
Inzago

Province of Milan
Client: Town Council of Inzago

Guidelines for drafting a resolution in accordance with the terms of L.r. 13/09 – Housing Plan (2009)
Liscate

Province of Milan
Client: Town Council of Liscate

Guidelines for drafting a resolution in accordance with the terms of L.r. 13/09 – Housing Plan (2009)
Novedrate

Province of Como
Client: Town Council of Novedrate

Guidelines for drafting a resolution in accordance with the terms of L.r. 13/09 – Housing Plan (2009)
Pognano

Province of Bergamo
Client: Town Council of Pognano

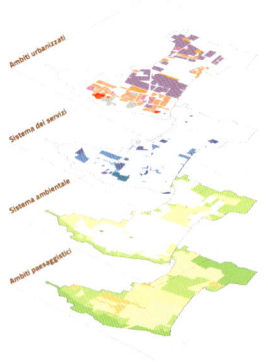
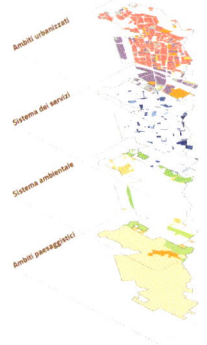
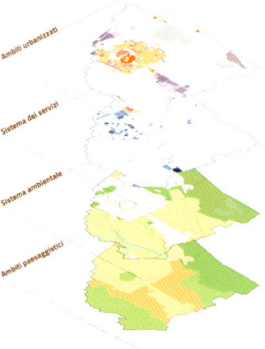
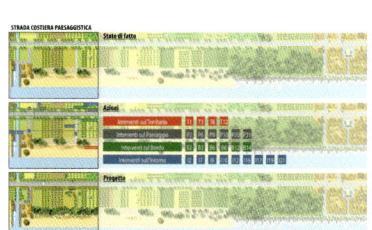

Territorial Information System – Municipal Territorial Management Plan (PGT) (2009)
Novedrate

Province of Como
Client: Town Council of Novedrate

Territorial Information System – Municipal Territorial Management Plan (PGT) (2009)
Verano Brianza

Province of Monza and Brianza
Client: Town Council of Verano Brianza

Territorial Information System Variance to Municipal Territorial Management Plan (PGT) (2009)
Cologno al Serio

Province of Bergamo
Client: Town Council of Cologno al Serio

Guidelines for environmental renovation of infrastructures (2009–10)
Regional Territorial Landscape Plan

Puglia Region
Client: Puglia Region

LIST OF PROJECTS

 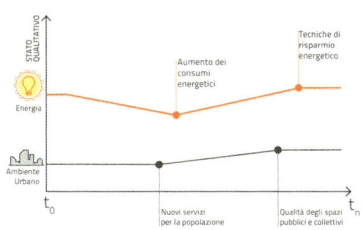  

Guidelines for drafting a resolution in accordance with the terms of L.r. 13/09 – Housing Plan (2009)
Verano Brianza

Province of Monza and Brianza
Client: Town Council of Verano Brianza

Strategic Environmental Assessment (VAS) Planning Document (2009)
Novedrate

Province of Como
Client: Town Council of Novedrate

Strategic Environmental Assessment (VAS) Planning Document (2009)
Canzo

Province of Como
Client: Town Council of Canzo

Ascertainment of applicability of Strategic Environmental Assessment (VAS) Planning Document (2009)
Cologno al Serio

Province of Bergamo
Client: Town Council of Cologno al Serio

  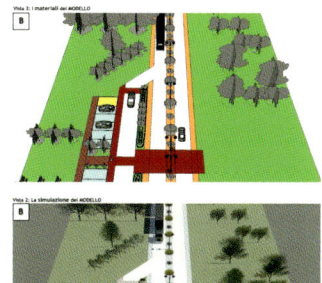 

Variance to Municipal Territorial Management Plan (PGT) (2009–11)
Cologno al Serio

Province of Bergamo
Client: Town Council of Cologno al Serio

Municipal Territorial Management Plan (PGT) (2009–12)
Verano Brianza

Province of Monza and Brianza
Client: Town Council of Verano Brianza

Urban Traffic Plan (2009–12)
Canegrate

Province of Milan
Client: Town Council of Canegrate

Municipal Territorial Management Plan (PGT) (2009–13)
Basiglio

Province of Milan
Client: Town Council of Basiglio

LIST OF PROJECTS

  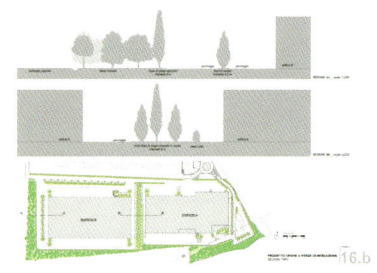

2010

Verification of municipal procedures as regards urban planning and TEM (2010)
Melegnano

Province of Milan
Client: Town Council of Melegnano

Strategic Environmental Assessment (VAS) Planning Document (2010)
Basiglio

Province of Milan
Client: Town Council of Basiglio

Ascertainment of applicability of Strategic Environmental Assessment (VAS) Single Office of Production Activities (SUAP) Procedure (2010)
Roncello

Province of Monza and Brianza
Client: Accademia SGR

Variance to Municipal Territorial Management Plan (PGT) (2010–13)
Pognano

Province of Bergamo
Client: Town Council of Pognano

Urban Traffic Plan (under way since 2010)
Inzago

Province of Milan
Client: Town Council of Inzago

LIST OF PROJECTS

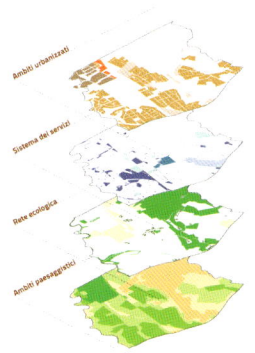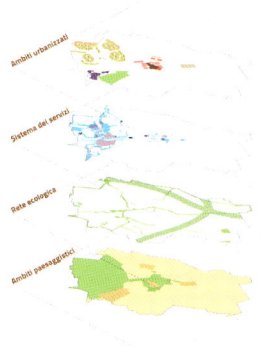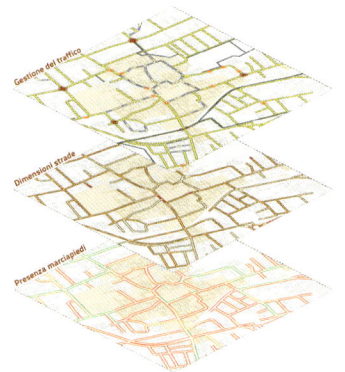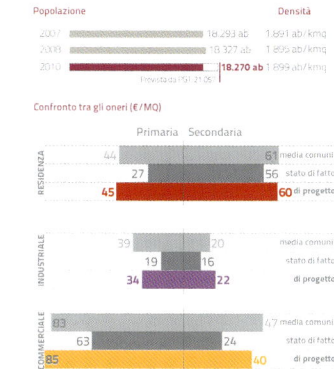

Territorial Information System (2010)
Mozzo

Province of Bergamo
Client: Town Council of Mozzo

Territorial Information System (2010)
Basiglio

Province of Milan
Client: Town Council of Basiglio

Register of roads (2010)
Inzago

Province of Milan
Client: Town Council of Inzago

Updating of urbanization costs (2010)
Melzo

Province of Milan
Client: Town Council of Melzo

LIST OF PROJECTS

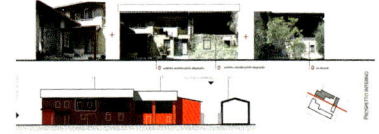

2011

Study of impact of Integrated Action Plan (PII) access road
Via Berlinguer (2011)
Opera

Province of Milan
Client: Town Council of Opera

Partial variance to Municipal Territorial Management Plan (PGT) (2011)
Vaprio d'Adda

Province of Milan
Client: Town Council of Vaprio d'Adda

Guidelines for drawing up plans for the renovation of farmhouses (2011)
Inzago

Province of Milan
Client: Town Council of Inzago

Ascertainment of applicability of Strategic Environmental Assessment (VAS) Planning Document (2011)
Inzago

Province of Milan
Client: Town Council of Inzago

Register of roads (2011)
Melegnano

Province of Milan
Client: Town Council of Melegnano

Strategic Environmental Assessment (VAS) Planning Document (2011)
Pognano

Province of Bergamo
Client: Town Council of Pognano

Strategic Environmental Assessment (VAS) (2011)
River Agogna contract

Province of Novara
Client: Province of Novara

LIST OF PROJECTS

Municipal cemetery plan (2011)
Inzago

Province of Milan
Client: Town Council of Inzago

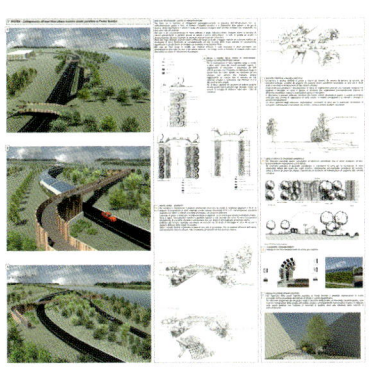

Feasibility study for new road system for Presezzo (locality of Ghiaie) – Bonate Sopra (2011)
Bonate Sopra

Province of Bergamo
Client: Vitali S.p.a.

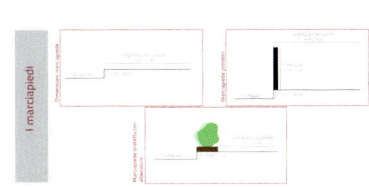

Municipal building regulations (2011)
Liscate

Province of Milan
Client: Town Council of Liscate

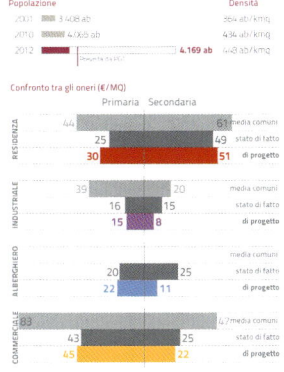

Updating of urbanization costs (2011)
Liscate

Province of Milan
Client: Town Council of Liscate

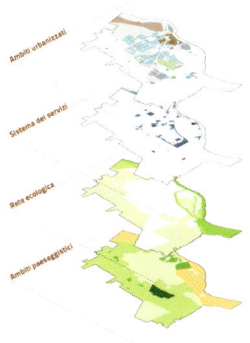

Territorial Information System
Partial variance to Municipal Territorial Management Plan (PGT) (2011)
Vaprio d'Adda

Province of Milan
Client: Town Council of Vaprio d'Adda

Provincial Territorial Plan (PTP) (2011–12)
Updating of analytical and descriptive tables

Province of Novara
Client: Province of Novara

Urban Traffic Plan (under way since 2011)
Melegnano

Province of Milan
Client: Town Council of Melegnano

LIST OF PROJECTS

  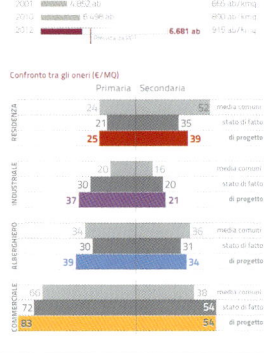

2012

Municipal building regulations (2012)
Cambiago

Province of Milan
Client: Town Council of Cambiago

Analysis of commercial system
Addition to Municipal Territorial Management Plan (PGT) (2012)
Opera

Province of Milan
Client: Town Council of Opera

Updating of urbanization costs (2012)
Cambiago

Province of Milan
Client: Town Council of Cambiago

 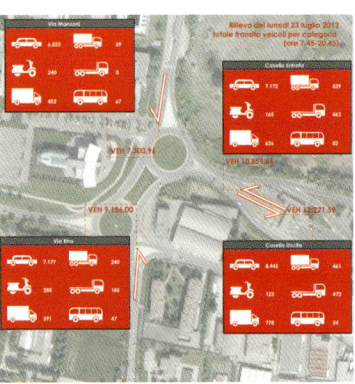  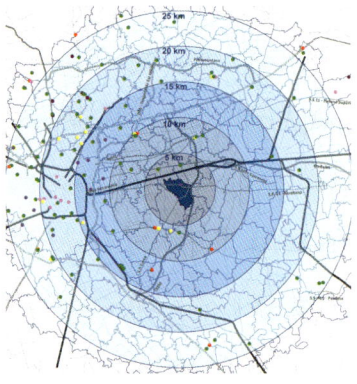

Register of roads (2012)
Verano Brianza

Province of Milan
Client: Town Council of Verano Brianza

Traffic survey (2012)
Fino Mornasco, Lainate, Trezzano sul Naviglio

Busto Arsizio
Client: Lidl Italia S.r.l.

Consultation on drawing up Municipal Territorial Management Plan (PGT) (2012)
Opera

Province of Milan
Client: Town Council of Opera

Analysis of commercial system
Addition to Municipal Territorial Management Plan (PGT) (2012)
Liscate

Province of Milan
Client: Town Council of Liscate

308

LIST OF PROJECTS

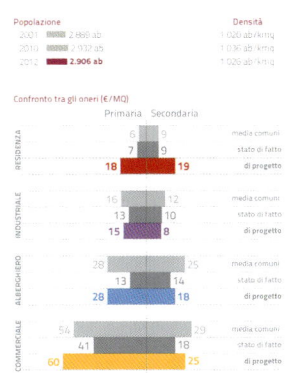  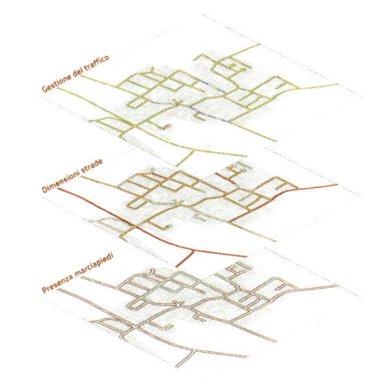

Updating of urbanization costs (2012)
Novedrate

Province of Como
Client: Town Council of Novedrate

Ascertainment of applicability of Strategic Environmental Assessment (VAS) Partial variance to Municipal Territorial Management Plan (PGT) (2012)
Cologno al Serio

Province of Bergamo
Client: Town Council of Cologno al Serio

Territorial Information System (2012)
Opera

Province of Milan
Client: Town Council of Opera

Register of roads (2012)
Pognano

Province of Bergamo
Client: Town Council of Pognano

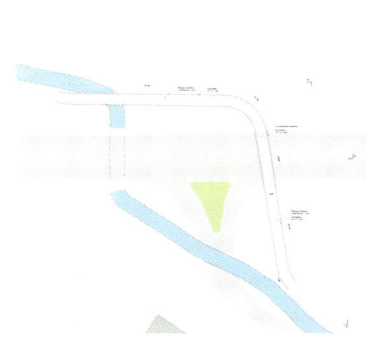 

Feasibility study for cycle bridge over the Rivoltana provincial highway (2012)
Liscate

Province of Milan
Client: Town Council of Liscate

Urban Traffic Plan (under way since 2012)
Verano Brianza

Province of Monza and Brianza
Client: Town Council of Verano Brianza

LIST OF PROJECTS

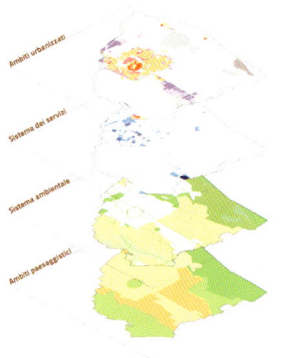

2013

Municipal building regulations (2013)
Basiglio

Province of Milan
Client: Town Council of Basiglio

Territorial Information System
Partial variance to Municipal Territorial Management Plan (PGT) (2013)
Cologno al Serio

Province of Bergamo
Client: Cologno al Serio

Ascertainment of applicability of Strategic Environmental Assessment (VAS)
Urban Traffic Plan (2013)
Inzago

Province of Milan
Client: Town Council of Inzago

Guidelines for the AT22 production area
(under way since 2013)
Verano Brianza

Province of Milan
Client: Town Council of Verano Brianza

310

LIST OF PROJECTS

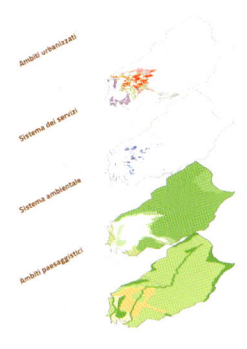 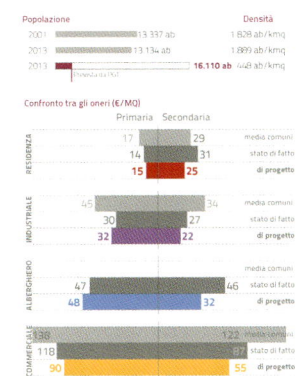  

Territorial Information System – Municipal Territorial Management Plan (PGT) (2013)
Canzo

Province of Como
Client: Town Council of Canzo

Updating of urbanization costs (2013)
Opera

Province of Milan
Client: Town Council of Opera

Definition of the monetization value for service areas (2013)
Opera

Province of Milan
Client: Town Council of Opera

Variance to the Municipal Territorial Management Plan (PGT) (under way since 2013)
Cambiago

Province of Milan
Client: Town Council of Cambiago

311

LIST OF PROJECTS

ARCHITECTURE

2005

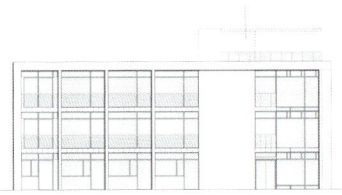

New office building (2005)
Trecate

Province of Novara
Client: Impresa CII – Guatelli

Functional renovation and restoration of Villa Albera (2005)
Oleggio

Province of Novara
Client: Carlo Albera

Restoration of Cascina Loreto (2005)
Oleggio

Province of Novara
Client: Bevilacqua

2006

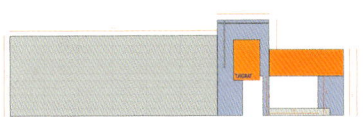

Factory building
Building permit (2006)
Romentino

Province of Novara
Client: TAIGRAF

Production plant
Feasibility study (2006)
Caponago

Province of Monza and Brianza
Client: DM Project & Affinity

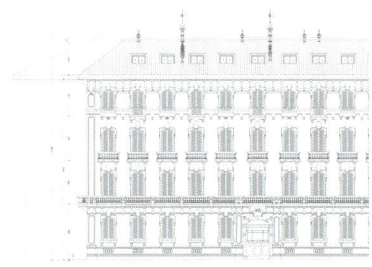

Feasibility study for functional renovation of a building on Corso Concordia (2006)
Milano

Client: Studio Turrini

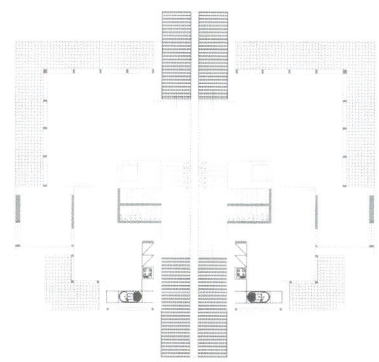  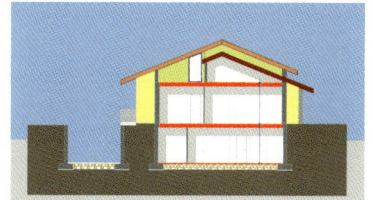 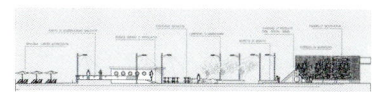

Preliminary project for tourist complex (2005)
Comignago

Province of Novara
Client: Impresa Tosi

Residential settlement (2005)
Oleggio

Province of Novara
Client: Impresa Bernardo Cuda

Development of Area B2 (2005)
Oleggio

Province of Novara
Client: Colombo family

Pedestrian access to beach (2005–06)
Marina di Carrara

Province of Massa Carrara
Client: Autorità Portuale Marina di Carrara

Feasibility study per functional renovation and restoration of the Argenteria Gangi building (2006)
Milan

Client: Studio Turrini

2007

Shopping mall
Executive plan (2007)
Cornaredo

Province of Milan
Client: Cotefa

Settala Strada Cerca area
Feasibility study (2007)
Settala

Province of Milan
Client: Marco Galbiati

Shed for agricultural activities (2007)
Grezzago

Province of Milan
Client: Agriverde S.r.l.

2008

Integrated Action Plan (PII)
Via Curiel (2008)
Melzo

Province of Milan
Client: Area Melzo Servizi Immobiliari S.r.l., Alhafin S.p.a., Cogeser S.p.a.

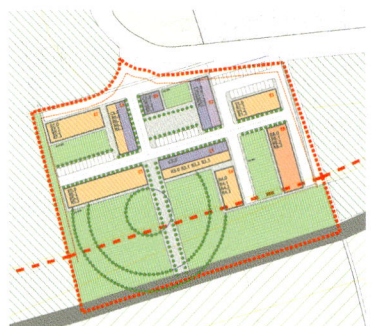

Feasibility study
Transformation area ARm6 (2008)
Cambiago

Province of Milan
Client: Town Council of Cambiago

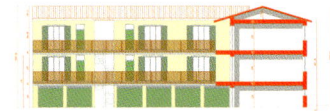

Preliminary project for renovation of the San Giovanni farmhouse (2008)
Oleggio

Province of Novara
Client: Impresa Bernardo Cuda

LIST OF PROJECTS

Single Office of Production Activities (SUAP) for enlargement of the railway freight station (2007)
Vignate

Province of Milan
Client: So.Ge.Mar

Project for the functional renovation and restoration of a farmhouse (2007)
Momo

Province of Novara
Client: Immobiliare Dellavalle

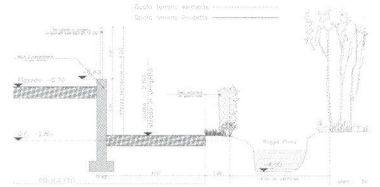

Single Office of Production Activities (SUAP) Tollgate area (2007–10)
Trezzo sull'Adda

Province of Milan
Client: Iniziative immobiliari S.r.l.

Single Office of Production Activities (SUAP) Furnace area (2007–10)
Trezzo sull'Adda

Province of Milan
Client: Iniziative immobiliari S.r.l.

Integrated Action Plan (PII) Former Pirelli testing area (2008)
Lainate

Province of Milan
Client: Della Frera

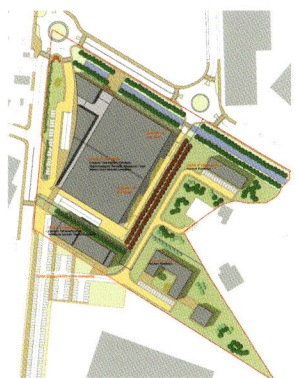

Integrated Action Plan (PII) Manzoni-Brodolini area (under way since 2008)
Rozzano

Province of Milan
Client: Giuseppe Frigo

LIST OF PROJECTS

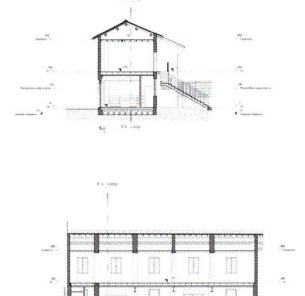

2009

Proposed Integrated Action Plan (PII)
Feasibility study (2009)
Pessano con Bornago

Province of Milan
Client: Gianni Colombo

Renovation of a commercial building
Notification of commencement (2009)
Cambiago

Province of Milan
Client: Livio Brambilla

Integrated Action Plan (PII) – Corte della Chiesa
(2009–12)
Roncello

Province of Monza and Brianza
Client: Corte della Chiesa S.r.l.

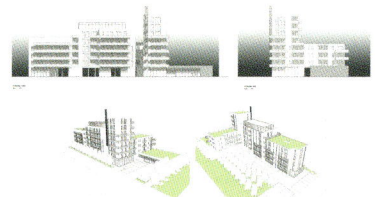

2010

Residential area of transformation ARm10,
execution (2010)
Cambiago

Province of Milan
Client: Edilbloque S.r.l.

Multifunctional complex
Proposal AP2 Zoning Plan (2010)
Vaprio d'Adda

Province of Milan
Client: Cover Development

CPE transformation sector
Feasibility study (2010)
Bresso

Province of Milan
Client: Künzi

LIST OF PROJECTS

 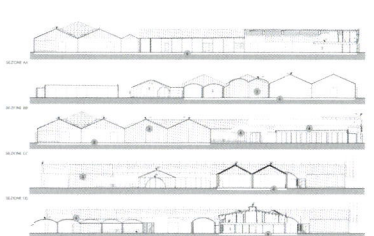 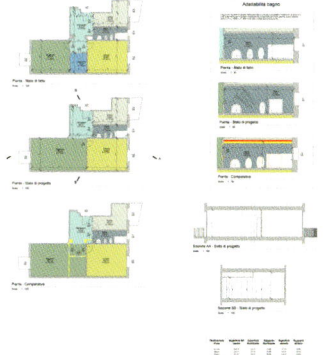 

Single Office of Production Activities (SUAP) (2010)
Melegnano

Province of Milan
Client: Accademia SRG

New gardening centre
Building permit (2010)
Desio

Province of Monza and Brianza
Client: Pilastro

Notification of commencement (2010)
Milan

Province of Milan
Client: Silvia Rossi

Integrated Action Plan (PII) – Core (2010)
Verano Brianza

Province of Monza and Brianza
Client: AR.CA S.r.l.

LIST OF PROJECTS

Integrated Action Plan (PII) – Montegrappa (2010)
Verano Brianza

Province of Monza and Brianza
Client: AR.CA S.r.l.

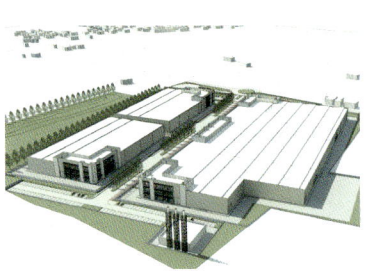

Integrated Action Plan (PII) – Cava Borgonovo (2010)
Verano Brianza

Province of Monza and Brianza
Client: AR.CA S.r.l.

Enlargement of artisanal building
Building permit (2010)
Pozzo d'Adda

Province of Milan
Client: VE.AN. S.a.s.

Cooperative building plan – Ecocity (2010–11)
Inzago

Province of Milan
Client: Town Council of Inzago

2011

Renovation of the former Cantina Sociale
Preliminary project (2011)
Villasalto

Province of Cagliari
Client: Town Council of Villasalto

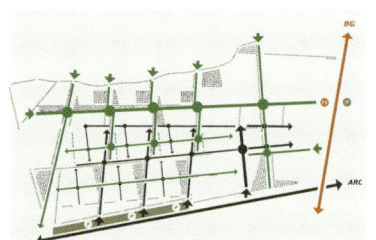

Project for conversion of a quarry into a residential area (2011)
Arcene

Province of Bergamo
Client: Vitali S.p.a.

Renovation plan for the Cascina Bindellera farmhouse
Feasibility study (2011)
Cassina de' Pecchi

Province of Milan
Client: Town Council of Cassina de' Pecchi

LIST OF PROJECTS

Integrated Action Plan (PII)
Former Linificio Nazionale factory
(under way since 2010)
Cassano d'Adda

Province of Milan
Client: Alauda S.r.l.

Renovation plan for Cascina Deserta farmhouse
(under way since 2010)
Peschiera Borromeo

Province of Milan
Client: Santa Croce S.r.l.

Building for commercial and service-sector activities Manzoni-Brodolini area
DIA – Executive plan (under way since 2010)
Rozzano

Province of Milan
Client: Giuseppe Frigo

New sports centre
Feasibility study (2011)
Cassina de' Pecchi

Province of Milan
Client: Town Council of Cassina de' Pecchi

Integrated Action Plan (PII) – I Platani
(under way since 2011)
Missaglia

Province of Lecco
Client: The Blossom Avenue Property S.r.l.

LIST OF PROJECTS

 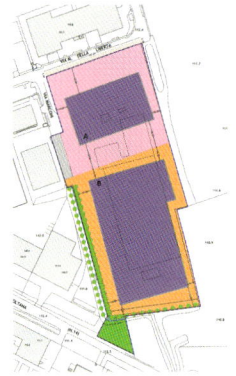 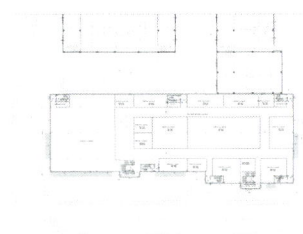

2012

Multifunctional complex
Building permit – AP2 plan (2012)
Vaprio d'Adda

Province of Milan
Client: Retail Development

Feasibility study for the former Danzas area (2012)
Liscate

Province of Milan
Client: Impresa Italiana Costruzioni Commerciali Industriali

Variance to the Rivoltana-Verona executive plan
Change of use (2012)
Liscate

Province of Milan
Client: Impresa Italiana Costruzioni Commerciali Industriali

Shopping mall (2012)
Minsk

Russia
Client: Structurama

Residential buildings (under way since 2012)
Missaglia

Province of Lecco
Client: CP – Investment S.r.l.

LIST OF PROJECTS

Renovation and change of use – Corso Europa (2012)
Missaglia

Province of Lecco
Client: Compagnia Immobiliare San Ferdinando S.r.l.

Proposal for execution of residential area of transformation – Feasibility study (2012)
Peschiera Borromeo

Province of Milan
Client: Santa Croce S.r.l.

Residential villas (2012)
Essaouira

Morocco
Client: Consonni Strade S.r.l.

Public housing (2012)
Kiev

Ukraine
Client: Structurama

LIST OF PROJECTS

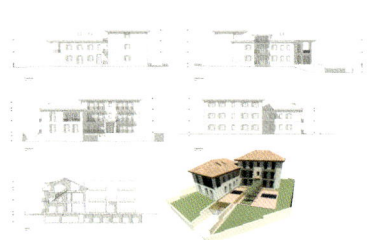  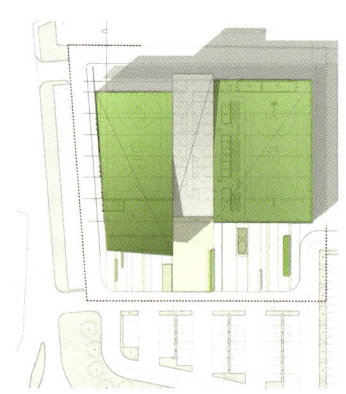

2013

Renovation of a building in the Contra district (2013)
Missaglia

Province of Lecco
Client: Compagnia Immobiliare San Fernando S.r.l.

SmeUP Base Field (under way since 2013)
Erbusco

Province of Brescia
Client: Sme.UP

Definitive project for the Palazzetto dello Sport sports complex (under way since 2013)
Opera

Province of Milano
Client: Town Council of Opera

**The Blossom Avenue Market
(under way since 2013)
Rozzano**

Province of Milano
Client: Anlus S.r.l.

LIST OF PROJECTS

INTERIOR DESIGN

2007

Working plans for the renovation
of an apartment (2007)
Sutri

Province of Viterbo
Client: Luciana del Giudice

  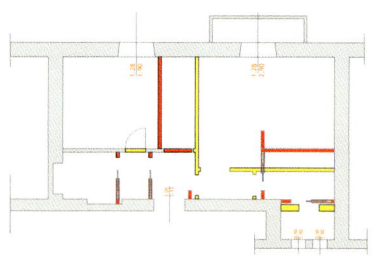

2009

Apartment on Via Giulio Romano (2009)
Milan

Client: Paglierani

Working plans for renovation of the Marogna
Mazzei residence (2009)
Milan

Client: Antonio Marogna, Alessandra Mazzei

Working plans for renovation of the Venturini
residence (2009)
Milan

Client: Cristina Venturini

Working plans for renovation of the Bassanini residence (2009)
Milan

Client: Luca Bassanini

LIST OF PROJECTS

2010

Working plans for a wine shop (2010)
Verano Brianza

Province of Monza and Brianza
Client: La Bottega del Vino e dei Sapori

La Gavetta restaurant (2010)
Milan

Client: La Gavetta S.r.l.

2012

Apartment on Via Vittorio Emanuele II (2012–13)
Siena

Client: Veronica Stocco

Apartment on Corso Italia (2012–13)
Milan

Client: Marco Facchinetti

List of Associates

Anzalone Davide Simone
Bartoletti Lorenzo
Battistessa Sara
Bensi Marco
Bonati Nicola
Borzacchiello Marco
Comai Alessio
De Stefani Luca
Fenghe Fabrizio
Ferrari Enrico
Ferrero Simona
Fior Marika
Galdi Raffaele
Gallina Francesca
Galluzzi Massimo

Gianatti Mara
Giovenzana Lorenzo
Grassi Mattia
Grossi Jacopo
Manzoni Francesca
Mattioli Guglielmo
Minardi Francesco
Morenghi Licia
Nemet Marco
Pignataro Tommaso
Salata Stefano
Sciuto Giovanni
Serra Paolo Emilio
Tirinnanzi Alessandro
Zilla Antonio